LIGHTS, CAMERA, FASTBALL

LIGHTS, CAMERA, FASTBALL

How the Hollywood Stars Changed Baseball

Dan Taylor

ROWMAN & LITTLEFIELD
Lanham • Boulder • New York • London

Published by Rowman & Littlefield
An imprint of The Rowman & Littlefield Publishing Group, Inc.
4501 Forbes Boulevard, Suite 200, Lanham, Maryland 20706
www.rowman.com

6 Tinworth Street, London SE11 5AL, United Kingdom

British Library Cataloguing in Publication Information Available

Library of Congress Cataloging-in-Publication Data Available

ISBN 978-1-5381-3862-5 (cloth : alk. paper)
ISBN 978-1-5381-3863-2 (electronic)

∞™ The paper used in this publication meets the minimum requirements of American National Standard for Information Sciences Permanence of Paper for Printed Library Materials, ANSI/NISO Z39.48-1992.

CONTENTS

FOREWORD

There once was a baseball team in Hollywood. Not only did it attract the famous film personalities to its games, but it was partially owned by a star-studded group of celebrities. The team was far ahead of its time in the presentation of games both on the field and in the early stages of television. There were cheerleaders composed of wannabe Hollywood starlets, beauty queens, and musical presentations as an opening act to the games.

Baseball truly had gone Hollywood.

The owner of the team was a good-looking man who arrived from Montana as a teenager, worked his way from an entry-level position to running a restaurant, married a movie star, and spent the majority of his time hobnobbing with celebrities while ultimately running one of the town's most popular restaurants: the legendary Brown Derby.

Some of the members of the team had looks that might have had them mistaken for movie stars themselves, and just for a little added attraction, they played some of their day games in short pants.

The managers of the team had Hollywood-type personalities in Fred Haney, who came from the radio booth to lead the team on the field, and the ever-colorful Bobby Bragan.

If all of this sounds like a film made in Hollywood, it isn't.

It is the true story of the Hollywood Stars baseball team, and writer Dan Taylor has done a masterful job in capturing both the story of the team on the field and the equally interesting story of the team and its primary owner, Bob Cobb, behind the scenes.

It all came to an end in 1958 when an even greater show came to town—the famed Dodgers arriving from Brooklyn—creating a big enough attraction to fill the Los Angeles Coliseum on occasion and changing both the geography and scope of Major League Baseball.

Taylor's storytelling of the last decade of the Stars carries special meaning for me because I became a fan of the Hollywood Stars when my family moved to Southern California from Ohio in the summer of 1950.

I was a teenager at the time and in the early stages of my love affair with baseball, a passion that would help propel me to a thirty-year career as an executive with the Los Angeles Dodgers.

I was so intrigued by the Stars and other teams in the Pacific Coast League, foremost being the Stars' archrival Los Angeles Angels, that as a freshman at El Camino College in 1953, it was an easy decision when I needed to select a subject for a paper as part of a feature writing class.

My interest was journalism as I tried to figure out the best plan to stay connected with sports, and particularly baseball, when it became clear—even at the community college level—that my athletic talent wasn't going to carry me far.

I decided to title my paper "Make Way for the Coast League," with the premise that the league could become a third major league. Much to my surprise, and probably to the surprise of my wonderful journalism professor, Mr. Bill Kamrath, my story was published by *Baseball* magazine.

Little did I realize then that some of the players I wrote about in the article would come to real life as close friends and even working companions during my days with the Dodgers.

I was presented an unbelievable opportunity to get to know these players as people and in some cases very close and lifelong friends, including Tommy Lasorda, Monty Basgall, Red Adams, Ben Wade, George Genovese, Johnny O'Neil, Gail Henley, Chuck Stevens, Tommy Saffell, Chuck Connors, and Gene Mauch.

Lasorda, of course, would become the legendary and Hall of Fame manager of the Dodgers. I met him when he was managing the Spokane team of the Pacific Coast League in 1959, and I was a writer for the newspaper in Long Beach, California. Our careers advanced and we are forever linked in hoisting the 1988 World Championship trophy.

Basgall and Adams became two of Lasorda's most trusted coaches, while Wade became the Dodgers' scouting director and Genovese, O'Neil, and Henley all served as Dodger scouts.

My friendships and working relationships with this wonderful group of individuals gave me an insight to life in the Pacific Coast League as Taylor describes it—playing in fan-friendly ballparks and enjoying the best possible weather, short travel distances, and long homestands enjoying wonderful, growing cities like Los Angeles, San Diego, San Francisco, and Seattle.

The player salaries in the PCL were close to what players were making in the major leagues, and a solid year all but assured a call to the majors.

Life was good for the players on the West Coast, and there was no better spot than Hollywood.

In many ways it seemed too good to be true for Cobb and his players, and it all came to a sudden stop with with the arrival of the Dodgers and San Francisco Giants of Major League Baseball.

In time there would be major-league teams in Oakland, Seattle, and San Diego.

Fan groups have tried their best to keep alive the memories of their Pacific Coast League teams and players, but more than a half century later interest has all but disappeared as the players from the PCL era have, with few exceptions, passed away.

In the Hollywood environment great stories from the past are always possible subject matter, and Dan Taylor has become the producer and director of a wonderful story of a baseball team that carried the perfect name of Stars.

—Fred Claire

Fred Claire was the executive vice president of the Los Angeles Dodgers while serving the team from 1969 to 1998. His story is captured in the book Fred Claire: My 30 Years in Dodger Blue. *A current book titled* Extra Innings *is a tribute to the City of Hope and describes Fred's dedication in assisting the medical center.*

ACKNOWLEDGMENTS

Words simply cannot convey the depth of my gratitude to Artie Harris. The introductions, many stories, and perspectives as well as your continual inspiration and friendship have been invaluable. It's hard to believe this book has achieved the light of day thanks to the assistance of a guy who grew up a staunch Los Angeles Angels fan and avowed Hollywood Stars hater. I am glad his aunt Florence entered John Van Ornum in Fred Haney's Knothole Gang and frequently took him to Gilmore Field. Those trips generated wonderful stories, which I thank you for sharing. You also offered beneficial perspectives and insights that were tremendous help not to mention great fun. I'm grateful for your friendship. Bob Walsh, you and the Cobb family have much to be proud of. I appreciate the enthusiastic sharing of your family's history. Eve, I cannot begin to express thanks enough for your dedication, support, and tireless work. Yes, it made for some very long nights, but this accomplishment has much to do with your skills, devotion, and diligence. Thank you.

A great many talented professionals offered their time, knowledge, and insights. My sincere thanks to Jim Gates, Cassidy Lent, and Claudette Scrafford from the National Baseball Hall of Fame and Museum; to Frances Kaplan of the North Baker Research Library at the California Historical Society; and to Faye Thompson and Seth Greenberg at the Margaret Herrick Library for their assistance. The Los Angeles Public Library, and in particular Terri Garst and Angela Charles, were of tremendous assistance. The *Los Angeles Times*, the *Sporting News*, the *Oakland Tribune*, *Variety*, the *Hollywood Reporter*, the Dick Dobbins collection, and Baseball-Reference.com were extremely helpful research resources.

So many in the baseball community, the entertainment industry, and the Hollywood Stars "family" extended their time, shared memories and stories, provided direction, and assisted with research. Many thanks to Bob Barisoff, Bob Bishop, Wes Breschini, Edd Byrnes, John Cavalli, Steve Cavalli, Ed Cereghino, Fred Claire, Stan Cline, John Cochrane, Joe Cooper, Mary Jane Dante, Bob Duretto, Arlo Engel, Eddy Erautt, Victoria Foran, Chuck Franklin, Robert Franklin, Jim Hardy, Joe Harper, Bruce Harrison, Roland Hemond, Gail Henley, Ed Hoffman, Clint Hufford, Marcelle Hufford, Bill Hunter, Mary Johnston, Denise Kelleher, Steve Kipnis, Terry Maalen, Dorothy McWhirter, Darrold "Gar" Myers, Mel Nelson, Rod Nelson, Irv Noren, Dennis O'Donnell, Sandy Oster, Paul Pettit, Bob Reiss, Larry Rubin, Mary Sarty, Robert Schweppe, Dorothy Scott, Art Shallock, Chuck Stevens, Bill Swank, Bill Turner, Cissie Walden, Barry Weinstock, and Woody Wilk.

The seeds for this book were planted by the late George Genovese. His pride at being a member of Hollywood's first pennant winner was infectious. Rare was the day when he didn't wear his 1949 championship ring. His many stories stoked both curiosity and research interest in this writer. What you've just read is its product. Thank you, George, and thank you, the reader.

1

"YOU CAN SELL IT OUT OF A HAT"

Patience had long ago ebbed. The small wood-paneled office on the second floor above the bustling restaurant had become a holding pen for a mixture of agitation and tinging anger. Bob Cobb stirred. Handsome, with dark wavy hair that was combed almost straight back, and immaculately dressed in a pressed dark suit with his trademark boutonniere, Cobb had agreed to meet a liquor salesman who was now late. A lack of punctuality did not bode well with Cobb, who rose each day at the crack of dawn to get to his restaurant before deliveries arrived. His plate, so to speak, was brimming. There were meetings, appointments, tasks to complete, and orders to approve, not to mention the continual matter of employees to direct. The owner of the immensely popular restaurant fidgeted behind his authentic American partner's desk. As Cobb shuffled documents, his right hand brushed a piece of paper that had been folded and stuffed beneath a side pad on the right end of his black leather desk blotter. It had been pushed there two days before, not out of disinterest but because of time constraints. Actually, Cobb did not know what the message was about. His lawyer had pressed it into his palm at a meeting. Cobb promised the man he would address it. Once back in his office, however, busyness became consuming. The folded paper was put in a place where it would not be forgotten, with the thought that he would to get to it when time allowed. On a desk that held the amount of clutter one would expect from the owner of the most well-known restaurant in the world, the invoices, proposals, and receipts that came in almost hourly had taken greater urgency and pushed the small scrap of nondescript paper further and further from Cobb's attention.

As the minutes passed, Cobb stewed that his schedule had been thrown off. His Irish ire, which would one day be bared to the world in an embarrassing fashion, grew.

Robert Howard Cobb was the living, breathing embodiment of self-made success. Clever, creative, and brimming with a desire to not just work but achieve, Cobb had learned the restaurant trade while working in his mother Mattie's boarding house in Billings, Montana. Throughout his youth he was as much at home on the back of a horse flinging a lariat as he was wielding a spatula and tossing flapjacks or turning eggs. The Cobbs were Midwesterners. His father, Charles, was an Ohioan; his mother was from Missouri. Young Robert was born in Moberly, Missouri, but the family, which also included daughter Shellie, moved to Montana by covered wagon when the children were young.

As with most boys his age, baseball was a favored pastime. Cobb relished outdoor challenges—fishing, horseback riding, roping—and became proficient with a rifle through competitive marksmanship. As a seventeen-year-old, Robert Cobb seemed destined to follow convention. Like many of the men in Billings, he took a job in the town mill. This wasn't just any local mill, though. Montana Sash and Door was one of the largest works milling companies in the entire Northwest. It operated out of a large, three-story, wood-frame building next to a lumberyard. Cobb's work ethic and ability to quickly understand tasks drew the notice of his supervisors. In short order, the teen was made assistant to the machine maintenance man. One evening in May, however, catastrophe would change the course of Robert Cobb's life.

Work at Montana Sash and Door had long since knocked off, and the employees had gone home for the night. The town's postmaster happened by the mill on his horse-drawn buggy when he noticed something amiss. Smoke was billowing from a window. By the time the town's fire department arrived in their newly purchased motorized firetruck, the entire building was engulfed in flames. Alerted to trouble by the wail of sirens, the townspeople flocked on horseback and on foot to gawk and satisfy their curiosity. Shock and concern spread about the community. As the intensity of the flames grew, so too did more problems. Embers from the blaze touched off smaller fires on wood-plank roads nearby. Inmates from the local jail across the street were hurriedly moved to a safer place of incarceration. So intense was the searing heat from the blaze that it blackened cottonwoods in a field next to the jail.

It was in the deep darkness of night that the glow of flames was finally doused. Despair was taking root in the men and women of Billings. Montana Sash and Door was gone, leveled. In the rubble were the remnants of dozens of completed projects that were to have been shipped the following morning. Two hundred fifty men slowly trudged home to the reality that they no longer had a place to work. As the firefighters picked up their equipment, a newspaper reporter noticed two despondent men sitting on a nearby curb. The younger man wiped tears from his reddened eyes. Next to him sat an older man, head in hands, crying. It was Robert Cobb and his boss.

In the aftermath of the fire, Cobb turned his thoughts southward—eleven hundred miles south, to be exact, to Los Angeles. While throngs were lured to Southern California by the bright lights and glamour of Hollywood, Cobb's interest was purely mathematical. With forty times the population of Billings, Los Angeles likely had many more employment opportunities. Thus, in 1919 at the age of seventeen, Robert Cobb packed his things and set out for a new beginning.

Once in Los Angeles, Cobb's goals were realized. He was quick to land work. His first job was as a messenger at Holman Bank. During summer months he picked up extra money as a barker, selling tickets for glass-bottom boat rides around Catalina Island. Employers recognized a magnetism to the young man. His personality drew people. Most of all, it drew their trust. In winter, when the tourist rush subsided, Cobb worked as a stock clerk for Haas Baruch Company, where he rose to company bookkeeper. Ambition next took him into banking and a job as a teller at Hellman Bank. Cobb got around town in a Model T that he had purchased for ninety dollars from "Big John" Coogan, whose son was the child star Jackie Coogan. The young man's cooking skills generated income as well. He drew on his Montana experience and cooked hamburgers in a popular Hollywood stand. In 1920 Cobb was hired as a checker at the dining room at the Lankershim Hotel. For the next five years he listened and observed, internalizing the ins and outs of the restaurant trade and, most of all, the likes, dislikes, and traits of its customers.

When Cobb met Herb Somborn in 1925, his life took another dramatic turn. Somborn was both enthusiastic and eclectic. His public recognition was as husband to the era's most glamourous film star, Gloria Swanson.

Within the business community Somborn was known as a multifaceted success. He had become a multimillionaire, first from the manufacture of shoes, then through real estate investment, and ultimately, the lure of Hollywood tugged. Somborn became a motion picture producer, then one of the industry's first film distributors. In 1925 Somborn cast his eye on the restaurant business. A friend had challenged him: "If you know anything about food, you can sell it out of a hat."[1] Conversations with Abe Frank, who managed the Ambassador Hotel; Wilson Mizner, a screenwriter; and cinema impresario Sid Grauman convinced Somborn to open an eatery. On July 16, 1926, Somborn filed incorporation papers and Brown Derby Wilshire Corporation was born. He secured a site at Wilshire Boulevard and Alexandria Avenue, which was across the street from the Ambassador Hotel, where he lived. Recalling his friend's words, Somborn then hired an architect with orders to design a building shaped like a hat. Rising from the roof was a neon sign that read: "Eat in the Hat." In all, Somborn sank $16,000 into the project. Once constructed, the unique structure housed a small, simple diner. It was called the Brown Derby. The menu consisted of just five items. Chili con carne was a particular favorite. Somborn kept the restaurant open twenty-four hours a day.

Somborn had liked the eagerness of the personable lad he saw cooking hamburgers on Wilshire Boulevard. He dropped by one day with the offer of a steady job. Robert Cobb accepted and in time found his duties to be all encompassing, if not overwhelming. He was the Brown Derby's headwaiter, buyer, bookkeeper, and receiving clerk. From a tepid beginning, Somborn's Brown Derby grew in popularity. Throughout the surge of success, Somborn's youthful protégé began to entertain the idea of opening his own restaurant. Whether spawned by workload, fatigue, or his own ambitious dreams, Cobb grafted to the ideas of a fast-talking entrepreneur and left Somborn's employ.

There could not have been a worse time in America to open a restaurant than 1928. The country was plunging into the Great Depression, and even though the motion picture industry's success buoyed the economy of Southern California, enthusiasm and savvy only went so far. Cobb soon found that his partner had been long on hyperbole but short on integrity. A gambling binge at a Tijuana casino lost all of his partner's money, including the $1,500 Cobb had invested with him. The fledgling restaurant, the Nickabob, met a swift demise. A contrite Cobb returned to

Somborn to ask for his old job back. The Brown Derby owner was a determined man with little tolerance for shenanigans or disloyalty. Somborn acquiesced with a test of Cobb's character: He hired the young man to wash dishes.

Cobb never complained. He rolled up his sleeves and savored a steady paycheck, careful to set aside a small amount to be able to indulge in his favored pastimes, among which were treks to Los Angeles's Wrigley Field to take in Angels baseball games. Cobb's contrition was exhibited through his hard work. Appreciation was shown in the extra shifts he took and the intensity of his efforts. Several months after Cobb was rehired, Somborn summoned him for a meeting. When the two sat across from each other, the protégé could read trouble in the body language of the Brown Derby owner. Somborn conceded that his restaurant was bleeding red ink. He was being sued for nonpayment of rent, the water bill hadn't been paid, and collectors were after installment payments on equipment. Somborn had appreciated the quick study Cobb had become and the many ideas the younger man espoused. He wondered whether Cobb was the man to turn things around. The men discussed ideas. Finally, Somborn told Cobb to put away his apron. He was promoted to general manager. Sixty days later the Brown Derby was operating in the black again, and Herb Somborn rewarded his eager protégé with a promotion to vice president.

The simple Wilshire Brown Derby did so well that Somborn and Cobb decided to expand the venture. They agreed it was time to move up and into the world of fine dining. The men rented an old motion picture studio near the intersection of Hollywood and Vine from Cecil B. DeMille and, on Valentine's Day in 1929, the men opened a second Brown Derby at 1628 North Vine. Their eatery couldn't have been more ideally located. Radio and motion picture studios, luxury hotels, and popular theaters were either on the block or just a short walk away. The intersection bustled. In addition to those who worked in the area, the many shows attracted hundreds to watch their performances.

The Hollywood Brown Derby was the antithesis of its predecessor. Where the Wilshire Brown Derby operated from a gaudy—if not cheesy—hat, the Hollywood Brown Derby was about quality and class. Its exterior featured a Spanish facade and flat tile roof. Inside, arched passageways led into the bar, banquet area, and dining room, where diners were able to eat in semiprivacy in one of several dozen leather-backed

Bob Cobb in 1934. Cobb was both suave and savvy. The business acumen that made his restaurant, the Brown Derby, one of the most famous in the world would transform the Hollywood Stars into baseball's most innovative club. ***Courtesy of the Bob Cobb Family Collection***

booths. Ornate chandeliers hung from a cantilevered ceiling. Every five feet, a derby-shaped sconce protruded from the wall. Cataracterum palms and an ice carving created in the theme of the day enhanced the restaurant's decor. In the center of each round table was a copper derby that, when opened, revealed an ashtray. These were the source of the bulge in more than a few coat pockets of men who left the restaurant having filched an eighty-dollar souvenir. Particularly unique to the Brown Derby were the phone jacks. Each booth had one. Tourists gasped at hearing a famous entertainer's name paged, followed by a maître d' hurriedly rushing a telephone to be plugged in at the celebrity's booth. The novelty of the feature added to the restaurant's allure. Directors and executives conducted business over lunch. Up-and-coming and wishful actors used the phones for pretense. Only once did Cobb have to seriously intervene regarding the use of the device. It occurred when a well-known madam had her girls paged in the restaurant on fight nights. "I have the greatest respect for your profession," Cobb said to the madam, "but, how would you like it if I set up a hot dog stand in your living room?"[2] The point was received, and the practice ended.

Bob Cobb turned Herb Somborn's second restaurant into a culinary palace and ultimately one of the most famous restaurants in the world. It became a magnet for movie stars and studio executives, who could stop in for a quick lunch, use the restaurant for a business meeting, or walk in after a day of shooting or recording. That convenience brought entrée into a haven of culinary flair. With his potential clientele in mind, Cobb had a much different vision for the second Brown Derby. He sought quality, luring Robert Kreis from the Pebble Beach Lodge to be executive chef, while Paul Posti joined as chef from the Statler Hotel in Boston. Together the men created sumptuous menus that changed with the seasons. Chicken-stuffed bell peppers, charcoal-broiled steaks, and deviled breasts of chicken would dot the menu in the fall. Winter could bring baked sugar ham, veal curries, and Parisienne sweet bread. Seafood wasn't declared just fresh; it was billed as "morning catch." Celebrities flocked. The Brown Derby became more than just a convenient watering hole. It grew into the place to go for a night on the town as well as the place for Hollywood's glamourous to be seen. On any given night the restaurant teemed with celebrity. One might find Charlie Chaplin and Groucho Marx cracking jokes while seated back-to-back in adjoining booths. The stunning Rita Hayworth would stride in to admiring glances and longing stares. Red Skelton routinely joshed with the staff, while across the room Spencer Tracy could be seen loquaciously entertaining friends.

Bob Cobb's ebullience was part of the Brown Derby's attraction. He was quick to greet customers. The man was dapper. He was rarely without a boutonniere in his neatly pressed suit. A newspaper poll of the best-dressed men in Los Angeles ranked Cobb third. Throughout a typical evening Cobb would make it a point to move from table to table with a smile filling his face. His, however, was a sincere and not phony or patronizing personality. He remembered tidbits about regulars, made certain to congratulate anniversaries and birthdays, and noted dining quirks.

Cobb knew that celebrities were particular in their tastes. They knew quality and appreciated class. He also knew that they would never complain, but if they weren't happy, they would not come back. The restaurateur was well aware that when Tyrone Power walked in the door, he was going to order boiled brisket of beef in horseradish sauce. Eddie Cantor would expect a hamburger steak. Gary Cooper wanted fried chicken, but he wanted his dry and not greasy. Cobb also knew which orders would upset his kitchen staff but insisted there could be no argument when George Raft ordered his steak smothered in catsup. When Wallace Beery ordered his customary corned beef cabbage, Cobb didn't want to hear his chef complain that it was not on the menu. Nor would Cobb accept any howls from the kitchen when Beery insisted they cover his sponge cake with catsup. "Our clientele like a tall story or a good gag with their hamburger," Cobb told a newspaper writer. "But without that better hamburger, they wouldn't keep coming back year after year."[3]

Celebrities didn't just enjoy eating at the Brown Derby; they embraced the place. Cobb found himself serving trout raised on Beery's farm in Studio City. Broccoli that came out of the kitchen was often from Robert Taylor and Barbara Stanwyck's farm in Brentwood. Corn, on occasion, came from Clark Gable and Carole Lombard's ranch in Encino. Dorothy Lamour summoned her mother from New Orleans to teach Cobb's chef the proper way to make shrimp creole. Pat O'Brien urged Cobb to add his Irish stew to the menu, and in time it became the Thursday night special. When the Brown Derby produced a cookbook, Jimmy Durante sent a copy to noted New York City restaurateur Toots Shor with a note urging that he read the book and learn something.

Cobb was also a stickler for quality and decorum. When Marlene Dietrich walked into the restaurant one evening wearing pants, Cobb kicked her out. He wouldn't let a woman wearing slacks dine in the Brown Derby for another thirty years.

In the early 1930s Hollywood was in its heyday. While much of America glowered from the apprehension and agony that seeped into homes during the Great Depression, motion pictures offered escape. In greater numbers than ever before, Americans suppressed their troubles with trips to the cinema. Newspapers in Los Angeles seized on this popularity and made a concerted effort to feed their readers the news, gossip, and tidbits about Hollywood's famous and glamorous. Gossip writers recognized the Brown Derby as a place with the sort of fodder that could fill column inches. Who was with whom in the Brown Derby became a regular notation in columns in the *Herald*, *Daily News*, and *Examiner*. Mollie Merrick often began her "Hollywood in Person" column with tales of whom she had been lunching with at the Brown Derby. Louella Parsons, the *Examiner* gossip columnist whose writing appeared in six hundred newspapers, often held meetings with her staff in the restaurant and claimed booth 52 for lunch for more than thirty years. Rare was the day when a Kendall Read or Lucille Leimert column in the *Times* failed to mention a celebrity couple that was seen dining in Bob Cobb's restaurant. Once Hedda Hopper began writing her acclaimed column in the *Times*, the Brown Derby became a regular source of information and inspiration. The publicity generated by the columnists further fueled the popularity of the restaurant. With many of the columns syndicated nationally to newspapers across the country, their notes made the Brown Derby as much a part of Hollywood lore as the actors and studios themselves.

Outside of the Brown Derby on the sidewalk, equally head-turning antics were a regular occurrence. People who were down on their luck sold gardenias at fifteen cents apiece. The corsages became a way to tell the tourists from the industry professionals who dined inside. An immigrant from Poland who called himself Vitch offered to sketch the celebrities in exchange for a cup of coffee and a bowl of hot soup. Cobb liked the man's work so much that he framed and mounted the charcoal sketches and hung them on the restaurant's walls. Over time, every wall would be filled with the caricatures, which would number more than one thousand. The works of the man, whose name was Icek Levkovitch, became part of the attraction of the Hollywood Brown Derby. For Cobb, the drawings became another matter for task. Each day he instructed a maître d' to scour the gossip columns, then separate drawings of couples who had broken up or filed for divorce and move together drawings of those who were now dating or had become engaged or married.

Star-struck movie fans, many of them tourists who hoped to catch a glimpse of or perhaps get an autograph from a movie star, gathered almost every night near the entrance to the Hollywood Brown Derby. Some got far more than a glimpse or an autograph. When two young girls approached actress Isabel Jewell for an autograph, they shared that they were from her small hometown in Wyoming. The fans were rewarded with the experience of a lifetime, a personally guided tour of Hollywood from the star of *Manhattan Melodrama* and *Lost Horizon.* Desperation sometimes overtook awe, as was the case of a young Oklahoma girl, Betty Brewer, who sang outside of the Brown Derby in hopes of being discovered. The musical notes reached the proper ear and earned a screen test, then a part in a movie. Brewer's performance in *Rangers of Fortune* led to a studio contract and ultimately roles in six motion pictures. More importantly, however, the work that came from the impromptu audition outside of the Brown Derby helped to take the girl's parents and five siblings off government assistance.

In 1931 Cobb broached the idea of a third Brown Derby restaurant with Somborn. He noted that many of their celebrity customers had moved to the area of Beverly Hills, Brentwood, and Bel Air, which were west of the Brown Derby's Hollywood location. Though the area was only five miles away, Cobb surmised that celebrities wouldn't venture far from home when they went out for dinner. The Hollywood and Vine restaurant would meet the lunch needs of the celebrity crowd, while a Beverly Hills location could become their evening destination. Somborn found a location, and the two men built a Brown Derby at Wilshire Boulevard and Rodeo Drive. The growth of office buildings and businesses in the area west of Los Angeles spurred the popularity of Somborn and Cobb's third restaurant, and in almost no time it, too, had become a profitable venture.

Through the early 1930s the Brown Derby continued to grow in both prominence and success. In the winter of 1933, however, stability cracked. Herb Somborn fell gravely ill. For many months he had been suffering complications from a kidney ailment. During the holidays Somborn was taken to Cedars of Lebanon Hospital, where doctors offered a grave prognosis. Cobb and Gloria Swanson, from whom Somborn had been divorced for eleven years, were frequent visitors. As Christmas drew near, Somborn asked doctors to move him from the hospital room to his apartment at the Beverly Wilshire Hotel. Two weeks later on January

2, 1934, with Bob Cobb at his bedside, Herb Somborn passed away. When Somborn's will was read a month later, 60 percent of his estate was put into a trust to go to his twelve-year-old daughter with Swanson once the girl turned thirty. Twenty-five percent was bequeathed to Cobb, along with management of the Brown Derby restaurants at a guaranteed monthly salary of $1,000. Victor Ford Collins, Somborn's attorney, was left 15 percent of the estate. Rather than accept Somborn's money, Cobb felt it most prudent to take ownership control of the Brown Derby restaurants. Together with Collins, he successfully negotiated an exchange of equity. Cobb gained the restaurants, and when she turned thirty, Gloria Swanson Somborn would receive the original Brown Derby that her father had started.

Cobb plunged his energies into the three restaurants. He expanded the operation to include catering. Soon it was not uncommon on a Thanksgiving morning to see Brown Derby trucks weaving their way through Beverly Hills, Holmby Hills, or the Sunset Avenue gate and into Bel Air with precooked holiday meals for celebrity customers. The month of June would see Cobb's trucks outside of country clubs, where they delivered Brown Derby meals to wedding receptions. When time allowed for recreation, Cobb accompanied Clark Gable and Harpo Marx to an area ranch where he engaged in his Montana passion for roping. When he could work in a day game at Wrigley Field, Cobb watched the Angels play. In the fall, time was always cleared to travel to Montana for a week of duck hunting.

Not even one month after Cobb had taken ownership control of the Brown Derby restaurants, he was taxed. On a Thursday afternoon, March 1, just after the height of lunch service had concluded, twenty-seven waiters walked out. Several hundred diners were aghast. Cobb recruited other staff to join him and wait tables for the duration of the day but soon found himself embroiled in a feud with the Waiters Union Local 17. The union demanded pay increases from the new owner. Cobb countered by firing the strikers and hiring replacements. Tempers and nasty tactics escalated. More than one hundred picketers were dispatched to all three Brown Derby restaurants. They blocked diners from getting out of their cars and from entering the restaurants. Employees were harassed and, in some cases, even followed to their homes. Workers were threatened that bombs might be hurled into the establishment. The union went to the

Screen Actors Guild and the Teamsters to ask that Cobb's celebrity customers and delivery truck drivers stay away from the Brown Derby.

Cobb fought back. He took legal action and petitioned for a restraining order to stop the picketers. Cobb argued that the fight wasn't about pay raises. He was willing to agree to the pay demands but insisted that what was truly sought was a closed-shop agreement—a pledge from Cobb that he would employ only union members in good standing as waiters, cooks, or busboys. This, Cobb explained to the judge, went against the National Industrial Recovery Act, a post-Depression policy by which every restaurant owner in Los Angeles had agreed to abide. Cobb added that the picketers' intimidation tactics had caused the Brown Derby to lose $20,000 in revenue. Cobb received his temporary restraining order and the picketing stopped. Not long after, the dispute was settled. No details were made public, and Cobb declared that the matter had been resolved in a way that pleased both sides.

Union ferocity was only one part of the challenges Cobb faced after assuming ownership of the restaurants. Competition came knocking as well. It heightened the owner's attention to detail and quest for continued success. In 1932 Sardi's, which had become a renowned New York dining establishment made famous, in part, by the gossip columnist and commentator Walter Winchell, opened a branch in Los Angeles on Hollywood Boulevard. Al Levy opened a branch of his successful restaurant chain down the street from the Brown Derby's Hollywood and Vine location. In 1936 a local comedian, Dave Chasen, opened a southern-style restaurant in Beverly Hills that developed a celebrity appeal.

Cobb not only weathered the storm, but his Brown Derby restaurants continued to prosper. The restaurateur's measure of distinction expanded one night from a peak of ingenuity. During a late-night conversation with his friend Sid Grauman, the men confessed to being hungry. Cobb retreated to the refrigerator. Taking stock of what he could find, Cobb pulled out leftovers—a head of lettuce, an avocado, a cold breast of chicken, a hard-boiled egg, some cheese, chives, watercress, tomatoes, two slices of bacon, and some of his chef Robert Kreis's French dressing. After throwing the bacon on the stove to cook, Cobb grabbed a knife and went to work. Minutes later he and Grauman were quietly devouring Cobb's concoction. The next day Grauman dropped into a booth at the Brown Derby for lunch. When he ordered a "Cobb salad," it threw the waitstaff and kitchen into a tizzy. No one knew what Grauman was talking about until their boss explained. The name stuck, and the dish was added to the restaurant's menu—but not, however, before a bit of flair was added: service on a cold plate with a cold fork and a gravy boat full of French dressing. Almost overnight, Cobb's creation became a sensation.

Cobb's restaurant evolved into more than just a celebrated eatery. It became ingrained into the fabric of celebrity life. When Clark Gable proposed marriage to Carol Lombard, he popped the question in booth 5 at the Brown Derby. Amos 'n' Andy could have chosen any restaurant to celebrate the anniversary of their act but did so in the Brown Derby with noted broadcaster Lowell Thomas.

The success of the Hollywood Brown Derby made Cobb a man in demand. Vendors saw the restaurant as a good account. It was good for business to say their product was part of the menu at the famous eatery. Sales representatives taxed Cobb's time and tried the man's patience.

As he waited for the overdue liquor salesman, Bob Cobb happened to spy the folded note that he had pushed beneath the pad on his desktop blotter days earlier. He fingered the paper, then pried it from where it was wedged. Cobb unfolded the note and his eyes widened at its words. Like a flash, he thrust his right hand to the telephone. He swiftly dialed the number to his attorney. Cobb's meeting was now forgotten, pushed aside by the urgency of the message on the note that now lay face up inches away. Bared was a handwritten question, one that unbridled such a powerful surge of yearning that the man could not phone his lawyer fast enough to deliver an answer. The note asked Bob Cobb if he wanted to buy a baseball team.

2

"NOT WITHOUT ME"

The dial on the black desktop telephone spun with an intensity fueled by urgency. Perhaps the youthful exuberance that coursed through Bob Cobb was its catalyst. After ten years of toiling over stoves, dealing with staff, negotiating prices, and haggling with temperamental chefs, Robert Howard Cobb had been presented with the opportunity to become involved in a venture that tapped his excitement.

Victor Ford Collins laughed that the venture was not about sponsoring a girls' softball team, as Cobb had cracked. No, a client of the lawyer was the owner of a team in the Pacific Coast League. The man was in a distressed situation with no choice but to sell his ball club. Things had to happen fast. Cobb was interested, and in a sign of the seller's desperation, the meeting to consummate a deal could take place in a matter of hours rather than days. Collins had used the seller's urgency to negotiate the purchase price from a prohibitive $100,000 to a more acceptable $40,000. A banker for the seller and the seller's primary representative had hammered out an agreement with Collins on the stipulations, terms, and legalese needed to complete the transaction.

Cobb was staring at a precipice the likes from which he had never before leaped. Collins had made explicitly clear that the food industry wizard was about to buy a mocked, downtrodden, laughingstock of a baseball team that didn't even have a place of its own to play in. Collins was well aware of the previous owner's attempts to build a ballpark. He told Cobb the price tag to construct such a park had been $100,000. The men hatched a plan: a share offering designed to raise $200,000.

The timing could not have been better to pursue such a strategy. Cash flowed about Hollywood like never before. The motion picture industry was riding a banner year. Moviegoers were buying tickets at the rate of eighty million a week. Both demand and salaries for directors, producers, and writers swelled. Filmdom's leading actors were awash in myriad offers, and there was excitement for films already in production for 1939 release, such as *The Wizard of Oz*, *Gone with the Wind*, and *The Hunchback of Notre Dame*.

On a chilly November morning in 1938, Cobb perused a list of friends. The first number he dialed was that of the film director Cecil B. DeMille. Cobb explained his idea. Words such as "partners" and "fun" were intermixed with "community service" and an insistence that "nobody is taking any profits."[1] He exuded enthusiasm and pitched the investment that was required: $7,500. No one could invest more. No one could pay less. With little question and without reservation, DeMille said yes. Boosted by the response, Cobb attacked the project with zeal. One by one he phoned each number on his list, everyone an icon in the entertainment industry—actors, directors, producers, and writers: Bing Crosby, Barbara Stanwyck, Robert Taylor, George Burns, Gracie Allen, Gene Autry, William Frawley, George Raft, William Powell, Raoul Walsh, and Joe E. Brown. None so much as batted an eye. Each eagerly said they would join in. And that's when Bob Cobb ran in to trouble—with his wife.

When Cobb shared the news of the venture, he was castigated by his missus. The man was taken aback. The look of consternation on his face made Gail Patrick smile mischievously and shriek, "Not without me. Not unless I can go in too!" Bob Cobb's facial expression morphed from shock to joy. With an ear-to-ear grin he replied, "Honey, it will be a pleasure. We'll be partners and have a lot of fun."[2]

Mrs. Robert Cobb left the conversation blissful. When Victor Ford Collins learned the news, he beamed, knowing that the involvement of Cobb's wife could only help to ensure the venture's success. The woman was far from a demure housewife lacking an identity of her own. She was one of America's rising screen starlets. The Alabama-born Margaret LaVelle Fitzpatrick was studying law with an eye to one day becoming her state's lieutenant governor when, in the summer of 1932, friends convinced her to enter a beauty contest. The Miss Panther Woman pageant was being staged as a promotional scheme by Paramount Publix Pictures to find a prospective starlet to be cast alongside Charles Laughton and

Bela Lugosi in *Island of Lost Souls*. More than sixty thousand young women applied. Kathleen Burke won and received the part. Margaret Fitzpatrick placed second. Her prize was a trip to Hollywood. It would change her life. She took her younger brother along. When she was introduced to Bill LeBaron, who had only recently taken over running the studio, Fitzpatrick was immediately offered a contract that would pay fifty dollars per week. "No, I must have seventy-five dollars and no cuts for up to a year," she snapped.[3] LeBaron was astonished by the woman's brashness. After a bit of back and forth, the studio executive gave in.

Fitzpatrick underwent several weeks of training. Speech lessons rid her of her Southern accent. Posture and poise lessons involved walking while balancing a book atop her head. Perhaps most significant was a name change. Margaret Fitzpatrick was out. She was now Gail Patrick.

Before the end of the year Patrick, née Fitzpatrick, had her first part as a secretary in *If I Had a Million*. Weeks later she wowed producers and crew with her riding and shooting skills in a small part in *The Mysterious Rider*. By the end of 1933 Patrick had been in eight movies. Her first significant role came in *Death Takes a Holiday* opposite Fredric March. It was in the spring of 1934 that Patrick earned her first leading role, playing a widowed mother opposite Randolph Scott in *Wagon Wheel*.

Patrick's compensation increased almost in step with praise for her work. From the early $75 per week she received on signing with Paramount, her contract was revised to pay $150 weekly. By the time she signed on to appear in *Mississippi* in 1935, Patrick was drawing $650 per week.

That year, following a day of shooting, Patrick accompanied friends to the Brown Derby for lunch. One of her companions introduced the actress to Bob Cobb. Instantly struck by the beautiful brunette, the beaming restaurateur stammered, "How happy I am to meet you."[4] Behind the smile beat the heart of a lovestruck adolescent. Cobb was smitten. Patrick swooned at the sight of Cobb's magnetic smile. His energetic personality and his natty attire, which was always accentuated by a red carnation, drew her attention. That Cobb was twelve years her senior did not dissuade the younger actress.

Cobb fell and fell hard. He was enamored with Patrick, in awe of her intelligence, captivated by her humor. The woman's cultured voice was magnetic and, of course, her striking beauty was enthralling. Like Cobb, Patrick was Irish. In almost no time Cobb and Patrick were seeing quite a lot of each other. Their doing the rumba at La Conga made the gossip columns. So, too, did their cozy dinner at the Trocadero, a birthday celebration at the Cocoanut Grove, lunch at Marcus Daly Café, and their trips to watch the horse races at both the Santa Anita Racetrack and Hollywood Park. When Patrick returned from a trip to the South, columnists were quick to note that it was Cobb who met her at the airport. Photographers made a point to grab pictures of the couple, and newspapers were all too happy to print them. A photo of the restaurateur and actress descending a staircase at the Academy of Motion Picture Arts and Sciences dinner showed Patrick glamorous in a long print maroon-and-white satin dress with a sable cape and Cobb in tuxedo, tails, and top hat. When photographed at the horse races, the picture that appeared didn't just show the couple together but was expanded to display their attire: Patrick in an attractive calf-length printed dress and matching hat, Cobb in a cream-colored double-breasted suit and fedora.

Also written about was the depth of their romance. Some gossip writers seemed to swoon vicariously along with Patrick, especially when they noted her regular receipt of flowers. Every Tuesday a large vase full of colorful flowers was delivered to the actress. The romantic gesture was to mark the anniversary of the day of the week on which Patrick and Cobb had met.

Throughout their dating and courtship, Patrick was kept busy by film opportunities and shooting schedules. As she tackled more and more projects, her reputation grew. So, too, did an appreciation for her character and demeanor. While fellow castmates and crew members would grouse about the egos, haughtiness, and ill-mannered temperament of some of the day's biggest stars, such traits were never mentioned about Gail Patrick. The woman became heralded throughout Hollywood for a kindness of spirit and largesse of heart. When Patrick learned that a child cast member in *Mad about Music* was the daughter of parents on government assistance, she hosted the family in her home over several weekends and provided them with support. Patrick leaped into action when her English secretary pursued American citizenship and beamed from the gallery as the woman took the naturalization Oath of Allegiance. When her home state University of Alabama football team was selected to come to Southern California and play in the Rose Bowl, it was Patrick who offered to host the team and stage a welcome dinner at the luxurious Hotel Biltmore. At Christmas the men at the post office came to expect

Patrick's annual arrival with her bundle of cards, seven hundred in all, and each with a handwritten personal letter to its recipient.

During the first week of December in 1936, Patrick was sent out of state on a multiweek tour to promote her latest film. On December 17, Patrick's American Airlines flight touched down at Burbank Airport. A longing, eager Cobb leaned against the fence, anxiously awaiting sight of Patrick. The restaurateur knew he never wanted to be apart from Patrick again, and when the two embraced, Cobb proposed. Knowing that Patrick had returned home for a large studio event and had to prepare for an upcoming picture, Cobb had hastily scraped together a plan. He arranged for a plane, and in such a hurry the couple didn't even bring along a toothbrush, Cobb and Patrick flew to Mexico and eloped in Tijuana. Patrick was due to begin work on a new film, *The Love Trap*, the very next morning. When the film's producer, B. P. Schulberg, learned of Patrick's wedding, he sent word that she could take the next twelve days off to enjoy a honeymoon.

Once the lovestruck couple returned to Los Angeles, they made a beeline for the county clerk's office on Figueroa Street, where they filed a notice of intent to wed. Cobb and Patrick made plans to marry in a local church on Christmas Eve, then honeymoon in Europe once the actress had completed work on the picture. As often happens with the best laid plans, Cobb's went awry. An outbreak of colds and influenza swept the area. Entire movie shoots were postponed because so many stars were stricken. Jury trials were put on hold due to the large numbers of ill judges. Before Cobb and Patrick could walk down the aisle and marry under California law, Gail Patrick was ordered to bed by her doctor. She, too, had come down with the flu. Cobb sought to brighten his wife's day with the gift of a new car at Christmas. But the virus and the ensuing changes it brought to the shooting schedule for *The Love Trap* meant the Cobbs were forced to cancel their honeymoon trip to Europe.

The couple settled into a five-bedroom, 3,327-square-foot home on Highland Avenue near Sepulveda Boulevard. But by the spring of 1937, the Cobbs became immersed in planning construction of a dream home in Brentwood on a site that was around the corner from Bing Crosby's Mapleton Drive estate and not terribly far from the ranch home of their friends Barbara Stanwyck and Robert Taylor.

The first few months of married life came and went at a harried pace. Cobb's restaurants continued to thrive. When Patrick wasn't ordering drapes or studying furniture swatches for the planned new house, she was on soundstages and sets shooting movies. Spring brought a contract to do *Stage Door* with "Ginge," her friend Ginger Rogers. Once that had finished, she was hired for a part in *Dangerous to Know*.

Patrick's celebrity grew through appearances on magazine covers in October and November 1937. Then, in December, as the Cobb's celebrated their first wedding anniversary, the couple also toasted Patrick's first leading role. Days later the *Los Angeles Times* trumpeted her selection as the lead in Paramount's *Angel in Furs*, a role which hiked Patrick's weekly paycheck to $1,500.

Cobb and Patrick became regulars on the red carpet at premieres. They joined the Bing Crosbys, the Pat O'Briens, the Dick Powells, and the Jimmy Cagneys at backyard swim parties and summer barbeques. Their own annual Christmas party became a coveted invitation. Guests received a tree ornament bearing their name and the date of the event. And, of course, during breaks in her motion picture shoots, Patrick would duck into the Brown Derby for lunch and the chance to spend time with her husband.

Whether at a premiere or a horse race, or while cozied up in a restaurant booth, the couple locked gazes. Their beaming smiles and cheek-to-cheek dances painted a blissful picture. In fact, one Los Angeles newspaper columnist labeled Patrick and Cobb "Hollywood's Ideal Couple."

In September 1938 Cobb expanded the Hollywood Brown Derby. With his wife's assistance he added on a private banquet room to the restaurant, and the couple debuted the new American Room with a lavish party. Patrick insisted that her close friend Carole Lombard bring her new beau, Clark Gable. The Don Ameches, the Henry Fondas, and Dorothy Lamour were among the many who attended.

It was three months later that Cobb was on the phone to many of these same friends with another invitation—to join him in buying a baseball team. In less than a day Cobb had lined up eighteen of the twenty partners he needed. He then directed Victor Ford Collins to complete the remaining details. Cobb and his assembled group of Hollywood stars were going to buy the Hollywood Stars.

3

"WHOLLY OWNED BY HOLLYWOOD PEOPLE"

The sweaters and jackets worn to the party seemed contrary to a January 8 temperature that much of the country would consider balmy but only residents of Southern California would complain was chilly. Apparel was just one example of a room painted in paradox. All about the American Room at the Hollywood Brown Derby, joviality flowed. The vigor of the men responsible for the gathering, cheerful to the edge of giddiness, contrasted greatly with the principal topic of the night: a baseball team that a columnist had once proclaimed "patrons have no use for."[1]

It had been one month since news first broke that Bob Cobb and his celebrity backers had agreed to buy the Hollywood Stars. During that time a few more movie stars, some business leaders, and a couple of renowned motion picture directors had been added to complete the partnership. Necessary funds were banked. The group had finalized plans, made hirings, and engaged companies to at long last construct a ballpark. Now with i's dotted, t's crossed, and the purchase complete, members of the press were assembled. As dinners were served to sportswriters from the *Examiner*, *Times*, *Evening Herald*, *Daily News*, *Citizen*, and *United Press*, Cobb and Victor Ford Collins effusively gave details of plans for a team few could previously associate with the word "excitement." The men depicted a bright future for a ball club many previously felt had none in Los Angeles.

The Hollywood Stars were a team that one sportswriter suggested played so poorly in 1938 it was as if the players did not care. Fans clearly didn't. So few bothered to show up for games that many felt it was inevitable the ball club would move to another town. The Stars' record, 77 wins and 99 losses, was the very definition of pitiful. In fact, it was a team so bad that it seemed bad luck was the only luck the Stars had. The team had to postpone a game when someone forgot to load the trunk with their uniforms and equipment onto the train during a road trip. One of the Stars' losses came via forfeit after umpires could not convince their manager to stop arguing.

The Stars' owner put so little money into the club that three players were released when the team was fined $1,100 by the league for its forfeiture. The club was run by a business manager with no baseball background and operated so poorly that when the man quit with two months left in the season, the move was applauded in print by sportswriters and columnists. Publicity was the responsibility of a man whose previous experience was selling crypts with a marine view for a mausoleum. Perhaps fitting, given the state of the 1938 Stars, the man's most celebrated brainstorm during the summer was a night in which blind and hearing-impaired fans received free admission to a Stars game.

Once the season concluded, the Hollywood Stars finished next to last in the eight-team Pacific Coast League. Their 1938 futility was nothing new. Over the previous nine seasons, while playing under three different names and in two different cities, the club had finished either last or next to last seven times.

If the exuberance of Cobb and Collins achieved anything, it was to deliver an elixir to the men who ran the Pacific Coast League, for the Hollywood club had produced little but headaches for the league over the previous two decades. It was somewhat ironic that the American Room of Cobb's Brown Derby, where the purchase of the ball club was announced, was ten miles from where the troubled team had originally been conceived.

It had been in the spring of 1909 that the team was launched as the Vernon Tigers. Inspiration for the team was a teetotal entrepreneur's scheme to promote sales of alcoholic beverages. In 1905 Vernon was incorporated to promote industrial development along railroad lines in the area. The small area located five miles south of downtown Los Angeles was an industrial town with railroad docks, meat packing plants, and just over seven hundred residents. That same year the Prohibition Alliance and the Anti-Saloon League began a quest to stop the sale of alcoholic beverages in Los Angeles. Seizing on the prospect of a dry Los Angeles, a railroad worker, Jack Doyle, used his life savings to lease land in Vernon and in 1907 build a saloon with a hundred-foot-long bar that employed thirty-seven bartenders to service customers. To lure people to both the small town and his bar, Doyle built a seven-thousand-seat outdoor arena for boxing and wrestling matches. Some of the biggest names in the sport—Jess Willard, Jack Dempsey, and Benny Leonard—fought in Doyle's ring. He staged local, regional, and even world title bouts.

Doyle's efforts gave ideas to Fred Maier. Head of the Los Angeles–based Maier Brewing Company, Maier saw baseball as a vehicle to increase beer sales. Already Maier's beer was the second most consumed beer in all of Los Angeles and sold 135,000 bottles of the product each year in both the city and six western states. Maier felt that baseball could help his company sell even more. Knowing that baseball fans drank a healthy amount of beer at games, Maier in 1909 built a ten-thousand-seat ballpark adjacent to Doyle's saloon and launched a ball club, which he tagged the Vernon Tigers.

A festive mood for the Tigers' first game took a tragic turn, however. During the Pacific Coast League team's debut on April 11, Maier fell ill. He was taken to the hospital suffering from what turned out to be his fifth attack of appendicitis. Doctors performed surgery, but Maier suffered a bad reaction to the anesthetic and died. Maier's brother, Eddie, took control of the brewery as well as the ball club. The man knew baseball better than the beer business, having pitched in high school and college. As a result, Eddie Maier paid particular attention to the Vernon Tigers. He worked to sign new ballplayers and used his connections to coax Hollywood celebrities such as Fatty Arbuckle, Tom Mix, and Buster Keaton to attend games. The ballpark's location adjacent to Doyle's saloon offered a passageway into the drinking establishment. Between innings it was not uncommon for players, such as Tigers left fielder Jess Stovall, to duck inside and cool off with a quaff of cold brew.

During the 1916 season Eddie Maier became embroiled in controversy. The Pacific Coast League accused the Tigers owner of violating professional baseball salary regulations. Maier protested, but one week after the season concluded, he announced his retirement from the game and sold his ball club to the former head of the rival Los Angeles Angels, Thomas J. Darmody.

The Darmody ownership was to be short-lived. In 1918 Maier declared he had yet to be paid by Darmody and took back ownership of the team. Maier let it be known that he would entertain offers for the club. Interested parties from Fresno, Hollywood, and Pasadena made pitches. Maier turned every one of them down. Then, in May 1919, Maier made a blockbuster announcement: He had sold the Vernon Tigers to the most popular actor in the motion picture industry, Roscoe "Fatty" Arbuckle.

Few in Hollywood could rival Fatty Arbuckle for box office appeal. In February 1919 Arbuckle had agreed to an unprecedented film contract. He was to make twenty-four pictures over three years for Lasky Corporation and be paid $3 million. Three months after signing the lucrative acting deal, Arbuckle sat in the office of Maier's attorney and agreed to pay $65,000 for the Vernon Tigers.

As soon as he was made president of the team, the Vernon Tigers became Fatty Arbuckle's toy. He took batting practice with the players. Photographers suited him in a uniform and posed the rotund comic with starlets. Donning a Vernon cap and jersey, the actor was photographed taking a bite out of a baseball. The photo would appear on a Zee-Nut series baseball card. Arbuckle took movie star friends on road trips. Sportswriters nicknamed the Tigers the "Fatty's" and the "Custard Pies" in reference to the owner's on-screen pie-throwing antics. Around the Pacific Coast League, "Fatty Day" was held whenever the actor came to town to see his Tigers play.

On the field the 1919 Vernon Tigers were a powerful team. Led by young sensation Bobby Meusel and former Brooklyn Dodgers pitcher Wheezer Dell, the Tigers won 111 games. They won a ferocious playoff series from the Los Angeles Angels to claim the Pacific Coast League pennant, then met St. Paul in the Junior World Series. Twenty-two thousand fans squeezed into the wooden Vernon ballpark for the championship game. Outside, more than five thousand fans were turned away. Those unable to get in missed watching the Tigers win to become champions of all of minor-league baseball.

During his divorce from baseball, tumult filled the life of Eddie Maier. Only a month after he sold the Vernon Tigers to Arbuckle, Prohibition became the law of the land. The sale of any beverage with an alcoholic content of more than 1 percent was banned. More than one thousand customers packed Doyle's saloon to gulp, guzzle, and sip one last time before the law went into effect. Breweries all across the country would be devastated. Many were forced out of business. Some concocted alternative products in order to survive. Stroh's turned to making ice cream. Pabst produced processed cheese spread. Coors made art pottery and ceramics. Anheuser-Busch recognized that people were producing homemade beer and sold them the necessary ingredients. Maier survived by selling "near beer," a product that contained a legal amount of alcohol.

Fatty Arbuckle had yet to pay Eddie Maier for the ball club, and after the Tigers' championship season, he asked to change terms of the deal. Arbuckle wanted to pay in installments. Maier grew angry and demanded cash. The actor refused, and when neither man would compromise, Arbuckle walked away from the ball club. Ownership of the Vernon Tigers reverted once again to Eddie Maier.

The Tigers fielded a powerful club again in the 1920 season. But during that summer startling tales began to emerge about unsavory actions by some of the Tigers players during their championship year. First baseman Babe Borton was accused of throwing games. Borton, who had played in the big leagues with the White Sox, Yankees, and St. Louis Browns, was accused of taking more than $2,000 from a Seattle bookmaker who followed the Tigers up and down the coast. It was claimed that during games in September 1919, Borton paid opponents to go easy against the Tigers. Maier asked the Pacific Coast League to investigate, and he ordered Borton suspended. Once the player had answered questions to the satisfaction of investigators, Maier booted Borton from the team.

In October a grand jury heard testimony in the matter. Players from Seattle and Salt Lake City told of being tipped off by Borton to pickoff throws and other Vernon strategies. Others revealed they were paid to give far less than their best effort. After two months of proceedings, the judge threw the case out. He announced that throwing baseball games was not against the law. However, the thirty-one-year-old Borton, who had batted .303 with fourteen home runs during the championship season, never played another game in professional baseball.

The Borton case soured Eddie Maier on baseball. He once again put the Vernon Tigers up for sale. The requirements of business were taking up much more of his available time. During the summer of 1921, a fierce competitor emerged to Maier's baseball operation. Multimillionaire chewing gum magnate William Wrigley Jr. bought the Tigers' chief rival, the Los Angeles Angels. Wrigley outbid moviemaker Hal Roach and Jack Doyle, paying $150,000 for the ball club.

Wrigley was one of the wealthiest men in America, with a fortune said to be worth 1/1700 of America's gross domestic product. Though based in Chicago, Wrigley had five residences around the country and particularly enjoyed Southern California. He owned controlling interest in Catalina, an island off the coast of Los Angeles. There he built a casino, a tile and pottery plant to take advantage of the island's clay and minerals, and launched a steamship line. Wrigley also loved baseball. In 1916 he bought a small stake in the Chicago Cubs, and in 1921 he became the team's principal owner. Adding the Angels gave him a team to follow while in the West and one that could aid in the development of prospects for his Cubs.

In 1924 Wrigley tightened his grip on the baseball market in Southern California. The chewing gum magnate built the crown jewel of minor-league ballparks at Forty-Second Place and Avalon Boulevard in south Los Angeles. It was a double-decked baseball palace that offered the most modern amenities in a Spanish-style architecture. The ballpark bore its owner's name—Wrigley Field.

With the Vernon Tigers' attendance and ticket sales having dropped year after year and the team's wooden ballpark becoming more dilapidated with each passing season, Maier gave in to the inevitable. He sold his ball club. The sale was a blockbuster. It involved the richest sale price ever for a team in the Pacific Coast League. Headlines broke on January 9, 1925, that Maier had received $225,000 for his ball club. The buyer was San Francisco banker Herbert Fleishhacker, who moved the Tigers to his hometown.

Herbert Fleishhacker was a prominent San Franciscan, a self-made success who had left school at the age of fourteen to work in his father's box factory. Herbert and his older brother, Mortimer, grew into the business and in savvy. An investment and quick flip produced a $300,000 profit for the brothers, a remarkable achievement in 1889. They then raised backing and bought paper mills and power companies before Herbert succeeded his father-in-law as president of Anglo & London Paris National Bank in 1908. A 1921 article in the *San Jose Evening News* said that Herbert Fleishhacker had an income of $100,000 per week. Fleishhacker did more than invest his money. The man was philanthropic. He founded the city's zoo and played a significant role in creation of San

Francisco's landmark Coit Tower. Fleishhacker also enjoyed sports. His son, Herbert Jr., had been national high school champion in the shot put in track and field. Later, Herbert Jr. starred in football and helped Stanford to the 1927 national championship. The senior Fleishhacker situated his new ball club in Recreation Park, a fifteen-thousand-seat wooden structure located in the city's Mission District, and renamed the team the Mission Bells. Two years later the team was renamed the Mission Reds.

Despite winning the pennant in 1929, the team consistently played second fiddle to the rival San Francisco Seals. The challenge of competing for attention from the Seals was further complicated in 1931, when the established club spent $1.2 million to build a palatial new ballpark, Seals Stadium. Made of concrete and steel, seating sixteen thousand, and featuring six state-of-the-art light towers to allow for night games, the ballpark was heralded as one of the finest in the country. The Reds arranged for Seals Stadium to be their home as well. But neither their play nor their business practices did much to make fans want to see their games. In the eight seasons that followed their pennant, the Reds finished in the second division seven times. Three times they finished last in the Pacific Coast League, and three times they ended the campaign in next to last.

Following the 1937 season, in which his team lost 103 of 176 games and was still unable to develop any measure of loyal fan following in San Francisco, Fleishhacker threw in the towel. He moved the ball club back to Southern California, where it was renamed the Hollywood Stars.

Fleishhacker's Stars were not the first incarnation of a Pacific Coast League team by that name. Not long after the banker had bought and moved the Vernon Tigers, Bill Lane pounced on the chance to become Southern California's second team. Lane had struggled for ten years to make a go of things in Salt Lake City. Following the 1925 season, he moved his team to Los Angeles and called them the Hollywood Stars.

Lane's Stars shared Wrigley Field with the Los Angeles Angels, but despite a pennant in 1930 and a couple of second-place finishes, his teams failed to make a dent in the support Wrigley's club enjoyed. In the winter of 1935 Lane became embroiled in a rent dispute with the Angels. To that point he had enjoyed a sweetheart deal. Lane's club played rent free and merely had to cover expenses incurred in using Wrigley's ballpark. But in 1932 William Wrigley Jr. died. His son Phil, or P. K., took control of the family empire. David Fleming was put in charge of running the Angels, and he demanded much more for use of the ballpark than the $8,000 Lane had previously paid. Lane was incensed. He told Fleming that the demand would cause him to lose money. When Lane investigated the possibility of moving his team to San Diego, Fleming mocked him. Lane became furious and intensified his queries of San Diego. When city leaders there agreed to build a ballpark, Lane applied for and received the necessary league approval to move.

Herbert Fleishhacker's dream of Southern California grandeur soured before it could take flight. Before his version of the Hollywood Stars had played their first game, Fleishhacker became embroiled in severe legal and financial turmoil. A group of French investors in Fleishhacker's bank sued him. They claimed that he had cheated them in a series of lucrative deals. Fleishhacker was accused of profiting from the purchase and subsequent sale of a large amount of steel. The investors claimed that the proceeds belonged to the bank and its investors. In another action, Fleishhacker was sued by bank investors who claimed that he had mishandled moneys derived from a lucrative sale of oil land in central California. A United States district judge ruled that Fleishhacker "violated his trust to the bank and the stockholders."[2] He was ordered to pay $651,579.71 in the Portland case and $735,872 in the oil land case. Just when Fleishhacker thought his storms had passed, the federal government indicted him for misappropriation of funds. The suits brought both scandal and scorn to the prominent San Franciscan.

Throughout the 1938 baseball season, Fleishhacker's San Francisco attorneys appealed the rulings. Little attention was paid by the man to his baseball team, and no money was invested in the team at all. Fleishhacker urged the team's business manager to find local investors, but none had interest. Rumors abounded late in the 1938 season that the baseball apathy shown by Fleishhacker and the lack of any movement toward building a ballpark meant the Stars would move back to San Francisco for the 1939 season.

Weeks after the 1938 baseball season had concluded, all of Fleishhacker's legal appeals were exhausted. By then the Internal Revenue Service had added a bill for $309,074 to the banker's obligations. The board of Fleishhacker's bank ordered him to resign. With his liabilities eclipsing $3.8 million, more lawsuits winding their way through the courts, and most of his assets in securities that fluctuated in value, Fleishhacker's attorneys recommended that he file for bankruptcy protection.

Two weeks after the rulings, on Monday, December 5, Fleishhacker traveled with his wife, May, to Los Angeles. A gossip columnist spied the man having lunch with his Los Angeles attorney, Victor Ford Collins, at Perino's on Wilshire Boulevard. Little did the reporter know that the dispirited Fleishhacker was being counseled on a strategy to liquidate his Southern California assets.

Already he had placed his estate in Atherton up for sale and made a suite in the St. Francis Hotel his family's residence. Over lunch with Collins, the attorney proposed the sale of the Hollywood Stars. A thirty-day option was agreed to, which would enable Collins to find a buyer. He had one specifically in mind. To hasten the sale and cease the banker's outgoing cash flow, Fleishhacker was persuaded to drop his asking price by more than half, to $40,000. Later that evening at a meeting of the Brown Derby board of directors, Victor Ford Collins pressed a folded note into Bob Cobb's hand. The note held news of the purchase opportunity. It was two days before the attorney heard from Cobb. When he did, it was from a man eager to learn more.

Twenty-four hours later, on December 8, the deal was done. While Cobb had assembled partners and raised much of the $200,000 necessary to purchase of the team, cover expenses, and pay for construction of a ballpark, Collins finalized the legal aspects of the transaction. Articles of incorporation were filed with the secretary of state. The Hollywood Baseball Investment Company would be led by Collins as president. Cobb would serve as vice president. George Young, the president of the successful Young's Market grocery chain and the Hollywood Park Turf Club, had become a partner and would serve as secretary-treasurer.

The Angels owned territorial rights to Los Angeles but had approved a twenty-year deal with Fleishhacker that allowed the Stars to operate in the region in exchange for 5 percent of the club's ticket sales income. Wrigley agreed to transfer that arrangement to Cobb's group. With finances raised and agreements complete, representatives of the seven other Pacific Coast League teams wired or telephoned their approval of the sale to league headquarters. "The Hollywood Baseball Association is wholly owned by Hollywood people," Cobb said to the sportswriters and reporters who gathered for the introductory dinner at the Brown Derby. He explained that none of the investors would receive any profit from the venture. Every penny would be plowed into ballpark improvements. "This is the spirit of the group," he said.[3]

Following the introductory dinner, the Cobbs wrapped their celebration of the new venture into an extravagant party to also mark their second anniversary. The night climaxed with Pat O'Brien and Cobb's mother singing Irish melodies while Barbara Stanwyck strained to learn the words. The couple continued the celebration a week later at Santa Anita, where they cheered victory by film mogul Louie B. Mayer's horse, Fly Bunny.

Privately, however, Bob Cobb's days churned at a hectic pace. There were people to hire, players to sign, contracts to be negotiated, and a bad ball club to improve. He had a deadline looming to submit a firm plan for a new ballpark. On top of that, the start of spring training was only seven weeks away.

4

"GO IN AND GET A UNIFORM"

The teenager found the gate open. The sound of bats whacking pitched baseballs echoed about the large stadium inside. Timorous at first, Jimmy Hardy soon felt excitement surge into a confidence that fueled his steps through the darkened tunnel. With each pace the sounds from the field grew louder until he was enveloped in sunlight and the activity taking place on the field burst into full view. On seeing the lush, green playing field, the fifteen-year-old felt a rush of excitement. With a baseball mitt on his left hand and sneakers on his feet, the young athlete from the nearby neighborhood stepped onto the field. Tentatively at first and then with more vigor, Hardy walked, then trotted toward a spot in the outfield, all the while expecting his intrusion to be noticed, stopped, and punished. When it was not, the teen became more emboldened. In almost no time he was racing to his left and moments later to his right, chasing after and snatching at the fly balls that were being hit by Hollywood Stars players during their batting practice. Spring training had reached its final few days. The Stars had moved their workouts into the football stadium in the southeast corner of Los Angeles's Fairfax District, which abutted Hollywood's southeast.

This venue, normally home to college and high school football and, more famously, midget automobile racing, Gilmore Stadium had been modified with a temporary backstop, a pitcher's mound, base paths, bases, and chalk foul lines to host the Hollywood Stars' final few days of training and then the team's first home series of the 1939 season. In the distance the sound of hammers driving nails gave rise to the impending completion of the team's much talked-about and anticipated ballpark, Gilmore Field.

Between each batted ball, Hardy glanced about and tried to suppress his awe. All around him were men, many of whom just six months earlier had been playing in the big leagues. The players had been bought, signed, or traded for during a frenetic ninety-day period after Bob Cobb and his backers had bought the ball club, then announced it would be planted in Hollywood. It was a ball club that played in the highest tier of minor-league baseball, whose ladder system reached from Class D ball in some of America's smaller towns and burghs to Class C, then Class B, and Class A, Class A1, and finally the top level, Class AA. The highest minor-league realm included three eight-team leagues: the International League, the American Association, and the Pacific Coast League, of which Hollywood was a member. Class AA was one step below the major leagues, and its teams were dotted with players who had played in the top flight or were prospects coveted by the men who scouted for its teams. The Pacific Coast League comprised teams in seven of the largest cities on the West Coast: Seattle, Portland, San Francisco, Oakland, Sacramento, San Diego, and Los Angeles. For a baseball-crazed Hollywood teenager like Jimmy Hardy, this was as good as if the big leagues had landed in his neighborhood.

It had all been uplifting, if not euphoric, to one Red Killefer as well. Killefer was a baseball lifer. As a player at the turn of the century, he carried two distinctions. He was the first man to bat in Chicago's Wrigley Field, and in 1916 he was traded for three future Hall of Fame players: Christy Mathewson, Edd Rousch, and Bill McKechnie. By December 1938 Killefer had been a minor-league manager for twenty-one seasons and skippered the Hollywood Stars.

When Killefer set out for New Orleans, host city of the 1938 Winter Meetings, he was a man handcuffed. Herbert Fleishhacker had made clear that there was no money available to buy new players. Killefer's only hope to improve the lowly Stars was to forge a tie-up with a major-league club that could send better ballplayers Hollywood's way. After a stopover in Chicago to speak with the White Sox, then a meeting with the Browns in St. Louis, Killefer arrived at his hotel in New Orleans to jubilant news. First was a phone call with news that his son, Tom, a Phi Beta Kappa student at Stanford, had been awarded a prestigious Rhodes Scholarship to Oxford University in England. Second was a surprise call from Bob

Cobb, who explained that he had just bought the Hollywood Stars. He wanted Killefer to continue on as manager. If he would, there was $50,000 at his disposal to buy new players. Killefer accepted then thrust into action.

While Killefer combed the Winter Meetings for ballplayers, Cobb taxed his normal responsibilities to assemble a baseball operation. With the everyday deftness used to stock the kitchens of his three restaurants, Cobb executed orders for one hundred dozen practice baseballs for spring training and one hundred dozen bats. Gail Patrick chimed with ideas for new home and away uniforms. It was imperative that a business manager be hired to run the day-to-day operation of the ball club. The hire had to be a man with experience to counter Cobb's naiveté. For almost two months Cobb received well-meaning suggestions from fans, business associates, and sportswriters. He solicited advice and tolerated unsolicited advice. As spring training loomed, he pondered ideas. It was early February when Cobb homed in on his candidate. The decision to hire Oscar Reichow would prove more fortuitous than he ever could have imagined.

Among Southern California's gaggle of baseball writers and sports columnists, Reichow was held in high regard. He was a roundish man of just past fifty whose pudginess, double-breasted suits, and round glasses gave him a professorial air. Though lacking any sort of formal educational degree, Reichow could school even the biggest of baseball experts on the inner workings of the game. Reichow had an extensive history in and around baseball. He was astute and well connected, with a long list of friends in the game—though that list did not, however, include the men who ran the Los Angeles Angels. Much of Reichow's early career had been spent in newspapers, where he began as a copyboy with the *Chicago Daily News* while barely out of high school. His rise was fast. From the role of sports department statistician, Reichow was made a sportswriter who covered area amateur sports. In 1910 Reichow was sent to New Orleans and tasked with covering the Chicago Cubs' spring training.

By the latter part of the decade, Reichow's byline began to appear in the widely read national publication the *Sporting News*. Following the 1919 World Series, Reichow was among a perceptive few in his profession to suspect that a handful of Chicago White Sox players had thrown games to the Cincinnati Reds. He was unafraid of taking on gamblers in print, and in 1920 he called out baseball for ignoring its gambling problem. In January 1920 the rampant spread of gambling on games and tales of fixes moved eleven team owners and the presidents of both the American and National leagues to seek a new leader for baseball. Reichow believed that Chicago federal judge Kenesaw Mountain Landis was ideal for the role. Reichow sought a meeting with the judge. Casual conversation in the judge's chambers left Reichow certain that Landis had an interest in that role. Seeking clarity, Reichow became direct. He asked Landis if he would accept the job if it were offered. "I could not say no if the position were put to me," the judge answered.[1] Reichow conveyed the news to the men vetting candidates and became an advocate for Landis in print.

Reichow's writing in the January 15, 1920, edition of the *Sporting News* was the first to float Landis as a candidate for chairman of the National Commission on Baseball:

> President [National League] Heydler speaks of desiring a man who is powerful, fearless and independent enough to reach out after any player, club owner, or official who by his act, association, or speech brings the national game into disrepute. The first thought is: Who is that man? In my opinion that man is Judge Kenesaw Mountain Landis.[2]

Reichow's column generated both curiosity and support for the judge's hiring. In February five names were submitted to the owners of the sixteen big-league clubs for consideration. They were New York State assemblyman Jimmy Walker, attorney John Conway Toole, former Princeton football star "Big" Bill Edwards, *Chicago Tribune* managing editor Harry Woodruff, and Landis, whom, it was noted, "some champion newspaperman put forward."[3] A decision was postponed until the postseason baseball meetings in November. Consensus built that "if one is selected it will be Harry Woodruff," Reichow wrote in March.[4]

Throughout the 1920 season, more cries rose to do something about the scourge of gamblers. In August, news spread that gamblers had fixed a game between the Philadelphia Phillies and the Chicago Cubs. Ban Johnson, president of the American League, went so far as to ask Congress to pass a law that would outlaw betting on baseball. On November 20, team owners assembled in room 1102 of the Congress Hotel in Chicago. Men who backed Woodruff said that Landis had withdrawn. Reached for clarification, the judge denied the claim. After more than two hours of quibbling and debate, William Veeck, president of the Chicago Cubs, emerged to declare that Landis had been selected to the post. Reichow was praised in the press as the new commissioner's champion.

During March 1923 Reichow traveled to California to cover the Cubs' spring training, which was now held on Wrigley's island, Catalina. During a morning workout Reichow became engrossed in conversation with William Wrigley. The chewing gum baron had long appreciated Reichow for advice he had given when Wrigley assumed control of the Cubs. As the men watched the team train, Wrigley asked Reichow if he would consider running his minor-league club, the Angels. With little hesitation, Reichow accepted. When the Angels arranged with a local radio station to broadcast games, Reichow agreed to handle the broadcast chores. Fans liked his work, which increased Reichow's popularity.

For fourteen seasons Reichow, as business manager, ran Wrigley's Angels. Under his stewardship the team grew into one of the premier organizations in minor-league baseball. During that span the Angels won three pennants and finished second twice. A new stadium was built that was considered the premier ballpark in all of minor-league baseball. Reichow's strategies helped the Angels engender a fan following that was both sizable and faithful. In 1932 Wrigley died. His son, P. K., assumed control. Prior to the start of spring training in 1937, word leaked that Reichow had become embroiled in a feud with Dave Fleming, whom P. K. Wrigley had made his point man to oversee the Angels. Reichow was reassigned to public relations duties and taken off the radio. A few months into the season, Oscar Reichow was summarily fired.

When news that Cobb had made Reichow the new Hollywood business manager reached the men who ran the Angels, the Stars were kicked out of the offices they had occupied in the tower at Wrigley Field. "All this makes for fine feuding," wrote one newspaper columnist.[5]

Once he began work for Cobb, Reichow stepped into a bare-bones operation. On many mornings he was the only one in the Stars' Gilmore Stadium office. Reichow juggled the tasks of at least three employees as he performed baseball duties, answered phones, and greeted both visitors and job hopefuls. During Reichow's first week on the job, a family friend, Edna Ward, arrived from Chicago for a visit. She had recently divorced and sought a change of scenery. Reichow's wife, Mable, suggested their friend go to the Stars office and "answer phones to help Oscar out."[6] Reichow and Cobb eagerly hired the woman on the spot, and Edna Ward would become a team fixture.

Reichow not only helped to take a great deal of the workload off Cobb, but he sped up the restaurateur's baseball education. One by one, key components of a baseball operation were put into place. With Wheaties cereal agreeing to be a primary advertising sponsor, Reichow and Cobb secured not one but two radio stations to carry Hollywood games. Joe Bolton, who had filled in on New York Giants broadcasts when not calling games for the Jersey City Giants during the 1938 season, was hired to handle the play-by-play for KNX. Mike Frankovich, the adopted son of actor Joe E. Brown, would describe the games for KFAC.

Arrangements were made with farm teams. Salina, a Class C club in the Western Association; Bellingham, a Class B team in the Western International League; and Big Spring, which played in the Class D West Texas–New Mexico League, would each take a small number of younger players who were under contract to Hollywood.

Buying players to improve the team, however, was paramount. Within hours of being phoned at the Winter Meetings, Killefer bought Bill Cissell from the New York Giants. The Boston Bees agreed to sell Bob Kahle for $7,500, then weeks later sent Harl Maggert to the Stars as well. Ed Chapman, a pitcher, joined from the Washington Senators. Those were the easy deals. Others were complicated and downright thorny.

No sooner had Cobb and company bought the Stars when they were paid a visit by Ernie Orsatti. In 1932 Orsatti earned votes for National League Most Valuable Player by batting .336 for the St. Louis Cardinals. During his career he had helped the Cardinals make four trips to the World Series, from which they came away with the winner's spoils twice. But baseball had always played second fiddle in Orsatti's mind to the perceived excitement of the motion picture industry. At the age of fourteen he had dropped out of school for full-time work as a gofer at one of the studios, then became a stuntman. Orsatti did automobile and boat stunts and even walked on the wings of airplanes. He plied his baseball skills for a studio team organized by the popular comedic actor Buster Keaton. It was Keaton, impressed by Orsatti's skills, who arranged for the stuntman and acting double to receive a tryout with the Vernon Tigers. Orsatti was signed and two years later, in 1927, was playing in the big leagues for the Cardinals.

Orsatti thought playing in front of his family and friends might be fun, so he informed the Stars of his interest to sign. The idea was appealing but would prove problematic. Though Orsatti had not played in three years, the Cardinals still owned his contract. When the president of the Sacramento Solons learned that Orsatti was making a comeback, he protested. The Solons had a tie-up with the Cardinals. Their owner pressed Branch Rickey, president of the Cardinals, that Orsatti should be assigned to his team and not a league rival. The outfielder insisted, though, that if he could not play for Hollywood, he would not play at all. Cobb offered $4,000 for Orsatti's contract. Rickey agreed to the deal and sent a telegram to confirm the agreement. Two weeks later Cobb, Reichow, and Killefer were outraged when Sacramento announced that they had obtained Orsatti's contract. The men complained to the head of minor-league baseball. Sportswriters skewered Rickey for reneging on his agreement with the Stars. Rickey responded that he had sent a telegram to the Stars but received no reply. He assumed that Hollywood had lost interest or forgotten about the deal and thus satisfied the request of Sacramento instead. Investigation into the matter determined that Rickey had indeed sent his confirmation telegram to the Stars—but to their old Wrigley Field address, where it sat unopened for two weeks. Once that error was discovered, Orsatti was awarded to the Stars.

When success at signing new players stalled, Cobb reached out to the motion picture industry for help. He enlisted actors William Frawley and George Raft to tap their many baseball contacts. Frawley was particularly friendly with the men who ran the New York Yankees. Raft, who had once been a batboy for John McGraw's New York Highlanders, counted Brooklyn Dodgers manager Leo Durocher among his friends. The actors phoned and sent telegrams to seek leads on available players and encourage favorable sale prices.

Promising amateur talent was snapped up. Cobb personally signed Carl Cox, a strong-armed seventeen-year-old shortstop who had impressed with a local amateur powerhouse, the Montebello Merchants. The Stars' chief scout, George Stovall, signed twins Tom and Jerry Downs, who had teamed with Jackie Robinson to bring a league championship to Pasadena City College. By the time Killefer, Reichow, and Cobb had finished signing players, thirty-nine would report to spring training. Among them was Everett Ellinson, a pitcher who drove all the way from the state of Washington in a 1913 Model T Ford. While Ellinson's sojourn made it into some of the papers, the headlines were about the one player who didn't show up: the Stars' most celebrated signing and important player, Babe Herman.

Floyd Caves Herman was big. He was big in stature at 6 feet 4 inches, big in lore, and carried a big baseball résumé. On the very first day of the Winter Meetings, Killefer pounced when he learned the Giants needed to clear older players from their roster. Yes, he was told, the Giants would be willing to part with Herman. The Stars' boss had managed Herman at the beginning of the future standout's career. When Killefer informed his new boss of the acquisition, Bob Cobb couldn't have been more pleased.

Babe Herman was both a local and a baseball legend, the type that sportswriters fawned over. In one day while at Glendale High, Herman won nine of fourteen events in a high school track meet; walked over to the baseball diamond, where he hit a home run; then played in his school's basketball game that night. In all, Herman left high school with thirteen varsity letters in football, basketball, baseball, and track and field. Herman's prowess led fledgling scout Gus Gleichman to offer a contract for $175 a month to play for a Detroit Tigers farm club, the Edmonton Eskimos in the Class B Western International League. Against the wishes of his mother, the teen withdrew from high school and began a professional baseball career. A league-leading .330 debut season brought an invitation to spring training with the Tigers.

Babe Herman showed up lugging a fifty-seven-ounce bat. Players howled with laughter. One pointed out that Babe Ruth's bat only weighed forty ounces. Herman blushingly grabbed a thirty-seven-ounce stick from the bat rack and was soon blistering baseballs through the remainder of spring. The Tigers were impressed but felt that given Herman's youth, he needed to play regularly and not sit on a big-league bench, so they farmed him out. The talented young player left camp with advice from Ty Cobb, who recommended that Herman not swing for the fences. "Swing for the pitcher's forehead," he urged.[7] The Glendale product also took with him a new nickname, "Babe," given to him by a Tigers coach. He then went to Omaha, where he put Cobb's advice to work and hit .402 in the Class A Western League.

In 1925, on the recommendation of their West Coast scout, Spencer Abbott, Brooklyn bought Herman's contract. The following season Herman burst into the big leagues by batting .319 and received votes for Most Valuable Player. In almost no time Babe Herman became a Brooklyn icon and one of the game's preeminent hitters. In 1929 his .381 batting average was second in the National League only to Lefty O'Doul's .398. The next season Herman hit .393 but was beaten out for the batting title by Bill Terry, who hit .401. Herman smashed 35 home runs that season, a Dodgers single-season record. He drove in 130 runs and was also second in the National League in stolen bases, with 18. "How that Babe can lay into the ball," his manager, Wilbert Robinson, marveled.[8]

Yet, Babe Herman was a dichotomy. Rather than laud Herman for his hitting deftness, some sportswriters chose to focus on his supposed daftness—like the time in 1930 when a fly ball purportedly hit him on the top of the head. Herman protested that the offender was actually Al Tyson, whose entry into the game had not been noted. And besides, Herman would add that the ball had hit Tyson on the shoulder. Then there were the base-running gaffes. Twice in 1930 Herman stopped to watch a home run and was passed on the bases by the hitter, who was thus called out. During a game in 1926 Herman tried to stretch a double into a triple, only to find two teammates occupying third base. When chided about doubling into a double play, Herman complained that nobody noted his hit drove in the go-ahead run.

Herman's teammate Charlie Dressen challenged anyone who considered Babe to be some dupe that the slugger was "nobody's fool."[9] Away from the game Babe Herman was both shrewd and astute. The traits made him wealthy. Among major-league outfielders, only Babe Ruth earned a higher salary than Herman during his big-league days. Herman invested those baseball earnings wisely. He owned property and a dozen money-spinning apartment houses. After buying an eighteen-and-a-half-acre spread eleven miles from his home in Glendale, Herman abandoned plans to make it a citrus farm and instead raised turkeys. In 1939 he parlayed the decision of President Franklin Roosevelt and several state governors to declare separate Thanksgiving holidays in many states into the sale of almost three thousand of his birds for one dollar apiece.

Herman's shrewdness was not born of mistrust or malice but rather a premium on fairness. After hitting .393 in 1930, Herman fought for a salary of $25,000. He settled for $19,000. A year later baseball's leaders, as one sportswriter explained, "took the jackrabbit out of the ball."[10] The new dead ball sent batting averages and home run tallies plummeting. Herman's average fell eighty points. Management cut his pay. Herman was furious. When he refused to accept what the team offered, Brooklyn traded him to the Cincinnati Reds.

Over the next six seasons, Babe Herman bounced among five teams. From the Reds ability to pry $75,000 from the Cubs for Herman to Pittsburgh's inability to afford Babe's salary, finances were at the root of many of the moves. Finally, in 1937 Herman returned to his original team, the Detroit Tigers. By 1938, injuries to his knees and waning skills had forced Herman into the minor leagues. But at the age of thirty-five, he was still productive. Herman batted .324 for Jersey City to finish fourth in the International League batting race.

To Bob Cobb, Babe Herman was more than just a hitter for the batting order. Herman represented a baseball version of what the motion picture industry called "star power." As the widely read columnist Hedda Hopper once explained, "Producers don't make stars. The public is the great star maker."[11] Babe Herman was an immensely popular player. The motion picture industry and its emphasis on star power was something Bob Cobb knew well. His wife, Gail Patrick, was under contract to Paramount Pictures, which had created and built its business on the concept. Paramount had seized on the popularity of Mary Pickford, Douglas Fairbanks, and Gloria Swanson to attract the financing needed to make its films and lure moviegoers to see its finished product. Star power had made Paramount the most successful and powerful of Hollywood's five major motion picture studios. "The movies are doing a great job of selling personalities to the public," Sacramento Solons owner Yubi Separovich noted.[12] Indeed, when Herman was signed, Bob Ray in the *Times* predicted the slugger "will add color to the Stars."[13] Babe Herman was a player whose hitting and popularity could change the Hollywood Stars from moribund to robust, both on the field and at the box office.

Babe Herman lived just six miles from the Stars' Gilmore Stadium office. He had been front and center at the area's winter baseball banquets. Sportswriters gushed that "Herman will be a slugging sensation for the Hollywood Stars."[14] Herman felt the enthusiasm that was building for the club. He gleaned from the newspapers what he represented to the Hollywood Stars. "The Babe has plenty of popularity appeal," Bob Ray observed in the *Times*.[15] When Herman and Cobb met for the first time, Babe Herman made sure Bob Cobb knew that he knew it.

If there was one thing Babe Herman could do as well as hit a baseball, it was negotiate. He arrived at Cobb's office in a dark suit, his blond hair parted above his left eye and slicked back. He puffed on a big cigar. Exuding confidence, Herman was friendly and engaged in small talk with the restaurateur. Once the conversation turned to money, Herman turned serious. In cavalier fashion he flicked ashes on Cobb's desk then insisted on a $7,500 signing fee and a contract that would pay what he had earned in the major leagues. The Stars' owner was flabbergasted. It was money Cobb did not have. No words, whether stern, cajoling, or even pleading, could make Herman budge from his demand. Thus, a tense holdout began.

When the thirty-nine signed ballplayers arrived in Elsinore in rural Southern California, they received a clear-cut vision of just how different things would be under Bob Cobb's reign. Their accommodation was the Amsbury Hotel, a luxurious retreat complete with a bathhouse, where players could ease the aches and pains from training in a spa and receive treatment from one of two masseurs. Meals were cooked by a French chef who had previously been employed to prepare William Wrigley's meals on Catalina Island.

Killefer liked the area. He was a proponent of hikes in the nearby hills and climbing mountains to get his team in shape. Every morning, players were in uniform and on the field by 10:00. They began with muscle stretching, then for the next two and a half hours engaged in a variety of drills that ranged from bunting to pickoff plays and fielding bunts. After a break for water and a snack, Killefer led his men to the hills, where they hiked for two hours. Nary a single player had energy for anything but a nap when they returned, and by 3:30 all thirty-nine men were usually sound asleep. For ten days Killefer whipped his players into shape. Sore muscles and blisters were in abundance as fitness levels improved and baseball skills rounded into shape.

Cobb brought some of the celebrity investors to Elsinore to watch workouts. It proved to be an eye-opening experience. The skills of many of the players generated excitement. The work habits of a few left the guests aghast. Particularly astonishing was George Puccinelli's habit of sitting down in the outfield grass when he was not involved in drills.

March 10 brought relief to many of the players. That morning the Stars packed their bags, bid Elsinore good-bye, and returned to Los Angeles to begin a schedule of exhibition games. The large oval football venue, Gilmore Stadium, would house training sessions that would lead up to Opening Day. A pair of intrasquad games gave the players their first chance to throw and swing bats with a greater degree of intensity. In the first intersquad duel, teenaged third baseman Carl Cox shone by belting a pair of ground-rule doubles into the right-field stands. A two-hour bus ride north for a game with the semipro Bakersfield Coca Colas and then south to Anaheim to play their fellow Pacific Coast League members, the Seattle Rainiers, netted a win, then a 5–2 defeat. A 9–4 win over the Chicago White Sox, who trained in nearby Pasadena, followed by a 9–4 win over the Sacramento Solons spawned optimism. Sportswriters lauded the Hollywood lineup. They predicted the Stars would have the best hitting attack in the entire Pacific Coast League. Their praise did little to lift Killefer's optimism, for the manager recognized that his pitching staff was weak. The Stars could only succeed if they heartily outscored their opposition. That could only happen if Babe Herman were in the lineup.

While the Stars went through daily drills, their celebrated new player was doing his workouts in Pasadena. With approval from Killefer, Herman trained with the Chicago White Sox at Brookside Park, which was not far from his home. The press eagerly reported that Herman was in the best shape of his life. Enjoying the attention of the writers, the former big-league star divulged that he had lost twelve pounds. As he read the almost daily reports of Herman's activities, Cobb laughed aloud one night to his wife about his negotiating session with the former big-league star. Herman, he told Gail Patrick, "was talking to novices."[16]

While Cobb and Reichow fretted over Herman, Killefer's fretting was focused on his pitching staff. Then he got a fortuitous break. Sixty-five miles east of the Stars' workout encampment, the Pittsburgh Pirates were training in San Bernardino. Their manager, Pie Traynor, had received merciless criticism from the press, who charged that the manager's easy-going nature was to blame for the Pirates' recent failings. On the night of Thursday, March 23, Traynor proved them wrong. When Ed Brandt missed curfew, Traynor kicked him off the team.

From 1931 through 1934, Brandt had been the Boston Braves' best pitcher and a standout in the National League. He was hardworking and well-liked by his Pittsburgh teammates. As soon as Red Killefer was able to track the pitcher down, he extended a contract offer and was delighted when Brandt accepted.

As the days grew closer to the start of the season, Cobb and Oscar Reichow took a tougher stance with Babe Herman's demands. They met with him on March 6, then again on the 27th. Both times Herman stood his ground. Now, with Opening Day looming, the men who ran the Hollywood Stars threatened to place Herman on baseball's suspended list if he did not sign by April 1.

In the final hours before the 1939 season was to begin, Bob Cobb pushed aside fretting over Herman, the head-pounding ringing of office phones, and the bustle of restaurant business to sit in the sunshine and watch his Stars workout in Gilmore Stadium. The team's compass point sat with Red Killefer on the hard, wooden benches in the grandstands. The men watched balls shoot around the field during batting practice and focused on the glove work of infielders, who crouched and reacted each time a fungo batted a ball in their direction. It was then that Cobb spied the intruder and asked, "Who's that kid out there at shortstop?"

Red Killefer was baffled. It wasn't one of his ballplayers, and no arrangements had been made for a tryout that day. On the infield below, Jimmy Hardy's concentration was broken by the loud voice of a Hollywood player. "Kid," the ballplayer said, "they want to talk to you up in the stands." Fearing a scolding, the youth timidly climbed the stadium steps. When the teenager reached the men, he nervously answered Cobb that he was a tenth grader at Fairfax High School, which was only about a mile away. He explained that he played baseball and football for the school and rambled about how excited he was that the Stars had come to his neighborhood. Pointing, the teen said that he had walked the six blocks from his home at 8215 Clinton to watch the workout.

"How would you like to be our batboy?" Cobb asked.

A look of surprise filled the boy's face. "No," the manager interrupted. "Let's make him the ball boy. They have a lot more responsibilities, and I think this boy is right for the job."

Owner and manager turned to the teen, who stood before them wide-eyed in shocked silence and disbelief. After a pause the boy finally blurted, "Yes, sir. I'd love to!" Cobb and Killefer broke into broad smiles.

"Okay then," Cobb snapped with a grin. "Go in and get a uniform!"[17]

5

"PLAY BALL!"

The heavy traffic that traversed north and south along Avalon Boulevard belied the normal serenity of a Saturday morning. A few yards to the west, the two small parking lots on East Forty-First and East Forty-Second had quickly filled, giving headaches to attendants who were made to wave away car after car and try to quell drivers' frustration. Men pushing lawnmowers and kids playing catch painted the picture of Saturday morning normalcy in the neighborhood. They were in the minority, however, far outnumbered by chattering masses who walked in the direction of San Pedro Street, brimming with eagerness.

A festive aura wafted about the homes, injected from the meetings of local and stranger. Cars of the interlopers bore the license plate frames of dealers as far away as Long Beach and Pasadena. Inside the Fords, Buicks, and an occasional Hudson were fathers and their excited sons, who had traveled from Inglewood, Burbank, West Covina, and Downey. Their journeys of anywhere from fifteen to fifty miles both stoked and satiated their eagerness.

To the youthful and juvenile in the neighborhood, this was a day to play practical jokes. It was April Fools' Day. To the many who trekked along Avalon Boulevard, however, April 1, 1939, represented one thing and one thing only: Opening Day of the baseball season. The magnet was the Angels' Wrigley Field. Its inhabitants portended optimism and the hope of a second straight Pacific Coast League pennant. Across the diamond on this afternoon, an air of curiosity hovered about the visitors, the Hollywood Stars. The team had been laughingstocks in 1938—losers of

99 games while the Angels were winning 105. But Southern California's second-fiddle club stepped into Wrigley Field giving a new impression. Apathy had been replaced by intrigue. Meekness had given way to strength.

Near the visitors' dugout on the first-base side of the large stadium, Bob Cobb and Gail Patrick nestled into their box seats. All about the couple were fans who pressed and squeezed through the large crowd and headed to where their ticket stubs directed. Cobb had been in this stadium dozens, perhaps hundreds, of times in the twenty years since he had arrived from Montana. This trip was different, though. Today's was not part of his escape from the frenzied pace of running popular restaurants. Rather, Opening Day of the 1939 baseball season represented Cobb's first game as the owner of a professional baseball team.

While Cobb was a bundle of nervous energy and his smile less free than usual, Gail Patrick beamed at the sight of the Hollywood players when they emerged from their dugout. She was especially pleased at their new uniform. Her creative thoughts had aided the design of the new, all-blue flannels. The actress admired the result—sleeves and pant legs adorned with white piping and collars highlighted by white trim. Across the chest, "Hollywood" was spelled out in white cursive letters. When the players turned their backs to the stands, fans saw the white outline of a star covering most of the space. The player's number was displayed within the star. The look was a dramatic change from the drab, gray appearance of the team in 1938. There were proponents who hailed Patrick's product as the most fashionable uniforms in baseball. There was, however, one exception—the pair of large white pockets on each player's derriere cheek. "They made small lads look broad," one newspaperman would write.[1] Still another chided that it gave players "a droopy drawers effect."[2]

A loud hum reverberated through Wrigley Field's concourse. A noticeable stirring and audible interest grew when one player in particular emerged from the first-base dugout. His picture had been in all the morning papers. Beneath the masthead on the front page of the sports section of the *Los Angeles Times,* the large headline screamed, "HERMAN SIGNS."[3] Below was a photo of the coveted slugger clad in the new Hollywood uniform and flanked by Cobb and Killefer.

The manager wasted little time writing Herman's name onto the fifth line of the Hollywood batting order. For Cobb, witnessing Herman scrawl his signature on the Hollywood contract brought a mixture of relief and exhilaration. The team principal confided to a select few that he had given in to Herman's demands, his budgetary objectives outweighed by the benefits of having the former Brooklyn Dodgers sensation in a Stars uniform.

When each of the thirteen-foot clocks near the top of Wrigley Field's ten-story tower read twelve o'clock, pregame festivities got underway. Announcements began to echo from the public address system. Joe E. Brown, the elastic-mouthed comedic entertainer, strode toward home plate, bat in hands, and beamed to the loud cheers of fans. Fletcher Bowron, the newly elected mayor of Los Angeles, waved to the crowd as he walked to the pitcher's mound. Eugene Biscailuz, the sheriff of Los Angeles County, tailed Brown, spun his baseball cap backward, then settled into a crouch behind home plate and held out a catcher's mitt. Bowron playfully delivered a pitch that whizzed frighteningly close to Brown's ear and made the actor bend like a pretzel to get out of harm's way. A look of feigned astonishment on Brown's face drew guffaws from the crowd. The mayor's next offering, grooved over the plate, was wacked by Brown into right field to a hearty roar.

It was only a matter of moments after home plate umpire Wally Hood cried, "Play ball!" that Hollywood showed one and all that more than their uniforms had changed. Frenchy Uhalt, the Stars' speedy center fielder, led off the game with a single to right field. After he was replaced on the bases by Bill Cissell, who had hit into a fielder's choice, Jim Tyack singled. Hope grew among the smattering of Hollywood fans in the large ballpark as George Puccinelli came to bat. Shouts of encouragement succumbed to groans, however, when a weak popup in foul territory was caught by the Angels' catcher for the second out of the inning. But before anyone in the stands or Angels dugout could breathe a sigh of relief, the announcement over the public address system wrought concern. Hearing that Babe Herman was now the batter evoked applause and optimism from the minority Hollywood backers if not concern among the home team's supporters, the more nervous of whom remembered a boast made by Herman that he would be the best player in the league.

Only an hour earlier, Babe Herman had groused at seeing where Red Killefer put him in the Hollywood batting order. Herman was superstitious. He relished batting third. But all of that was a mere afterthought as he stepped into the batter's box. Anticipation, curiosity, and respect rip-

Babe Herman brought instant credibility to the once moribund Stars when he joined the team in1939. Herman was a fan favorite for six seasons before rejoining the Brooklyn Dodgers in 1945. ***Courtesy of the author***

pled through the stands. Eyes studied the vision of greatness, noting the small wad of leafy chewing tobacco that swelled his left cheek. Ever meticulous, Herman made it a practice to take time to assume his stance. He shuffled his feet in the dirt of the batter's box until he was confident that he had achieved firm footing. Herman's hands gripped the base of the bat just above the knob. He took two practice swings, then brought the bat to a comfortable resting position, eight inches in front of his stomach. The thirty-four-and-a-half-inch-long tan Hillerich and Bradsby model bat, weighing just under thirty-four ounces, was angled slightly over Herman's left shoulder. Concentration brought his upper torso slightly forward. Herman took a third practice swing. The elbow-length sleeves of his jersey flapped in unison to the movement. The tensing of his biceps was concealed by the long, dark blue sleeves of a McAuliffe undershirt worn to ward off the chill of the day. Once Herman was finally set, he turned his head to the right and fixed his gaze toward the pitcher. The number 9 on the back of his jersey within the white outline of a large star was pointed almost directly at Bob Cobb and Gail Patrick in their private box.

Watching his prized acquisition, Cobb alternated balling his fists then clutching and rubbing his hands in unconscious nervousness. Patrick shook two dozen lucky rabbits' feet that were clutched in her left hand. As Cissell and Tyack stepped away from first and second base, Scow Thomas began his motion. An instant after a high, hard fastball rolled from his fingers, a loud thwack filled the air. All about the large baseball stadium fans rose, mouths open and eyes widened to the flight of the ball. In right field Johnny Moore sprinted across the green grass, drawing ever closer to the wall until the ball shot over the brick barrier and crashed off a car in the parking lot. A loud cheer went up from the Hollywood faithful. Bob Cobb yelled in jubilation; his wife squealed with delight. The first time Babe Herman had swung a bat in a game as a member of the Hollywood Stars, he had slugged a three-run home run. Not one of the Cobb's movie industry friends could have conceived of a story with such theatrics.

The Stars' lead would last for just three innings. In the bottom of the third, the Angels erupted to score six times. Their onslaught against the putrid Hollywood pitching staff raged for twenty-five minutes. During the surge, Red Killefer summoned Ed Brandt from the bullpen. Rather than stifle the Angels' uprising, the former Boston Braves ace enflamed it. Two hits tacked three runs on the scoreboard and robbed the left-hander of his composure. When Brandt barked his displeasure at an umpire's call on a close play an inning later, he was kicked out of the game. Though the ejection compounded their woes, Hollywood's veteran lineup did not capitulate. When Herman singled in his second turn at bat, it prompted the Angels to walk the Stars' new star intentionally in each of his successive trips to the plate.

In the fifth inning Hollywood closed the gap to 7–6. One of the intentional walks to Babe Herman would extend the Stars' half of the seventh inning and backfire badly for the Angels. Bill Norman was sent to pinch-hit with the bases loaded. He made Angels outfielders chase a double that emptied the bases of Cissell, Herman, and Spence Harris to give Hollywood the lead, 9–7. Three and a half hours after the game had begun, a 10–9 Hollywood triumph was jubilantly celebrated with raised cocktails and storytelling in the Brown Derby. The following morning's press would laud the Stars and tell Southern California that a new era in area baseball had begun.

On the season's second day, the Stars split a doubleheader with the Angels and rode acclaim from the unexpected success against their vaunted rival into the first professional baseball games ever to be played in Hollywood.

In their dealings with Earl Gilmore, Victor Ford Collins and Bob Cobb had extracted an agreement to use his football stadium until their new ballpark was completed. Space was made beneath the stands for an office. As long as Gilmore Field was under assault by laborers, plumbers, electricians, and plasterers, the Stars would play their home games on a makeshift diamond in Gilmore Stadium. Fortunately for all involved, this would encompass only one home series, seven games.

To call Gilmore Stadium's baseball configuration makeshift was an embellishment. Adventuresome, precarious, and even dangerous might have been more appropriate. Squeezing an adequate playing field into the football stadium proved challenging. After studying layouts, it was decided to place home plate where the west sideline and the south seven-yard line of the football setup met. The first-base line angled and met the bag where the ten-yard line for football would be. The pitcher's mound rose from the twenty-yard line. There were no dugouts. Players and coaches would be made to sit on football benches. The playing field was encircled by a twenty-foot-wide, oval-shaped dirt track normally used for automobile and motorcycle racing. Where the track ran along the right-field fence, outfielders would have to be mindful of a slight embankment in the dirt. The stadium's oblong shape produced a peculiar outfield dimension. The distance from home plate to the right-field fence was a mere 275 feet, which was 60 feet closer than in almost any other ballpark in the Pacific Coast League. It was decided that balls landing in the right-field stands to the right of section 12 would be doubles and to the left would be home runs. Sportswriters dubbed the cozy den the "Punch Bowl."

When players, coaches, and members of the Stars' staff arrived at the stadium on April 4, reactions for the first-ever home game of the Bob Cobb ownership regime were quite diverse. Both managers spied the short distance from home plate to the right-field fence and almost immediately decided to stack their batting order with left-handed hitters to try to take advantage. Bob Cobb, on the other hand, seethed. For weeks the stadium groundskeepers had worked diligently to produce a playing field that met Pacific Coast League standards. But forty-eight hours before the first game, a rodeo had been held in the stadium. The activities undid all of the hard work and left a substandard playing surface.

By the first pitch at 2:15, a combination of curiosity and enthusiasm drove thirty-five hundred fans into the oval. Among them sat celebrities Cesar Romero, Roscoe Karns, and George Raft. Unlike at traditional home openers, there was no fanfare. At Cobb's insistence, no red-white-and-blue bunting was hung. No celebrity flung a wild first pitch. Cobb wanted that revelry saved for the inauguration of Gilmore Field in four weeks' time.

Fans applauded Babe Herman for being the first to take advantage of the stadium's short dimensions to hit a home run. Awe abounded when George Puccinelli smashed a ball high into the air and well over the scoreboard atop the left-field stands, 360 feet away. Their blasts were highlights of Hollywood's third triumph in four games, 9–5. Twenty-four hours later, Ed Brandt pitched Hollywood into first place by retiring seventeen Portland batters via ground-ball outs. The 4–3 victory was secured on a run-scoring single by Babe Herman.

When young Rugger Ardizoia firmed Hollywood's hold on first place in the Pacific Coast League by pitching the Stars to a 6–1 win on Friday, their fans had seen the rejuvenated team win six of its first eight outings. It was then that the wheels came off the bandwagon. The Stars fell into a long losing streak. Malaise struck during the doubleheader that concluded the series with Portland. Even though Babe Herman hit two home runs, one of which cleared the right-field stands, Hollywood sent nine thousand fans home disappointed when they lost both halves of the doubleheader, 8–5 and 12–8. The team then packed trunks and suitcases, and players boarded a train at Union Station to begin a three-week road trip that would take them to Sacramento, Seattle, and Portland. In Sacramento they took on a team that had yet to win all season but inexplicably turned the tables and made back-to-back Gilmore Stadium defeats grow into a seven-game losing streak.

By the time Hollywood reached Seattle, the adoration of Southern California baseball fans, not to mention that of the press, had switched teams. While the Stars struggled, the Angels had won nine games in a row, grabbing first place and, with it, the bulk of the headlines and column inches in the six Los Angeles–area newspapers.

Red Killefer bemoaned Hollywood's pitching. Ed Chapman was getting chased early from starts. Ed Brandt was inconsistent. Wayne Osborne was getting hit. The only pitchers who gave the manager any satisfaction were a pair of rookies, Rugger Ardizoia and Bill Fleming. Rugger Ardizoia was a chunky, hard-throwing San Franciscan son of Italian immigrants. He had signed with the Mission Reds as a seventeen-year-old in 1937. Ardizoia spent the 1938 season pitching for Bellingham in the Class B Western International League. During spring training in 1939, Killefer saw an improved pitcher. His faith in Ardizoia was rewarded when the nineteen-year-old pitched a four-hitter and beat Portland, 6–1, in his first start of the 1939 campaign.

As good as Ardizoia's debut for the Stars was, Bill Fleming's first start for Hollywood was even better. It was a shutout win over Seattle. Bob Cobb, Oscar Reichow, and Red Killefer never tired of telling how fortuitous Hollywood was to land Bill Fleming. The twenty-four-year-old pitcher was the nephew of the man who ran the Stars' chief rival, the Los Angeles Angels. Back in the spring of 1934, David Fleming arranged a tryout for the boy, but the Angels' manager wasn't impressed and sent him on his way. Several months later the younger Fleming tried out for the Mission Reds. The talent-strapped club signed him to a contract and assigned him to pitch for a minor-league club in Muskogee, Oklahoma. In 1938 the Reds placed Fleming with their farm club in Bellingham, where he won twenty games in the regular season and three more in the playoffs. He finished the season with an earned-run average of 1.79, the second lowest in all of baseball.

When the Stars reached Seattle, Bob Cobb and Gail Patrick were guests of honor at the city's new ballpark. Two days into their stay, Patrick was summoned home for filming. The couple put their car on a train bound for Los Angeles and flew home. Before leaving, Cobb gave Killefer the okay to obtain pitching help. The manager convinced the St. Louis Browns to sell Bob Muncrief and bought Johnny Bittner from the New York Yankees. Further communication with the Browns gave hope for still more pitching help. Lou Tost had shown enough promise with the 1938 Stars that he was purchased by St. Louis. By the closing days of spring training, the left-handed pitcher was struggling to make the American League club. After Tost surrendered a game-winning home run in an exhibition game with Cleveland, the Browns agreed he needed more seasoning and, on April 10, returned the pitcher to Hollywood.

As the road trip wound to a close, Muncrief was the first of the newcomers to pay dividends. In his first game for Hollywood, he pitched the Stars to a 6–5 win in Portland. The outcome wasn't decided, however, until Babe Herman stroked a run-scoring double in the ninth inning. Ardizoia pitched the Stars to a 5–2 victory, which helped Killefer's crew to salvage a split of the six-game series.

While the loss of eleven of twenty games on a three-week road trip would send most teams headed for home wallowing in failure, the Hollywood Stars were hardly a picture of dejection. The train ride back to Los Angeles was filled with a level of merriment that was uncharacteristic after such losing. The players' card games were more jovial than usual. Storytelling was dotted with louder belly laughs. None was as loud, though, as the climax of shenanigans during the trip played by the team pranksters. Gloom from defeat was pushed aside by the anticipation of what lay ahead. A new day was about to dawn. Once home, the Hollywood Stars would settle into a brand-new ballpark, one that would forever change the reputation of the ball club and, in the years to come, would also change baseball.

6

"A FEW STEPS AHEAD OF THEM"

Through more than two decades the idea of Hollywood's very own baseball stadium had been floated, conceptualized, and practically promised to the area's ardent baseball fans. It was a dream touted so consistently that fans couldn't help but feel akin to an Argonaut in a sailor bar under assault from a flirtatious nymph or the recipient of one of George C. Parker's many pitches to buy the Brooklyn Bridge.

Bill Lane was the first. When he moved his team from Salt Lake City in 1926, he vowed that one day it would play in a ballpark in Hollywood. For nine seasons he cajoled fans and asserted to the public that his team would call Hollywood home. It never did. When Herbert Fleishhacker moved the Mission Reds to Southern California in 1938, he announced that his ball club would make Gilmore Stadium its home. Then reality hit. Closer inspection proved that playing a full season of baseball in the football stadium was implausible. Sportswriters and columnists tempted and teased with rumors and projective suppositions. Everyone from movie studio mogul Louie B. Mayer to recently retired New York Yankees slugger Babe Ruth was said to be involved in one plan or another that involved the purchase of a Pacific Coast League team and its placement in a newly constructed ballpark in Hollywood. When none ever materialized, it left fans callous and wary that it might ever be realized.

On February 13, 1939, the years of rumors and off-the-mark reports faded into history. Under a sunny sky Bob Cobb and Victor Ford Collins thrust steel spades into dirt on Earl Gilmore's land in a display of reality. Doubt was pushed aside; skepticism, dispelled. A ballpark was finally coming to Hollywood. Groundbreaking for the new park was done hastily and without fanfare. Once concluded, the motors of tractors came to life, and work began to level the ground. In most quarters the occasion drew praise, but at least one sportswriter heaped scorn on Cobb, excoriating him for failing to hire a publicist who might have turned the event into a more celebrated occasion. The serial entrepreneur answered that only the first game in the new ballpark would be worthy of such festivity and vowed that the event would indeed be one to remember.

To most, Cobb had found the ideal spot for his ballpark. Earl Gilmore's 264-acre plot had become an entertainment destination for thousands around the region. On the west side of the property, at Beverly and South Fairfax Avenues, was Gilmore's football stadium. The stadium was home to the Loyola University and Pepperdine University football teams and also to the Los Angeles Bulldogs of the American Football League. On Thursday nights, auto racing brought throngs to watch the 300-horsepower midget cars roar around the stadium's track. Tuesday nights meant motorcycle races. The stadium hosted rodeos and political rallies, and in 1934, the Three Stooges filmed *Three Little Pigskins* in the stadium. At the far east edge of the land was the Pan-Pacific Auditorium. The University of Southern California and University of California, Los Angeles played their basketball games in the Pan-Pacific. The Los Angeles Monarchs played their Pacific Coast Hockey League games in the building. When the Ice Capades or Harlem Globetrotters came to town, the venue was a lure for fans. If a boxing match was of a caliber that the Olympic Auditorium or Pan-Pacific Auditorium couldn't hold the expected crowd, it was staged instead at Gilmore's stadium. Gilmore's complex was, quite simply, the biggest single sports center in the world.

Victor Ford Collins had actually seized upon the idea for the site during the summer of 1938. He initiated discussions with Gilmore, only to put their talks on hold while Herbert Fleishhacker dealt with his legal problems. Once the club had been successfully sold to Cobb, he eagerly renewed the discussion and found Gilmore to be a willing, if not stern, partner.

Earl Gilmore was the sixty-one-year-old son of a rags-to-riches success named Arthur F. Gilmore. In 1903, while drilling a well for water on his 256-acre dairy farm, the senior Gilmore struck oil. Soon derricks dotted the family acreage. Gilmore bought more land and ultimately expanded his property to more than two thousand acres. When Arthur died in 1918, Earl, then thirty-two, took over the family business. The younger Gilmore had a promoter's zeal. Hearkening to his father's prophesy that one day every American would own a horseless carriage and Gilmore's oil would make them run, the younger Gilmore built an empire of gas stations. At its peak, three thousand Gilmore gas stations would dot towns, highways, and street corners throughout the western states. Gilmore Oil became the largest oil company on the West Coast. The twenty-four wells on the family property were producing eight thousand barrels of oil per day. Annual sales reached $45 million. Earl Gilmore's castle was the 5,900-square-foot adobe home in which he was born, at 6301 West Third Street, across from his property. A Stanford graduate, the younger Gilmore was innovative, the first to introduce a self-service gas station that offered a discounted price to customers willing to pump their own gasoline. Gilmore called it the "gas-a-teria." He marketed the different grades of gasoline by color and stressed clean, family-friendly gas stations.

In 1934, with his main oil field beginning to dry up, Earl Gilmore expanded his business interests. He constructed the twenty-thousand-seat football stadium. During the Depression, Gilmore noticed that farmers routinely parked along the perimeter of his property on Third Street near Fairfax Avenue. They were selling items they had grown or made, such as produce and knitted goods. One afternoon Gilmore stopped by to talk with the farmers. He proposed to build a series of covered stalls just to the south of his stadium and asked if they would be willing to pay fifty cents a day to rent a stall from which they could sell their goods. Eighteen agreed. Gilmore then cleared a baseball diamond from his land at Third and Fairfax, constructed the stalls, and called the site the Farmers Market. The popularity of the venture led Gilmore to partner with two developers and construct restaurants, shops, and other structures that further commercialized the northeast corner of the family land. The Farmers Market became a popular destination and a $16-million-a-year enterprise.

Earl Gilmore was a man whose name was in the newspapers nearly every day. He sponsored everything from a circus to radio shows and auto races. Indianapolis 500 cars and airplane racers bore both the Gilmore Oil name and its distinctive red lion logo. Gilmore loved sports. He was an accomplished skeet shooter, a licensed pilot, a member of the California State Fish and Game Commission, and for five years served as president of the Turf Club at Hollywood Park Racetrack. But of all the sports Earl Gilmore enjoyed, he loved baseball most.

Gilmore wasn't frivolous. He was calculating and drove a hard bargain. Negotiations between Collins, Cobb, and Gilmore grew taxing. The man proposed a complex plan. He offered Cobb a ten-acre tract for his ballpark, which he would lease to Cobb for twenty years. Gilmore would oversee construction and cover half of the $200,000 cost needed to erect the ballpark. But in exchange he wanted 10 percent of the Hollywood Stars' ticket revenues during the twenty-year lease period. The oil mogul insisted on all of the money the team derived from parking on his property for their games. He also demanded all of the money the team received from advertising on the outfield fences in the ballpark. Ever the promoter, Gilmore had one more requirement. He wanted the ballpark to carry his name—Gilmore Field. With no alternative and little time to waste, Cobb and Collins agreed.

For eight weeks following the February groundbreaking, passersby on Beverly Boulevard or West Third Avenue witnessed progress daily. Heavy equipment gave way to skilled laborers. Piles of lumber and drywall shrank. As they did, a foundation, frames, and finally siding rose. Cobb had ordered his ballpark to be made of wood. Experience from attending games at the concrete-and-steel edifice of Wrigley Field had taught him that the chill from nighttime fog was exacerbated by both. It was a discomfort he wanted to spare Stars fans. As Opening Day neared, there was still considerable work to be done. It was only after Cobb signed off on expanding construction from one eight-hour shift to three and sending work whirring around the clock that the new venue's character came into view. Finally, on the evening of May 1, 1939, the public got to see Hollywood's very own ballpark for the first time. On arriving, fans were treated to a spectacular art deco exterior design. Large letters on the third-base and first-base side of the structure spelled out "Hollywood Stars," flanked by two large stars.

Cobb's open house brought a horde. Whitey Meyer, Gilmore Field's newly hired head usher, showed people around. The concession stands were opened, and hot dogs, peanuts, and popcorn given away for free. It was quickly apparent that this was no ordinary ballpark. The venue was intimate. The builders, Mickey Reed and Forest Stanton, former college ballplayers, had designed the park with fan satisfaction in mind. Each tier of seating was twelve inches higher than the one below so fans' view of

When it opened in 1939, Gilmore Field drew praise for its comfort and fan amenities. ***Courtesy of Larry Rubin***

the game would not be blocked by the person seated in front of them. The ballpark's intimacy was inescapable. From the first-base and third-base lines to the front row of seats was a mere twenty-four feet. The distance from home plate to the backstop measured just thirty-five feet. "Not many foul balls will be caught for outs," one Hollywood player remarked.[1]

The first six rows of seating were box seats—320 boxes in all—which contained anywhere from four to eight seats, depending on the buyer's wishes. The Gilmore Field boxes were unlike those offered in any other ballpark in the country. Each had a back and sides for privacy, with a small counter on which to set food and eat. The boxes were modeled after those popular with wealthy and celebrity patrons at the Hollywood Park Racetrack and the Hollywood Bowl entertainment venue. Almost every box was bought by a season ticket holder: celebrities, motion picture moguls, and business leaders, in most cases. Unlike the method used at every other ballpark in both the major and minor leagues to identify box seats—a number and letter stenciled on a piece of wood—at Gilmore Field a small plaque with a gold engraved nameplate told which box belonged to Walt Disney, where George Raft was to sit, and which box was for Groucho Marx and his family. Behind the 2,254 box seats were grandstand seats. Eight thousand were originally planned, but the number was later scaled back slightly. Bleachers completed the seating structure. They extended from the end of the grandstands to each foul pole and held in the neighborhood of two thousand fans. The original plan for Gilmore Field totaled seating for 12,500. Once construction concluded, Cobb would settle for 10,000.

At Gail Patrick's urging, two ladies' lounges were constructed. Both mirrored the finest in any of the area's theaters or cinemas. They featured powder rooms with lace curtains and offered free powder and puffs, sterilized combs and brushes, sewing needles and thread, and several mirrors of both the full-length and small variety. The room was staffed

The Stars built Gilmore Field with their celebrity fans in mind. The ballpark featured boxes that were unique in baseball, offering their celebrity owners a degree of privacy. *Courtesy of Larry Rubin*

with two attendants to keep things well stocked and clean, and to serve the female fans. Beneath the stands was a VIP lounge, a private room that offered pregame entertainment and privacy for the Stars' celebrity fans. Cobb's idea was for a band to play in one corner while a bar offered cocktails in another. Before night games a buffet dinner was to be made available.

An elite designer, Avery Rennick, was enlisted to construct a luxurious office that Cobb and Collins could use when at the ballpark. The product was the President's Room. On seeing it for the first time, one Hollywood player remarked that he thought the room was an apartment. Its walls were covered in knotty pine and the floor was carpeted. The men could work from behind an Early American desk-and-chair combination. The room was decorated with a four-tier bookcase, a grandfather clock, and a piano. Framed Walt Disney caricatures adorned several of the walls.

The one area of the ballpark's operation that fans probably expected to exceed traditional norms surpassed even that—food service. Cobb had hired Jacobs Brothers, an East Coast food service company, to handle the sale of food and souvenirs in Gilmore Field. The company assigned a savvy young manager named Danny Goodman to handle the Gilmore Field operation. Goodman was sent west from Newark, New Jersey, where he had profitably run the concessions at the Newark Bears ballpark. It didn't take long, however, for Goodman and Cobb to clash. Goodman, understandably, was under profit margin directives from Jacobs Brothers. He was instructed to take advantage of his employer's ability to buy hot dogs, peanuts, and other items for the concession stands in large quantities and at low prices from their preferred vendors. Cobb, on the other hand, placed a premium on quality.

The men argued over just what foods would be served in Gilmore Field. On his visits to other ballparks, Cobb had been appalled to see sloppy vendors selling what he called "Chinese peanuts and sleazy hot dogs on papier-mâché buns."[2] He insisted that Gilmore Field offer skinless hot dogs that he wanted sold from charcoal heaters. Cobb demanded the hot dogs be served on real milk buns and sold for a dime. Peanuts were to be jumbo-sized and hot. Coffee was to come with real cream and sugar. He wanted it sold out of gallon thermos bottles. Checkers were to call back the coffee vendors every twenty minutes and replace their product with a freshly brewed batch. Cobb would serve the same ice cream as in his restaurants—"except," he said, "with a slightly smaller butter-fat content."[3]

The attention to detail given the food offerings was matched by the emphasis on the materials used to make up Gilmore Field. In almost every town in minor-league baseball, fire from carelessly tossed matches and cigarettes was a threat to the local ballpark. Cobb insisted that the wood used in Gilmore Field be made fireproof. During the public tour of the ballpark, fans were given a demonstration of the result. George Young doused a pillar with gasoline while Cobb unleashed a blow torch. Onlookers nodded, gasped, and applauded as the effort failed to ignite so much as a single spark.

Night baseball was new to the minor leagues. It had only been initiated in the major leagues in 1935. Cobb, Collins, and Oscar Reichow were insistent that a majority of Hollywood games be played at night. Fans who toured Gilmore Field saw a playing field illuminated as if it were daytime. The ballpark featured a new product of General Electric: lights that were surrounded by reflectors to enhance illumination of the field. In all, eight towers were raised that featured 204 arc lights of 15,000 watts. Tom Curtis, the superintendent of the new ballpark, was especially proud of the large feature that loomed above the Gilmore Oil sign to the right of the center-field wall—an electronic scoreboard. He beamed that the lights could be seen through fog and would offer almost instantaneous declaration of official scoring decisions. A large gong was set up that would chime at the end of an inning the number of runs Hollywood had scored. Later during the inaugural season, a second, much smaller gong would be added to ring the opponents' tally.

Jim Fitzgerald, once a major-league groundskeeper, was brought out of retirement to lay out the field. He built Gilmore's dimensions to feature deep power alleys, 40 feet deeper than in Wrigley Field across town. The rest of the field bore a standard layout, 335 feet from home plate to both foul poles and 407 feet from the plate to dead-center field. As was his custom, the last thing Fitzgerald did on the job was to bury a dollar bill before embedding home plate into the earth.

Of all the ballpark's facets and features, perhaps what Cobb stressed most was an emphasis on cleanliness and a quality of behavior rarely, if ever before, stressed in the game. Workers were hired to patrol the park, both inside and out, to sweep up cigarette butts, pick up dropped wrappers, and discard other debris. Ushers were made to wear uniforms of navy blue slacks, a white dress shirt, and a navy blue tie covered by a dark blue blazer adorned with gold buttons. Atop each man's head was a white peaked cap with a black leather visor. Vendors were clad in a white shirt with bow tie. Their shoes were to be shined, their hair combed, and their faces clean and devoid of facial hair. The vendors would meet and go through dry runs before every game, where it was stressed that they be polite, saying, "Thank you" and "Excuse me." When it was announced that the ballpark would employ cigarette girls, six hundred hopefuls applied. Fourteen were hired. Like the other vendors, each was schooled in the appropriate actions and clad in a smart, clean uniform.

The sneak peek of the new ballpark culminated with on-field announcements. A tarpaulin covered home plate, and an orchestra played while fans toured the venue. Finally, Cobb stepped to the microphone and, under the illuminating beam of the park's new lights, glowed as he praised the construction team and thanked the many people who had made the long-held dream come to fruition. As fans filed out, it was apparent that while P. K. Wrigley had a colossus, the largest stadium in all of minor-league baseball and one that was perhaps worthy of a big-league tenant, ten miles to the east Bob Cobb had constructed a gem.

The following day sportswriters and columnists used words such as "ornate" and "modern" to describe the new ballpark. One wire service writer typed that Gilmore Field featured "a grandstand that will be studded with movie kings and queens and overflowing with glamour gals."[4]

By 10:00 on the morning of May 2, 1939, a large throng massed outside the main entrance to Hollywood's marvelous new ballpark. The first pitch would not be thrown for more than four hours. Anticipation overpowered practicality. Hope intersected reality. Once the gates opened, professionals and housewives, laborers and grandmothers streamed into the new structure to experience the realization of what had been long rumored and wished for. None balked at paying ten cents to rent a seat cushion. Unlike at other ballparks, Cobb wanted brightly colored seat cushions—lavender, red, pink, or yellow—and charged twice the going rate of Wrigley Field. Programs were snapped up faster than barkers could beckon. That they, too, cost a dime—double what the Angels asked—failed to slow the line of buyers. The Stars would face Seattle. Festive red, white, and blue bunting hung over the front railing from right to left field and lent significance to the event. Once inside, those who had not been at the previous night's preview were almost instantly awestruck. The bandleader and actor Rudy Vallee, behind large sunglasses, shot home movies with a 16mm camera. "Slapsie Maxie" Rosenbloom, the boxer turned actor, proudly pointed out the nameplate on his box to friends. Heads swiveled left to right and back again while wide eyes drew in the marvel.

When players trickled from the dugout, more evidence of the team's panache was displayed. "Colorful" was a word easily conjured to describe Hollywood's new home apparel. The white home uniforms featured elbow-length red sleeves. A two-inch-wide red strip circled the collar and ran down the front of the jersey. On the left breast was a blue star. Within the star was a white block *H*. The design was surrounded by a thin red outline of a star. A large outline of a star filled the back of each jersey, with the player's number featured within the star. The Hollywood players wore red caps. Each quarter panel was bordered by a white stripe, and a white star emblazoned the cap's front.

Once the 2:15 p.m. start time drew near, the smartly attired ushers steered people to their seats. As Clark Gable's ex-wife Ria settled into her seat behind home plate and Buster Keaton paused his chat in the box seats with Ernie Orsatti's wife, pregame festivities began on the field. The merriment was pure Hollywood. First, Gail Patrick strode toward the pitcher's mound to loud applause dotted with whistles and a few scattered catcalls. Joe E. Brown emerged from the Hollywood dugout, sporting an oversized mitt on his left hand and his customary wide smile. Finally, Jane Withers, the twelve-year-old box office star, carried a bat almost as big as she to home plate. Each time Patrick would wind up to throw the ceremonial first pitch, Brown turned and ran in mock fear, filling the air with laughs. Finally, with Withers holding the large bat, her hands six inches apart, and Brown extending his gloved hand, Patrick heaved the ball toward the plate to a jubilant roar from the stands.

Members of the North Hollywood Kiwanis club then paraded onto the field and presented the stadium with an American flag. The Hollywood American Legion drum and bugle corps escorted the flag to center field. Once it was raised, as it snapped in the midday breeze, Victor Ford Collins, then Bob Cobb, and finally Oscar Reichow made welcome speeches from a microphone that had been set up at home plate.

As an overflow crowd of more than ten thousand fans watched, nine large white placards on which stars were painted were rolled to the infield. What the fans could not see was that behind each placard was a tiny car driven by one of the nine Hollywood starters. Once the large placards were finally aligned around the infield, the players leaped through them to loud applause.

On KNX radio, Joe Bolton introduced the players to his audience—George Puccinelli in left field, Frenchy Uhalt in center field, and Bill Norman in right field. On the infield were Tim Marble at third base, Joe Hoover at shortstop, Bill Cissell at second base, and Babe Herman at first base. The catcher was Jimmie Crandall. Wayne Osborne stood atop the mound, poised to deliver the pitches.

Under a bright afternoon sky, anticipation meshed with advent to produce elation. It was only minutes into the contest that Cissell sent fans young and old scrambling after the first foul ball. It sliced into the stands behind first base, where it was snatched by baseball enthusiast Bill Schroder. It was a souvenir so cherished that Schroeder would sleep with it under his pillow for decades.

Hollywood put the new electronic scoreboard to its first test. In the bottom of the first inning, the Stars loaded the bases. With two outs, Marble lined a single to center field that scored two runs and elicited wild cheering and applause throughout the new ballpark.

Bob Cobb alternated his time between sitting in his box with his wife and walking around the ballpark to check on the operation. The man was rarely able to take a half dozen steps before being stopped, offered congratulations, and made to shake hands. By the middle innings, with his hand and arm sore, Cobb sought refuge in the press box. His stay did not last long. In the top of the seventh inning, Seattle rallied to score four runs and tie the game. Cobb hollered loudly, like many in the stands. His actions, though, drew rebuke from his own public relations director, who kicked the Stars' vice president out for violating standard baseball policy that prohibited rooting in the press box.

Seattle added three more runs in the top of the ninth inning for an 8–3 lead. Few among the throng were driven to leave, however. Their faith was rewarded with a drama-filled bottom of the ninth. First Hoover singled, then Ernie Orsatti pinch-hit and doubled. Spence Harris brought both men home with a single to right field. With two outs and the score 8–5, Hollywood managed to load the bases. Puccinelli, who had already tallied two hits in the game, came to bat. From every box, grandstand seat, and spot in the bleachers, fans rhythmically clapped and stomped their feet trying to spur "Pooch" into a hit that might tie or win the game.

A fly ball off the meat part of his bat drew yells, but the noise turned to groans when the ball's trajectory slowed and it fell back toward earth and into an outfielder's mitt for the final out of the game.

In some newspapers, reports of the inaugural game in Hollywood were pushed from the headline by news that New York Yankees star Lou Gehrig had taken himself out of the lineup, thus ending his streak of consecutive games played at 2,130. Most of the Los Angeles papers did give big billing to the Gilmore Field debut game. All offered glowing praise of the new ballpark.

After the inaugural, Cobb announced that all of the Stars' games during the week would be played at night, with an 8:05 p.m. first pitch. "Why some big leaguers fight it [night baseball] is beyond comprehension," he said.[5] Day baseball would be reserved for the weekend. Thursday nights would be ladies' nights, but Cobb broke with Pacific Coast League tradition and refused to let women in for free. "If you give your product away, your customers are persuaded that it is worth just what they pay—nothing," he explained to a sportswriter.[6]

A little more than twenty-four hours after Puccinelli's game-ending fly-ball out, the big lights were turned on, and the Stars and Seattle contested Gilmore Field's first night game. "It looks like a lovely evenin'," remarked Shine Scott, the Hollywood trainer.[7] He was right. Hollywood scored four runs in the first inning and four more two innings later to win, 9–4. Babe Herman earned a pair of slacks for smacking the first triple in the new ballpark. Frenchy Uhalt scored a pair of shoes for getting Gilmore Field's first hit, a sport shirt for its first double, and a hat for scoring the ballpark's first run. Bill Cissell took home a silk shirt for being the first to steal a base in the new park.

A crowd of forty-five hundred saw the Stars beat Seattle, 8–3, in the third game of the series, and they won the following night as well, on a Babe Herman home run. Success, atmosphere, and great weather helped to draw an overflow crowd of thirteen thousand to the series finale, a Sunday doubleheader. Herman arrived at the ballpark in an almost giddy mood. His latest batch of turkeys had hatched. He boasted that it was a bumper crop. After winning four of seven from Seattle, Hollywood split the pair of games and left for San Diego. Within the offices, smiles abounded at the accountant's figures. They showed that the team was 400 percent ahead of the home attendance figure of the 1938 Stars after a similar number of home games.

As the team took to the road, Red Killefer had worries. In spring training the manager had been confident that his team would hit. It was the pitching staff that worried him. True to his belief, by mid-May Spence Harris was leading all Pacific Coast League hitters with a .410 batting average. Babe Herman's .360 mark was eighth best in the league. One columnist called Hollywood's the most dangerous batting order in the Pacific Coast League. During the inaugural series in Gilmore Field, Killefer's men had scored thirty-nine runs over the seven-game series. In the latter half of May, fortunes turned.

The Stars lost five of six against Oakland and plunged into the second division of the standings. Killefer's pitching staff was abysmal. The ballyhooed buys had turned into busts. Ed Brandt hurt his pitching arm and was released. Ed Chapman proved ineffective and was also let go. The youthful prospects Bill Fleming and Rugger Ardizoia impressed but were inconsistent. Neither Lou Tost, Bob Muncrief, nor Johnny Bittner was a solution. It seemed for a stretch that anytime a PCL club cut a pitcher, Hollywood brought them in for a trial. In almost every case, it didn't take Killefer long to realize why the previous club had sent the hurler on his way. Young pitchers were brought up from the lower minor leagues and given opportunity. None could deliver. Finally, out of desperation, Oscar Reichow boarded a plane and set off around the country. He watched games, visited clubs, spoke to scouts, and looked high and low for pitching help. Upon his return, Reichow shared with a sportswriter that he had never seen such a dearth of pitching talent in all his years in professional baseball.

By mid-June the Stars had fallen to sixth place in the eight-team Pacific Coast League. That's when the bats failed. Ernie Orsatti couldn't crack the outfield lineup and was released. With his best days clearly in the past, Harl Maggert was sent to Oklahoma City. Despite the losses, fans were entertained and enamored by their local baseball team. Big crowds filled the new ballpark. Sunday doubleheaders proved especially popular. Some crowds took the staff by such surprise that Cobb himself would roll up his shirt sleeves and pitch in to sell tickets. The press warmed to the ball club. Sportswriters tossed about nicknames for the team. "Sheiks," "Film City Nine," "Flickerville Nine," "Cinema City Nine," and "Twinklers" were most commonly used. The latter was ultimately shortened to what would become the most commonly used of the nicknames, the "Twinks."

Babe Herman rekindled memories of his great years with Brooklyn by swinging his hickory bat in menacing enough fashion to challenge for the league lead in doubles, home runs, and batting average. Frenchy Uhalt was an acrobat in center field, evoking loud cheers with diving catches on the green turf and leaping grabs up against the outfield wall. Slugfests and pitchers' duels enthralled. But few games were as compelling as Hollywood's June 27 battle with the rival Los Angeles Angels. The eight thousand fans who filled box and grandstand seats for Gilmore Field's first battle of the "Civil War" rivalry sat glumly as the Angels scored ten times in the second inning and built a 12–0 lead. Those who did not leave were rewarded with a game that *Los Angeles Times* sports columnist Bob Ray hailed as the greatest he had ever seen. Hollywood stormed back to score once in the fourth inning and three times in the fifth; then, after the Angels had scored their thirteenth run in the top of the eighth inning, the Stars scored six times in the bottom of the inning and then three more times in the ninth to tie the game. Seventeen-year-old rookie Carl Cox was inserted to play third base and slammed two line-drive singles and a double. The fans delighted in crying out the run tally each time the gong was rung from the press box. In the tenth inning Hollywood loaded the bases but failed to score. Two more innings were played before a Hollywood error and a single by the Angels' pitcher, Ray Prim, brought two runs home, and the Angels prevailed, 15–13, in twelve innings.

July began with what could later be reviewed and noted as a bad omen. While on the field during pregame drills, Bob Cobb was struck in the face by an errant throw. He spent the next several days nursing a badly swollen and painful jaw that would ultimately require surgery. Later that night Babe Herman was struck on the hand by a pitch and suffered a broken bone. The injury ended his season. Within days injuries would beset the Stars like a plague. During a series in Oakland, Frenchy Uhalt was stricken with a bad case of food poisoning. His physician ordered bed rest, and he missed a week of games. Spence Harris, the team's leading batter, pulled a muscle in his back while swinging and was shelved for several weeks. Reichow and Cobb accepted an offer from Dallas of the Texas League and sold George Puccinelli. Jim Tyack was called up from the low minors to replace the veteran slugger. In one of Tyack's first games with the team, the rookie suffered a concussion in a base-running collision and was hospitalized for several days. After he recovered and returned to the lineup, the young outfielder ran into a bleacher railing at Gilmore Field and came away with an injured ankle.

The lack of quality pitching and the injuries to key hitters saw the Stars plummet into last place. It was only from winning five of the last seven games of the season that they managed to crawl into sixth place and finish the season with an 82–91 record. None of the team's woes, however, would drive fans away. Big crowds filled Gilmore Field throughout the summer months. By the end of the season attendance was 225,000—almost double what the 1938 Stars had pulled into Wrigley Field. Revenue from food and souvenir sales doubled from 1938. "Biggest average revenues in the entire Jacobs chain," Cobb crowed. Though unhappy about the team's finish in the standings, Cobb was elated with the first season result. He chortled to an interviewer that when the major leagues came to study his operation, they "will find Hollywood a few steps ahead of them."[8]

7

"CLEAN UP THAT MOUSE TRAP"

Following his first season in professional baseball, Bob Cobb was the golden boy of minor-league ball. In December, at the game's annual wintertime convention, he was awash in congratulatory handshakes and backslaps. All about the luxurious Edgewater Beach Hotel on Chicago's Michigan Avenue, reporters—local and even one from the *Sporting News*—squired Cobb to gain time for an interview. Men from every level of the game sought a chat in order to glean ideas from the man whose creativity and determination had helped turn the Hollywood club into a pioneering operation.

During the meetings Oscar Reichow was able to arrange an invitation for his boss to have lunch with the commissioner of baseball, Judge Kenesaw Mountain Landis. Cobb was elated at the prospect. He was nervous when the appointed time arrived and he and Reichow reached the door to Landis's hotel suite. When the commissioner appeared in the living room of his suite, Cobb felt more excitement than he ever had at meeting a movie star or celebrity. Landis, on the other hand, did not share the demeanor. The commissioner could be best described as grouchy. "I'm Judge Landis," the septuagenarian said.[1] Cobb was momentarily amused by a self-introduction coming from such a widely known figure. While the men shook hands, Cobb tried not to snicker at the man's disheveled white hair, which he thought looked akin to a fright wig.

The three men sat down to lunch, but before anyone could take a bite of food, Landis erupted in anger, "Do you know Bert the Barber, the Miller Boys, Nick the Greek?"

Reichow shook his head from side to side. Cobb, honest to the core, tried to shade the truth. "I guess they're gamblers," he said sheepishly.

"You know damned well they are!" Landis roared across the table. "There's a lot of gambling in your ballpark. Now, clean up that mouse trap, or I'll close the place."[2]

While the accusation was of little surprise to Cobb, the threat and tenor of the commissioner was startling. Cobb knew full well that Gilmore Field was rife with gamblers. Wrigley Field was, too. But what, he wondered, could be done about it?

The illegal activity within Gilmore Field had hit a zenith during the middle of the 1939 season. With almost every pitch, orders could be heard barked about the stands. Wagers were readily seen taken. "A five says this pitch is a home run," a man would shout, to which another would snap, "A buck that it's a strike."[3] Some wagers were upward of $1,000. In the middle of the bettors, a man with bills of several denominations squeezed between his fingers noted the cries. The actions made parents who were seated nearby uneasy, especially when profanity was hollered. Children marveled at the sight of actual dollar bills changing hands. A few fans mustered the courage to approach the head ushers, Whitey Meyer or Mel Morrison, to complain. By and large, most of the Stars' staff treated the gamblers simply as a minor nuisance.

The seriousness of the grandstand gambling heightened in midseason. At the same time that scouts from the St. Louis Cardinals, Boston Red Sox, New York Yankees, and Chicago Cubs were in the stands at Gilmore Field to study Hollywood pitcher Bill Fleming during a July 22 game, a detective from the Los Angeles County Sheriff's Department was scrutinizing, too. The detective was glued to the actions of some of the city's biggest and most notorious gamblers. When the detective gave a predetermined signal, members of the department's vice squad pushed their way into the ballpark. The deputies hauled more than a dozen men away. When one resisted, he was beaten. Two men oblivious to the raid, standing twenty feet apart, argued loudly over what odds should be set on a particular activity. They were arrested, and each was charged with a felony. One of the men would later be banned by a judge from attending games at Gilmore Field for two years.

The raid on Gilmore Field came as part of a cleanup of the leadership of both the city and county of Los Angeles. Throughout the 1930s, Los Angeles was a city awash in corruption. Whether out of sight in back rooms, warehouses, and homes or in public places such as country clubs and even in hotel suites, gambling syndicates staged dozens of illegal games almost every night around the city. So rampant was the gambling and prostitution that the New York mob dispatched Bugsy Siegel westward to try to take control and funnel profits in their direction.

The corrupt activities were entwined with law enforcement and politicians. A 1937 grand jury report alleged that bookmakers and madams funneled a percentage of their profits into political campaign funds. In exchange, lawmakers turned a blind eye, and the activities went on unabated. Jurors were told that the city had an estimated two hundred gambling dens, more than two thousand slot machines, and eighteen hundred bookmakers.

On January 14, 1938, the trajectory of the illicit pendulum changed. That was the night that a private investigator named Harry Raymond agreed to go to the store for his wife. He unlocked his Boyle Heights garage and climbed into his car. When he pressed his foot to the accelerator, a bomb that had been wired to the engine exploded. Raymond was badly injured.

The ensuing weeks brought investigations that uncovered the involvement of a special Los Angeles Police Department intelligence squad in the bombing. The graft and corruption within the force and in political offices was laid bare. Repeated revelations led to a recall effort, and on November 16, 1938, Frank L. Shaw became the first mayor of a major American city to be booted out of office by a public recall election. Two days after the election, James E. Davis resigned under fire as the chief of police. The resulting effort to clean up the department saw 245 officers fired, many of whom held senior rank. In January 1939, a total of 66 commanders were made part of a sweeping number of transfers. Five weeks later, a reorganized Central Vice Squad began a ferocious crackdown on gambling with a series of raids on bookmaking operations.

Almost nightly for months, the squad unleashed raids throughout the city. Siegel was driven from town and instead shifted his operation to Las Vegas. The officers cajoled sources for information, interrogated those arrested, and when necessary, used battering rams to knock down fortified doors. Back-alley gambling dens, hotel rooms, a special cruise ship, and even a church were raided and gambling operations busted. The squad confiscated slot machines, roulette wheels, and poker chips. They broke up dice games, card games, and even sports betting operations.

Investigations uncovered fixed horse races at Santa Anita after a raid found jockeys and movie stars partying with evidence of tips being shared.

The illicit activity tore apart celebrity marriages. The actress Ginger Pearson told a judge that her husband "absolutely refused to work. All he would do was gamble."[4] She was granted a divorce. Dancer Evelyn Kay similarly testified in superior court, "My husband spent nearly all his time gambling."[5] She, too, was granted a termination of her marriage.

Raids, arrests, and convictions went on for months. Salacious newspaper coverage dragged the depth and breadth of the illegal activities from darkened dens. Bit by bit, law enforcement felt it was reining in the illicit activity. But there was one place in Los Angeles where gambling continued right out in the open. It took place in plain view of children. It involved celebrities and common folks alike. It was going on in the stands at every Hollywood Stars home game in Gilmore Field.

By the time the 1940 season began, Cobb had taken the commissioner's warning to heart. He kept an eye on the grandstands, and he asked head ushers Meyer and Morrison to do the same. To their dismay, the wagering flowed unabated. If anything, the scrutiny had made it more sophisticated. Aware of probing eyes, the men moved their wagering from the box seats to a less conspicuous place. On some nights it might be in the upper levels of the grandstands behind first base. Other nights they would congregate down the left-field line, away from prying eyes and ears, near a chain-link fence that separated the grandstands from the bleachers. The bettors positioned lookouts to offer warnings should law enforcement enter the ballpark or an usher approach. Players knew full well what was taking place. They were bemused to see the actor George Raft often sitting in the middle of the activity. "He's betting against us," a Hollywood infielder shrieked.[6]

Unbeknownst to Cobb, an effort had been launched three weeks after the 1939 baseball Winter Meetings aimed at tackling the Gilmore Field gambling problem. The mayor of Los Angeles assigned a detective, Wallace Jamie, to secretly study the problem. Throughout the 1940 season, beginning with exhibition games in March through the conclusion of the campaign in October, Jamie attended every home game in both Wrigley Field and Gilmore Field. He was a keen observer and made copious notes. In November he submitted a report that shocked the men in charge of both the Angels and Stars as well as heads of local law enforcement.

The detective detailed the sophistication of the ballpark gambling. Jamie charged that gamblers appeared to wager with inside knowledge from Stars and Angels players, noting that when specific players came to bat at certain times of a game, wagers on that player to strike out could reach as high as $600.

Jamie's work led to the discovery of a one-hundred-phone bookie joint above an ice plant near Santa Monica Boulevard and La Brea Avenue, just outside of the city limits. The operation moved more than $20,000 per day and had avoided being shut down by paying $100 bribes to the police officers who had discovered its location. A separate investigation raised equally disturbing information. Around the time of Jamie's report, the head of the California Horse Racing Board revealed that a gambling probe by his agency had led to a ring of illegal betting at both the Los Angeles–area ballparks. The horse racing probe found evidence that gamblers fixed races at Hollywood Park and Santa Anita Park. They then used the large winnings from those races to bet at Stars and Angels games. The horse racing investigation said the gamblers would operate in the daytime at the racetracks, then move to the ballparks at night. Once at the ballparks, the bettors would wager with celebrities, particularly the movie stars who were regulars at Gilmore Field. Jerry Geisler, chairman of the California Horse Racing Board, said, "Either the gamblers must be run out of these sports or the sports will be ruined."[7] Jamie's report was turned over to the district attorney with hopes that it would be presented to the grand jury and charges would be brought.

When the 1940 season got underway, six men who were reputed to be major gamblers went on trial in Los Angeles. The six were charged with fixing horse races at Hollywood Park. Throughout the four-month trial, not a single word was mentioned to connect any of the men with betting on local baseball. Actors Don Ameche and George Raft received subpoenas to testify and were implicated in the wagering that took place. In late May the trial went to the jury. For several days the jurors wrestled with the decision. After five days one of the six men was found guilty, while another was acquitted. In July the other four defendants struck deals. Each agreed to plead guilty to a lesser charge of contributing to the delinquency of a minor and was fined $1,000.

Early in the 1941 season, the effort to stamp out baseball gambling in Los Angeles ensnared a player. The morning before he was to pitch against the Hollywood Stars, Julio Bonetti of the Angels was seen reaching into the passenger window of a new car and accepting money from the driver, a reputed gambler. Later that day the gambler offered bets on Hollywood. That night, with Bonetti pitching, two Angels errors in the fifth inning helped Hollywood to take a 4–3 lead. Bonetti came out of the game for a pinch-hitter after toiling for eight innings. The game went extra innings, and Hollywood triumphed, 10–4. Once the Angels were made aware of Bonetti's association with the gambler and the man's betting, they launched an investigation. The pitcher denied any wrongdoing. But throughout a two-month probe, investigators said, Bonetti's story changed. On July 2, the head of minor-league baseball banished Bonetti from the game. A month later the pitcher applied for reinstatement but was denied. Julio Bonetti never played professional baseball again.

Despite the trial and the Bonetti banishment, gambling in the local ballparks did not stop. Gilmore Field was far from the only ballpark where illegal betting wreaked frustration on the management. It was rife in many of the stadiums throughout the Pacific Coast League. Across town at Wrigley Field, the Angels hired a private detective to note gamblers and their actions, then turned his information over to the district attorney's office. One Angels game with Sacramento had to be stopped when a fistfight broke out in the box seats between a gambler and a police detective caught taking the man's picture. W. C. Tuttle, president of the Pacific Coast League, seethed at the ongoing shenanigans. "Open wagering on strikes and balls and hits is offensive to the average fan," Tuttle told the teams. "It has to stop!"[8] It didn't.

During the 1942 season, a national sportscaster broke a story that claimed Judge Landis was so incensed by the out-of-control gambling in Gilmore Field's grandstands that he had given Cobb and Reichow thirty-six hours to clean it up, or he would close the ballpark down. Reichow insisted to the local press that the ball club had received no such notification. Tuttle checked with Landis and found the report to be untrue.

The private detective hired by the Angels photographed gamblers, and the team's management sent the images to Cobb and Reichow as well as to area law enforcement. Ushers were put on alert and told to boot the men out of the ballpark if they were caught in Gilmore Field. Raids continued. One staged during a Sunday doubleheader netted twenty arrests. Paul Zimmerman, the sports editor for the *Los Angeles Times*, railed in print that "loudmouthed gamblers make a damned nuisance of themselves."[9]

Cobb and Reichow were pushed to extremes. They cut off phone service in the ballpark between games of doubleheaders to prevent gamblers from accepting wagers or phoning bookmakers. Special operatives were hired to monitor the activity, with Meyer and Morrison ordered to take action when it got out of hand. Announcements were made during games: "If any man does not conduct himself as a gentleman and gambles or swears in this park, please notify an usher at once or an officer, or give all of the details to the office, as we are determined to stop this practice and ask your help."[10]

The actions of Cobb, his staff, and the authorities could barely put a dent in the illegal goings-on. It wasn't until the ensuing months and the outbreak of a major world event in December 1941 that the flow of baseball gambling in the Gilmore Field stands would recede to a mere trickle.

8

“WE’RE BOTH IRISH”

The freneticism and euphoria that carried Bob Cobb and the new owners of the Hollywood Stars into their inaugural season was but a distant memory eleven months later. Whatever angst, frustration, or ire, the construction of Gilmore Field and the assembly of a ball club wrought paled in comparison to the fury that exploded in March 1940.

A mere two weeks before the Stars were slated to launch the Pacific Coast League season, the *Los Angeles Times* revealed that the city attorney was considering a court injunction to stop the Stars’ season opener from taking place. Ray Chesebro claimed the team’s games constituted a public nuisance. The headlines brought cries of political grandstanding. Earl Gilmore was furious. He claimed the idea was a pressure tactic by the city to annex his land.

Across town the Angels were incensed. “If they can kick Hollywood out, they can kick us out,” said Dave Fleming, the team’s president.[1] “Where will they stop if they are going after public gatherings?”[2] Harry Williams, the secretary of the Pacific Coast League, admitted to reporters, “I am amazed. This is the first time in the history of baseball, so far as I know, that a baseball park has been sued for being a public nuisance.”[3] When a sportswriter reached Cobb for comment, the restaurateur wondered where it would all end. “If a crowd, automobiles parking on streets, and noise constitutes a nuisance and can be stopped simply because someone wants them stopped, the American Legion Stadium in Hollywood is just as vulnerable as we.” He added, “And so is Hollywood Bowl and its singing and music programs, to say nothing of the sunrise Easter services."[4]

Chesebro refused public comment, but four days before the season's first pitch was to be thrown, he filed suit in superior court. While Gilmore and Cobb cried politics, the crux of the matter actually stemmed from one angry housewife. Alice Newberry said she and many of her neighbors were fed up. They had had enough of the fans parking their cars in front of their homes. The loud whirring of the midget auto racers in Gilmore Stadium, rumbling from ice machines, and frustrations from congested traffic exasperated homeowners not just mere yards away at Stanley and Oakwood but those at Sweetzer and Melrose more than a mile and a half away as well. Baseball, it turned out, was what finally pushed the neighbors to take action. The sports-heavy schedule and long season brought the annoyance of loud crowds, public address cries, bright lights, celebratory fireworks, and gong chimes into their homes for seventy-five nights over five and a half months. Newberry took her gripe and those of her neighbors to City Hall.

Just two weeks after the 1939 season concluded, the complaints were brought before the Los Angeles City Council. It was pointed out that thirty thousand people living adjacent to the Gilmore property were affected. A request to take action was put to a vote, but the majority of council members rejected the idea. Steven Cunningham, who represented the district where the Gilmore complex was, pressed on. He funneled the matter to the Public Health and Welfare Committee, which indicated a willingness to take up the matter.

Victor Ford Collins was irritated by the city's action. He noted that the Stars had followed proper procedures when Gilmore Field was built. The team's president and attorney told reporters that the ball club had received just one notice of complaint from the city. He pointed out that many of the items listed as problems were easily fixable, but several were not. Parking could not be made free as a way to stop people from parking their cars on neighborhood streets. The Stars and the Pacific Coast League refused to impose a curfew that would stop games at 10:30 p.m. Collins also said the team was limited in what it could do to prevent noise from the public address system from invading the nearby neighborhood.

Forty-eight hours before the season's first game was due to begin, the Seattle Rainiers checked into the Knickerbocker Hotel wondering if they would be playing in Gilmore Field on Saturday afternoon, March 30.

While the Rainiers lounged at their hotel, lawyers were hard at work. Attorneys for Earl Gilmore, Victor Ford Collins on behalf of the Stars, and two assistant attorneys for the City of Los Angeles spent three successive days in negotiations. When they finally broke, the men notified the city council that they were confident that the problems could be resolved to the neighbors' satisfaction.

Gilmore agreed to test out a new muffler system on the race cars in his stadium. Collins had acquiesced to many of the noise concerns for Gilmore Field. Batters would only be announced the first time through the order, and then the public address system would be turned off. Fireworks and the gong would be curtailed, and work would begin right away to try to retrain the beacon of the lights away from homes. Rather than implement a 10:30 p.m. curfew, Cobb, Reichow, and Collins agreed to move up night games. They proposed beginning at 6:15 rather than 8:30 p.m. City leaders were pleased with the plan and Chesebro was ordered to withdraw the lawsuit. The season opener would go on as scheduled.

At ten minutes past two o'clock on Saturday, March 30, comedic actress Gracie Allen flung the ceremonial first pitch to get the 1940 season underway. Her radio and marital partner, George Burns, made sure everyone within earshot knew that he was in the front row to offer encouragement, albeit behind the backstop screen. The day that was almost spoiled by a lawsuit was instead dampened by gray skies and defeat. The following day a break in the weather brought hope that the teams could squeeze in a doubleheader between showers. Several gallons of gasoline were poured on the muddy infield, then lit ablaze to try to dry the dirt. The groundskeeping frenzy and a break in the weather allowed Hollywood to register its first win of the season, 4–1. Just as the second game was about to begin, a heavy downpour let loose. The teams agreed to call it a day and head for their next scheduled destinations.

Few could have known that the aggravations of the fight with the city and the frustrations brought about by bad weather to open the season foretold the kind of year that lay ahead. In almost no time the Stars were plummeting toward the bottom of the Pacific Coast League standings. Keen to change the team's fortunes after its disappointing 1939 season and to generate more publicity, Cobb and the board of directors had fired Red Killefer. Though the man had another year on his contract, Collins tried to lessen the Stars' payout by negotiating a settlement. "Just stack that money right up in front of me," Killefer demanded, unwilling to accept one penny less than he was owed.[5]

The man Hollywood hired to replace Killefer was Bill Sweeney. It had been no secret during the 1939 season that Bob Cobb was enamored with the Portland manager. Each time the Portland club came to Los Angeles, Cobb invited Sweeney to lunch at the Brown Derby. Sweeney was personable and immensely popular with the press—just the man who could generate notices in columns and write-ups in the six area daily newspapers. Sweeney was also animated, a baseball showman, and the sort of character fans would find entertaining.

Prying Sweeney from Portland wasn't easy. The team's owners refused to release their manager from his contract. Their stance did not change until Sweeney himself told them he wanted to go to Hollywood. Talks began with the proposal to trade a player or players for the manager. Portland demanded two of Hollywood's best players. Reichow was reluctant. Finally, Cobb wrote a check for $10,000 and bought out the final year on Sweeney's Portland contract.

What Bob Cobb didn't realize was that he had bought a baseball oxymoron. On one hand, Bill Sweeney was an amusing story spinner who was quick with the quips. He would produce smiles and laughs when he sat down with sportswriters. Though Sweeney did not progress beyond the eighth grade in school, men who had employed him marveled at his astuteness. His tactical savvy and psychological skills produced winners. Yet the qualities that made writers laugh and drew admiration from his bosses were overshadowed by a turbulent side. Bill Sweeney was mean. The simplest mistake by a player would trigger a fiery rage. His coaches shook their head at things he said and did toward players. As mean as he was toward his players, he was downright nasty to umpires. When he ran onto the field to dispute a call, the first words out of his mouth were often, "I ought to punch you right in the nose!"[6] During such arguments his face would turn deep red. It made fans give him the nickname, "Ol' Tomato Face."

Cobb and Hollywood's fans got a large dose of the rage that Sweeney could unleash just three weeks into the 1940 season. During a game against San Diego in which the Stars won, Hollywood's Bill Cissell slid into home plate and spiked the Padres' catcher. As Cissell started to trot toward the dugout, the San Diego pitcher hurled choice words in his direction. Sweeney heard them, raced toward home plate, shoved Cissell out of his way, and began throwing punches at the opposing pitcher. Players from both teams rushed to join the fray, and soon Sweeney was surrounded. With his head down, the manager wildly flailed his arms, trying to throw punches at anyone in a San Diego uniform. Finally, two of his own players wrapped their boss in a bear hug and dragged him from the fray.

When he joined Hollywood, Sweeney declared himself the team's first baseman. This pushed Babe Herman, bad legs and all, into right field. The new manager was quick to earn the fans' adulation when he belted a home run over the left-field fence that helped to win the Stars' second game of the season. But the win would be an April rarity—May, too. While Sweeney was hitting over .300, Frenchy Uhalt and Babe Herman struggled. Three weeks into the season, Herman's batting slump and poor fielding put him on the bench.

The losses ate at Cobb. He began using the back door to enter his restaurants to avoid the jibes of friends and customers. The Stars' owner wondered aloud to employees why his players weren't hitting. Fans, on the other hand, were not dissuaded. Forty thousand streamed through the Gilmore Field turnstiles during a seven-game series with the Angels to begin May. By the middle of May, Reichow beamed at reports that showed the club was 25 percent ahead of its attendance totals at the same time in the 1939 season.

Finally, on May 19, fortunes seemed to turn. After a pair of rookies struggled to hold the job, Joe Hoover took over at shortstop and played so well that big-league scouts came to check him out. At that same time Bill Cissell amassed a fourteen-game hitting streak. Bill Sweeney suffered a back injury, which pushed Babe Herman off the bench and back to first base. In an ensuing twin bill against San Francisco, Herman slugged his first home run of the season. He also doubled twice, singled, and drove home four runs. His performance helped Hollywood to a pair of wins that lifted the club's record above .500 and into the first division.

But what was to become commonplace for the club throughout the season manifest once the Stars had climbed into fourth place. Every time the team went on a run, they would fail to sustain the success and fall into a hole. Six consecutive defeats in Seattle knocked the Stars back into the second division. Once they broke the losing streak, they went on to win seven in a row, only to fall back into yet another slump. Woes extended off the field. Babe Herman had disaster strike his turkey enterprise. Herman had kindly offered an out-of-work relative a job to look after his ranch, particularly when baseball took him on the road. But in July many of Herman's turkeys became ill. Within days a virus would claim a quarter of his five-thousand-bird flock.

Throughout the summer the team sought players. Oscar Reichow moaned that he had cash to spend but could find no one willing to sell him hitters. Prospects were pulled up from lower-level minor-league clubs. Several arrived to infuse quick help, only to soon see their productivity dwindle, confirming that they were not yet ready to succeed at the Pacific Coast League level. Not even the two dozen rabbits' feet that Gail Patrick clutched in her front-row box could change the Stars' fortunes. The team's seesaw swings continued throughout the summer. Finally, Sweeney reached a breaking point and erupted in such outlandish form that his relationship with the Hollywood board of directors was irreparably damaged. After a game in which Hollywood had lost for the seventh consecutive time, Sweeney strode into the Gilmore Field pressroom. He had been incensed by the team's play and the loss. To calm himself, he guzzled a bottle of beer before meeting with sportswriters to answer their questions. As he often did, "Tiny," the Gilmore Field security guard, entered the room to hear what Sweeney had to say. On this night the man was sporting a brand-new pistol. "Let's see it," Sweeney beckoned.[7] The manager looked the .38 over, then pointed the gun toward the ceiling. He squinted as he focused on the sight. Suddenly a loud bang filled the room, followed by the sound of shattering glass. The room fell both quiet and dark. Tiny flicked on his flashlight. Sweeney calmly handed the revolver back to the security guard, bid the sportswriters good night, and left the room. His shot had obliterated the room's lone light, Bob Cobb's expensive chandelier.

Injuries became a burden. Sweeney himself had to be hospitalized in July. He had suffered injuries to his ribs in a collision while trying to break up a double play in a game against the Angels. Days after Sweeney told reporters that he was confident the team could squeeze into the playoffs with a strong finish over the final five weeks of the season, Babe Herman pulled a leg muscle. He would not play again during the 1940 season, and Hollywood was doomed to a sixth-place finish.

If the season had not cascaded hopes and impressions deeply enough, an even more shocking revelation soon would. One month after the season ended, Angelinos awoke and unfolded their newspapers to a large photo of Bob Cobb and Gail Patrick dancing cheek to cheek. The picture of a happy couple belied the large headline above. It read, "Gail Patrick Files Suit for Divorce from Cobb."[8] As if a bad year could not get worse, tumult in their household pushed the couple to a breaking point. "Another Hollywood illusion of the happily married couple was shattered yesterday," wrote the *Los Angeles Times*.[9] Cobb moved out of the family home and took an apartment on Hayvenhurst Drive, minutes from his office in the Hollywood Brown Derby and two miles from Gilmore Field. Friends of the couple were stunned by the revelation. Few saw the action coming. "We were for so long extremely happy that it is with the greatest of regret that I am filing this complaint for divorce," Patrick said in a statement to the press.[10] "There is little that I can say," Cobb responded, "except that I am exceedingly saddened."[11] The press later learned that Patrick had charged Cobb with mental cruelty in the divorce action.

Three weeks later the couple appeared before a judge in superior court. Patrick painted a picture of Cobb as temperamental and at times volatile. The actress answered her attorney's questions in a somber and often inaudible voice.

"Did Mr. Cobb on numerous occasions tell you that he no longer wished to remain married and that you should obtain a divorce?"

"He did."

"Did he allow you to make social engagements and then refuse to join you?"

"Yes."

"And for reasons that weren't your fault, would he become angry and ignore you for several weeks at a time?"

"Yes."[12]

Patrick shared that her husband's actions had caused her to become nervous and ill. Under questioning from the judge, the celebrated entertainer acknowledged having known Cobb for two years prior to their 1936 wedding. "And knowing his disposition, you married him anyway?"

Patrick paused, turned toward the judge, and replied, "We are both Irish."

The judge nodded. "I understand," he said, then granted the decree.[13]

9

"THE COAST LEAGUE HAS BEEN FAST ASLEEP"

The squeal of tires braking on hard pavement filled the air. Heads turned and attentions perked to the loud, sickening sound of two heavy cars crashing into each other. When the concerned reached the scene of the accident, they found one of the drivers in great pain. It was several agonizing minutes before police and then an ambulance arrived. As the attendants loaded Emmit O'Brien Harrison onto the gurney for the trip to a nearby hospital, no one could have known the seminal moment that was taking place, the life paths that were about to be altered, and the dreams that would change. Harrison had suffered a badly broken leg. The accident would plunge his six-member family into despair, struggling to make ends meet. With Harrison unable to work, his wife's role would change, forced by fate to become the family breadwinner. The family angst forced the Harrison's youngest son to wrestle with whether to surrender glory for practicality. It came at a time when the Hollywood Stars were about to embark upon a controversial new plan.

It did not take Bob Cobb long into his ownership of the Hollywood Stars to become steeled by a conviction. Whether it was confirmed by the frustrations of 1940, when the Stars offered cash aplenty but could find no one willing to sell to them a capable outfielder, or just his own experience watching semipro baseball around Southern California, Cobb became convinced his club had to develop its own talent.

Southern California was an area that teemed with baseball talent. Some of the best players in the big leagues—Bobby Doerr, Bob Meusel, and Bob Lemon—were from the area. Parks, playgrounds, and schoolyard diamonds from Pasadena to Long Beach and Santa Monica to West Covina were regularly buzzing with pickup, youth league, and semipro games. The region's sunny, warm weather gave twelve months of playing opportunities, all of which helped young players hone their skills.

Once Cobb gained an understanding of baseball finances, the knowledge merged with his appreciation for the level of baseball talent in Southern California to form a strategy. To acquire the best players possible, teams such as Hollywood had long been at the mercy of big-league clubs. They had to buy players, usually those the big-league clubs no longer wanted. Discarded big leaguers, however, were often players on the downside of their career. Young players, on the other hand, offered a more cost-effective and beneficial way around this cycle of reliance. With a patient approach and sound development, a club could lessen its reliance on major-league discards. The younger players could also become a future source of revenue. Big-league clubs had a history of paying tidy sums to minor-league clubs for promising young prospects. "The Coast League has been fast asleep," Cobb told a local sportswriter. "It has permitted the majors to come in and steal our material."[1] With these factors in mind, Cobb hit on a plan—aggressively sign young Southern California high school and college prospects and develop their skills via his very own farm system.

Every team in the Pacific Coast League had some sort of arrangement with one, two, and in some cases, three lower-level minor-league clubs. Each, eager to add talent, would agree to take a small handful of the PCL clubs' young prospects. Neither Hollywood nor many other clubs in the Pacific Coast League had bothered with trying to sign top graduating high school or college players. To do so would mean bidding against big-league clubs and their deep pockets, which was a futile exercise. Instead, clubs like Hollywood annually sought to sign a half dozen or fewer lesser-tier high school or college prospects with the hope that three or four seasons of development in the lower minor leagues would produce a contributor. What was status quo was not good enough in the eyes of the men who ran the Hollywood Stars. Instead, Cobb and Oscar Reichow hit on a plan to get the very best area prospects. They became talent raiders.

The idea to aggressively pursue local talent was buoyed by the praise for Carl Cox. The teen had handled himself so well during spring training in 1939 that Red Killefer decided not to farm him out but keep him on the

Hollywood ball club. The youngest player in the Pacific Coast League, eleven years younger than the league's average age of twenty-eight, Cox played sparingly. When he did get onto the field for Hollywood, the prospect held his own. In a late June start against the Angels, the teen stung a trio of line-drive singles, scored three runs, and handled a pair of plays deftly at third base. "He'll become a sensation in a year or two," wrote Bob Ray in the *Los Angeles Times*.[2]

The signing of more players with skills like Carl Cox was the goal, but to do so meant acting before the big-league scouts could make their offers. Hollywood decided on a controversial plan. They would sign young prospects before they completed school. Their first such target was Bill Gray. The twenty-year-old was a strapping 6-foot-2-inch first baseman at UCLA whose swing could send a baseball hurtling awe-evoking distances. A native San Diegan, Gray and his good friend Ted Williams had filled their free time as youths and adolescents by playing baseball while their mothers journeyed to Mexico to save souls for the Salvation Army. During the summer of 1938, while playing in amateur games in Wrigley Field, Gray had befriended Hollywood first baseman Ced Durst. The collegian confided to the former New York Yankee that he was thinking of dropping out of school in order to play pro ball. Durst introduced Gray to Killefer. With little money to spend on players, Killefer never followed up. During the off-season Durst became the manager of the San Diego Padres and alerted his new employers to Gray's intentions. Gray's college coach, Marty Krug, happened to moonlight as a scout for the Detroit Tigers. Once he learned that the first baseman did not plan to return to school, Krug traveled to San Diego and urged the young talent and his parents to agree to sign a contract with Detroit. In the meantime, the Brooklyn Dodgers got wind of Gray's availability. Their scout, Ted McGrew, offered Gray $4,000, but the deal was thwarted when the Dodgers' president, Larry McPhail, refused to allocate the money. Gray instead signed with San Diego. When Killefer and Cobb learned of the agreement, they complained that San Diego had "stolen" Gray from them. It was a claim that Durst laughed off. Inexplicably, though, San Diego released Gray after five months of minor-league ball. Hollywood responded quickly and signed the budding slugger.

After the college season concluded in June 1939, Hollywood again raided. They signed Don Wolin, a slick-fielding, strong-armed nineteen-year-old shortstop from Compton Junior College. Like Carl Cox, Wolin played sparingly through the remaining weeks of the season. Both would undergo intense tutoring, though. Hollywood coach Glenn Wright, himself a former standout shortstop with the Pittsburgh Pirates, would hit sixty balls to the boys each day and sit with the prospects in the dugout during games to discuss positioning and defensive strategy.

High school players were not permitted to sign with big-league clubs until the completion of their graduation ceremony. It was a policy that dated back to 1920 and a voluntary covenant the major leagues had made with the minor leagues that it would not sign so-called sandlot players. On January 14, 1921, this proposal became section 8, article V of the Major-Minor League Agreement. To Cobb and Reichow this was an agreement that limited the actions of major-league clubs only. Nowhere could they determine that the rule barred minor-league clubs from signing sandlot players.

Hollywood launched a strong-minded pursuit of young talent. They signed Freddy Cochrane, a talented high school outfielder. A tip led the Stars to Sacramento, where they plucked a seventeen-year-old high school catcher from right under the noses of their league rival Sacramento Solons. During the spring of 1940, there were few high school players in all of Southern California better than Bill Barisoff. As stellar on the mound as he was with the bat, Barisoff was dreaded by opponents and coveted by big-league scouts. That he attended Riis High School, the city's reform school, did not deter regard or interest. In six league games Barisoff allowed only five earned runs. He struck out 55 batters in 40 innings and batted .588 at the plate. Among his games that made headlines was one in which he came one out from pitching a perfect game. Following the school year, Barisoff was honored as the Southern California baseball player of the year in a ceremony at a Los Angeles Angels game. He achieved all this as just a sixteen-year-old high school junior. The Angels, hoping it would help their parent Chicago Cubs sign Barisoff, gave the player a trip to San Francisco as a reward for the honor. Scouts from the Detroit Tigers, Cleveland Indians, New York Yankees, and St. Louis Browns extended congratulations and cajoled the boy's mother. Therein lay the problem. Ana Barisoff was an immigrant from Russia. She was a confectioner who worked over a copper kettle and marble slabs all day at a store on Western Avenue, where the candy she made came from the recipes of the store's namesake, Mary See. Ana Barisoff was set in the ways of the old country. She was not enamored with her son's baseball activities and was both confused by and suspicious of the men who came around from baseball teams to sweet-talk her. Bill Barisoff's high school coach offered to serve as a buffer between the woman and the scouts. He urged that the men come back in a year, when the boy would be a senior. The big-league teams agreed. The Hollywood Stars did not.

Money was scarce in the Barisoff household. The Stars' offer of a signing bonus was enticing. Finally, three weeks before spring training was to begin, Barisoff dropped out of school and signed with the Hollywood Stars. The signing spawned ire and alarm. The New York Yankees and Brooklyn Dodgers voiced their displeasure to the commissioner's office. The Los Angeles Angels sent their scouts, Dutch Reuther, Joe Gaddini, and Clarence Brooks, to area high schools, where they gave talks to the school baseball teams and urged players to resist the temptation to leave early for money.

Six months after Hollywood landed Barisoff, the Stars set their sights on an even bigger prize. Eddie Harrison was the most heralded high school athlete in Los Angeles. A football sensation, Harrison's skills in the fall of 1939 helped to lure crowds of ten thousand or more to Gilmore Stadium whenever his Fairfax High team played. Sportswriters called him "Torpedo." Even the revered Olympian and pro athlete Jim Thorpe came to see him play. Rare was the Saturday morning during football season when Harrison's picture wasn't prominent in at least one of the area's newspapers alongside a story of his Friday gridiron exploits. Once spring arrived, Harrison pitched and played the outfield for his high school team. He was named All-City in both sports, and recruiters from several colleges were keen to land his talents.

Eddie Harrison was the product of an athletic household. His older brothers, Ralph and Hal, played amateur and semipro baseball. They pitched batting practice to the boy, honing their younger brother's eye for curveballs, which would set Eddie apart from his high school teammates, who struggled with the pitch. At the center of the Harrison household was Eddie's mother, Lulu. Orphaned by a house fire in her native Rome, Georgia, at the age of four, Lulu Harrison treasured the family unit. Her daughter, Helen, and three sons were the center of her universe. She, in turn, was both their rock and the family glue. The family had struggled through the Depression. Steady work never came easy for her husband,

Emmitt. Now, incapacitated by the car accident, Emmitt Harrison was again unable to provide, which threw the family into tumult.

Her husband's accident left Lulu Harrison with little choice but to seek work. Eddie Harrison chipped in too. The teen took on part-time jobs to help his family. He caddied at Wilshire Country Club, where he carried the bags for judges and lawyers, many of whom never missed a chance to try to coax the teen to play football for their alma mater, the USC Trojans.

Whereas only eighteen months before, the arrival of the Hollywood Stars meant excitement in the Harrison's neighborhood, now the ball club loomed in a different way. Relief. A way out of the family's financial distress. One of Eddie's closest pals was Jimmy Hardy, who was the ball boy for Hollywood. In time, the Harrisons' difficult financial plight became known to the men in charge of the Stars. They arrived at the Harrisons' residence at 5530 Monroe Avenue with a contract and a bonus offer. It was all overwhelming. For several days Eddie pondered whether to make college football or professional baseball his future. It wasn't long before sportswriters got wind of the offer. Articles and column notes soon appeared, but the "will he or won't he" chatter only added to the burden carried by the young standout. Eddie's high school football coach, who had a potential championship team on his hands, urged the seventeen-year-old to remain in school. Lulu Harrison stressed that she wanted her son to go to college. But it pained Eddie to see his mother wracked by fatigue from working, running a household, and caring for her disabled husband. For four days Eddie went back and forth over the matter. He pondered possibilities and wrestled with his own dreams and aspirations. On June 28, he reached a decision. Eddie Harrison signed the contract offered by the Hollywood Stars.

The very next night Harrison heard cheers from the Gilmore Stadium fans when Bill Sweeney sent him into the game as a late-inning defensive replacement. He was the youngest player in the Pacific Coast League, two years younger than San Francisco's Farris Fain and ten years younger than the average age of players up and down the league. A week after making his professional debut, Harrison's importance to the Stars would grow significantly. During Hollywood's Fourth of July game, Sweeney was involved in a collision on the base paths. He suffered injuries to his ribs and back that put him in Santa Fe Hospital for several days. Coach Glenn Wright became acting manager. Sportswriters typed that Wright would move Babe Herman to first base and replace him in the outfield with the veteran Spence Thompson. He didn't. Instead, when Wright presented his lineup card to the umpires for the Stars' July 5 game with the Angels, it had Eddie Harrison's name seventh in the batting order and playing left field.

It didn't take Gilmore Field fans long to see the skills that had dazzled the Stars' scouts, coach, and manager. In the bottom of the sixth inning, Harrison shot a ball past the shortstop for a base hit. He scored after being advanced to third base. One inning later Harrison came to bat with two outs and two runners on base. He sent a drive bounding between the center and right fielders that reached the wall. Harrison did not stop running until he was safely at third base with a triple and two more Hollywood runs were shown on the scoreboard. By the end of the night, the seventeen-year-old had been responsible for half of the six runs Hollywood scored in the team's 8–6 loss. "Last night's contest was featured by . . . the fine stick work of Eddie Harrison, seventeen-year-old former Fairfax High player who patrolled left field for the vanquished Stars," wrote *Los Angeles Times* sports editor Paul Zimmerman.[3] The following night Harrison continued to generate excitement. He sent a triple to the wall at the base of the scoreboard in right center field, then later scored on a teammate's hit.

When Portland came to town, the series was promoted in the *Times* with a large photograph of Harrison smiling to words from the Stars' acting manager Wright. That night the Fairfax High product showed the toughness that had made him a standout on the football field. While he was at second base, a teammate singled. Harrison took off in an all-out sprint. Convinced that he could score, Harrison ignored Wright's signal to stop at third base. As he raced for home plate, Harrison realized the ball would arrive an instant ahead of him. The rookie lowered his left shoulder and laid a football-style block into the Portland catcher. The blow from the two-hundred-pound teen sent the catcher sprawling, and the ball squirted from his mitt. Hovering above the two bodies, the umpire thrust his arms aside to signal Harrison safe. Once the catcher had collected himself, he erupted with rage at the audacity of the bold rookie. Harrison returned the verbal venom. In an instant, teammates raced from both dugouts to surround the quarrelers, with many adding their own jibes to the fray. At the umpire's urging, Harrison's teammates steered their

The Stars found a loophole in baseball signing rules and used it to nab local high school sensation Eddie Harrison. The prized prospect jumped into the starting lineup as a seventeen-year-old. ***Courtesy of Bruce Harrison***

young outfielder back to the dugout while fans cheered the display of brazenness and zeal.

Just as he had done in his debut series against the Angels, the former prep standout had hits in each of Hollywood's first four games with the visiting Beavers. But at the height of Harrison's inaugural success, things would suddenly change. After a six-night stay, Bill Sweeney was released from the hospital. The Stars' skipper returned to Gilmore Field the following evening, where he visited with Wright and the players. Sweeney then watched from the stands as his team lost their eighth game in a row, 2–1. The losses had dropped Hollywood into seventh place, and fan attendance shrank. After being a spectator for one night, Sweeney retook the reins of the ball club. In the manager's first game back at the helm, Hollywood ended its losing streak. Babe Herman launched a three-run home run over the right-field wall and Bill Fleming pitched a two-hit shutout to propel Hollywood over Portland, 4–0. In the win Harrison had yet another hit.

Over the next three games, however, Eddie Harrison went hitless. There were miscues in the field, the failure to fully extend and snag a catchable fly ball, a futile lunge for a liner that got by him to score a run and lead to another. Sweeney sought help from management. Another player. A better bat. Jack Rothrock, a former Boston Red Sox and St. Louis Cardinals outfielder, was available. At Sweeney's urging, Rothrock was signed. When the Stars arrived in San Diego to begin a series with the Padres on July 16, it was Rothrock and not Harrison who was in the lineup and playing left field. "Young Eddie Harrison isn't ready to play regularly in this league yet, and rushing him along too fast isn't going to do him any good," wrote Bob Ray in the *Times.*[4] Was it Ray's opinion, or was he repeating the words of Bill Sweeney? Regardless, Eddie Harrison would not get into another game for the rest of the 1940 season.

Not long after Sweeney's July 4 injury, Babe Herman pulled a leg muscle. For help, Bill Gray was summoned from the Salina Millers of the Class C Western Association. There, he had been batting .300, and on arriving at Gilmore Field he was thrust into the Stars lineup. Gray raised eyebrows with two hits in his first game and three more the following night. One month into his tenure with the Stars, Gray cemented himself into Gilmore Field lore. It happened in a game on August 25, during the second half of a doubleheader against the Seattle Rainiers. In the bottom of the sixth inning, the tall, strapping slugger came to bat against Les Webber, who was being scouted for possible signing by the Brooklyn Dodgers. With a loud thwack, Gray sent a ball hurtling into the bright afternoon sky. Necks craned, and with each foot the ball traveled, eyes grew wider and mouths more agape until the well-mashed sphere flew over and disappeared beyond the scoreboard to the right of centerfield. The point where the home run vanished from view was 420 feet from home plate, and the scoreboard was 22 feet high. "Gigantic," wrote one sportswriter.[5] "Cleared the barrier with plenty to spare," typed another.[6] Envy tugged as Babe Herman marveled. It had been his goal to achieve such a Bunyanesque feat, but neither he nor anyone else who ever wore a Hollywood Stars uniform would manage to duplicate it.

As pleased as Cobb was with the contributions and performances of Harrison and Gray with the Stars as well as Cox, Wolin, and Barisoff in the minor leagues, the signing of top-area prospects was only half of his goal. Development was essential. Oscar Reichow laid out plans to Cobb for a minor league whose teams would strictly be affiliated with clubs in the Pacific Coast League. The men took their idea to a meeting of Pacific Coast League team owners in San Diego. It was met with a mixture of cautious interest and outright enthusiasm. Cobb pointed out that teams were following Branch Rickey's lead and corralling talent. The St. Louis Cardinals president, a trained lawyer, had hit on the idea to buy minor-league clubs and thus gain ownership of every player under contract to that club. This eliminated the costly bidding that was involved with buying players. By 1940 the Cardinals owned all or part of thirty-one minor-league clubs. Five pennants and three second-place finishes from 1926 to 1934 had spurred rivals to follow Rickey's lead. Where the Brooklyn Dodgers had one minor-league affiliate in 1934, they had eighteen in 1940. The New York Yankees were affiliated with fourteen clubs. Cleveland and Pittsburgh had ties to ten clubs, and the Washington Senators were affiliated with nine.

Cobb and Reichow reminded their fellow owners that outside of the five Pacific Coast League cities, no others in California had minor-league baseball. San Jose, Fresno, Bakersfield, Santa Barbara, Riverside, San Bernardino, and Anaheim were growing. Each had a suitable ballpark in which to play, and their population portended a favorable fan base. The men tossed ideas back and forth throughout the winter of 1940. They recruited friends and business associates to own clubs in the proposed league. Finally, in August, men from six communities each agreed to deposit $1,000 with the National Baseball Association for a club in the new league. At a meeting on August 31 at the El Tejon Hotel in Bakersfield, it was agreed to call the league the California League. Minor-league baseball's governing body had granted the league Class C standing. Inaugural cities would be Bakersfield, Fresno, Riverside, San Bernardino, San Jose, and Santa Barbara.

By the time the league began, on April 18, 1941, membership and affiliations had changed. The new ballpark in San Jose was not complete, so the club would operate as the Merced Bears and field a team with players supplied by the Oakland Oaks. San Diego aligned with the Anaheim Aces. The Los Angeles Angels had a tie-in with the Stockton Flyers. Sacramento was connected with the Fresno Cardinals and had allowed the St. Louis Cardinals to also use the club as a farm team. The Bakersfield Badgers received players from the San Francisco Seals, and the Riverside Reds were partly owned by and tied up with the Cincinnati Reds. The Santa Barbara Saints drew the ire of Cobb when they announced they would be a farm club of the Brooklyn Dodgers. The deal broke an agreement to associate not just with Hollywood but only with clubs from the Pacific Coast League. Spurned by Santa Barbara, Hollywood elected to own its own minor-league club and turned instead to San Bernardino.

Babe Herman lobbied to be the San Bernardino manager. Cobb, however, was convinced that there was more baseball in Herman's thirty-eight-year-old body and more hits in his bat. In January another Hollywood outfielder, Jack Rothrock, got the job instead.

The launch of the new league was well received. In Fresno, a crowd of 4,500, which included Branch Rickey, packed the ballpark for opening night. More than 2,500 poured into Santa Barbara's newly constructed Laguna Park. In Merced, the Bears' Opening Day almost became calamitous. The team's starting pitcher was stopped for speeding while on his way to the ballpark, then promptly taken before a traffic judge. When the player explained that he couldn't afford the cost of the fine and the problem that going to jail would cause, the judge made a deal with him: Pitch the Bears to an Opening Day win, and the fine would be waived. He did, and it was.

Hollywood's new farm club began play in an aura of fanfare. Bob Cobb chartered a bus and filled it with several of his movie star pals, who journeyed the seventy miles east to watch the San Bernardino Stars make their California League debut against Riverside. Art Gleeson, the new team's general manager, arranged for Battery C of the 65th Coast Artillery at nearby Camp Haan to attend the game. Whistles and catcalls abounded from the servicemen when Susan Peters, a lovely young Warner Brothers actress who had been named the league's "sweetheart," was introduced and waved to the crowd. Rothrock's nine won and got off to a hot start. By the end of the first month, they were leading the league. Bill Barisoff was the ace of the pitching staff, with seven wins against just one defeat. Manny Perez, who had impressed a Hollywood scout by pitching a fourteen-inning shutout in a semipro game, was signed and shone for San Bernardino. Fred Cochrane led the league in runs scored and would bat leadoff in the league's All-Star Game. At the end of June, however, things fell apart. San Bernardino and Riverside had struggled with dwindling attendance. Promotional ideas were tried to boost ticket sales. Tickets were offered to men in the military for just twenty cents. Ten-dollar ticket books were sold. Reichow confided to the *San Bernardino Sun* that the team was $12,000 in debt. He urged civic support for the team. Nothing worked. On June 28, the Riverside club folded amid deep financial losses. With no neighboring rival, San Bernardino did the same. "I regret very much that such action on the part of the Hollywood club was necessary," Oscar Reichow said.[7]

While Reichow and Cobb paid off debts, closed out the books, and arranged for San Bernardino's players to join other clubs, the Hollywood Stars sputtered. Bud Abbott and Lou Costello's hilarious "Who's on First?" routine performed from home plate on Opening Day had been a rare highlight through the first half of the 1941 season. By June the Stars were mired in fifth place, twelve games out of first. When the calendar turned to July, results became worse. They trailed the league leaders by eighteen and a half games and sat in sixth. If there was a silver lining in the 1941 season, it was the play of Babe Herman. Curiously, Bill Sweeney had not played Herman during the first two weeks of the season. It was not until the press began to nudge the Hollywood manager about the omission that Herman got on the field. Once he did, the veteran went on a tear.

Employing his usual superstitions—spitting on the end of his bat, then pounding it with his fist after he had taken the first strike; ignoring the number four, which he considered to be bad luck; and insisting that he bat third in the order—Herman entered the month of May with a .400 batting average. Defying his age, Herman's play at first base was stellar as well. He showed range and dexterity that many believed age had siphoned. The tattered old glove that had been given to him seven years before by the Cardinals' Jim Bottomly seemed possessed of magic.

On June 26, a large crowd filled Gilmore Field to celebrate Babe Herman's thirty-eighth birthday. The day began with news that Herman had been selected to play in the Pacific Coast League All-Star Game. That evening, before appreciative fans, a large birthday cake was rolled onto the field. The Helms Foundation presented Herman with its Athlete of the Month Award for his play during May. Civic leaders showered the Hollywood first baseman with gifts. Sportswriters gave him a large turkey. It was only after the game that Herman learned the writers had arranged for the bird to be swiped from his Glendale ranch. Among those who stepped to the microphone to say a few words was Sacramento manager Pepper Martin. The former St. Louis Cardinals star grinned and said, "I'm glad to see this ceremony for the Babe, who served his apprenticeship in the National League."[8] Herman erased Martin's smile when he hit a double to drive in a run. The blow put Herman's batting average at .382, which led the league and helped Hollywood defeat Sacramento, 10–3.

Following the festive game, Hollywood went on a torrid run. The Stars won fifteen of their next twenty-two games. Throughout August and into September, the team pursued a spot in the playoffs while Herman chased a batting title. Wins over Sacramento during the final week of the season secured the necessary fourth-place finish. Herman completed the season with a .346 average, which topped the Pacific Coast League.

The league employed a Shaughnessy playoff format, which paired the fourth- and first-place finishers in one semifinal and the teams that finished the regular second and third in the other. Winners of the two series would then meet in the final of the President's Cup. Hollywood's fourth-place finish matched them against the regular-season pennant winners, the Seattle Rainiers, in a best-of-seven series. The teams split the first four games. On a wet and chilly evening September 29 in Seattle's Sick Stadium, Babe Herman put Hollywood on the cusp of the league title series. In the top of the first inning, Herman doubled to put two runs on the scoreboard. In the ninth inning, with the score tied, Herman singled, then scored a run to spark a five-run Hollywood rally. The Stars won, 7–2, to take a 3–2 series lead.

The following night the teams were to conclude the series with a doubleheader. Wind and rain whipped Seattle throughout the afternoon.

By game time the field was wet and even muddy in spots. Umpires ordered the game to go ahead, a decision that infuriated Bill Sweeney. In a show of protest Sweeney coached third base while wearing rubber boots and a rubber raincoat. Neither the umpires nor the league president found the manager's antics amusing. In the dreary weather, Hollywood's hitters could not solve the Seattle pitching, and the Stars' season was ended by a pair of 2–0 shutouts.

Sweeney's Seattle antics drew the ire of the Hollywood board. To them it was the final straw. They had endured tantrums and tirades from the field boss throughout the summer. After a game against Oakland in which Hollywood blew a 12-run lead and lost, 14–13, Sweeney went berserk. He smashed windows, chairs, and several bats in the clubhouse. The manager mocked Reichow and Cobb to sportswriters, angry that the men would not make the trades he wanted. Sweeney ranted privately to trusted members of the press that he was not consulted when Reichow bought new players. Days after the 1941 season concluded, the Hollywood board of directors held its annual meeting. The men emerged to announced that they had agreed not to offer Bill Sweeney a new contract. Oscar Vitt, the former Cleveland Indians skipper, was hired to manage the club. So contentious and so irreparable was the club's relationship with Bill Sweeney that nobody bothered to phone him with the news.

10

"A DAY THAT WILL LIVE IN INFAMY"

The appearance of a large orange sun over the San Gabriel mountains gave credence to predictions that Sunday, December 7, would be much warmer than usual, perhaps as high as the mid-80s. At kitchen tables throughout Southern California, men unwrapped their morning newspaper to an image of Betty Grable, beaming while clutching the fruits of a Christmas shopping excursion. The seductive actress's curvaceous left leg stretched from car seat to pavement, adeptly posed by the picture's photographer. In Bel Air, Brentwood, and the Hollywood Hills, some of filmdom's biggest stars were sleeping off the aftereffects of a lavish fundraising party that had been held the previous night at the Beverly Hills estate of Baroness de Kuffner.

While it had been six weeks since the Hollywood Stars and Los Angeles Angels had put away their uniforms and equipment, baseball still raged about the area. Company teams and other semipro clubs took advantage of the warm winter weather to continue the summer pastime. As the morning hours waned, players from clubs that spanned leagues throughout Southern California gathered their gear and readied for Sunday play. The day's biggest game would be a matchup of teams from two aircraft manufacturing plants, Lockheed and Vega Aircraft Company. Such was the significance that the meeting would be held in Wrigley Field and heralded as "Aircraft Day." Proceeds from the game would benefit the recreation facilities at the two plants. It was of such importance to Vega Aircraft Company that Red Barrett, a former Cincinnati Reds standout, was recruited to pitch.

As the noon hour approached, a steady stream of cars turned into the parking lots around Earl Gilmore's football stadium. The Pacific Coast League champion Hollywood Bears and the winners of the American League, the Columbus Bulls, were to play for the Little World's Cup. It was at about that time when a seemingly idyllic, tranquil Sunday was pierced by tumult and laced with fear.

It happened at 11:22 a.m. Housewives who regularly tuned their radios to hear "Over Our Coffee Cup," a weekly broadcast by First Lady Eleanor Roosevelt, were first to gasp at the shocking news. John Hughes on KFWB radio broke in with yet another report. Finally, H. V. Kaltenborn over the NBC radio network announced that "Japan has made war upon the United States without declaring it."[1] In rapid-fire succession, bulletins and further reports shot from radios in apartment kitchens and mansion dens, in restaurants and stores. Rattled drivers became distracted. Some took their eyes off the road to turn the volume knob, while others pushed buttons to find a station that might offer more details. *Los Angeles Times* reporter Bill Henry was on his way to work when the news crackled from his car radio. While he tried to digest what was happening, he was struck by the almost melancholy sight of fathers calmly playing catch with their sons in front of their family home, unaware of what was happening in the Pacific. Then, in sharp contrast a mere two blocks away, Henry noticed two young women sobbing, clearly jarred by what they had just heard on the radio.

Each news update brought further details of the attack by the Japanese Imperial Navy upon the Hawaiian base, Naval Station Pearl Harbor, and nearby Hickam Field. There were many casualties, the announcers said. Transfixed in front of radios, families fretted about loved ones who were serving, while others feared what might come next. Each word from the commentators rippled horror, confusion, and anger about the city.

In contrast to the fear and worry that gripped homes, eighteen thousand football fans cheered wildly in Gilmore Stadium when the public-address announcer declared that the United States was at war with Japan. Their cheers were quickly hushed, however, when reverberating words instructed all active members of the military as well as those who worked for the fire and police departments to report for duty at once. Men in uniform and those with plans to join their ranks would soon fill Pershing Square in downtown Los Angeles. A tense mood prevailed. Tables were quickly set up in the park, and workers began to sell defense bonds. Each passing hour brought more information and with it new orders and actions. By nightfall, searchlights scanned the sky. Large ack-ack guns were moved into position and pointed at the ready should enemy aircraft be spotted. The navy ordered a blackout of all dwellings within a fifteen-mile radius of San Pedro Harbor. Frank Burris, commissioner of the Federal Communications Commission, sent word that all Los Angeles radio stations were to broadcast for only one minute at a time every half hour. The shutdown would last for nineteen hours and was intended to throw off any Japanese bombers that might try to use radio signals to track a course to Los Angeles.

When the workweek began the next morning, consternation reigned. In factories, restaurants, and office buildings, many workers kept an ear trained to their radio for updates. Neither the Hollywood Bears' 21–9 win nor Vega Aircraft's 3–2 triumph over Lockheed before 1,506 fans was a topic for conversation around water coolers. Productivity came to a halt when President Franklin Roosevelt addressed the Congress. More than 90 million Americans were transfixed to the president's description of December 7 as "a day that will live in infamy."[2] Many were heartened while others fretted when Roosevelt asked the Congress to pass a declaration of war. Thirty-three minutes after the president's seven-minute speech, war was declared in a vote of 388 to 1.

War planners quickly sprang into action. By Monday night their meetings had delivered orders that brought change to local businesses. Retail stores and shops near the coastline were told to close by 4:30 p.m. Factories located close to the coast halted their overnight shifts. Brightly lit restaurants like the Brown Derby were ordered to turn off neon signs and cover windows.

Only two days before the attack on Pearl Harbor, baseball had wrapped up its annual Winter Meetings. More than one thousand club owners, operators, managers, and coaches had gathered in Jacksonville, Florida. Victor Ford Collins had vowed to "take the rubber band off the cash wad" to acquire pitching.[3] Oscar Reichow and new manager Oscar Vitt walked the halls, chatted up old friends, and gathered information while trying to make deals. But war had now thrown baseball into confusion. Within forty-eight hours of Roosevelt's declaration, two of the game's biggest stars had joined the war effort. Hank Greenberg had only been discharged from the army on December 5, but four days later he reenlisted and told reporters, "We are in trouble, and there is only one thing for me to do."[4] The very next day Cleveland's ace pitcher, Bob Feller, took the Oath of Induction and joined the navy. Many more ballplayers would soon follow.

Tensions around the world escalated. By midweek, three days after the Japanese attack, Germany and Italy declared war against the United States. Military leaders knew they would need more men to fight two wars—one in the Pacific and another in Europe. Only one year earlier, the United States had fewer than two hundred thousand men in uniform. Its military was outnumbered by those of more than twenty other countries. In response, Roosevelt had proposed a draft. Men between the ages of twenty-one and thirty-five were required to register and, if selected, serve one year in the armed forces. Now the War Department asked Congress to change the ages for eligibility and the length of service. It agreed and set the registration range to include all men between the ages of twenty and forty-four. If drafted, service would last the duration of the war plus an additional six months.

Volunteerism became paramount. In Southern California, the county sheriff issued an urgent call for civilian defense volunteers. More than three thousand doctors were recruited to respond should Los Angeles be bombed. Bob Cobb was among those to heed the call for help. He agreed to be a director of the United Service Organizations (USO).

The shock of Pearl Harbor continued to resonate when the holidays arrived. Christmas and New Year's were celebrated by celebrities in a far more subdued fashion than usual. Actor Spencer Tracy pruned his trees. Academy Award nominee Jeannette MacDonald threw a New Year's party not for friends and fellow entertainers but for soldiers. Producer Henry Sherman cooked up a western barbeque for one thousand members of the 165th Regiment. Many actors eschewed the limelight for quieter festivities. Mickey Rooney and his fiancée, Ava Gardner, skipped plans to dine at a posh restaurant and ate, instead, with Rooney's family. Clark Gable and his wife, Carole Lombard, sequestered themselves at a duck club in Northern California.

Early in the new year, baseball wondered what it would or should do. The Michigan State League, the Coastal Plains League, and the Big State League pondered shutting down, fearful that enlistment and conscription would leave its teams without sufficient numbers of players to field teams. Others wondered what sort of wartime rules would be enacted and how they would impact their operations. In the Pacific Coast League,

Gilmore Field was a playground for the biggest names in the motion picture industry. Clark Gable and his wife, Carol Lombard, were regulars before the tragic death of the actress. ***Courtesy of Snap/Shutterstock***

club owners and operators got their first indication in a cable from the league's secretary, Harry Williams. "Massing of people may be prohibited for public safety," Williams warned.[5] Quietly, an even bigger question loomed. Would there be baseball at all in 1942?

It was with that question in mind that Judge Kenesaw Mountain Landis sent a letter to the president to ask what baseball should do. The very next day a response came from the White House: "I honestly feel that it would be best for the country to keep baseball going." President Roosevelt explained that "everybody will work longer hours and harder than ever before. And that means they ought to have a chance for recreation and for taking their minds off their work even more than before."[6]

With clarity at hand, W. C. Tuttle called together Pacific Coast League club owners and executives for a special meeting during the first week of February. Bob Cobb began the meeting with a pronouncement that any uniformed member of the military would be admitted to games at Gilmore Field free of charge. He further added that the Stars' board of directors would pay the state and federal tax on their tickets. The meeting tackled challenges posed by the war. A projected shortage of players prompted a vote to reduce rosters from twenty-five players to twenty. The army had asked teams to cap crowds at five thousand per game because of a shortage of law enforcement officers able to handle crowd control and traffic issues. It was a request the army would later reconsider. Spring training was shortened. Considerable discussion was given to how proposed gas rationing and use of trains for military transportation might affect the way teams made their road trips.

All around Los Angeles, as in the rest of the country, normalcy was pushed aside. The shock of war entered homes and apartments on a daily basis in the form of newspaper articles about attacks and sieges in Europe and in Asia. More heinous notice came via telegram or a knock at the door bringing tragic news about a loved one. On January 17, six weeks after America had plunged into war, a shocking war-related tragedy jarred Bob Cobb and the entire Hollywood motion picture community.

An ambitious plan to raise money for the war effort had begun. It enlisted the help of actors and other entertainers. All around the country, the sale of war bonds took on many forms, such as rallies, purchase incentives, and prizes. Bing Crosby produced the song "Road to Victory" to help promote the effort. Two weeks into 1942, Carole Lombard responded to a request to headline a statewide war bond rally in her native Indiana. Lombard was one of the most popular actors of the day, and her appearance drew a big crowd to the state capitol. The day was resplendent in nationalism. Flag ceremonies and speeches brought cheers. Inside the Capitol Building, Lombard gave an autographed picture to each person who bought a war bond. By the end of the day, $2,107,513 had been raised from the actress's efforts. The next day Lombard changed her plans to travel home by train. She was anxious to return to her husband. A couple in the airport heard the actress's mother ask her daughter not to fly, a request that went unheeded. Together with her mother and her husband's publicist, Lombard boarded a TWA DC-7 for the flight home. That evening at the Lockheed Air Terminal in Burbank while awaiting his wife's arrival, Clark Gable received a telegram from his publicist to say that the plane was refueling in Amarillo, Texas. It was behind schedule. The flight would stop to refuel next in Las Vegas. As the time approached 8:00 p.m., Gable anxiously checked his watch. The plane was due to land in Burbank at any moment. It never appeared. Word spread through the airport of an accident near Las Vegas. A frantic Gable chartered a plane. Once in Las Vegas he was directed toward Olcott Mountain, thirty miles southwest of town. When he arrived, Clark Gable found mayhem. The plane had veered seven miles off course and slammed into the side of the mountain. Lombard, her mother, Gable's publicist, and fourteen soldiers headed for training were among the twenty-two people on board who were killed.

News of the crash knocked the war off the front pages of newspapers across the country. "Not since Knute Rockne was killed in 1931 has an airline fatality shocked the nation as Carol Lombard's," wrote Tom Treanor in the *Los Angeles Times*.[7] The industry that America turned to for escape in tragic times was itself enveloped in tragedy. "It seems impossible to believe," said Joseph Been, the executive vice president of RKO Pictures.[8] "I am so unbelievably shocked that I don't know what to say," actor William Powell told a reporter.[9]

Bob Cobb, like many in Hollywood, was shaken by the news. He considered Clark Gable and Carole Lombard to be great friends. The couple became engaged in his Hollywood Brown Derby restaurant. In fact, many fans liked to ask for the specific booth number in which Gable had proposed to Lombard—booth number 5. The first time Lombard and Gable were seen in public as a couple was at Gilmore Field, where they watched the Hollywood Stars. They were baseball fans and spent many a summer evening cheering the Stars. Such was their friendship that only days after the tragedy, Cobb received a phone call. The gravelly voice at the other end was that of the downhearted Gable. For three days he had remained at the mountainside throughout the recovery effort. Now he had returned, escorting his wife's body from Las Vegas by train. Gable was phoning to ask if Cobb would serve as usher at Lombard's private funeral.

The service followed the request Lombard had made in her will. It was private. The public was barred even from roads that led to the Methodist Church in Westwood Hills. Police shooed away photographers. Fewer than fifty people were permitted entry to the chapel. Many spent the entire service weeping.

In the days that followed, grief was coupled with consternation. Executives at United Artists pondered how and when to release Lombard's recently completed film, *To Be or Not to Be*. Gable confided to friends that he could not bear to return to the couple's ranch on Petit Avenue in Encino and debated whether to put the spread up for sale. Perhaps inspired by Lombard, a new attitude prevailed about Hollywood. Countless entertainers—Ann Southern, Bette Davis, Dorothy Lamour, Harold Lloyd, and Kay Kayser among them—plunged into new roles, ones dedicated to assist the war effort. Joe E. Brown's wife prepared 165 dozen cookies a day for service canteens. Spencer Tracy invited soldiers at a nearby listening post to drop by his North Hollywood home on Sundays to swim in the pool. Joan Crawford, who replaced Carole Lombard in *He Kissed the Bride*, donated her salary from the film, $112,000, to the Red Cross and the Navy Relief Fund.

Beyond Hollywood's borders were thousands, millions of people troubled by the war who sought both solace and optimism. More than ever before, Americans would turn to motion pictures as an outlet. They would also come to embrace baseball for escapism. From the tragic death of Carole Lombard, a lesson was born that would be embraced throughout the war years by the entertainment industry and by baseball as well. It was put quite succinctly by the syndicated columnist Hedda Hopper, who wrote, "Giving joy to others makes you forget yourself."[10]

11

"A SWEET PROSPECT"

The mere sound of the door's creak was enough to produce a knot in Oscar Reichow's stomach. In the weeks that followed America's entry into the war, the daily delivery of mail to Gilmore Field seemed to bring nothing but bad news. Edna Ward could see the consternation on her boss's face as well as in his mannerisms and through his speech. Conversations between the Hollywood business manager and the new skipper, Oscar Vitt, were difficult. It seemed as though each time the men spoke, Reichow was the bearer of more bad news. It often meant there was yet another player the manager would not be able to write onto his lineup card, use as a pinch-hitter, have as a reserve to come off the bench, or help out of the bullpen.

First came a letter from Ed Cole. Reichow had spent hours and hours at the Winter Meetings seeking pitching help. He came away with Cole, a former St. Louis Browns hurler whom Reichow was convinced would be a mainstay of Hollywood's 1942 pitching staff. Cole wrote, however, that he had received his draft notice and was entering the navy. The very next day came another letter, this one from Bill Gray. "I've enjoyed my two seasons with Hollywood more than any other period of my life," he wrote. "I am proud to trade my uniform for one with Uncle Sam."[1] Just like that, Reichow had lost a key pitcher and a blossoming power hitter who had posted a .282 batting average over ninety games in 1941.

The notices from Cole and Gray would only be the beginning. Each day thereafter seemed to bring similar letters and more losses. Within two weeks Cootie Thompson, Carl Cox, Freddy Cochrane, Johnny Bittner,

Bill Atwood, and Gene Thompson notified the club that they were entering the armed forces. Reichow even lost his assistant when Richard Sheary was conscripted.

Conscription wasn't the only cause for the exodus. Well-paying defense jobs also cut into the Stars roster. The team's catcher, Bill Brenzel, would join the hundred thousand men who were lured by good pay to work in shipyards. Ron Smith declared himself through with baseball to take a job with a defense contractor. Les Powers answered an urgent call for teachers and told the club he would only play on weekends until the school year ended in June. "We'll have to get help," Reichow told reporters.[2] The Hollywood business manager sent cables and typed letters to dozens of fellow team operators in search of players. He became so desperate for help that he authored a column that ran in the *Sporting News* in which he proposed that big-league clubs reduce their rosters to seventeen players. This would make more players available for clubs in the minor leagues. His idea was ignored.

Amid the chaotic search for players came another storm. It involved Babe Herman. At the Winter Meetings, Cobb and Reichow were startled to learn that Herman had joined with Los Angeles businessman Edward "Dunk" Farrell to try to buy the Portland Beavers. Their offer was turned down. The men sought to negotiate further, but talks reached a dead end. Now, as the calendar drew closer to the start of spring training, Herman made pronouncements to the press that puzzled and angered members of the Stars' board of directors. When asked about the off-the-field pursuit, Herman told sportswriters he had asked Hollywood for his release in order to pursue a managing job but was refused. Cobb and Reichow said that this was all news to them.

In January, matters with Herman took an even more infuriating twist. The slugger declared that he had been cheated and was through playing for Hollywood. "He has not told us that," Oscar Reichow answered the *Los Angeles Times*.[3] The Hollywood board saw the bluster as merely Herman's latest holdout, an attempt to extract a higher salary. Herman saw it differently. "If I don't get that bonus I was promised, my baseball career is over," he declared.[4] Reichow, Cobb, and the entire Hollywood board was baffled by Herman's pronouncement. None had any idea what the popular slugger was talking about. Victor Ford Collins agreed to look into the matter. He soon reported back that the bonus had been promised by the team's former manager, Bill Sweeney, who never made anyone else aware.

The angst that enveloped Reichow led the Stars' business manager to take an extra-hard stance when players wrote or phoned to extract higher pay. No call, though, was more perplexing than one from Wayne Osborne. When the pitcher labeled Reichow's salary offer unfair, the Hollywood business manager exploded. As Reichow launched into a tirade, Osborne stopped him with a reply that left the Hollywood business manager speechless. "Baseball may have a rough year ahead," Osborne began. "It seems to me with things the way they are, it [the money offered] was too much."[5]

It wasn't long before stress began to affect Reichow's health. Two additions, though, enabled the Hollywood business manager to smile and brought rare off-season elation to the Hollywood front office. One in-

In many cases the movie stars were as enamored with the Hollywood Stars players as the players were of them. Here actor-singer Gene Autry (left) swaps work clothes with Stars outfielder Babe Herman (right). ***Courtesy of Los Angeles Herald Examiner Photo Collection, Los Angeles Public Library Photo Collection***

volved one of the biggest names in baseball. The second brought to Hollywood a prospect many felt had the potential to become a big name.

At the conclusion of the 1941 season, the Chicago Cubs had released Charley Root. For sixteen seasons Root had been a mainstay of the Cubs' pitching staff. In 1927, his second season in the major leagues, Root won twenty-six games to lead all National League pitchers. He was popular with the press and a favorite of Cubs fans. Root occupied a unique place in baseball lore. He was the man on the pitcher's mound during Game 3 of the 1932 World Series, when Babe Ruth supposedly pointed to center field and predicted he would hit the next pitch for a home run. "Never happened," Root would snap whenever he was asked about it.[6] Root's version of the event was that teammates in the Cubs dugout had razzed Ruth unmercifully throughout the series. Of the incident in question, Root explained that after he had rifled two fastballs past the Babe for strikes, Ruth stepped out of the batter's box. According to Root, the Yankees slugger responded to his hecklers by raising his right arm and, with one finger extended, shouted, "Boys, I've got one strike left."[7] His mighty swing connected with Root's next pitch, a changeup six inches inside and low. The pitcher was stunned by how far Ruth hit it, 440 feet for a dramatic home run. As Ruth rounded third base, he laughed and made a two-hand gesture at Cub players in their dugout. Of all the reporters covering the game that afternoon, only Joe Williams, in an article in the *New York World-Telegram*, suggested Ruth's home run was a "called shot." Root said to a Hollywood player, "If he would have done that, I would have drilled that fat SOB between the eyes!"[8] Anyone who thought Root's talk was hyperbole hadn't heard Babe Herman talk about the pitcher's tenacity: "You know those felt buttons [atop a baseball cap]? He knocked five of 'em off my cap, and he's my best friend!"[9]

Through their joint ownership with the Chicago Cubs, the Los Angeles Angels were felt to hold the inside track to land the pitcher. In fact, despite being approached by a handful of major-league clubs, Root did contact the Angels about a job. Team president Dave Fleming and manager Jigger Statz offered Root the chance to be a coach and pitch from time to time. Root thanked the men and said he wanted to think things over.

While the Angels waited, Root tended to his off-season endeavors—more than three hundred head of cattle on his thousand-acre ranch south of San Jose near the central California coast. Like his good friend Herman, Root had invested his earnings wisely. He was a shrewd negotiator as bidders at the annual Great Western Livestock Show could attest. There, Root regularly rubbed elbows with heiress Doris Duke and actor Clark Gable.

By December the wait turned to negotiating. Root and the Angels went back and forth on salary and a signing bonus. Finally, in January, the Angels threw in the towel. Fleming told sportswriters they were simply unwilling to pay what the pitcher wanted. As soon as he read the notice, Bob Cobb seized on the opportunity. Oscar Reichow was dispatched to the pitcher's Hollister ranch. Root played hardball. He insisted that tending to his cattle kept him busy and that he was happy to make ranching his new career. Reichow returned to Los Angeles without an agreement. He told the press that Hollywood had made a "bona fide, substantial bid," adding, "Charley is undecided whether he wants to play minor league ball."[10]

Four days later Root traveled to Los Angeles to take part in an annual baseball players golf tournament. After shooting a 92 at Brentwood Country Club, the Chicago Cubs all-time winningest pitcher dropped by the Stars office. Root resumed discussions with Reichow about a Hollywood contract. When after several minutes the door to Reichow's office opened and the two men emerged wearing smiles, Edna Ward knew she was going to be asked to prepare a contract. "We are tickled to death to get Root," Reichow told a reporter. "We feel proud in having one of the most colorful personalities in baseball as a member of our gang."[11]

On March 7, the normal uptick in enthusiasm that traditionally accompanied the team's first exhibition game swelled from the completion of an intense quest. The headline on the front page of the *Los Angeles Times* sports page trumpeted, "Stars Sign Boy Pitching Wonder." Only twenty-four hours earlier, Eddie Erautt and his father, Bill, had stepped into the Stars' offices to handshakes and smiles. Sight of the pair had brought jubilation to Oscar Vitt, for the Hollywood manager had coveted the precocious sensation for almost two years.

The teenaged Erautt had been the clubhouse boy—shining shoes, handling chores, and laundering uniforms—for the Pacific Coast League's Portland Beavers. It was a job that had been handed down from his brother Joe when the older Erautt signed with the Detroit Tigers. Joe Erautt had received the job from Johnny Pesky when the young shortstop signed with the Boston Red Sox. Between chores, Eddie Erautt would train with the Beavers' players. His powerful right arm quickly caught the eye of Oscar Vitt, who was at the time the Portland manager and was not alone in budding adoration. "We're going to get you," Lefty O'Doul told the sixteen-year-old before his San Francisco Seals played the Beavers.[12]

Vitt cleared his schedule to watch Erautt pitch in an American Legion game for Kamm's Kids. In a pregame conversation with the team's coach, Wade Williams, Vitt was told that Erautt was far and away one of the best American Legion pitchers in the Northwest. Williams said the boy had poise to go along with his blazing fastball, and was physically maturing and putting on weight. After he had watched the teenager pitch, Vitt concurred and proclaimed that Eddie Erautt would be the best pitcher in the Pacific Coast League in two years' time.

It soon became clear the Lincoln High School senior would have suitors well above the level of the Pacific Coast League. The Brooklyn Dodgers dispatched scouts to watch him pitch. Heralded New York Yankees talent hunter Joe Devine traveled from his home in the San Francisco Bay area to evaluate the young sensation. One thing everyone quickly learned was that Eddie Erautt's father would be no pushover when it came to negotiation.

Bill Erautt was the child of Hungarian immigrants and had grown up in Canada, where his sport of choice was ice hockey. His skills took him to the semipro level. Shortly after the birth of Joe and before Eddie was born, Bill and his wife, Katherine, moved their young family to Oregon, where they settled in the southwestern Portland neighborhood of Multnomah. He taught his boys the game of ice hockey, but in time baseball became the family's sport of choice. On nights and weekends Bill Erautt worked as a ticket taker at the Beavers ballpark while his sons worked in the clubhouse and cavorted on the field.

Because Eddie was part of the winter graduating class of Lincoln High School, teams could not begin contract negotiations with him until late January. Once it was permitted, the Brooklyn Dodgers made a bold strike, offering a $12,500 bonus. Dodgers general manager Larry McPhail suggested he was prepared to go higher. "No," Bill Erautt instructed his son. "I want you to sign with an independent club."[13]

Almost from the day in October 1941 that he was hired to manage Hollywood, Oscar Vitt regaled Bob Cobb and Oscar Reichow with tales of Eddie Erautt. He called the young sensation "the second Bob Feller"[14] and raved that Erautt was "a sweet prospect."[15] Vitt stayed in touch with the family and cajoled the Erautts. He convinced the pitcher's father that he would look after his son. Prodded by his manager, Cobb offered the largest signing bonus the team had ever pledged to an amateur player: $6,500. Bill Erautt held out for more. Knowing how coveted his son was and that Hollywood was likely to one day reap a windfall from the sale of Eddie's contract to a big-league club, Bill Erautt demanded 50 percent of the future sale price. Cobb and Reichow agreed to the demand and Eddie Erautt signed with the Hollywood Stars.

Despite the woes and frustrations of trying to assemble a roster, Hollywood ripped off seven consecutive wins to begin the exhibition season. They beat college teams and fellow Pacific Coast League members, and had rousing wins over the Pittsburgh Pirates, Philadelphia Athletics, and Chicago Cubs. Erautt pitched impressively in a 4–1 win over a USC team that would go on to win its league title. After pitching well against the Chicago Cubs, Erautt was approached by Chicago's ace pitcher, Claude Passeau, who said, "Kid, you're going to be a great pitcher. Just be yourself."[16]

The euphoria of landing Root and Erautt was only temporary. By the time March ended and Opening Day arrived, Reichow had been able to add only three new regulars to the ball club. His additions did little to sway the prognosticators, who predicted a dismal sixth-place finish for Hollywood in the 1942 season. Reichow had pushed himself beyond the brink. The stress and fatigue of an unending and futile talent hunt finally took its toll. While the Hollywood Stars were buttoning up their jerseys to begin the season, Reichow lay in St. Vincent's Hospital undergoing treatment for pneumonia.

12

"THE TERRIBLE TWINKS"

Trepidation and uncertainty shrouded all of professional baseball as it entered its first season with the country at war with Germany and Japan. Few, if any, could guess what lay ahead in the coming weeks of spring and summer 1942, yet almost everybody pondered. Politicians sought to use the game as a vehicle for diversion and normalcy, though everyday life was anything but. Governor Culbert Olson declared April 2–5 Baseball Week in California, and Los Angeles mayor Fletcher Bowron declared April 2 Baseball Day in the city.

When eight o'clock struck on the night of April 2, Gilmore Field erupted into a display of patriotism. First, the California Mechanized Cavalry staged a military equipment demonstration on the diamond. Five minutes before the game was scheduled to begin, the stadium was darkened. A single spotlight illuminated the American flag and two members of the National Guard, who raised the colors in center field to the sounds of the national anthem played by an army band.

A crowd that exceeded the requested five-thousand-person cap on public gatherings applauded and cheered the California governor as he strode to the mound, rolled up his shirt sleeves, and flung the season's ceremonial first pitch not once, not twice, but three times before he was finally able to come close to home plate. Hundreds of soldiers, sailors, and marines in uniform graced the grandstands alongside celebrities such as Joe E. Brown, Betty Grable, Deanna Durbin, and Robert Taylor.

As stirring as the exhibitions were, the undisputed star of the night was Charley Root. The forty-three-year-old turned back the hands of time. He pitched eight scoreless innings, walked only one batter, and struck out seven. "I hit against Charlie back when I was with the Giants," said Oakland's player-manager Johnny Vergez, "and I can tell you his fast one still takes off."[1] More than 6,500 fans were abuzz as they left the park after watching Hollywood beat Oakland, 3–2.

The season-opening win was merely a temporary mask on a bad ball club, camouflage that was ripped away over the ensuing week as the Stars lost four of their next five games. Each loss stirred fans and sportswriters, who groused that the Stars had done nothing to improve the ball club. Board members countered that the club had $50,000 to spend but could find no takers. The most exuberance shown in Gilmore Field through the first month of the 1942 season came when news was announced during a game against Seattle that a squadron of B-25 bombers under the command of General Jimmy Doolittle had successfully bombed Tokyo. A crowd of more than eight thousand fans cheered the announcement wildly for almost five full minutes.

Four days into the season Babe Herman got the itch. He contacted Oscar Vitt, and the new manager stressed how badly he needed the slugger. Board members and management conferred. Ideas designed to please Herman were bandied about. Meetings were held with the player in the team's Gilmore Field office. Finally, on April 8, Babe Herman ended his holdout. Whether purely coincidental or part of negotiating wizardry, the renowned slugger emerged as a Hollywood stockholder. Careful to avoid violating baseball rules against player ownership, Herman placed his share in a family member's name. Game programs would feature an advertisement for "Babe Herman's Blue-Ribbon Turkeys."

Bob Cobb agreed to buy turkeys from Herman's ranch to serve at his Brown Derby restaurants. George Young, the secretary-treasurer on the Hollywood board of directors, also agreed to buy turkeys from Herman's farm for sale by his grocery distribution company. Young offered Herman market counsel to help him determine how many poults and pouts to buy each year.

With the ink on the agreement barely dry, Herman hurried to Union Station to catch a train for Sacramento to join up with the team. For a week he worked his way back into shape. On April 17, Vitt sent Herman to bat for the first time in the 1942 season—in the bottom of the ninth inning with the bases loaded. The wily veteran worked a walk to force in the winning run as the Stars beat Seattle.

While Herman honed his batting eye, Root anchored the Hollywood pitching staff. He won seven of his first eight starts. Sportswriters theorized that the onetime Chicago Cubs sensation may have recaptured some of his major-league magic. The area newspapers made it a point to note when Root would be the starting pitcher in games at Gilmore Field. Fans responded. Box office receipts doubled and in some cases tripled whenever Root was on the mound. A crowd of eight thousand saw him beat the Angels on April 19. Seven thousand filed through the turnstiles for Root's May 6 start, and a near-capacity crowd of ten thousand cheered as Root pitched Hollywood to a 13–1 win on May 10. The attendance figures proved Cobb's theory that the star system wasn't just a motion picture phenomenon.

Rivals noted that Root had recaptured the zip on his fastball. His own manager lauded Root's grit and determination. "He's setting a fine example for the rest of our pitchers," Oscar Vitt said.[2] "The safest predictions a fellow can make is that Charley Root," wrote *Los Angeles Times* columnist Paul Zimmerman, "is hurling his way back into the Major Leagues."[3]

Together, Herman and Root helped to spin the turnstiles. Herman had almost instantly become a fan favorite upon joining the Stars. His young daughter marveled at the way fans would swarm after games for a handshake or an autograph from the man who was "just my daddy."[4] Herman patiently made time for any and all. It was not surprising to sportswriters who recalled the tale of a 1930 game when a heckler in St. Louis had hollered that Babe was "yellow." Infuriated, Herman started after the fan. He was stopped in his tracks when the man extended his hand, said he merely liked to rile opponents and apologized. After the game, Babe took the fan to dinner.

Babe Herman endeared himself to Hollywood's fans with his first-swing home run in 1939, but if that hadn't done it, an incident against the rival Angels in September 1940 surely did. That afternoon, Peanuts Lowrey cracked a home run and gleefully pranced about the bases. As he did, however, the base umpire frantically waved his arms and bellowed that the home run did not count. He had called time-out. In their dugout the Angels were at first puzzled then furious at the loss of a run. The umpire explained that Herman had asked for time to be called because he couldn't find his sunglasses. The Angels fumed and pointed out that they had been perched atop Babe's cap.

When Chicago released Charley Root, Hollywood pounced and signed the Cubs' all-time winningest pitcher. ***Courtesy of the Mark Macrae Collection***

Neither Herman nor Root, however, could change the Stars' fortunes. When May arrived, the Stars were in the second division, seven games out of first place. In mid-May the depths of the team's woefulness reached a zenith. Hollywood lost nine consecutive games, during which they managed to score a grand total of just five runs. Fielders were awful. They made nine errors during the streak. Hitters were worse. They batted a pitiful .161 in the losses. After the initial few weeks of the season, the club was never close to the .500 mark. In fact, much of their summer would be spent stuck in seventh place. One columnist took to calling the team the Terrible Twinks. Members of the board of directors chafed at the nickname and other criticisms from the press. Some of the men openly quarreled with sportswriters before and after games.

Through it all, Oscar Vitt proved he was the right man at the right time for the Hollywood Stars. He knew little could be done about his team's lack of talent and held his tongue. Criticized in previous managing stops for being too harsh on his teams, Vitt shielded his players from the ire and anger and kept the club loose. The Stars' manager had few peers as a baseball storyteller. Whether by a quick quip or regaling a group of sportswriters with a yarn, Vitt's humor helped to push aside the drudgery that came with covering such a bad team.

Babe Herman's bad knees cut into his productivity. "Creaking Babe Herman can't play regularly," Al Wolf wrote in the *Los Angeles Times*.[5] Vitt had little choice but to use him primarily as a pinch-hitter. When Herman did see action, he was a marvel. His two-run home run sparked a June win over Portland. Given an emergency start due to a teammate's injury, Herman slammed three hits in a 2–1 loss to Seattle. By mid-June, Herman had far and away the highest batting average in the Pacific Coast League. What took some of the luster off the .377 mark, however, was that he had played in only thirty-six of Hollywood's eighty-seven games and in those games had come to bat just sixty-nine times.

While Root's pitching and Herman's hitting drew cheers from the fans, two rookies were turning heads in the dugouts. Manny Perez was the first dividend from Bob Cobb and Oscar Reichow's grand scheme, the California League. A product of Long Beach Poly High School, Perez had pitched three seasons for St. Louis Browns farm clubs but was released in the winter of 1939. A Hollywood scout saw Perez pitch in a local semipro league and signed him for the Stars' California League team in San Bernardino. In the new league's inaugural season, Perez was a marvel, winning twenty-four games. Vitt did not know what to expect of the young pitcher entering spring training but was impressed enough to keep him on the ball club. Five days into the 1942 season, Vitt summoned Perez from the bullpen in the second inning of a game against Oakland, with Hollywood trailing, 3–0. The right-hander wiped clean his spectacles, then induced a double play. Perez shut out the Oaks for the next seven innings and allowed just two hits. The performance so impressed Vitt that he moved Perez into his starting rotation, and the rookie responded by pitching a three-hitter to beat Sacramento. Later in the summer Perez blanked Seattle on a two-hitter. In all, Perez would make twenty-six starts and win fourteen games.

The gem of the Stars' rookie class, however, was Eddie Erautt. Despite the club's struggles, Vitt stuck to his plan to bring the teen along slowly. He only wanted to pitch Erautt in relief during his first season in pro ball. In Erautt's first professional outing, the teen flung two scoreless innings in Sacramento before he allowed a game-winning run. Two weeks later in Seattle, Erautt endured a similar fate when he surrendered the winning run in the bottom of the ninth inning of an otherwise impressive relief appearance. On May 8, at the urging of coach Johnny Bassler, Vitt gave Erautt his first start. Early errors put Hollywood in a hole, and the kid didn't make it through two innings.

Though Hollywood had only eight pitchers on their club, Erautt saw little action. Concern for the teen's confidence was a major reason why. The bulk of Erautt's work consisted of pitching batting practice. Most felt that one day soon, however, he would produce glowing headlines for the Stars. One that he did manage to generate during the 1942 season came from an innocuous occurrence—an arrest. On a morning in late May, Erautt and Oscar Vitt's son Bob hiked into the Hollywood Hills, where they used the young Vitt's BB gun to shoot cans. The teens were spied by officers in a patrol car and arrested. After a reprimand at the station, the boys were released to the Hollywood manager. "Eddie said he was sharpening his eye," Oscar Vitt said to a reporter. "We'll see if he's improved his aim one of these days soon. If so, I'll rig up a shootin' gallery for my whole pitching staff!"[6]

Soon after the incident, the Chicago White Sox offered to place Ed Weiland with Hollywood. This meant one of the Stars' pitchers would have to go. In terms of productivity Eddie Erautt was the most likely; however, when Erautt signed, it was with the guarantee that he would not be farmed out. Vitt had a conversation with the teen's father, who agreed that a drop to a lower minor-league level would be best for his son's development. When a club in Salem, Oregon, forty-five miles south of the Erautts' Portland home, expressed interest in taking on the young pitcher, the loan deal was struck. Eddie Erautt joined the Salem Senators of the Class B Western International League for the remainder of the 1942 season.

World War II's effect on baseball was a continued shortage of available players. The shortage made leagues go on hiatus or even fold and teams close up shop. At the end of June, it brought a temporary end to Cobb's California League. Bakersfield had struggled to find players. Santa Barbara was forbidden by a nighttime blackout rule to play home games after dark. San Jose played before a mostly empty ballpark. When the league shut down after its games on June 28, one of its brightest young stars was Eddie Harrison. He was fourth among the league's batters with a .313 average and second in triples with seven.

At Gilmore Field, frustrations at trying to acquire players and generate wins was joined by the daily quest to learn how the ongoing war would affect the team's operation. In June military leaders had discussed a nighttime blackout on the West Coast. The men were concerned with how to protect shipping interests along the California coastline. At the outset of the war, all nighttime vehicle traffic on coast roads and highways was banned. Lights in homes, restaurants, and other buildings along the shores from Santa Barbara to the California-Oregon border were ordered blacked out at night. The concern was that the lights would silhouette ships against the shore and make them potential targets for enemy submarines. In May, military leaders ordered a study of all lighting that shone out to sea along the West Coast. Even though both Gilmore Field and Wrigley Field were fifteen miles inland and their lights were blocked by hills, the Office of Civilian Defense expressed concern. The lights, they felt, could reflect off cloud or fog banks. Travel became a concern also. Owners and operators of the eight Pacific Coast League clubs were worried that train schedules might be curtailed. A plan to shorten the season was discussed in the event rail travel was affected.

Throughout the summer the Stars became a key supporter of the war effort. Tickets were given to fans who bought war bonds or donated blood, scrap metal, or rubber. Salutes to generals Jimmy Doolittle and Douglas MacArthur were held. Reserve Officers' Training Corps (ROTC) members were involved in ceremonies before and during games. The Stars broke Pacific Coast League protocol and played midweek exhibition games with semipro clubs to raise money for the war effort. Especially popular were the pregame concerts led by popular band leader Rudy Vallee and his United States Coast Guard band. Saturday games were designated Young Patriots Day. Youth thirteen and under were admitted free, received gifts, and were given the opportunity to meet military heroes who were home on leave from the war.

During the second half of the season, injury added to the team's problems. So many Stars regulars were sidelined that a backup catcher and a shortstop became starters in the outfield. Fatigue hit Charley Root. It had been seven seasons since Root had last taken regular pitching turns. In mid-June Root's performances reached a high point. He fired a two-hitter at Portland, then, in his next start, pitched no-hit ball for five innings. It would be the last successful outing Root would enjoy.

Following the near no-hitter, Root was chased to the showers after giving up five runs through three innings. Four days later he blew a five-run lead and lost. In the start after that, the former Cubs' ace let a seven-run lead slip away after three innings. Columnists who had once praised the former Cub now suggested Root should pitch only in Sunday double-headers.

In July, sportswriters selected Root to pitch in the Pacific Coast League All-Star Game. With the Hollywood Stars chosen to host the event in Gilmore Field, a spectacular show was staged. Cowboy actor Roy Rogers and his band entertained before the game. Operatic star Margaret Phelan sang the national anthem. An overflow throng of eleven thousand squeezed into the wooden ballpark. On a night of celebration, the loudest cheers were reserved for Charley Root. Pacific Coast League president W. C. Tuttle had suggested that the south manager, Ced Durst, make Root the starting pitcher. Throughout the week leading up to the game, Durst pondered whether to comply or start Angels ace Ray Prim. When Oscar Vitt pitched Root in San Diego the afternoon before the All-Star event, Durst's decision was made for him. Prim got the call. Root would work in relief. A loud roar greeted the Hollywood hero when he finally did come into the game in the seventh inning. Root pitched a scoreless frame that helped to preserve a 3–1 win for the south.

On the morning of August 5, Pacific Coast League baseball took its biggest hit yet from the wartime policy changes. The long-feared dimout order was handed down. Lieutenant General J. L. DeWitt of the Western Defense Command and 4th Army ordered nighttime dimouts for eighteen counties in the state of Washington, fourteen in Oregon, and fifty in California. Beginning on August 20, 1942, all brightly lit signs and outdoor illumination were ordered to be extinguished at night until the end of the war. Streetlights were to be darkened. Headlights on automobiles could be no more than 250 candlepower. Failure to comply meant a one-year prison term or a fine of $5,000.

No team anywhere in baseball ushered out night baseball in a more grandiose fashion than the Hollywood Stars. On the night of August 19, the Stars staged a "Good-Bye Lights" party. The team covered their uniforms with luminous paint. Baseballs were likewise made phosphorescent. The plan was to pull the switch and turn the lights out in the ballpark between games of the doubleheader. In the dark Hollywood's uniforms and the baseballs would glow. That's the way it was supposed to work. It didn't. After the Stars beat Oakland, 7–0, the park was made dark. To the chagrin of the Stars, the paint did not work. The sting of the failed gimmick was dulled by a 9–2 victory. After the game, Stars president Victor Ford Collins cracked, "The Hollywood Stars have not been shining too brightly this season, so I suppose we might say that a dim-out is nothing new to us."[7]

Throughout the final month of the season, the club experimented with start times to try to determine which suited fans best. Only 594, including actor Oliver Hardy, came to their first weekday game, a 3:00 start. When the club opted for a 1:30 first pitch, it drew more than 5,500 fans.

Only one burning ambition prodded the Stars over the final six weeks of the season: to stay out of last place. Desperate for talent, the club called up its heralded 1940 signing, Bill Barisoff, from Dallas in the Texas League. In his first game with the Stars, the now-nineteen-year-old prospect stung a single in a ninth-inning pinch-hit appearance against Sacramento. Two days later Barisoff pitched Hollywood to a 6–1 win over Calship Marine in a fund-raising exhibition game. Barisoff's versatility was valuable. Vitt used him to pinch-hit and pitch in relief over the final five weeks of the season.

On the final day of the 1942 season, Barisoff and Manny Perez rewarded the faith shown by the men who signed them. In the first game of a doubleheader, Perez pitched a twelve-inning shutout as Hollywood won its 75th game of the season, 1–0, over Portland. After a brief intermission it was Barisoff's turn to shine. He held the Beavers at bay through five innings. In the sixth, a pair of walks and a pair of hits initiated a Portland rally. Vitt removed the rookie from the game that would ultimately be the 103rd that Hollywood would lose during the season, 7–5.

Barisoff's performance, however, could not generate optimism for the 1943 season. Twenty-four hours before the pitcher's performance, a group of men had assembled in front of home plate in Gilmore Field. With fans watching, each raised his right hand and took the Oath of Induction into the United States Coast Guard. Among the new inductees was Bill Barisoff. He would never pitch for the Hollywood Stars again.

13

"WE FELLOWS WILL WIN THIS FIGHT!"

During the first year of World War II, professional baseball in small towns and rural burghs fought a losing battle. America's entry into the war was not met with initial success. For weeks newspapers and radio stations reported a steady diet of bad news. In the Pacific, seventy-six thousand US and Filipino soldiers surrendered to the Japanese at Bataan, the largest US surrender since the Civil War. America's defense of the Philippines crumbled, and President Franklin Roosevelt ordered General Douglas MacArthur to evacuate. South of Hawaii, the American aircraft carrier *Saratoga* was torpedoed by a Japanese submarine. During the Battle of Coral Sea, nineteen Japanese aircraft attacked the USS *Lexington* and damaged the carrier so severely that its crew of 2,735 were forced to abandon ship. One month later, during the Battle of Midway, the USS *Yorktown* and the USS *Hammann* were torpedoed and sank.

The American military totaled almost four million men by the end of 1942. Generals urged more. They wanted ten million. One profession affected by the demand for able-bodied men was baseball. While many clubs in the lower half of the minor leagues struggled to find players, the American public not only needed but insisted the game continue. A survey that appeared in the *Sporting News* polled more than one hundred thousand readers on whether baseball should cease until the end of the war. A vast majority urged to keep the game going.

When teams reconvened for spring training in March 1943, baseball's shortage of players was palpable. Seventeen leagues had closed up shop. All were Class C and D leagues with member clubs in small towns. In all,

1,429 minor-league players had either volunteered for or been drafted into the armed forces. The numbers directly led 124 minor-league teams to go out of business due to a lack of available players.

Columnists suggested that what was now a problem of the lowest levels of the minor leagues might soon reach the game's higher levels. Days before spring training was to begin, that theory was given credence. The Texas League startled many when it announced it had no choice but to go on hiatus. Predictions were made that the Pacific Coast League might be next, but for a different reason. Day baseball, the naysayers crowed, would plunge the league into bankruptcy. The owner of the San Francisco Seals grabbed headlines when he proclaimed that the league was out of business. Charlie Graham's declaration drew the ire of fellow club owners. "Graham is just a crepe hanger," the owner of the Sacramento Solons fired back.[1]

Of pressing concern to the Hollywood Stars in the early days of March 1943 was who would manage their ball club. Unhappiness with Oscar Vitt equaled his loathing of the men who were displeased with him: the Hollywood board of directors. "Too many suggestions from the boys up front," Vitt complained to friends.[2] His complaints reached the ears of sportswriters. Oscar Reichow was whispered to be the culprit. A columnist in the *Oakland Tribune* brought the rumor to light, writing that Reichow "doubled in brass as field manager."[3] George Young and Victor Ford Collins negotiated to buy out the remaining year on the manager's contract. It was only days before spring training when Vitt agreed to a $4,000 settlement. When news broke, Babe Herman quickly threw his hat in the ring for the job, but the board of directors had another man on the ball club in mind. They hired Charley Root. "We made the change for reasons of economy," said Collins. "We wanted a player-manager."[4]

When spring training began, Charley Root had a problem. Only five members of his pitching staff had any professional experience at all. One was Root himself. Another was eighteen-year-old Eddie Erautt. While a full roster of players was of concern to the board, the management, and the manager, finding enough workers to staff the games at Gilmore Field weighed just as heavy. Danny Goodman had entered the army, and it was a challenge to find anyone as skilled and astute to oversee food and merchandise sales. So many ushers had joined the war effort that the Stars resorted to a never-before-used workforce to handle the task: a team of female usherettes. Gone, too, were many members of the groundskeeping crew. Bob Cobb solved that problem by buying a tractor so that one man could drag the infield smooth before games instead of the four-man crew normally employed for the task.

Not only were many of the fans' favorite players away serving Uncle Sam, but many of the most ardent celebrity fans were, too. Five weeks after the attack on Pearl Harbor, Jimmy Stewart was commissioned and by fall was training to be a bomber pilot. Not long after, Alan Hale enlisted in the coast guard. By May 1942 Ronald Reagan was also in the Army Air Corps. In July of that year, Gene Autry joined up and was soon training to pilot C-109 tankers. After completing work on *National Velvet*, Mickey Rooney joined the army. Robert Taylor enlisted in the Navy Air Corps. In August a still-grieving Clark Gable signed up with the Army Air Corps. George Raft became scarce from Gilmore Field after he assembled a group of boxers and launched "Cavalcade of Sports," a traveling boxing show that he took to military installations around the United States.

Also absent from Gilmore Field was perhaps the Stars' biggest fan, Joe. E. Brown. Within weeks of America's entry into the war, the popular comedic actor received a letter from a friend, Art Reichle. The UCLA baseball coach was now a lieutenant stationed in Alaska. Reichle wrote to say that many of the men at the base missed baseball. They had no equipment and thus couldn't play. He asked if Brown would help. Brown turned to the Hollywood Stars, and on February 20, 1942, the comedian flew to Alaska carrying dozens of bats, baseballs, mitts, and full catcher's sets. While there, he entertained the men and came away from the visit moved and motivated.

Brown plunged into an endeavor unlike what any entertainer had done before. He would travel the globe to entertain American troops. Brown would pay for it all himself. He wanted to do more, to bring recreation to American troops as well as entertainment. When he shared his idea with Bob Cobb, the Hollywood Stars' principal eagerly pledged support. The team staged an exhibition game with the Angels in Wrigley Field. More than five thousand fans turned out. Babe Herman capped the day with a home run to make the Stars winners, 4–3. Even more importantly, $25,000 was raised for Brown's Military Sports Equipment Fund.

Throughout the 1942 season, the Stars urged their fans to donate sports equipment for Brown's effort. Baseball had launched a "Bat and

Ball" drive, and the *Sporting News* magazine was also creating a similar program. Both agreed to donate to Brown's project.

Sports equipment wasn't all that Brown sought. The actor called on Hollywood studios to send used projectors to military bases around the world so that the troops could watch movies. Once he had gathered more baseball gear, Brown set out on an exhaustive tour. Flying aboard army bombers, Brown traveled to deliver baseball gear and stage shows for troops in Hawaii, on Midway Island and Christmas Island, New Caledonia, Guadalcanal, Tulagi, the New Hebrides, and New Zealand before he reached Australia. On the Fiji Islands the crowd for his show included one thousand native Fijians. On Guadalcanal, a US Marine approached with tears in his eyes. He handed Brown a gift, a knife, and said, "I got two with that."[5] An outfit presented the comedian with a confiscated Japanese sniper's rifle. Native chieftains loaded Brown down with bananas, coconuts, and even shark's teeth. Wherever there were American troops, Brown entertained. He staged one-man shows on the backs of army trucks and in hospitals, and if he happened across troops on bumpy dirt roads, he wasn't shy about breaking into hilarious skits.

At home, Brown's wife fretted. He wrote often to assure her that he was all right, with the exception being one letter that explained he had a bunch of mosquito bites. The couple communicated in code. Brown was forbidden to reveal where he was. To allay his wife's worry, he would substitute the initial of his middle name with that of the island or country he was in at the time.

Brown's efforts were slowed but twice. The first occurred when he broke out in hives after receiving a vaccine for yellow fever. The second was far worse. It came when the horror of war tragically struck home.

On October 8, 1942, Brown had just completed a show when he was approached with shattering news. There had been a plane crash. Brown's oldest son, Don, was the pilot and did not survive. Don Brown had been a letter-winning football and basketball player at UCLA before he entered the Army Air Corps. He had risen to the rank of captain and was squadron commander of the First Fighter Squadron. It was while Don Brown was on a training mission ten miles southeast of Palm Springs that the tragedy occurred. Joe E. Brown was devastated. He hurried home to be with his family. Dark glasses hid red eyes when he stepped off a plane at the Lockheed Air Terminal in Burbank. His youngest son, Joe L., who

Festive, celebrity-studded ceremonies opened Gilmore Field in May 1939. Before the first pitch (left to right) Los Angeles mayor Fletcher Bowron, Stars -president Victor Ford Collins, Bob Cobb, and comedic actor Joe E. Brown. ***Courtesy of the Bob Cobb Family Collection***

was about to enter the Marine Corps, met the actor and whisked him quietly past a throng of waiting reporters and photographers.

The war put added burden on thousands of Southern California families whose sons or fathers were serving. As the Hollywood Stars went through spring training drills, concern was a companion to both Babe Herman and Charley Root. Herman's son Bob was an army lieutenant and a tank commander. Similarly, Charley Root's son, Charles, was an army private and about to complete basic training at Camp Roberts.

Rallies and supportive activities took place all around Los Angeles. During the summer, thousands massed outside of City Hall for a Red Cross blood drive. The throng cheered loudly when it was announced that 61,133 people had rolled up their shirt sleeves to donate blood. The cheers were even louder when Chief Boatswains Mate Lester Pulliam limped on stage with the aid of crutches. He was hobbled by injuries he had suffered in the Japanese attack on Pearl Harbor. Pulliam sparked a loud roar when he proclaimed, "We fellows will win this fight!"[6]

The winter of 1942–1943 brought baseball more difficulty in its quest to find players. The Stars responded with a renewed push to sign high school prospects. "This looks like a splendid opportunity for players in their teens," Victor Ford Collins said.[7] At Oscar Reichow's suggestion, the Hollywood Rookie School was launched. The clinic and tryout showcase was a concept Reichow had created in 1933 when he ran the Los Angeles Angels. The Stars' version was run by Babe Herman, who taught baseball fundamentals and skills to 165 teens. While Herman headlined the rookie school program, Marty Krug, the Stars' head scout, scoured the region's semipro leagues and high schools for talent. Krug knew where to find prospects. He had been the baseball coach at UCLA from 1937 through 1939 and knew the area's programs and coaches well.

The results of Herman and Krug's work were several exciting young prospects. Seventeen-year-old Danny Hile was first to be signed. Hile was a left-handed pitcher who had twice been all-league fullback at Venice High and averaged nine strikeouts per game on the diamond in the spring of 1942. Buzz Knudsen, a tall, left-handed pitcher who was also seventeen, was signed from nearby Fairfax High. Better still was another Fairfax pitching product Hollywood landed: Al Yaylian, who was the 1942 City Player of the Year. Jim Hill addressed the team's need for catching help when he was signed off the campus of Los Angeles City College. Following the 1943 season, the Stars would also ink Les Barnes, a seventeen-year-old infielder from Alhambra High School, and seventeen-year-old first baseman Gordon Goldsberry from Ontario.

It was one of Babe Herman's discoveries who made the biggest impact. Thomas Oscar Davis caught Herman's eye during the Hollywood Rookie School. He signed on with the Stars a mere three weeks before Opening Day in 1943. Davis was a smooth-fielding, line-drive-hitting shortstop with an arm that propelled a baseball to first base as if it were shot from a cannon. The seventeen-year-old had shone at El Monte High School and with the semipro powerhouse Montebello Merchants. The teen was known to friends by the name formed from the first letter of his first, middle, and last names: Tod. "He'll be a big help to our ball club," Charley Root said after watching Davis for the first time.[8]

A travel ban made teams conduct spring training closer to home. Rather than retreat to Elsinore, Ontario, or Riverside as in years past, the Stars drilled in Gilmore Field. The absence of major-league and Pacific Coast League clubs training in Southern California posed a challenge to scheduling exhibition games. The Stars instead prepared with games against teams from area military bases and the company teams of defense contractors. Many of the games were fund-raisers. One in particular against the Service Stars lured an overflow crowd of eleven thousand into Gilmore Field. The visitors' lineup was dotted by major leaguers, and it was the three hits, including a two-run double, by one of them—Joe DiMaggio—that won the game, 5–2.

Club owners had agreed to shorten the Pacific Coast League season by a week and a half. No games would be played at night. Hollywood opened the 1943 season in San Francisco. Before a crowd of fifteen thousand at Seals Stadium, Tod Davis slammed two hits in his professional debut. A week later, the young sensation had three hits in his first game at Gilmore Field. It wasn't long before Root was including the young shortstop when asked who he felt were the best big-league prospects in the Pacific Coast League. Covetous major-league scouts would soon turn up to make their own evaluation of the teen as well.

Undeterred by the rationing of gasoline and tires, fans flocked in record numbers from all over Southern California to attend games at Gilmore Field. Winning and losing had little to do with it. The rival Angels were clearly the class of the league. Hollywood, on the other hand, looked destined for another second-division finish. What rivaled the Angels' pennant pursuit for gripping drama and helped to lure fans to Stars games was the hitting of a previously unheralded Stars outfielder, Johnny Dickshot. The thirty-three-year-old, whose nickname was

One of the best of the young prospects Hollywood signed was Tod Davis. He soon became known for much more than the peculiar spelling of his name, exciting fans with his stellar play. ***Courtesy of Mark Macrae Collection***

"Ugly," opened the season in extraordinary fashion. Able to see the ball better, he said, because of day baseball and more fit from a liquid diet, Dickshot amassed a remarkable hitting streak to begin the season. When April turned to May, he had managed a hit in every game. His batting average was .477, tops in the Pacific Coast League. Dickshot's hitting streak and the Los Angeles Angels' winning streak vied daily for top billing on the sports pages of the six Los Angeles newspapers. When the Angels win streak was ended at a record 20, Dickshot's hitting streak kept on going.

On May 21, Dickshot hit two home runs to extend his streak to 33 consecutive games. The following afternoon, in the fourth inning in a game against the Angels, Dickshot dropped a bunt down the third-base line. The play at first base was close. Many of the 3,500 fans and several reporters in the press box were convinced the throw pulled the first baseman's foot off the bag. Umpire Wally Hood, however, called Dickshot out. The Stars' star did not come close to a hit the rest of the afternoon, and his impressive streak ended.

The signing by Hollywood of young prospects proved fortuitous through the summer of 1943. Tod Davis became a mainstay. Jim Hill took on the catching chores. Danny Hile and Buzz Knudsen took turns on the mound before each received his draft notice.

Veteran players offered helpful instruction to their teenaged teammates—along with mischievous initiation. Rare was the game when one of the young players returned to his cubicle in the Stars clubhouse after the final out and did not find his shoes nailed to the floor or his clothes tied in knots. In hotels on road trips, a smack to the face by a soaking wet towel flung across the room might awaken a rookie from slumber. Yet for all of the tomfoolery Babe Herman, Pappy Joiner, Charley Root, or Johnny Dickshot never hesitated to stop a rookie after batting practice, pull a young player aside in the dugout, or sit down next to one of the teens in the clubhouse and share a tip, offer advice, or pass along a word or two of encouragement.

A combination of advice, experience, and maturity sprang one particular Hollywood prospect to the head of the class. During spring training Eddie Erautt proved to Charley Root that he had learned and grown from his 1942 experiences. In an exhibition game he mowed down a navy team made up of former big-league ballplayers and convinced his manager that he was ready to take regular turns in Hollywood's pitching rotation.

Three weeks into the season the eighteen-year-old confirmed that notice when he shut out San Diego. On June 3, Erautt pitched scoreless ball for ninc innings, only to lose his shutout and the game, 1–0, in the tenth. But on June 16, the growing reliance on Erautt was burst when the talented teen received his draft notice and was made to join the armed forces.

While the young prospects turned heads, it was the old veterans who evoked the loudest cheers. Charley Root won fifteen games and hurled fifteen complete games. No moment in the 1943 season evoked more fan hysteria than a whack in a September game against Sacramento by Babe Herman. The popular slugger smashed a line drive to right field that tangled up the overzealous Sacramento right and center fielders in pursuit. As the fielders pried themselves apart then chased down the baseball, sixty-five hundred fans screamed deliriously, hoping their voices might propel the forty-year-old Herman to run faster. Herman, bad knees and all, chugged around the bases before the ball could be relayed from the outfield. His inside-the-park home run made Hollywood victorious, 4–3.

Throughout the season Johnny Dickshot engaged in a spirited duel with the Angels' Andy Pafko for the Pacific Coast League batting title. Dickshot was atop the charts for the first five weeks of the season. Pafko then surpassed him and led the batting race to the final week of the campaign. With three days remaining in the 1943 season, Dickshot had four hits in a game with San Diego while Pafko was held hitless in Seattle. This pushed Dickshot atop the batting title chase by the narrowest of margins. The next afternoon, Dickshot went 1-for-4 while Pafko hammered out three hits to regain the lead. Newspaper headlines ballyhooed their duel to promote the final day of the season. In Seattle, Pafko went hitless in three turns during the first game of a doubleheader. He came back to collect three hits in the second game. Dickshot went 2-for-7, one hit shy of being enough to claim the batting crown. Pafko narrowly took the crown, .356 to .352.

The ban on night baseball was devastating to some clubs, Sacramento especially. The Solons regularly played before paltry crowds. On many days there were no more than 150 people in the stands. In all, the club drew just 30,000 fans for the home half of their 155-game season. When the Los Angeles Angels announced that they had drawn 222,439, the team's management was praised by columnists in several Los Angeles newspapers. One week later, when the Hollywood Stars completed their last home game, the announcement of their season attendance drew astonishment. With an uncompetitive club that was never in the pennant race at all, Hollywood shattered their single-season attendance record with a tally of 324,982 fans. The figure represented an increase of more than 30 percent over their previous best, the 1941 playoff season.

That the attendance record was achieved in the face of such hardship proved to baseball that the Hollywood Stars were more than just a novelty, a team with celebrity ownership and celebrity fans. They were a progressive, innovative club led by men who were changing the way teams operated.

14

"DON'T WORRY ABOUT HIM"

The steps were confident and purposeful. Each was made amid the shroud of noise, a mixture of cheers and applause born of excitement and frenzy, hope and promise, none of which was heard by its intended recipient. The noise makers included classmates, neighbors, buddies, and just plain fans. Some had been driven to Gilmore Field by an almost unprecedented media buildup, keen to see for themselves whether this teenaged pitcher really was as good as billed and if he could help make the Hollywood Stars a winner. Only days before, on the morning of April 9, 1944, the front page of the area's largest newspaper, the *Los Angeles Times*, covered Hollywood's Opening Day prominently. A large photo of Joe E. Brown awaiting the ceremonial first pitch filled the center of the first page of the sports section. The column inches to the right contained a large article about Hollywood's dramatic 2–1, ninth-inning win over Seattle that launched the season. Down the left-hand side, however, the paper's columnist, Braven Dyer, did not pen a customary insight about the game but rather chose to share with readers that "local baseball fans will see a brilliant young pitching prospect in action for Hollywood."[1] Four nights later, tease became satiation.

Stadium lights added to the illumination, if not the brilliance. The War Department had given its okay to resume night baseball. From the Stars dugout, older, far more experienced players admired that the seventeen-year-old stepped up onto the pitcher's mound with total calm. He took the pearly white baseball in his right hand and began to massage it with his palms. His mannerisms showed a precocious poise. It was as if the pitcher were about to face a rival high school or a foe from the area's semipro leagues and not a thirty-year-old who was a nine-year veteran of pro ball, a forty-one-year-old with extensive experience with the Detroit Tigers and Boston Red Sox, or a thirty-six-year-old who had been a regular with the Boston Braves. Hollywood had never before seen a pitcher quite like Clinton Earl Hufford.

It was just days after Hufford passed from sixteen to seventeen in late August 1943 that he first stepped on a pitcher's mound in Gilmore Field. Marty Krug had been tipped off to Hufford and invited the teen to the ballpark for a tryout. The seventeen-year-old was a friend of Tod Davis. He had attended Pasadena High School. When Hufford arrived for the August audition, Krug, Charley Root, Oscar Reichow, and Bob Cobb watched intently. Each noted how calm Hufford seemed. "Don't worry about him," his father, T. V., said. "Nothing seems to bother him."[2] Days later Krug showed up at the elder Hufford's gas station with a Hollywood Stars contract and $500 cash, a signing bonus for his son. The teen eagerly scrawled his name on the paper. A day later a furious New York Yankees scout turned up and fumed, "Don't you know it's against the rules for teams to sign seventeen-year-olds?" T. V. Hufford shrugged and replied, "No one said anything."[3] In the days that followed, the Huffords would hear similar complaints from other major-league scouts, all of whom, like the Yankees, had wanted to sign the boy—but properly, upon his graduation from high school.

Clint Hufford was a pitching wonder. He was 6 feet, 2 inches tall and weighed 195 pounds. The sensation had been schooled from a young age by his father who was a former semipro catcher. When the elder Hufford formed a semipro team of his own, Clint was its standout until, at the age of sixteen, the mighty Montebello Merchants began efforts to woo the teen to their side. When Hufford joined the area power, he paired with a boy a year younger, Irv Noren. Together they gave the team an almost unbeatable one-two pitching punch. The teens alternated starts, and over a forty-two-game season, Hufford won ten and lost just once. Hufford and Noren became fast friends. They often drilled, worked on fundamentals, and played small-sided ball in Pasadena-area parks. Sometimes another area talent, Jackie Robinson, would ask to join their games of pepper.

When spring training opened in February 1944, Charley Root took Hufford under his wing. "He was the only one who ever helped me,"

When the Stars signed talented high school pitcher Clint Hufford, teams such as the New York Yankees protested. *Courtesy of Mark Macrae Collection*

Hufford told an interviewer.[4] Under Root's tutelage the boy's crackling fastball was soon complemented by a sinkerball and a sharp bending curve that could humble the fiercest of men.

The Hollywood Stars opened the 1944 season filled with optimism. Bob Cobb had sought to keep his 1943 club together. Confident that the Stars were poised for improvement and a playoff berth, he ordered Reichow and Root not to sell any players. Just three weeks after the 1943 season ended, the plan went awry. The Chicago White Sox offered three players and cash for Dickshot's contract. It was an offer the Hollywood board of directors could not turn down.

On opening night fans paused to take in a new feature in the Gilmore Field concourse, an Honor Roll. The board displayed the names of the twenty-four Hollywood Stars players who were away serving in the military. The thrill of the team's narrow Opening Day win soon faded. The Stars lost three straight games to Seattle, with two of the losses coming in humbling high-scoring outbursts by the opposing Rainiers. It was on Thursday night, April 13, that Charley Root sent Clint Hufford to the mound to make his professional debut.

More than a dozen of Hufford's high school classmates cheered noisily from the Gilmore Field grandstands. While the pitcher's father hollered encouragement, Hufford's mother clutched her purse nervously. "I did not hear any of it. I was too focused," the pitcher would later say.[5] Inning after inning, Hufford walked off the mound as another zero went up on the visiting team's side of the scoreboard. After nine innings the game was a scoreless tie. Hollywood had managed just one hit, a single Hufford himself had struck. In the top of the tenth inning, Hufford again kept Seattle off the scoreboard. In the home team's half of the inning, Tod Davis belted a line-drive single to center field. Jim Hill beat out a bunt single that advanced Davis to third base. Del Jones then raised the noise level in the ballpark with a single to right field, which scored Davis to win the game, 1–0. Hufford's debut was called "impressive, to put it mildly," by Al Wolf of the *Los Angeles Times*.[6] Charley Root told John B. Old of the *Los Angeles Herald-Express* he considered Hufford to be "the best developed kid I've ever seen," adding, "He's an exceptional prospect."[7]

Four days later Hufford held the Los Angeles Angels scoreless through the first five innings in Wrigley Field. In the sixth inning, the Angels' own seventeen-year-old sensation, Roy Smalley, smacked a double that scored two runs and sent Hufford and the Stars to defeat. Root sought to ease pressure on the young hurler by working him out of the bullpen with an eye to only occasional starts. In May, Hufford got one of those occasional starts and again flashed his potential by throwing an impressive three-hitter to beat Portland.

Along the way Hufford's flashes of promise were accompanied by reminders of inexperience. Brought on in relief with the bases loaded and nobody out against Oakland, Hufford calmly induced an infield popup and a comebacker to register two outs. As quickly as Hufford looked invincible, he imploded. He balked to allow a run; then, on back-to-back pitches, Oakland baserunners successfully stole home.

To show he had not lost faith in his teenaged phenom, Charley Root used Hufford in relief again the very next afternoon. The young right-handed pitcher entered the game with one out in the fifth inning and proceeded to complete the game without allowing a run. He permitted just two hits. Throughout the summer Hufford would alternate between starting and relief roles. On Memorial Day he pitched Hollywood to a win over Oakland, 7–2. Two weeks later he earned his eighth win with a perfect relief appearance against Sacramento.

The young Stars were like kids in a candy store. None was awestruck, but all reveled in being professional baseball players. Girls flirted with the naive teens outside of ballparks and in hotel lobbies. "We thought they wanted tickets to go to the ball games," Hufford said. "We didn't know any better. We were just having fun playing baseball."[8] Root sought to build a mentoring environment by pairing the teenaged Stars with veteran players as their roommates while on the road. The idea floundered. The veteran players knew full well what the hotel lobby flirting was all about. When one came down the hallway toward his room with a girl on each arm and saw his teenaged roommate, the veteran asked, "Which one do you want to sleep with?"[9] After the naive teammate replied that he wasn't interested in going to sleep, he was made to find another room for the night.

The Pacific Coast League had entered the 1944 season with a new leader. Clarence Rowland was a former Chicago White Sox manager who later became business manager for the Los Angeles Angels. Rowland was known throughout the game by the nickname "Pants," for an incident in his youth in which he wore his father's work overalls to play in a game, hit a triple, and ran completely out of the pants while sprinting around the base paths. Despite carrying a comical nickname, Rowland was all business. He brought to the job a greater optimism and higher degree of ambition than had previously been exhibited by league presidents. During the middle of the 1944 season, Rowland worked to sow positivity among club owners and management. He was insistent that the war would soon end. Rowland stressed his case by pointing to American successes in the Pacific theater—the seizure of Saipan, the bombing of Japan, and the liberation of Guam. Clubs could only hope that it might mean an end to the loss of their players. Neither happened. With World War II in its third year, the military returned to the United States Congress to ask for more soldiers, pilots, and sailors. Congress agreed to lower the draft age to eighteen. Four weeks after Rowland's efforts to raise hope among the clubs, on August 21, Clint Hufford turned eighteen, received his draft notice, and was lost to the Hollywood Stars.

Still, there was confidence that the core of the Hollywood Stars would remain intact. Many of the players were married and had young children and thus were low conscription priorities. Two of the team's best young players, Jim Hill and Tod Davis, did not meet military service standards. Hill had been classified 4-F. Davis had been exempted from military service because of a perforated left eardrum. After Congress modified policies to provide the military with more men in the fall of 1944, both Hill and Davis received status review notifications. Hill was ordered to undergo two days of physical exams, while Davis was told he was to be reviewed for reclassification and conscription. The Stars were relieved when Hill's status did not change. They were shocked when Davis's did, and he was soon conscripted. "That kid was on the threshold of the majors," Buck Fausett sighed.[10]

Oscar Reichow's ongoing quest for talent produced a pair of midseason deals with the Cincinnati Reds. While the goal was to gain immediate help, little did Reichow know that one of the acquisitions would impact the ball club for years to come. On May 11, Reichow purchased Francis Kelleher, a muscular yet soft spoken twenty-eight-year-old outfielder. He was from Crockett, a tiny town of two thousand people, which was a company town of the C&H Sugar Company and located thirty-five miles northeast of San Francisco. Kelleher had been classified 2-A, which made him eligible for the military draft. Thinking he would soon be conscripted, Kelleher elected to skip spring training and instead stay at home and spend time with his wife and children. All the while the expected summons from the Selective Service Board never arrived. Convinced they would soon lose the outfielder, Cincinnati didn't mind parting with Kelleher. Once Hollywood struck the deal, Kelleher was convinced to play until he received his draft notice. It never arrived.

The Stars had lost six games in a row when Kelleher joined the ball club. Almost immediately the new left fielder became the favorite of Hollywood's fans. At 6 feet, 2 inches and 195 pounds, Kelleher drew doubletakes with a distinctive batting stance and swing. Before beginning his swing, Kelleher would lift his left knee to almost a ninety-degree angle. The brief kick enabled him to better time opposing pitchers. Kelleher's play after his arrival ignited a Hollywood tear. The new slugger hit .450 in his first seven-game series, which concluded with a game-winning single in the ninth to help Hollywood beat Portland, 5–4. Three nights later Kelleher brought cheers from 10,758 fans at Gilmore Field with three hits. While pitchers struggled to find a pitch that Kelleher did not like, sportswriters learned there was one thing he was not happy about—being called by his given name in print. The new Hollywood left fielder preferred Frankie to Francis.

By the time the Stars boarded a train for home after a June 4 win in Oakland, Hollywood had won seven of eight games, fifteen of twenty-two, and had soared to third place to become a serious contender for one of the PCL's four playoff spots. Two days later, however, the optimism and enthusiasm paled against world events. On the morning of June 6, 1944, Hollywood's hot streak came to an abrupt standstill. Angelinos awoke to bulletins that blared from radios with news of an all-out Allied invasion on beaches in the northwest of France. President Franklin Roosevelt urged Americans to go to church or simply stay home. Bells tolled all around Los Angeles. Three women in Huntington Beach took turns ringing one large bell for a solid hour. Men and women of all ages huddled around radios for updates. Bundles of newspapers would barely land in front of newsstands before grasping hands snatched every copy. Readers devoured details beneath the large headlines like the one in the *Los Angeles Times* that simply screamed in bold "INVASION!" When he reached his office, Oscar Reichow was quick to notify the radio stations and newspapers that the Stars would not play that night, "in deference to the boys who are making that grand fight in France."[11]

Reichow had kept abreast of Hollywood's men in the service through correspondence. Throughout the season letters would arrive from players stationed in faraway posts. Occasionally articles appeared in newspapers or the *Sporting News* with information about a member of the ball club. One such article made laughter fill the Stars clubhouse. It detailed Eddie Erautt's machine-gun training at Camp Roberts. The drill was abruptly ended when Erautt's shots obliterated the target, a radio-controlled model airplane, something that had never before been done.

Not all of the notices brought good news. Freddy Cochrane, who had been a tail gunner on a B-17 in the European theater, was undergoing treatment for scarlet fever at Wadsworth Hospital in the Sawtelle Veterans Home. Cochrane would never play professional baseball again.

Hollywood faced a gaping need at third base. In the spring Oscar Reichow had identified a player to fill it: Buck Fausett of the Cincinnati Reds. The Reds, whose West Coast scout was a frequent visitor to Gilmore Field, knew exactly what compensation to seek. At his urging, the Reds asked for the contract of Eddie Erautt. Reluctantly, Reichow agreed. Terms enabled the Reds to buy Erautt's contract for the sum of $35,000, but only one year after the pitcher had returned from the war.

While Kelleher continued his torrid hitting in July 1944, Hollywood's hot play cooled. A game-winning home run to defeat Sacramento vaulted Kelleher to the top of the Pacific Coast League batting charts. His .339 average bested those of his teammates Babe Herman and Butch Moran. All the while, Reichow held his breath that the military would not come calling for Kelleher. Over the final six weeks of the season, Hollywood slipped from playoff contention. First, Moran was injured, spiked on a close play at first base and forced to miss two weeks of action. Then he was suspended by the Hollywood board of directors after he demanded an immediate pay raise and refused to play unless his demand was granted. Pitching became a problem as well. Charley Root slumped from his stellar fifteen-win form of 1943 to just three wins in 1944. "I'm not foolish enough to think I can go on pitching full games year after year," the forty-five-year-old pitcher-manager conceded.[12]

On September 9, with Hollywood having plunged to sixth place and teetering on the end of their playoff contention, manager Root made a strategic blunder that so flummoxed the local media and outraged the board of directors that it led to the end of his tenure with the club. The Stars had won the first game of a doubleheader, beating the Angels, 12–7. Among the heroics was a home run by Kelleher. Between games, Kelleher was lauded with a trophy for being voted Hollywood's Player of the Year.

In the second game Hollywood trailed, 5–3, in the fifth inning. Kelleher came to bat with a runner on second base and one out and was instructed by Root to bunt. When he did, he popped the ball up in front of home plate. Angels pitcher Don Osborn made a frenzied dash to catch Kelleher's bunt in midair. Osborn then spun and threw out the Stars' runner, who was trying to scramble back to second base. The double play ended any threat to score and also the inning. One sportswriter labeled Root's call for a bunt "the all-time boneheaded play," while another bellowed, "What in the world were they thinking?"[13] The defeat ended Hollywood's playoff aspirations.

Though his wasn't as pronounced as the team's fade, Frankie Kelleher's late-season decline cost him the Pacific Coast League batting title. He finished with a batting average of .328. When the mathematicians calculated it out, his was second best to Oakland's Les Scarsella. A furious August and September hitting frenzy by the Oakland outfielder put his batting average at .3288, a fraction above Kelleher's .3285. Kelleher led the league in runs batted in with 121 and home runs with 29. Eighteen-year-old Tod Davis was fifth in runs batted in with 77. When the votes were tallied for the league's Most Valuable Player Award, Kelleher wound up second, just two points behind Scarsella.

A final tabulation did not fare well for Charley Root, either. During the summer, the board had extended a new contract offer. The offer came when Hollywood was playing well and contending for a playoff spot. It was a contract that covered two years. Root, however, surprised the board by rejecting the terms. Not long after Root's decision, the club went on a losing streak and plummeted to sixth place. The board chose not to resume negotiations.

Hollywood finished in the second division, in sixth place with an 83–86 record. Adding to the frustration of losing was that their rivals, the Angels, won the regular season with Bill Sweeney at the managerial helm. Then there were complaints about the manager's behavior, specifically his habit of scolding players with profanity outside the dugout and within earshot of women and children. Letters were received by the club and, worse, appeared in print. "I thought Root reached an all-time low in handling ballplayers by bawling them out in that fashion," penned a box holder. “I’m certainly not disgusted with the Stars, but I am with Root,” another fan wrote.[14]

No sooner had the season ended when rumors appeared in print that Root would not be retained. It was not until the club’s November board meeting that the matter was acted upon, and Charley Root was dismissed. Columnists up and down the West Coast couldn’t help but dot their stories by recalling the extension that had been offered back in July. Root, they wrote, should have taken the deal.

15

"DIDN'T WE MAKE A FORTUNE?"

When the Hollywood Stars stepped from their train in San Francisco, they walked into a swarm of activity. It was the kind of scene they had become used to in trips to the city in the previous three years. Men in military uniforms ran to catch trains. Wives, mothers, and girlfriends hugged loved ones and the newly inducted. Anxious men flung olive-colored duffel bags onto carts. On this second Monday of May in 1945, however, the mood was different than before. There was an air of jubilance and far more smiles than they'd seen in a while. It took one of the players to spy a newsstand to learn why. Blaring from a newspaper rack was a large headline from an extra edition that read: "WAR OVER." Germany had surrendered.

While the fighting in the Pacific continued, Germany's capitulation brought relief, if not joy, to millions of Americans. In addition, for men in professional baseball it brought a belief that normalcy, or at least some semblance of it, would soon return to their game.

The challenge to find ballplayers had grown impossible by the 1945 season. The rosters of Pacific Coast League clubs were filled mostly with men who were either 4-F, physically unable to meet military standards, too old for the draft, and, in some cases, still too young to be drafted. The Los Angeles Angels, the most vociferous complainers about Hollywood's raiding tactics, had signed two teens of their own—fifteen-year-old catcher Bill Sardi and sixteen-year-old pitcher Richie Columbo. Hollywood not only continued its pursuit of teenaged talent, it expanded its efforts. The Stars exploited the immense interest in semipro ball throughout

Southern California by creating a team of their own, the Junior Stars. Calling Gilmore Field the team's home diamond proved a lure to talented players. Marty Krug, Hollywood's head scout, managed the club, and he signed two seventeen-year-olds: Rowe Wallerstein, a pitcher from Fairfax High School, and Bob Duretto, a hard-hitting outfielder from Franklin High School.

The offseason brought the drama of another manager search. No sooner had Charley Root been fired when newspaper writers floated a bevy of intriguing names to whet the appetite of Hollywood's fans. Casey Stengel and Fred Haney were mentioned, but neither had interest in the job. Babe Herman, on the other hand, wanted it desperately. "Maybe I'd be a flop as a manager," Herman told the *Los Angeles Times*, "but I'd sure appreciate a chance. I've been in baseball all my life, so I ought to know a little about it by this time."[1] The Hollywood board settled instead on Buck Fausett. There were several factors that drove the decision. One was experience. Fausett had been a player-manager at Little Rock in the Southern Association in 1943. Another factor was talent retention. While Fausett was eligible for the big-league player draft, major-league teams had agreed that they would not select anyone who was a player-manager. Reichow pointed this out to the board, which helped to drive their decision in Fausett's favor.

In his frustration with the board's decision, Babe Herman quit. He was offended that he wasn't given greater consideration for the job. Any idea that it was just another of Babe's holdout ploys was quickly quashed when he told a reporter, "No more playing for me. I've got a bad knee."[2] Herman asked for his release but was refused. As the season progressed, Herman tended to his 3,200 turkeys and 4,000 incubating eggs.

For Bob Cobb, the troubles of his ball club were but a few that filled his world. The war had brought difficulties to the restaurant business. There were shortages. Items such as meat and sugar were rationed under government supervision. The rationing of gas kept many at home and away from ball games and dinners out.

One beacon of light for Cobb came in the form of a glamorous woman who had entered his life. Sally Wright lived in the same building as Cobb. The woman was sixteen years the restaurateur's junior. She was vivacious, tall, and striking. In her twenties Wright had been a model and appeared in newspaper and magazine ads and on billboards as Miss Chesterfield. Within the industry she carried the nickname "The Figure."

Wright was three years removed from a marriage to a wealthy Midwest department store heir. Their divorce had been messy and became fodder for the press when she had her estranged husband jailed for violating a judge's order.

Cobb and Wright dated on and off for more than two years. During that time Wright saw others, including Clark Gable. Cobb, however, had an ally in his pursuit—the woman's eleven-year-old daughter, Peggy. The girl liked Cobb, so much so that messages from other suitors would fail to reach her mother. Cobb's, though, always found the woman's eyes and ears. It was Peggy Wright who was responsible for the subterfuge. When Cobb and Wright went out on dates, Bill Frawley agreed to babysit. The actor would often spend the evening teaching Wright's daughter how to throw dice in a hallway of the building.

Prior to the start of spring training on February 28, Cobb married Sally Wright in a private evening ceremony at the home of a friend in the coastal town of Carmel. Cobb called his bride "the love of my life," adding, "She makes my world work."[3] The new Mr. and Mrs. Cobb settled into a home in tony Bel Air, which had been designed by the renowned architect Robert Finkelhor and was both expensive and expansive.

It was not many weeks later that the Cobbs were joining neighbors, friends, and family members to celebrate the end of the war in Europe. The biggest celebration came on June 9, when Los Angeles welcomed generals James Doolittle and George S. Patton home from the war. One million Angelinos cheered the men as they paraded in jeeps through the city's downtown streets. That evening 105,000 filled the Los Angeles Coliseum for a show of pageantry and celebration. Actor Jack Benny emceed the event. Jeannette MacDonald sang an emotional rendition of the national anthem. Bette Davis recited a poem written by General Patton as a prelude to the introduction of the revered military leader. The large crowd roared with delight at every sentence delivered in the speeches given by the two heroic generals.

As Los Angeles feted the military champions, the Hollywood Stars were being pummeled, 12–2, in San Diego. Such was the picture of their season. Where the 1944 campaign had been dismal for the Stars, 1945 was abysmal. Much of the summer was spent mired deep in last place, "so deep in the Pacific Coast League cellar," one columnist wrote, "that they may strike oil."[4]

On July 3, Oscar Reichow received a surprising pair of phone calls. The first was from Babe Herman to again ask for his release. It was a request that Reichow denied. The second phone call came shortly after. This was from Branch Rickey, president of the Brooklyn Dodgers. He asked what it would take to purchase Herman's contract. The Dodgers were in a fight for the National League pennant. The club sat on top of the standings, but their archrivals, the New York Giants, were nipping at their heels. Rickey needed a player who could fill in, pinch-hit, and once in a while play first base or in the outfield. Herman had been startled to receive Rickey's phone call. "Can you still hit the ball?" the Brooklyn executive asked. Herman, who hadn't swung at live pitching in ten months, answered, "I guess so, but I can't run a lick."[5] Reichow and Rickey quickly came to an agreement. Rickey then offered Herman a salary of $10,000 to play the last three months of the season.

On the afternoon of July 8, with the Dodgers trailing St. Louis, 6–2, in the seventh inning, Leo Durocher sent Babe Herman to the plate to pinch-hit. Ebbets Field erupted in cheers for the return of one of the Dodgers' all-time favorites. It had been fourteen years since Herman had last worn the Dodgers flannels, and he was now forty-two. The man astounded onlookers when he laced the second pitch he saw into center field for a single that drove home a run. He later scored, but the Dodgers fell short and lost, 6–4.

Herman had hits in three of his first four pinch-hitting appearances and drove in runs in three of his first five. In Pittsburgh on July 15, Herman socked a pinch-hit home run in the eighth inning, then Durocher entrusted him to finish the game in right field. A month later Herman belted a run-scoring double off Pittsburgh's Preacher Roe. It would be Herman's last hit in professional baseball. Two days later during batting practice in Chicago, Herman was smacked on the kneecap by a pitched ball. The injury left Herman in such pain he could not play again in the 1945 season. Quietly, Herman packed his belongings, announced he was retiring, and boarded a train for home. In thirteen big-league seasons, Babe Herman amassed a career batting average of .324, an on-base percentage of .384, and 181 home runs. In six seasons with Hollywood, his batting average was .323. Herman's former manager, Bill Sweeney, called the local favorite "a natural hitter," then added that Herman could hit "even if he has to be brought to the plate in a wheelchair."[6]

On Tuesday, August 14, Hollywood's players dressed at their lockers. An important game with Sacramento lay ahead, one that was critical if they were to get out of last place. In one area of the room, Mel Steiner shuffled a deck of cards, hoping the sound might entice a teammate or two into a game of blackjack. Trainer Doc Meilke exchanged barbs with one of the team jokesters. The clattering of metal spikes on concrete flooring said the manager was leaving his office for the dugout. Idle chatter and clubhouse hijinks were brought to an immediate halt by the unmistakable sound of a news bulletin on a clubhouse radio. The announcer introduced the president of the United States. Harry Truman proceeded to declare that Japan had surrendered. The war was over.

A mile and a half away, at Hollywood Boulevard and La Brea Avenue, people ignored vehicle traffic to spill into the streets and celebrate. In downtown Los Angeles, nine miles from the ballpark, so many people clogged the streets that traffic was at a standstill for hours. The revelers waved flags and tooted horns. A bellboy in the Hotel Biltmore poked his head out of a door and shouted, "Is it true?"[7] In the Hollywood Canteen, every serviceman enjoying respite grabbed an actress and planted a kiss to celebrate. In the stands at Gilmore Field the fans were practically giddy. Though their team had blown an early lead and would trail most of the night, losing, 5–4, the fans were full of merriment at news of the war's end. Only once all night was there silence from the box seats and grandstands. That came when the public-address announcer asked fans to pause for a moment of silent reflection and pray.

Prayer may have also been tried by at least a few of Hollywood's fans to help the team change its fortunes as summer approached fall. Entering September, the Stars were dead last in the standings, thirty-six games out of first place. Few games would illustrate their calamitous 1945 season better than the September 11 tussle with the San Francisco Seals. After trailing for eight innings against Seals thirty-game winner Bob Joyce, Hollywood scored two runs in the bottom of the ninth inning to even the score. Hopes of a win grew when the Stars advanced Mel Steiner to third base with just one out. Buck Fausett sent Bob Duretto to pinch-hit, and the seventeen-year-old lofted a fly ball to center field. Before any of the 2,662 fans in Gilmore Field could rise to cheer the rookie's game-winning sacrifice fly, Steiner tripped and fell while dashing for home plate and was tagged out to end the inning. The game would need another six innings to decide before San Francisco prevailed, 5–4.

Once the final out of the final game of the 1945 season was made, the Hollywood Stars had failed to extricate themselves from last place in the Pacific Coast League. The record, 73 wins and 110 losses, was the worst under the Bob Cobb ownership group. Their final standing meant little to the team's most ardent supporters. In fact, it actually gave reason to celebrate. Jack Benny, George Burns, and Groucho Marx and his brothers, along with Jimmy Durante and Joe E. Brown, booked a banquet room at the Beverly Hills Hotel and threw a party—a last-place party.

Cobb, Reichow, and Fausett were guests of honor. Dozens of actors, including Ronald Reagan and William Frawley, howled at the jokes that ricocheted around the room. Jack Benny quipped that he had been lucky—extremely lucky—to have been in Germany all season and hadn't seen a single game. Fausett was given the gift of an expensive wristwatch. The entertainers presented each player with a leather billfold. In a jab that captured the tenor of the night, George Burns brought down the house when he joked, "We all love the Hollywood Stars. And why shouldn't we? Didn't we make a fortune this season betting against them?"[8]

16

"THE BOY WONDER"

It was an almost daily occurrence at airports and on docks. From New York to Alameda, San Pedro to Boston, smiles beamed brightly and cheeks were smeared with lipstick. Loved ones burst with euphoria as they hugged, kissed, or exuberantly shook hands with a man in uniform. With the signing of surrender treaties, ships that carried between five hundred and almost seven hundred men journeyed through rough winter seas to bring soldiers and sailors home from war. For six months planes and ships ferried the 5.5 million enlisted men back to families, jobs, and careers. Thirty-four of those men were contracted to play baseball for the Hollywood Stars.

On Monday, February 18, 1946, Buck Fausett greeted twenty members of the Hollywood Stars to the first day of spring training. The team once again occupied the diamond in Ontario. Travel restrictions during the war years had anchored most clubs close to home for spring training. Seven Pacific Coast League clubs and five big-league teams had resumed their prewar routine and would train in Southern California.

The regular docking of transport ships and arrival of military planes brought more players back to the Hollywood Stars. Beneath a bright Ontario sun, Bob Kahle shook hands with teammates he hadn't seen in four years. Art Lilly and Roy Joiner hadn't been away as long but still bore wide grins upon greeting old teammates. Not all would complete their service commitment and play in 1946. Tod Davis had written Oscar Reichow to say that he was in Okinawa and expected to sail soon for Korea as part of the occupying force. His note included a request for two bats and a dozen baseballs so that he could take advantage of free time and play some ball. A letter from Clint Hufford let the Stars know that he was serving in the Philippines and frustrated not to have played ball since leaving the states.

There was glum news among the once-prized prospects who were home from the war. Bill Barisoff returned from the coast guard with an injured shoulder. The decision was made to release the once-promising pitcher. Eddie Harrison chose not to return at all. The once-celebrated Stars' signee had elected to join the workforce and was toiling in the film lab at Paramount Pictures by day while folding linens at night at the Roosevelt Hotel. His real ambition was to seize on the opportunity he felt the growing housing market presented and get into real estate.

Within ten days of the opening of camp, the Stars' ranks had swelled from twenty to forty. Not long after, eight more arrived. Fausett was forced to run drills in three shifts to accommodate the growing roster. Exhibition play began impressively, particularly in games with big-league clubs. Hollywood rallied for two runs in the ninth inning to beat the Pittsburgh Pirates, 7–6. There were nods and pursed lips, the sort of body language that told of favorable opinions, after the Stars beat the St. Louis Browns. "That group is a better team right now than we had at any time last year," Fausett said to John Old of the *Herald-Express*.[1]

The manager pressed Oscar Reichow for one more addition. Fausett felt one more starting pitcher would make the team a pennant contender. Two weeks before the start of the season, Fausett's wish was granted when a forty-ninth member of the club, Eddie Erautt, was released from the army and soon after arrived in Ontario.

Erautt had left as a raw prospect. Fausett, Reichow, and Cobb now saw a man, a young pitcher who had physically matured and been buffed into a gem by high-level wartime ball in the Pacific. The men in charge of the Stars had read tidbits in the *Sporting News* during the war that told of Erautt's success in service games against experienced major leaguers. He was no longer the eager eighteen-year-old who had departed in 1942 but a stocky, strong adult of twenty-one. New teammates like shortstop Johnny Cavalli marveled at Erautt's "great fastball and really good control."[2]

Enthusiasm at Erautt's appearance quickly took a back seat to serious decision making in the final days of spring training. Twenty-six players had to be trimmed from the roster by Opening Day. Pondering the cuts was plagued by legal ramifications. In 1944 the government had enacted the Servicemen's Readjustment Act, more commonly called the G.I. Bill. Among its provisions was one that, with stipulations, guaranteed a returning serviceman his job back. An employer who had taken a returning serviceman back was not permitted to fire the veteran for one year. Baseball had adopted its own policy. No player, according to the commissioner, could be sent to a lower classification for either thirty days of a training session or for fifteen days of a season once they had rejoined their team. If the conditions were violated, the team would owe the player the difference in the salary he had previously earned with the club and the wage the lower classification club would pay. "Every effort will be exhausted to find a place in organized ball for him," Stars president Victor Ford Collins said of the players they would have to cut.[3]

At baseball's convention in December 1945, eleven leagues that had gone dormant during World War II announced plans to resume. Throughout the early weeks of 1946, Reichow fielded almost daily calls from fellow club operators who were in search of players. Managers for the Cubs, White Sox, Pirates, Browns, and Athletics visited Hollywood workouts looking for ballplayers who could fill needs. The inquiries and interest helped Reichow to place players and trim the Hollywood roster. Among first to go were young players who had filled in admirably during the war years but lacked the talent to beat out returning service veterans. Jim Hill lost the catching job to Al Unser and was optioned to Little Rock. Mel Steiner was sent to El Paso. Danny Hile joined on with Pocatello, and Buzz Knudsen with Fresno. It was the opinion of many managers, coaches, and scouts that most of the returning servicemen would need a season or two to regain their form. Bill Gray was one such prospect and was sent to a Class B club in Spartanburg, South Carolina. Art Lilly would be kept for the first month of the season, but once Glen Stewart proved to be the superior second baseman, Lilly was dispatched to Class B Yakima.

The first ripple in the legal tide pool would indirectly involve the Hollywood Stars. On February 24, the Stars bought Tony Lupien from the Philadelphia Phillies. Within days the Harvard-educated first baseman penned a letter to the commissioner that argued his sale violated the G.I. Bill. The Phillies contended that Lupien would be paid the $8,000 that he would have made had he played for them. Hollywood agreed to pay Lupien $5,000, and the Phillies would put up $3,000. The amount represented the highest salary in all of minor-league baseball. Money, though, was not Lupien's issue. He argued that he did not receive a fair chance to win back his old job with the Phillies. After giving thought to the long odds of winning a court fight, Lupien dropped the matter and reported to Hollywood.

What further complicated the challenge of trimming Hollywood's roster was a deal Reichow had struck during the off-season with the Pittsburgh Pirates. The major-league club had agreed to send up to a half dozen players to the Stars. So, just as Reichow and Fausett were feverishly working to reduce the numbers of players in camp, Tommy O'Brien, Cully Rikard, Art Cucurullo, Xavier Rescigno, and Hank Gornicki arrived from the Pirates.

The literal and figurative rays of sunshine that accompanied Opening Day of the baseball season were doused when not one, but two days of heavy rain drenched Los Angeles and postponed Hollywood's games with Portland. While Buck Fausett wondered what to do with his pitching staff, his counterpart, Marv Owen, worked to keep the Portland players occupied in their hotel. At Gilmore Field, Max Samuels fretted about what he would do with 150 dozen hot dog buns if the final game of the brief homestand were washed out as well.

On Sunday, March 31, the rains let up. More than 9,500 eager baseball fans poured into Gilmore Field for the start of the 1946 season. The actors, businessmen, and everyday Joes cheered their Stars as they split a doubleheader with Portland. The games proved to both Fausett and the fans that Butch Moran, Lupien, Rikard, and O'Brien would make a productive middle of the batting order. Pitching, however, was another matter.

It was on April 6 that the real bright light in the 1946 season emerged: Eddie Erautt. Fausett had given the young hurler two relief stints to knock the rust from his years away in the service. On Opening Day, Erautt had thrown two stellar innings and pitched impressively four days later in Sacramento. The performances convinced Fausett to give Erautt a start, and on Saturday, April 6, the manager learned why Oscar Vitt had called him "a second Bob Feller."[4] For each of the first five innings, Erautt's fastball was searing. The host Solons could not touch it. The scoreboard operator at Sacramento's Edmonds Field had the easiest job in the world. All he had to do was hang a zero on the home team's side of the scoreboard. By the time the game entered the bottom of the sixth inning, Hollywood had staked its young sensation to a 5–0 lead. In the bottom of the sixth, however, fatigue set in. Erautt lost his command and his fastball lost its wicked movement. Sacramento rallied to score three times. When the Solons initiated another rally an inning later, Fausett took his prized phenom out, but not before Erautt had struck out a half dozen batters.

Fausett handed Erautt the ball five days later, and the young fireballer was even better. Erautt took a shutout into the ninth inning against Seattle. It was in the ninth that Cliff Mapes managed a triple, then scored on an infield out to spoil Erautt's gem. In all, eleven Seattle batters went down on strikes in Hollywood's 4–1 win. The young sensation reeled off a string of even more impressive performances. The following week Erautt beat Seattle again. This time it was by shutout. He followed with a two-hitter and blanked the Angels, 8–0. In a 10–0 shutout win over Sacramento, Erautt contributed a three-run home run.

Even in defeat, Erautt was near invincible. A 2–1 loss in Oakland came only after Stars shortstop Johnny Cavalli made two errors, both of which plated Oaks runs. When Erautt lost a 1–0 game in twelve innings to Oakland, Emmons Byrne of the *Oakland Tribune* called the performance "a red-hot pitchers' duel all the way."[5]

The success of Erautt and the Stars brought big crowds. Gilmore Field's single-game attendance record was smashed on April 14 when 11,923 squeezed into the park. It was a mark that lasted only three weeks, until Reichow and Cobb had the idea to rope off a section of the outfield just in front of the fence to create a standing-room area. This enabled two thousand more ticket buyers to be accommodated. Once again Gilmore Field seemed a haven. Many of the actors were back from the war. Jimmy Stewart was again in his box near first base. Clark Gable was attending regularly, and Ronald Reagan was in the stands more often than not. Away from the field, gossip columnists resumed writing about movie stars in the Brown Derby after they had spent the war years filling their columns with notes about the dining habits of officers' wives in Cobb's palace.

While Eddie Erautt's performances filled the box office coffers, efforts to sign and develop further young prospects were dealt two significant blows. A month after the 1945 season had concluded, the California League was approved to resume by the National Association. But by January 7, when owners from six cities had secured ballpark leases and paid membership deposits to the league, Pacific Coast League clubs were shut out of their affiliation plans. Major-league clubs had recognized the value of developing prospects in sunny, warm California. They had swooped in, made better offers, and received affiliation agreements. The league that Bob Cobb had so tirelessly worked to create had been snatched away.

The second blow was inevitable. During meetings in December, the National Federation of State High School Athletic Associations urged the commissioner's office to put a stop to the signing of nongraduated players by minor-league clubs. It received no opposition. On February 2, the proposal was ratified as part of a new Major-Minor League Agreement. The rule stated that "no player from schools in the National Federation of State High School Athletic Associations can be signed until his class graduates."[6] Hollywood's raiding days were over.

Detours to Cobb's development quest became the smaller of the headaches he endured in 1946. In late May a lawsuit filed in Seattle plunged worry into just about every club owner in minor-league baseball. Early in the season the Seattle Rainiers had released their former second baseman, Al Niemiec. Niemiec had rejoined the team after three years in the navy. A conversation with Hollywood first baseman Tony Lupien convinced Niemiec to sue. He claimed the Rainiers violated the G.I. Bill. Four weeks later a federal judge ruled in Niemiec's favor and ordered the Rainiers to reinstate the infielder. The ball club refused. Their owner insisted Niemiec was inferior to the second baseman they had. Niemiec was made a counteroffer. The Rainiers' owner proposed a sales job with his brewery at the same salary he would have received playing ball—$2,888.50. Begrudgingly, Niemiec accepted.

The ruling brought a flurry of similar lawsuits. Three would be filed against the Stars. Bill Barisoff and Buzz Knudsen demanded wages they felt they were owed under the G.I. Bill. Art Lilly sued for reinstatement. Victor Ford Collins, the team's president and attorney, took a unique stance from other clubs. He argued that the ball club was exempt from terms of the G.I. Bill because its players were seasonal workers. Only full-time employees, Collins pointed out, were afforded the guarantee.

Throughout the spring and early summer, the Hollywood Stars felt the brunt of a postwar housing crisis that rippled through Southern California. With thousands of veterans returning and still more who had served or worked defense jobs in the area electing to stay, apartments and houses became scarce. City leaders were exasperated. They urged builders to construct forty thousand homes and apartments. It was easier to order than execute. The effort became bogged down by regulations and slow production of needed materials. The angst directly affected Hollywood and its players. Foremost among them was manager Buck Fausett. After a futile search for a place to live, Fausett set up a trailer in the parking lot at Gilmore Field until he was forced by the city to move. Three players, Eddie Erautt, Earl Escalante, and Ben Guintini, came up with a resourceful solution. Unable to find a place to rent, they made the home-team clubhouse at Gilmore Field their home. Futility pushed others to extremes. Bill Atwood, the Stars' backup catcher, was so frustrated by his unsuccessful search for suitable living quarters for his wife and young daughter that he quit the team and returned home to Georgia. The housing problem experienced by players became so desperate that Cobb and Oscar Reichow offered a free season pass to anyone who would provide living quarters to a Stars player.

In late May the Stars faced more than just a minor headache. A national railroad strike threatened the club's ability to get to an upcoming road series. The Brotherhood of Locomotive Engineers and the Brotherhood of Railway Trainmen ordered workers to walk off the job on May 19. Management tried to fill voids, but passenger service was thrown into disarray. Many scheduled trains were delayed or even canceled, and those trains that did manage to keep to their schedules were packed. Relying on a bus as an alternative was impractical for the Stars. It was true that teams in almost every other minor league traveled by bus, but none covered the wide expanse of the Pacific Coast League. A road trip to Portland, for example, meant traveling more than 1,000 miles, and when the trip ended with a week of games in Seattle, there was a 1,200-mile journey back home to Hollywood. It was 400 miles to Sacramento and 376 to the San Francisco Bay area. The growing crisis taxed the patience of the Hollywood management. Seats on trains out of Union Station were at a premium. With a May 27 travel date to San Francisco fast approaching, Bob Cobb seized on an idea. He met with executives of Western Airlines to explore the prospects of transporting his ball club to San Francisco by air on a charter flight. Though growing in popularity with the public, air travel had been eschewed by professional baseball. "There is the question of safety," said American League president William Harridge.[7] The men feared catastrophe, one that could wipe out an entire ball club. Cobb pointed out that the military had ferried men about by plane during the war. He frequently flew, and without reservation. So it was that a day after being pushed back toward the cellar with 8–5 and 10–0 losses to the Angels, Hollywood's players were driven to Lockheed Air Terminal in Burbank and boarded a plane to become the first team in minor-league baseball to fly by charter to an away game. When they arrived home after Eddie Erautt had shut out the Seals, 2–0, and outdueled the league's best pitcher, Larry Jansen, so heavy was the praise for the trip that Cobb vowed to change the way the Stars traveled: a Western Airlines sign would be painted onto the outfield fence at Gilmore Field, and the Stars would use the company's planes to make charter flights for travel to many of their away games.

On May 24, controversy seeped into the club's offices at Gilmore Field. It was on that day that the Chicago White Sox fired their manager, the popular Jimmie Dykes. During twenty-two seasons Dykes had been among the best players in the American League, and in twelve years as the manager he had produced the team's best results in a quarter century. Dykes spent his off-seasons living in Hollywood, and his storytelling provided regular meal for the Southern California press. No sooner had the White Sox let Dykes go when Vincent X. Flaherty wrote in the *Los Angeles Examiner* that Dykes "can be the manager of the Hollywood Stars anytime he chooses." He added that the popular Dykes would be the "best thing that ever happened to the Hollywood club."[8] Victor Ford Collins steadfastly denied the rumors: "You have my word of honor on that."[9] Only two weeks earlier, a Los Angeles newspaper columnist had reported that the Stars' board of directors had met and made plans to fire Buck Fausett. George Young angrily denied the report and insisted that no such discussion of Fausett had taken place at the meeting. Fausett was shaken by the latest outburst. He went to the board of directors and offered to resign. It was unanimously rejected. The rumors troubled some in the clubhouse. "A really nice guy," said the team's shortstop, Johnny Cavalli. "Everybody liked him."[10] In truth, Fausett was too nice, reluctant to criticize his players and hesitant to discipline them. A small handful of veteran players who were of a dubious nature took advantage and walked all over the manager.

Denials by board members did little to slow the runaway freight train of Jimmie Dykes rumors. Excitement grew at the prospect of Dykes taking over the Stars. Further fanning the flames of speculation, Dykes was unreachable, away on his first vacation in thirty years—a fishing trip in the Adirondacks—and thus unable to deny the rumors. The more the

Stars remained planted in fifth place, the more rumors churned of an impending change.

Two ever-growing numbers became a focus of attention throughout the latter half of the 1946 season: Eddie Erautt's win tally and the rising numbers of strikeouts he was racking up. In the young sensation's final start in the month of July, he blanked San Diego, 1–0, for his twelfth win of the season. With it came selection to pitch in the Pacific Coast League All-Star Game. Sportswriters who covered the league also voted Tony Lupien and Hollywood catcher Al Unser into the game. The game's format would pit All-Stars from seven PCL clubs against the league leaders, the San Francisco Seals.

In Erautt's first start of August, he fired a three-hitter that silenced the Angels, 11–0. In the win, he boosted his league-leading strikeout tally to 166. What also brought smiles to the Hollywood brass was that another overflow crowd, 11,749 fans, had come to watch Erautt pitch. The series with the Angels had seen more than 59,000 fans attend the seven games. Team accountants began to project that the season could shatter the club's attendance record and might even eclipse a half million fans.

Throughout the summer the board's meddling with the manager grew. After losses, Fausett would be summoned to answer to board members. Some nights the meeting would last as long as an hour and a half. The pressroom at Gilmore Field sat next to the room where the board would assemble after games. Sportswriters witnessed the summonses and were flabbergasted at the practice. Out-of-town writers ridiculed the Hollywood board. "Second guessers of the rankest sort," wrote Lee Dunbar in the *Oakland Tribune*.[11] On a night when Fausett was beckoned, a sportswriter hollered, "If you're going to fire him, do it in time for the morning editions!"[12]

On August 3, Buck Fausett brought an end to the tensions. He asked to meet with Reichow and Cobb, then shared that his brother had bought the Albuquerque Dukes, a Class C club in the West Texas–New Mexico League. Buck's brother wanted him to invest and become player-manager. Fausett agreed and handed in his resignation.

Five days later the rumors came to fruition. Jimmie Dykes was hired to manage the Hollywood Stars. His initial plan to stay out of baseball for the remainder of the season changed during a round of golf in Las Vegas with Cobb, Reichow, and Collins. The men extended a generous contract offer with bonuses for attendance achievements, earning playoff berths, and winning a pennant. Dykes accepted the job and flew to Portland to take over the club. When he met his players for the first time, he received a start. The men were dressed more fashionably than any big-league players he had ever managed. "I thought I was on a movie lot," Dykes told a reporter. While the players changed into their uniforms, Dykes noticed many appeared overweight. The new manager's astonishment grew to anger. "You guys are the fattest bunch of bohunks I ever knew," he railed.[13] He accused the players of spending too much time at the beach and drinking too much beer. Dykes vowed to impose afternoon workouts and banned trips to the beach.

The new manager was able to calmly acclimate as Eddie Erautt pitched Hollywood to a 4–1 win in Dykes's first game at the helm. It was Erautt's triumph that started the club on a five-game win streak to leapfrog San Diego into fourth place. Soon, belief grew that the Stars could achieve a spot in the playoffs.

During the third week of August, the league took a break for its All-Star Game, played before more than fourteen thousand fans in San Francisco's Seals Stadium. In the sixth inning, with the game scoreless, Eddie Erautt strode to the mound. The young hurler failed to shine. After two infield hits, a clean single, an error, a fielder's choice, and a sacrifice fly, the league-leading Seals had plated three runs off the Hollywood sensation. It was the only scoring in a game in which San Francisco triumphed, 3–0.

Once the season resumed, Hollywood lost five of their next seven games and fell back into fifth place, one spot below playoff qualification. Dykes initiated changes. He shuffled the batting order. The former White Sox skipper also instructed his players to take more chances. Specifically, he wanted Tony Lupien, Johnny Cavalli, and Bud Stewart to make better use of their running speed and try to steal bases.

With four weeks left in the season, Hollywood's playoff hopes looked morose. They trailed the fourth-place Angels by six games. Sacramento was red hot and drawing closer and closer to the Stars in the standings. Erautt took the ball in the series opener against the Solons. With Bing Crosby among those shouting encouragement from the stands, the budding ace injected life into the club by whiffing ten and winning his fifteenth game of the season, 6–2.

The next morning Oscar Reichow fielded a phone call from Cincinnati Reds general manager Warren Giles. The Reds wanted to exercise their option and take Eddie Erautt to Cincinnati then and there. Reichow resisted. He had dealt with the same request from Giles back on May 14 and reminded the Reds' boss that their agreement called for Erautt to remain with Hollywood for the entire 1946 season. The Stars, Reichow insisted, were intent on sticking to the terms of the deal.

Following Erautt's win over Sacramento, Hollywood went on a tear. The Stars won thirteen of their next sixteen games and soared into third place. The budding sensation was the winning pitcher in four of those games. Consensus around the league agreed with Braven Dyer when the columnist wrote in the *Los Angeles Times* that "Erautt is the most promising young pitcher in the Pacific Coast League."[14] On September 12, a crowd of more than 7,000 fans flocked to Gilmore Field to watch Erautt hurl a two-hitter and earn his nineteenth win of the season. The attendance count put Hollywood's total for the season at just under 500,000. The next night, as fans pressed through turnstiles, Bob Cobb and Oscar Reichow stood poised near the main entrance to the park. They waited for a signal from the ticket takers. When one pointed to a tall, slender man who wore a tan shirt and black slacks, Cobb and Reichow approached. They informed Harry Mitchell that he was the 500,000th fan to attend a Stars home game that season. Flashbulbs popped to commemorate the occasion, and Mitchell, an announcer at CBS, was presented with a free pass to all of Hollywood's home games in the 1947 season. The Stars would finish the season with a home attendance of 513,441, almost 200,000 more than they had ever drawn before.

Eight important games in Seattle were all that stood between the Stars and a berth in the Governor's Cup playoffs. The series began ominously. Hollywood lost the first three and had lost four of five before Eddie Erautt pitched them to an 11–2 victory. It was a momentous win for Erautt, his twentieth of the season, making him the first Hollywood pitcher ever to achieve that total. Eight strikeouts helped to push Erautt's season total to 234, the best in the entire Pacific Coast League.

The following night the celebration of individual accomplishment gave way to team achievement. When Cully Rikard worked a bases-loaded walk in the top of the eleventh inning, Hollywood scored the go-ahead run and beat Seattle, 4–2. The win secured third place and a spot in the Governor's Cup playoffs.

Hollywood's challenge in the playoffs was stiff. The Stars drew the regular-season champs, the San Francisco Seals. Their closest chance at a win in the series came in Erautt's start in game two. Through six innings the young pitcher was invincible. Neither team to that point had been able to score. In the seventh, a single, a walk, and an error allowed San Francisco to score the first run of the game. The Seals scored twice in the eighth. In the top of the ninth, Hollywood rallied. Three successive singles with nobody out cut the Seals lead to 3–2. But the Stars could muster nothing more and came up short. They were swept in four games, while San Francisco went on to claim the league crown.

Hollywood's turnaround invigorated its fan base. The season was profitable. In addition to box office revenue, the club received $35,000 from Cincinnati for Eddie Erautt's contract, and two other players were purchased by the Pittsburgh Pirates. Bob Cobb declared that every penny of the profits would be plowed into making improvements to Gilmore Field. He had plans for bigger things in the ball club's future.

17

"THE BUSINESS IS NOT FOR SALE"

The hard marble floor amplified sounds and made it almost impossible for Bob Cobb not to hear the many people who called out his name. Regardless of where he was in the Hotel Biltmore—in a hallway standing next to the tapestry-covered walls or in the banquet room beneath the lavish chandeliers—the celebrated restaurateur and vice president of the Hollywood Stars was continually approached. Autograph seekers shoved papers and pencils. Reporters sought interviews. Few men were more in demand during the baseball Winter Meetings in December 1946 than Robert Howard Cobb.

In six short years Cobb's Hollywood Stars had burst from apathetic to admired, one of a very small handful of minor-league clubs to draw more than a half million fans in 1946. Hollywood's attendance was only thirteen thousand fewer than what the American League's St. Louis Browns had managed to draw. The more than one thousand delegates at the meetings were astounded by figures recited by Danny Goodman. Back from the army and again running the Gilmore Field concessions operation, the clever New Yorker shared that those half million fans had consumed 20 tons of hot dogs and 19 tons of peanuts, drank 50,000 gallons of beer and 46,000 gallons of soda pop, and also enjoyed 165,000 cups of ice cream and 100,000 boxes of Cracker Jack. Jimmie Dykes boasted to reporters that the Stars had made $4 million in 1946, a figure Cobb would neither confirm nor deny

The timing of the meetings arrival in Los Angeles couldn't have been better. The Pacific Coast League had completed a banner season. Clarence "Pants" Rowland, the president of the Pacific Coast League, sought to capitalize on the league's success. A table was set up in the Biltmore to display examples of the innovativeness of his member clubs. Brochures, programs, and other promotional materials were laid out to showcase the work of Hollywood and other clubs in his league. Cobb's operation was envied, and with good reason. But the envy of one of the legends of the game was far greater than all the rest.

Bob Cobb eagerly agreed when Hank Greenberg asked to meet. Greenberg was undeniably one of the greatest players in baseball. Twice, in 1935 and again in 1940, he had been selected Most Valuable Player in the American League. Greenberg was a hero to a great many fans of the Detroit Tigers. When World War II was declared, Greenberg became the first major-league player to enlist in the armed forces, and he missed the next three seasons. Following the war, in 1946 Greenberg led the league in home runs with 44 and also topped the American League with 127 runs batted in. But during stretches of the 1946 season, Greenberg had struggled. He was thirty-five, and his legs didn't allow him to continue playing in the outfield. He was the highest-paid player in the game, earning $60,000 per season, yet fans who had once cheered him without hesitation showered Greenberg with boos. The fans' reaction and his February marriage to Caral Gimbel, the heir to the Saks and Gimbels department store fortune, had made the slugger ponder life after his playing days.

Greenberg's new wife longed to live in Southern California. Hank Greenberg had been giving considerable thought to buying a ball club. The two aspirations drove the player to contact Cobb. Neither man would say what transpired when they met. Cobb and members of the Stars' board of directors denied to reporters ever having been approached by Greenberg. H. G. Salsinger, sports editor of the *Detroit News*, reported with firm conviction that Greenberg had offered Cobb $500,000 for the Hollywood Stars. It was a sum higher than what had ever been paid for any minor-league ball club before. Joe Williams of the *New York World-Telegram* cornered Greenberg at a dinner. The slugger confirmed that he wanted to buy a ball club, and Williams wrote that Greenberg had, in fact, made an offer to Cobb that was rejected. Dan Daniel, too, reported in the *Sporting News* of Greenberg's bid to buy the Stars. Daniel quoted the former All-Star, "I have a chance to buy into another team in the Coast League but am not interested in anything outside of Los Angeles."[1] Greenberg was referring to an inquiry from the owners of the Portland

Beavers. When pressed by Al Wolf of the *Los Angeles Times,* a member of the Hollywood Stars' board of directors insisted, "The business is not for sale."[2]

While Hollywood's board of directors had no intention of selling their ball club, selling players was another matter. Since their first season in charge, Hollywood had become prolific sellers of talent. The *Sporting News* heralded, "The Hollywood Stars have become one of the largest marketers of baseball talent."[3] Late in the 1940 season, deals were struck that sold the contract of Bill Fleming to the Boston Red Sox for $25,000 and two players. Rugger Ardizoia was sent to the New York Yankees for $35,000 and three players. Bob Kahle was sold to the Philadelphia A's in a straight cash swap. Following the 1941 season, Hollywood reaped $50,000 from the sale of Lou Tost to the Boston Braves, Johnny Barrett to the Pittsburgh Pirates, and Cliff Dapper to the Brooklyn Dodgers. In the fall of 1942, their California League find, Manny Perez, was purchased by the Chicago Cubs for $15,000, while Joe Hoover was bought by Detroit and Frank Kalin by the Chicago White Sox. The sale of Eddie Erautt to the Cincinnati Reds netted the Hollywood board $35,000.

Hollywood's knack for finding and developing talent made Gilmore Field a regular summer stop for the scouts of several big-league clubs. Heading into the 1947 season, those talent evaluators had circled three names on the Hollywood roster for further evaluation: Tod Davis, Carl Cox, and Clint Hufford.

During spring training in Ontario, it was Tod Davis who was quick to make a good impression on Jimmie Dykes. Davis had returned from the service more physically mature, sporting both added weight and confidence, some of which came from winning the heavyweight boxing championship of his army division. In an intrasquad game he slammed three balls over the outfield fence and smacked a fourth off the 421 mark in dead-center field. "Tod Davis is the best young shortstop prospect I ever saw," Dykes's coach, Harry Danning, gushed during the exhibition season.[4]

Carl Cox had returned from military duty in Japan suffering from malaria. It took him awhile to regain both his health and his batting eye, but his fielding gave Dykes reason to consider moving Davis to third base in order to play Cox at shortstop.

Clint Hufford's pitching skills had been responsible for his delayed discharge from the army at the end of World War II. While serving as part of an occupying force in Japan, the young private pitched for the 8th Army Chicks in the Occupation League. On a September afternoon Hufford was startled to receive an order handed down by General Robert Eichelberger, commander of the 8th Army and head of the occupying forces. A challenge had been made. The Supreme Allied Commander, General Douglas MacArthur, had challenged a team from Eichelberger's 8th Army to a game against a team from the 6th Army. Eichelberger wanted Hufford to pitch for his side. "Win," the general said, "and you go home right away."[5]

No sooner was the final out of the spirited contest recorded, and Hufford had pitched his side to a 9–1 win, when a captain approached and pointed to a jeep. "Get in," he said. "There's a plane waiting for you."[6] Still in baseball garb, Hufford was driven onto an air base and up to a waiting plane. Officers shouted their displeasure as the captain ushered the private onto the plane ahead of them, and a day later he was home in Southern California.

Evidence was overwhelming that the 1947 Hollywood Stars had the potential to be a prolific hitting team. In six consecutive exhibition games Frankie Kelleher smashed six home runs. With Dykes choosing to sit in the stands, where he chomped a cigar and observed, Kelleher belted a two-run home run to help Hollywood defeat the manager's former team, the Chicago White Sox, 5–4. Kelleher's grand slam was the highlight of an 8–6 win over Portland. In spite of the slugger's spring hitting, dark clouds led to ominous predictions for the 1947 season. "The road is going to be steeper and rockier this year than last," wrote Al Wolf in the *Los Angeles Times*.[7]

Before the season began, Hollywood's board of directors celebrated one of the club's biggest victories of the season. It came in a courtroom. Clubs throughout baseball had been beseiged by players who sued for pay and or reinstatement with claims of noncompliance with the G.I. Bill. Hollywood used a defense that was far different from those of other clubs. The argument that Bill Barisoff, Buzz Knudsen, and Art Lilly were seasonal and not full-time workers and thus not covered by the G.I. Bill resonated with US District Judge Charles C. Cavanah. So much so that Cavanah ruled in favor of the club and against the players.

The schedule maker put Hollywood on the road for the first two weeks of the season. He may have been doing Hollywood's fans a favor. Rather than actually witness the team lose four of its first five games, they could imagine things were better than they really were as they listened to Sam Balter's radio re-creations. The hitting of Frankie Kelleher and Tod Davis offered hope. Kelleher drove in eleven runs over the first fifteen games. At the conclusion of the series in San Francisco, Davis had hammered out eleven hits in three games. His hitting and play in the field moved Jimmie Dykes to exclaim, "He has everything it takes to be a great star in the major leagues."[8] By the time the ball club returned home, however, things were dismal. The Stars occupied sixth place in the standings, courtesy of nine losses in their first fourteen games. Even worse, on the final day of the road trip Kelleher was involved in a collision in the outfield that left him with torn tendons in his right hand. The injury would keep Hollywood's best player in the dugout for the next nine weeks.

A freshly painted Gilmore Field with colorful bunting hung from railings; comedic actor Eddie Bracken, fresh from his first starring role in *Ladies Man,* tossing the ceremonial first pitch; and most importantly, an eleven-inning, 3–2 win over first-place San Diego pleased 9,132 fans. The next night, however, the Stars learned firsthand that their fans were tired of losing and watching bad baseball. Jeers rained on the players throughout a 10–4 loss. Fielders who committed four errors and pitchers who surrendered ten hits and seven walks earned particular ire. When Don Ross lost a fly ball in the lights that let two runs score in still another Stars loss to San Diego, management tried to placate fans by announcing the Gilmore Field lights would be inspected and overhauled.

Over the following week, however, results failed to improve and fans became even more demonstrative. After an 11–4 loss to Sacramento to begin a doubleheader, most of the 10,234 fans left in disgust before the second game began. Not even piping in "Babe Ruth Day" ceremonies from Yankee Stadium over the loudspeakers could persuade the fans to stay. The fans who left missed seeing Clint Hufford pitch Hollywood to a 5–4 win to salvage a doubleheader split.

With the team floundering, two player acquisitions were made that changed the Stars' fortunes. The first came on April 25 and was a product of both Oscar Reichow's tenacity and his acumen. While scouring rosters following the 1946 season, Reichow had become smitten with a power-hitting outfielder on the Burlington Bees in the Class C Carolina League. Gus Zernial was a 6-foot-4-inch, 215-pound Texan who slugged 41 home runs, drove in 111 runs, and batted .336 during the 1946 season. All the more impressive was that Zernial's productivity had come after missing the 1943, 1944, and 1945 seasons while serving in the navy in the Pacific. Reichow first tried to acquire Zernial in the minor-league draft after the 1946 season. His quest was trumped by the Cleveland Indians, who nabbed the outfielder in the major-league draft. Under draft rules, selected players had to remain in the big leagues for one season or become available for selection by other clubs. When Reichow noticed a box score in the *Sporting News* that showed Cleveland had shipped Zernial to its Baltimore farm club, he put in a claim and was awarded the slugger's contract for $6,500. Implanted in Kelleher's left-field spot, Zernial made Reichow look like a genius. He had three hits in his first game, amassed seven runs batted in after three games, and following his first ten games with Hollywood, Zernial had belted four home runs, driven in seventeen runs, and sported a .487 batting average. "Watch out for the great Zernial," touted Braven Dyer in the *Times*.[9] Stars' radio announcer Fred Haney affectionately nicknamed the new left fielder "Ozark Ike" after the lumbering hillbilly character in the newspaper comic strips.

If there was a negative to Zernial's play, it was his fielding. He found the lights at Gilmore Field particularly troublesome. On several occasions Zernial lost sight of balls that crossed the bright arc lights and subsequently fell to the turf untouched. The problem was remedied by a teammate who pointed out that Zernial wore his hat navy style, pulled back with the bill pointing at an upward angle. Once the teammate showed Zernial how to use the bill to shield the lights and their glare, the outfielder's fielding problem almost immediately went away.

While Zernial's hitting helped matters, it was poor pitching that kept Hollywood stuck at the bottom of the Pacific Coast League standings. "As soon as our pitching improves, we won't lose as many ball games," Dykes told a crowd at a sports luncheon.[10] Trades were made and poor performers were released, but still the team's fortunes failed to change. When Xavier Resigno developed a sore arm, first baseman Tony Lupien urged Dykes to pick up his friend George "Pinky" Woods. The two were natives of Vermont and former teammates with the Boston Red Sox. Reichow looked into it and in mid-May arranged with Indianapolis for Woods to join Hollywood on a thirty-day trial. It didn't take Reichow that long to exercise his option and buy Woods's contract outright.

Woods was an imposing man, 6 feet, 5 inches and 225 pounds. He had been signed by the Red Sox after going undefeated in two seasons at Holy Cross College. An unfortunate by-product of a diamond mishap detoured his path to predicted pitching prominence. During a 1942 game Woods had singled, and on his attempt to stretch the hit into a double, he was spiked by the opposing second baseman. He neglected to have the wound treated. Weeks later, pain and swelling sent Woods to a doctor. A bad infection was diagnosed, and Woods suffered the amputation of his big toe and part of the ball of his right foot. He recovered and spent three seasons pitching for the Red Sox. In 1945 a sore elbow shelved the hurler. The team doctor recommended surgery, and a procedure to remove bone chips was performed. In spring training Woods proclaimed the operation had given him a "brand new arm."[11] His performances failed to impress the Red Sox, and Woods was sold to Indianapolis. The move infuriated the veteran. He refused to report, then vowed to retire from baseball. After a change of heart Woods pitched primarily in relief for Indianapolis in 1946. The following spring, however, it grated on the pitcher that he had no future with the Red Sox. When the opportunity was raised to join the Hollywood Stars, Pinky Woods eagerly accepted. Woods almost immediately became the best pitcher on the Hollywood staff. He won his first five starts with the club. On June 22, a 3–2 loss to Seattle snapped the streak, but the side-arm flinger beat the Los Angeles Angels five days later on a 3–0 shutout to help Hollywood escape from the cellar and climb into sixth place.

A pair of young pitchers showed promise. It took Clint Hufford a while to regain his sharpness after being away in the war. After three impressive relief-pitching appearances, Hufford was given a start, and on April 12 he pitched Hollywood's first complete game of the season. He received no support, though, and lost, 2–0. Six days later the twenty-year-old beat San Diego, 3–2, on another complete game. Through the first two months of the season, Hufford's would be the only complete games registered by a Hollywood pitcher. Perplexity with his corps of relief pitchers made Dykes give opportunity to another young pitcher who rose to the challenge, Al Yaylian. The diminutive left-hander from Fairfax High School rewarded his manager with a string of strong performances.

On June 8, fans and sportswriters were surprised to see Leo Durocher turn up at Gilmore Field for a Sunday doubleheader. The Brooklyn Dodgers' manager was serving a one-year suspension from baseball for a series of alleged misdeeds that included consorting with gamblers, accruing gambling debts, and defying a judge by marrying actress Laraine Day in Mexico before her divorce decree was issued in California. Upon news of his suspension, Durocher traveled to Los Angeles, where he stayed with a friend, the actor George Raft. Together with Day, Durocher took in the Stars' game from box seats behind first base. This would turn into regular outings to Gilmore Field. A few days after Durocher's initial appearance, Edith Gwynn wrote in the "Rambling Reporter" column in the *Hollywood Reporter* that she had dined with the suspended skipper and that he wanted to become manager of the Stars. Pressed by sportswriters, Durocher backed away from the claim and said his proclamation the previous spring still stood; he wanted to be the manager of the Brooklyn Dodgers until the day he died.

On June 15, Frankie Kelleher was cleared to resume action. Gus Zernial was moved to right field and Kelleher returned to left field. He also returned to the torrid hitting he had been showing throughout spring training and the first two weeks of the season. Over the next six weeks Kelleher socked eleven home runs and drove in fifty runs. A fourteen-game hitting streak pushed his batting average to .364.

The appearance of Patsy O'Rourke, the head scout for the Chicago White Sox, raised eyebrows, if not outright concern, around Gilmore Field in July. Oscar Reichow fretted that O'Rourke might have interest in Kelleher. It soon emerged that O'Rourke had been dispatched to evaluate Tod Davis. The Detroit Tigers sent a scout to Gilmore Field as well. Not long after, the Tigers offered $10,000 not for Kelleher or Davis, but for Tony Lupien. The offer was rejected. Detroit increased its pursuit by adding three players to their previous cash offer. Again, the pitch was turned down.

Throughout the summer, frustrations simmered at the team's inability to mount a charge toward a playoff spot. The Stars fell to the bottom of the Pacific Coast League standings before managing to climb a couple of notches into sixth, where they would ultimately finish. While the poor win-loss record failed to generate awe, statistics did. The 1947 Stars set a half dozen batting records, including for home runs with 113, runs scored with 920, and runs batted in with 855. Gus Zernial finished third in the race for the league batting title with a .344 average. Tony Lupien wound up one spot behind him, hitting .341. After missing more than two months of the season due to injury, Frankie Kelleher wound up ninth in hitting and also smashed 21 home runs. Equally impressive were the turnstile counts. Sportswriters had noted during the summer that it was almost impossible to get a box seat for a game at Gilmore Field. For a second consecutive season, more than a half million fans had streamed into the Stars' ballpark.

Lupien was named league Most Valuable Player by the *Sporting News*. On September 5, fans feted the popular first baseman. Biggest of the many gifts given was a new car. When the balding standout tipped his cap to thank the fans, loud laughter erupted from all about the ballpark. The stunt revealed a toupee, which was also one of the tributes Lupien had received.

Personal and attendance accolades aside, disdain shrouded the Stars' Gilmore Field offices. For the seventh time in the nine seasons of the Bob Cobb group's ownership, the Stars finished in the second division. Sportswriters jabbed and chided. Some did so less subtly than others. For all the well-earned praise for innovation, the ownership and management of the Stars was becoming known more for its failure to field a contending ball club. Such was the mood of the press and ardent fans that one columnist penned, "Thank goodness Danny Goodman's peanuts and hot dogs are first division."[12]

18

"GIVE 'IM MY REGARDS WHEN YOU SEE HIM"

The noise began as a few handclaps from a smattering of observant fans. The sound aroused curiosity. Heads quickly turned. Eyes darted. As the ovation grew, shoulders were nudged. Fingers pointed. Recognition of the hulking figure with the herculean reputation took but mere seconds. As acknowledgment spread, more than nine thousand fans rose to their feet, clapped their hands, whistled, and shouted with adoration for the man who slowly moved toward a box in one of the front six rows of Gilmore Field. No announcement was needed. Everyone recognized the figure. And why wouldn't they? It was Babe Ruth.

Each of the two home runs that Frankie Kelleher hit on that May 2 afternoon generated applause that paled when compared to the welcome given the immortal former Yankee. If they were completely truthful, dozens of fans would admit they never saw Kelleher lead Hollywood to victory over the rival Angels that day. They were jockeying to get their program, baseball, or a scrap of paper autographed by their idol. Ruth obliged everyone.

Only the evening before, Ruth, along with his wife, daughter, and son-in-law, had climbed from the Chief after the train had pulled to a stop in Union Station following its cross-country excursion. For the next two weeks the iconic former ballplayer was to make daily trips to Enterprise Studios and assist the director, Roy Del Ruth, and the actor who was to portray him, William Bendix, as they sought to produce a motion picture about Ruth's life.

While the long strip of gelatin emulsion generated by a month's filming would capture the story of the great slugger's life, his visit to Gilmore Field burned permanent memories in the minds of hundreds of admirers and devotees across three generations. Ten-year-old Les Boxer and his father sat in the box directly in front of the former slugger. They were moved by the man's aura and the depth of reverence his iconic status wrought. As Ruth signed the youth's baseball, young Boxer was struck by the legend's ashen skin and that the man's once-commanding voice now barely rose above a whisper. Another of the youthful admirers, Barry Weinstock, couldn't get over the sight of the once-hulking hero tightly wrapped in a heavy overcoat on a seventy-degree day. He had no idea that it shielded a body shrunken by the ravages of cancer or that Ruth's flat cap hid a head of hair made sparse by the disease.

Reporters jockeyed for Ruth's attention along with the autograph seekers. The former Yankee great apologized for the raspy sound of his voice. He explained that while in Los Angeles he was to undergo a procedure that would block nerve pain and restore his normal sound. Some asked for a prediction for the 1948 Yankees. "Look pretty good," he chortled.[1] Inevitably the subject turned to Charley Root, Ruth's one-time World Series nemesis, who had once managed the Hollywood Stars. Ruth chirped, "How is Charley? I hear he's managing Billings this season."[2]

As Hollywood struggled through the 1948 season, Billings, Montana, was very much at the forefront of Hollywood's management. Though Bob Cobb had lost his pet project, the California League, to major-league clubs, he still burned to build a farm system for the Stars. That hunger led him to his adopted hometown of Billings. The appearance of Oscar Reichow at the Pioneer League's annual meeting during the winter of 1947 was the first tip-off that Hollywood had something up its sleeve for the Montana town. In short order Cobb and Reichow launched a push to convince the league to add two teams and put one of them in Billings. Cobb plunged into the quest with the aplomb he had poured into his purchase of the Hollywood Stars. He set a goal to raise $100,000 through a three-pronged plan. The Hollywood Stars contributed $25,000. Cobb then turned to his movie star friends and convinced Bing Crosby, Cecile B. DeMille, Barbara Stanwyck, Robert Taylor, and William Frawley to buy shares in another third of the project. Finally, Cobb turned to the Billings business community to become involved. He was overwhelmed

In May 1948 Babe Ruth took in a game at Gilmore Field. Before the game he posed with Stars sluggers Gus Zernial (right) and Frankie Kelleher (left). ***Courtesy of A.F. Gilmore Company***

by the response. Shares were priced at $100, and nobody was permitted to purchase more than ten. First, the owner of the town's largest department store bought in, then the president of the local livestock commission joined. A prominent attorney invested, followed by the owner of three drugstores and the general manager of the finest hotel in Billings. Archie Cochrane, a local auto dealer, agreed to join the group. He brought along his brother, Mickey, the former All-Star catcher for the Philadelphia Athletics. Within just a few days, Cobb's efforts had assembled 140 local investors. "Never in the ten years that I have been connected with Organized Ball have I found more enthusiasm for a team than right here in Billings," Cobb beamed to a local reporter.[3]

Athletic Park, the local American Legion ballpark, was upgraded to include box seats, locker rooms, concessions stands, umpires' rooms, and seating for 4,200. An agreement was struck that made the Billings ball club a farm team for the Hollywood Stars.

The seven-year-old Pioneer League, which was comprised of six clubs in Utah and Idaho, agreed to expand. After studying road maps and rain schedules, the league initially focused on two Montana towns, Butte and Great Falls. Cobb stepped up his efforts and tirelessly touted Billings. When city leaders in Butte declined to get involved in the league, Billings received its invitation to join.

Archie Cochrane was made president. Harry Voelker was recruited from the Houston Buffaloes to run the day-to-day operation. On Cobb's recommendation, the club hired Charley Root as manager. And then there was the quest to come up with a name for the team. A contest was launched, and one thousand suggestions poured in. Club stockholders narrowed the list, then voted three-to-one to name the new team the Mustangs.

At the same time Babe Ruth was soaking the applause of fans in Gilmore Field, Bob Cobb was the recipient of an ovation from six hundred people at the first "Welcome Mustangs" banquet in Billings. The town's mayor told those who turned out that the new ball club was "one of the finest things ever to happen to this city."[4] The Billings project was part of a bigger plan Cobb carried. As such, he struck arrangements with three other minor-league clubs: Denver of the Class A Western League, Las Vegas in the Class C Sunset League, and Buck Fausett's Class C Albuquerque club in the Arizona–New Mexico League. Hollywood would provide a handful of prospects to each and in return would receive first crack at signing up to two players that were owned by the clubs. The deals, along with the investment in the Billings Mustangs, at last gave Hollywood its own farm system.

The Billings experience, however, was a frustrating one for Charley Root. Cobb and Reichow had boasted that they would give the team a roster of players who would finish in the upper half of the standings. It did not. Once-heralded Hollywood signees Rowe Wallerstein and Les Barnes were assigned to the club. When Wallerstein pitched well, Las Vegas exercised a clause in their agreement with Hollywood and claimed the Mustangs' most productive hurler. Barnes hit well, but debilitating injuries he suffered in an automobile accident when he returned home from the war had robbed him of his quickness. Root ultimately moved him to third base.

Opening night was in Pocatello, Idaho, and it gave a glimpse of what was to come. The Mustangs were clobbered, 13–0, and would go on to lose their first six games. Defeat didn't dampen the town's excitement, though. Athletic Park was renamed Cobb Field, "since he was so instrumental in bringing organized professional baseball to Billings," explained Harry Voelker.[5] On May 3, just under thirty-three hundred fans roared with delight as their Mustangs put a 13–0 pasting on the visiting Salt Lake City Bees in the home opener. Cheerable moments, however, would be few and far between that summer. The Mustangs wallowed in or near last place throughout most of the season. The team's pitching was so bad that Root, just months away from his fiftieth birthday, activated himself and pitched three games in relief.

On August 17, Root pushed open the glass door and walked into a coffee shop for breakfast in Boise, Idaho. He unfolded the local newspaper and was greeted with a bold headline that announced the death of his longtime antagonist, Babe Ruth. For eighteen years Root had simmered every time he read in print that Ruth had pointed to center field to boldly predict where he would send Root's next pitch during the third game of the 1932 World Series. The man bristled at being better remembered as a participant in an event that never happened instead of as the winningest pitcher in the history of the Chicago Cubs.

From Hollywood teammates to Billings players, by reporters and fans, Root was asked often if Ruth did, in fact, call his shot. Each time Root would shift the large chaw of chewing tobacco in his cheek, let fly a stream of brown spittle, then state, "Most certainly did not."[6] Root had confronted the Babe about it once. His angry question was greeted with laughter and, the pitcher claimed, an admission that Babe liked what the tale had done for his reputation. When the former Cubs pitching standout learned that producers in Hollywood planned a motion picture about Ruth's life, he consulted a lawyer, who threatened a lawsuit should Root's name be used or claims of the called shot made part of the film.

Revelations after Ruth's passing said throat cancer took the legendary slugger. His voice had been made raspy and softened by a sinus tumor that pressed against nerves. No operation would have saved the Babe or restored his voice to normal. While Ruth hadn't known that he was being ravaged by cancer and that it was terminal, reporters did. The men held off from reporting the news, knowing, as one said, "it would break him down."[7]

As Root read the newspaper accounts, he thought of the Babe that only those close to the man truly knew. For all of the excesses and bluster, he was a generous lug with a heart as big as the world. The thoughts took Root back three months to Oscar Reichow's visit to Billings. Reichow told the Mustangs' manager that Ruth had visited Gilmore Field. When asked about Charley, he said, "Give 'im my regards when you see him."[8]

While Cobb was reveling in the launch of professional baseball in Billings, 1,200 miles away enthusiasm at Gilmore Field was waning. Once again, the Stars put a product on the field that had little hope of contending for a first-division finish. Injuries rippled through the roster. During one stretch, Jimmie Dykes had just seven able-bodied pitchers at his disposal.

Fans were unhappy. Criticism flew. Dykes was on the receiving end of much of it. Sportswriters who early in the summer had been polite in their description of defeats now held little back. Some became unreserved in their criticism. They used words such as "weak" and "inept" to describe the team. One nicknamed the players "winless wonders."[9] Another writer took the Stars to task by calling them the Hurricanes, because the team had "blown so many leads."[10] It was reported that players disliked Dykes. One visiting scout told a reporter that he didn't think the Hollywood manager was giving it "the old college try."[11]

A boy's naiveté and quick wit gave players the rare chance for a laugh at their manager's expense. A Hollywood player had chided the team's batboy, the son of Frankie Kelleher, to lose some weight. "Take a few laps around the park," the player teased. Eight-year-old Bobby Kelleher turned to the rotund Dykes and snapped, "Come on let's go," which evoked howls from nearby players.[12]

Go is what Dykes ultimately did. Rumors made their way into print of a schism growing between the Hollywood board and the manager. Some complained about his cigar-smoking habit during games. Others grumbled at a lack of any apparent fire. Still more questioned his subdued personality. Grumbling grew in thc clubhouse when the manager put a stop to the practice of providing sandwiches between games of doubleheaders. It made its way into print when the manager fined Joe Krakauskas for drinking a soft drink in the clubhouse.

On August 28, Dykes became embroiled in a contentious meeting with the board of directors. The Stars had lost seventeen of twenty-two, and eight games in a row. Board members were tired of the losing. Dykes was tired of their criticism. Emotions and tempers reached a crescendo that burst when the manager barked that he quit and stomped out of the room.

In the clubhouse the clattering of the manager's spikes interrupted newly acquired shortstop George Genovese, who was unpacking at his locker. "Kid," Dykes said, "you shoulda got here a little sooner. You might have saved my job."[13] When pressed by sportswriters, Dykes launched a parting shot at his former employers. "I did the best I could with the material the front office was able to get for me, but that wasn't good enough," he said. Board members fired back. When asked about a potential successor, one said, "Whoever he is, he won't be a manager as lenient with his players as Dykes. That was Jimmie's trouble—too easy on his players."[14]

Manager was added to the duties of Hollywood's second baseman, Lou Stringer. But after just three weeks on the job, the Stars accepted an offer from the Boston Red Sox, who were desperate for a second baseman, and Stringer was sold. Hollywood's coach, Mule Haas, took over the team the final week of the season.

One of the season's few bright spots was the play of Gus Zernial. A two-home-run game on Opening Day launched a prolific season. On June 6, he hit two home runs in one inning. During the final weekend of the season, Zernial hit a grand slam one day, then two home runs the next to give him 40 for the year. Zernial added a staggering 156 runs batted in and a batting average of .322 to his 1948 credentials. It was enough to send him on his way to the big leagues. The Chicago White Sox eagerly bought the slugger's contract.

In sharp contrast to Zernial's stellar season was Pinky Woods. Though he led all Pacific Coast League pitchers in strikeouts through most of the summer, the knuckleball hurler topped the league in three dubious categories: most hit batters, most walks allowed, and most wild pitches. He was second in the league in hits surrendered. Woods finished the season as the first pitcher in Hollywood Stars history ever to lose twenty games.

Amid the losing and disdain there was just one man truly justified to celebrate once the last out of the season had been made. Months before, at the conclusion of spring training, Bob Hoenig had written a column in the *Hollywood Citizen-News* in which he made a prediction of the final standings for the 1948 Pacific Coast League season. After Gus Zernial's late home run binge had helped to push Hollywood from seventh into a sixth-place finish to conclude the season, Hoenig was heralded. From Oakland's winning the pennant to Sacramento's last-place finish, Hoenig had correctly picked the finish of all eight teams over a sixth month, 188-

game schedule. The Bureau of Measurement Analysis at UCLA put the odds of the sportswriter's achievement at 40,320 to 1.

19

"LET ME HAVE IT FOR THREE YEARS"

Tension in the room was palpable. The end-of-season gathering of the Hollywood Stars' board of directors all too often had involved discussion of a new manager. This was the tenth such meeting in the history of the group's leadership and the fifth time that Misters Cobb, Ford Collins, Young, Frawley, Reichow, and the rest had used the gathering to ponder whom to select. To some in the room, the task was part of usual management routine. For others, the club's frequent managing changes were an embarrassment that had to stop.

The club's frequent hirings and firings had brought derision from fans and the press. The criticism in columns that appeared in both Los Angeles newspapers and national baseball publications sullied the ball club's otherwise sterling reputation. Bob Cobb had been especially pilloried by newspaper columnists. And then there were the rumors. Each time a manager was fired, the men had to field questions from friends, family, fans, and most of all, reporters who wondered just who the next field boss would be. After Jimmie Dykes resigned, the newspapers were machinated. Yankees great Red Ruffing, they said, wanted the job. Rip Collins, who had been recently fired by San Diego, was claimed by one newspaper to be the board's safe choice. Kiki Cuyler was reported in another to be a cinch. When the board met on November 4, it was George Young, the secretary-treasurer, who had had enough. He insisted that the job must go to one man, and one man only: Fred Haney.

If ever there was a baseball man who could be considered something of a local legend in Southern California, it was Fred Haney. Hollywood's fans knew Haney as their team's radio announcer, and a very good one at that. In 1943 Haney heard rumors that a lack of advertising sponsors threatened to knock Hollywood's radio broadcasts off the air. Haney thought of all the servicemen in hospitals who enjoyed listening to baseball on the radio, so he went to Bob Cobb with an offer to call the games for free. Haney enlisted Bing Crosby's help and landed a sponsor to underwrite the expenses. Next, Haney proposed a knothole gang for kids. With ardent promotion during broadcasts, the club came to number more than six thousand members.

In truth, Fred Haney's baseball résumé listed far more than his popular radio signoff of "rounding third and heading for home." A burning tenacity had propelled him to overcome his diminutive 5-foot-6-inch stature and become a heralded high school athlete. He not only dazzled as a quarterback on the football field and shone on the baseball diamond at Polytechnical High School in downtown Los Angeles, but he won titles in swimming and excelled in water polo. So successful were Fred Haney and his brothers that the school gave its playing field their family name. It upset some in his family when, after graduation, Fred Haney entered professional baseball. His brother Carl had been a standout at USC, and Fred was urged to take the college route as well. But after three seasons in the minor leagues, Fred ascended to the Detroit Tigers, where he played third base and batted .352. "One of the greatest hustlers I ever saw," said his manager, Ty Cobb.[1]

In 1939 Haney's dugout role changed to that of manager. He was hired to lead the St. Louis Browns. The club Haney inherited was abysmal, devoid of much talent. It finished the 1939 season with one of the worst won-loss records ever recorded, 43–111. A twenty-four-win improvement in 1940 sparked high expectations for the 1941 season. Those expectations proved Haney's undoing. When his Browns got off to a slow start, fans, stockholders, and board members became enraged. After wrestling with the decision through three sleepless nights, on June 5, the Browns' president fired Haney, who took the news hard. He accepted an assignment to manage the team's farm club in Toledo, Ohio. Following the 1942 season, though, Haney quit, frustrated that he had not been permitted to make player moves.

Fred Haney returned home to Southern California and his wife, Florence, and daughter, Patricia. He owned a successful liquor store and ran it with the same doggedness he employed on the baseball field. When a

For six seasons former Detroit Tigers player and St. Louis Browns manager Fred Haney was the immensely popular radio voice of the Hollywood Stars. ***Courtesy of Terry Maalen***

man tried to steal a case of beer from the store, Haney chased the culprit for two blocks before he finally caught up with the man and threw a punch that decked the bandit.

The lure of baseball continued its hold on Haney's attention. In 1944 he took on a new role in the game—broadcaster. Haney called both Los Angeles Angels and Hollywood Stars games over KMPC radio. He handled the home games, while Paul Flanagan constructed re-creations of the two teams' road games. The former manager's announcing style was best described as homespun and easy. He offered anecdotes and explanations of strategies and moves that were drawn from his years of experience in the game. As one columnist expressed, "He just talks it to you."[2] In time Haney came to be heralded as the Pacific Coast League's most popular broadcaster. For four seasons Haney was the toast of Los Angeles. Then, controversy struck. Days after the 1947 season ended, P. K. Wrigley fired Haney as the voice of the Los Angeles Angels. He claimed that the popular former big leaguer didn't offer support of his club on the air. Behind the scenes was another story. The Cleveland Rams pro football team had moved to Los Angeles. The ad agency that owned broadcast rights to the Rams games pushed for the Rams broadcaster Bob Kelley to handle Angels broadcasts as well.

Both the Angels and local newspapers were deluged with letters of protest from angry fans. Wrigley vowed to keep Haney off the airwaves altogether. He feared that the popular mic man would pull listeners with him if he were to call just the Stars' games. Columnists came to Haney's defense and skewered the Angels' owner. Bob Cobb realized opportunity. He announced that he would do all he could to ensure that Haney broadcast every Hollywood game, home and away. The team switched radio stations to KLAC, and companies that had previously advertised on KMPC's broadcasts of Stars and Angels games followed Haney to his new spot on the radio dial.

Fred Haney's name had come up during previous managerial discussions in the Hollywood board room: first when Charley Root was fired, then again when the board hired Jimmie Dykes. Haney certainly had the characteristics that Bob Cobb looked for in a manager. He had managing experience and was a good baseball man, popular with the press, personable, and filled with a sense of humor. Fred Haney loved nothing more than a good practical joke. To have a conversation with him was to laugh at a gag or two, often a bit off-color. His wife, Florence, a devout Catholic, cringed when he told his jokes to priests. Family members laughed about an occasion when she rose to leave the room as her husband began a joke, only to hear him say, "Don't worry, Florence. This one's clean!"[3]

The first time Haney was considered for the Hollywood job, he was not interested. His liquor store was doing well. After Buck Fausett's firing, Haney was dissuaded by the extent of the board's meddling. He had also gained an understanding of the team's problems. When he was queried about the job, he said he would only consider it if he had full control of player acquisition and a multiyear contract. His were demands that Bob Cobb would not agree to.

George Young's persistence in the winter of 1948 made Cobb agree to meet with Haney. When they did, the job was discussed and finally offered. Haney told Cobb that he would think about it. When contacted later by a reporter, Haney said he had turned Hollywood's offer down. "I positively will not accept the job on a one-year contract," he declared.[4]

When the board met days later, Young was demonstrative. He angrily pounded a fist on the table. His voice rose as he thundered that Haney was the best man for the job. Cobb agreed to another meeting with Haney. There he was prodded. "You've been running the club for ten years and haven't done a darned thing. Let me have it for three years and see what I can do," Haney urged the Stars' vice president.[5] Cobb left the meeting with reservations. Haney left without a job offer.

Again, Young pressed his case. He urged the board to accept Haney's terms. Victor Ford Collins agreed to negotiate with Haney. He came back to the board with parameters of a deal: an annual war chest of $250,000 to sign and buy players; the ability to spend up to $10,000 on a single player without the need to go before the board of directors for approval; a fixed player payroll of $160,000, which would be the second highest in the Pacific Coast League; and an annual salary of $15,000, the highest paid to any manager in the league. It was unlike any deal given a manager in the ten years of the Cobb ownership group's reign.

When the board agreed and extended a formal contract offer, Haney asked for two weeks to think it over. In actuality he wanted to secure one last element that he felt was imperative—a tie-up with a better major-league club than Hollywood had aligned with in the past. Haney's target: the Brooklyn Dodgers. He placed a phone call to the Dodgers' general manager, and after Branch Rickey replied that he was interested, only then did Fred Haney accept the Hollywood job.

Haney's hiring was heralded in the local press. "The dark ages at Gilmore Field may be over," wrote *Los Angeles Times* sports editor, Paul Zimmerman.[6] "Haney Hailed as New Hollywood Hope," trumpeted the

When Bob Cobb moved Haney from behind the microphone to the role of manager of the Stars for the 1949 season, the Stars enjoyed a dramatic change. Here Haney signs his 1950 contract. ***Courtesy of Terry Maalen***

headline in the *Sporting News*.[7] "Haney is really 'Mr. Big' when it comes to player deals," wrote *Long Beach Press Telegram* sports editor Frank Blair, who added, "Don't expect a one-year miracle at Hollywood, but in a couple of years under the new liberalized policy, Haney may lift the Stars out of the second division and have them fighting for the flag."[8]

There was agreement between management and manager in the need for a better major-league tie-up. Frustration had swelled over past agreements. Deals with the St. Louis Browns, Pittsburgh Pirates, and Chicago White Sox had been one-sided. Little came from the big-league partners in the way of talent, but each extracted first crack at a Hollywood prospect.

While Hollywood was committed to find a better big-league partner, Bill Veeck arrived in Los Angeles in search of a new top farm club. His Cleveland Indians had just won the 1948 World Series. Veeck proclaimed that the primary reason for his trip was to appear on the radio show of one of the team's investors, actor Bob Hope. But the Cleveland Indians' president arranged a side trip to meet with Bob Cobb. Veeck explained to Cobb that the relationship with his top farm team, the Baltimore Orioles, had broken down. He wanted to align with a team in the Pacific Coast League. Was Hollywood interested? Cobb and Veeck agreed to talk further.

Three weeks later Cobb had a meeting on his calendar with Cleveland's newest investor and vice president, Hank Greenberg. The intent was to renew discussions about a tie-up with Greenberg's ball club. Their meeting was cordial but ended quickly. The necessity of the meeting actually ended when Greenberg saw headlines in the morning papers at the newsstand near his hotel. "Haney Signs Star Contract," was accompanied by a photograph of Haney and Victor Ford Collins seated at a table in the Brown Derby. Bob Cobb stood behind the pair. Greenberg knew the Haney hiring would be a deal killer for his boss. Bill Veeck would insist that a Cleveland man manage his top minor-league team. Cobb, too, had reservations about a deal with Veeck and Greenberg. He was not in favor of Veeck's insistence that Cleveland be able to recall any player on twenty-four-hour notice. "Where would that leave us with our fans?" Cobb asked.[9] He shook Greenberg's hand and the two men parted amicably.

The ink had barely dried on his contract before Fred Haney was working with the fervor of a whirling dervish. Banquets from Long Beach to Bakersfield beckoned. Haney gave insight into the magnitude of the work that lay ahead. "We have 38 men on our reserve list," he said, "and there are only seven players out of that number that I want on my ball club. The team has to be rebuilt."[10] When Haney wasn't speaking to a group, he was speaking into a microphone on one of many local radio sports programs, all of which stoked interest in the Hollywood Stars.

It was after his hiring that Haney told Cobb of his conversations with Branch Rickey. The news was not received well. Bob Cobb considered Rickey to be "slick and sanctimonious,"[11] but agreed to Haney's request that the sides meet. An initial tête-à-tête came days before Thanksgiving at the Whitcombe Hotel in San Francisco, where Cobb, Haney, and Collins met with Rickey's son, Branch Jr., who oversaw the Dodgers' farm system. Cobb was, to say the least, startled when the younger Rickey offered a full working agreement and a $20,000 annual payment to the Stars. The offer failed to erase Cobb's apprehension of dealing with Rickey, however. The sides talked for eight hours and at 2:00 a.m. reached a tentative agreement. Despite the impressive numbers and promises, Cobb remained wary. He wondered aloud if the deal truly had the blessing of Rickey Jr.'s father. A phone call was immediately placed to Brooklyn. A somewhat groggy Branch Rickey invited Cobb and Haney to visit, and the next morning the men were on a plane bound for New York.

Trepidation accompanied Cobb during the taxi trek to the Dodgers' offices at 215 Montague Street. "Hide your pocketbooks or he'll have 'em all before you get out of the room," the driver snapped.[12] Cobb's objective was to determine the trustworthiness of Branch Rickey. He peppered the Dodgers' president with questions. None was about their agreement but rather player deals Rickey had made with other clubs. The Dodgers' boss sized up Cobb's intent. He surmised that he had been painted in a bad light by men in the Pacific Coast League who had come out on the short end of a trade or player purchase made with Rickey. The man carefully explained his side of each case that Cobb raised. He showed copies of correspondence that supported his position. Branch Rickey then signed a blank agreement and calmly handed the paper with a pen to Cobb and suggested he fill in the terms he wanted. It was a common Rickey ploy, but it worked. Cobb bought in.

Fred Haney closed the deal with the insistence that any player Brooklyn provided to Hollywood be young, talented, fast, and hardworking. The manager did not want his club to be a haven for older players, as many Pacific Coast League clubs had become. Rickey agreed. Together he and Cobb rose from their chairs. As the men's palms met, their handshake became a seminal moment in the history of the Hollywood Stars. "I expected to meet a horse thief," Cobb would later say to a reporter. "What I did meet was one of the great gentlemen of our time."[13] The meeting would steer the ball club in a new direction. Losing and frequent manager changes were to become a thing of the past.

Days after Thanksgiving, Haney was feted at the annual Friars Club banquet in Los Angeles. "As I look into your smiling faces, I see more ex-Hollywood managers than I have ex-wives," cracked George Jessell to get the event underway.[14] The night featured a raucous roast with Haney the target. Comedic actor Lou Holtz deadpanned, "I don't know anything about baseball. How could I? After all, I've only been watching the Stars play for ten years."[15] At the culmination of the evening, Haney and Cobb introduced Branch Rickey Jr. The men announced that Hollywood and the Brooklyn Dodgers had reached a twenty-year working agreement. The three hundred who were gathered erupted in thunderous applause.

Following the annual baseball winter convention in December, the changes began. So daunting was the workload that Haney recruited Paul Jeschke, the team's batboy, to be his personal assistant and handle paperwork. The roster was torn to shreds. Haney bought two pitchers, Glenn Moulder from the Chicago White Sox and Jack Salveson from Oakland. Not certain that George Genovese was ready for Class AAA ball, Haney made a trade with Seattle for Johnny O'Neil. By Christmas another half dozen players had been sold or optioned out to other clubs. In January Branch Rickey Jr. visited and asked if four young players who lived on the West Coast could train with Hollywood. Should Haney like any of them, he could take them. One would turn out to be surprisingly good: Jim Baxes, whom Haney would use at third base.

In early February, more players were dispatched by Brooklyn. The transaction brought a much-needed left-handed pitcher, Art Shallock. With new players in tow, Hollywood opened spring training in a new location, San Fernando, which was only twenty-two miles from Gilmore Field. The locale offered Haney, Cobb, and company more convenience. Hollywood's celebrity followers regularly trekked to watch workouts. Afterward they would share drinks with the players in a bar across the street from San Fernando Park. Once exhibition games began, the Stars won their first five. Optimism, if not enthusiasm, grew. Through it all Haney remained poker-faced. Ifs, maybes, and could-bes dotted his conversations. Two weeks before Opening Day, Haney and Cobb flew to Florida to observe the Dodgers' spring training workouts. Eight days later they returned with five players. Among them was a starting catcher, Mike Sandlock, and a starting outfielder, Herb Gorman.

As Opening Day approached, only six holdovers from the 1948 Stars remained. Seventeen newcomers filled the roster. While equipment trunks were loaded and players packed for the trip to San Diego and Opening Day, twenty-six hundred miles away an angry confrontation was about to send one more player Hollywood's way. He would be the best player the Stars suited up in the 1949 season.

On the diamonds that made up the Dodgers' spring training complex outside of Vero Beach in north Florida, Irv Noren seethed. In 1948 Noren had batted .323 for Fort Worth and been named Most Valuable Player in the Texas League. When he arrived in Vero Beach for spring training in

February 1949, Noren felt that his Fort Worth performance should merit a shot with the Brooklyn club. Instead, Noren found himself one of almost five hundred prospects, hopefuls, projects, and roster fillers who played on one of the twenty-four teams, identified by a color rather than name, in the Brooklyn farm system. "I don't even know where the big club is," Noren complained to teammate Don Newcombe. "I want to meet with Mr. Rickey," he demanded of a Dodgers coach.[16]

Noren had been a Southern California sensation, a standout on the football field and baseball diamond at Pasadena High School. He shone as a pitcher with the semipro Pasadena Merchants. It was in basketball, however, where Irv Noren wrote his prep headlines. He was the California Interscholastic Federation Player of the Year and the apple of the eye of dozens of college coaches. Uncle Sam got to Noren first. Basketball and baseball endeavors paused while he spent three years in the military during World War II. Upon his discharge from Fort MacArthur, Noren enrolled at Pasadena City College and averaged twenty points per game during the winter basketball season. Before he could entertain college offers, an enticing proposition lured Noren into professional basketball. Along with a Pasadena friend, Jackie Robinson; another two-sport standout, George Crowe; and Stanford All-America Art Stoefen, Noren joined the fledgling Los Angeles Red Devils. Following two impressive games against the Chicago American Gears, in November 1946 Noren and Stoefen were recruited to join the National Basketball League powerhouse. Noren was paid $100 per game to play alongside the premier player of the day, George Mikan.

Noren's basketball pursuits did not dissuade baseball scouts. Their interest in the Pasadena pitcher remained high. The Boston Red Sox and New York Yankees expressed interest. A meeting with Tom Downey of the Brooklyn Dodgers would change Noren's career path. "I'll pay you five," the veteran scout declared. "Five what?" a puzzled Noren asked. When Downey responded $5,000, the two had a deal.[17]

A strong suggestion from Branch Rickey that Noren focus on just one sport ended the young man's basketball pursuits. Another change came when he was moved to the outfield. A .363 season for Santa Barbara in 1946 brought the almost unheard-of jump from Class C ball to Class AA. After his MVP season of 1948, Noren expected another big jump, this one into the big leagues. That it did not happen pushed him to a face-to-face showdown with Branch Rickey.

When Rickey revealed his plan to assign Noren to one of the organization's top farm clubs, Montreal, the outfielder blurted, "I won't go there."

Rickey was momentarily startled. "What will you do?" he asked.

Noren explained that his father owned a Swedish bakery that made "very good Swedish bread." The ballplayer said that he and his older brother planned to sell their father's bread nationwide.

Rickey fumbled for a response, then asked Noren to come back to his office the following morning. When he did, the Dodgers' boss proposed that Noren play for Hollywood. Flushed with excitement at the prospect of playing at home, Noren eagerly agreed. "There's just one thing," Rickey added. "Hollywood opens in San Diego in two days. We want you there."[18]

As Noren and his wife hastily packed their things to begin a cross-country drive, Fred Haney's herculean off-season rebuilding effort had concluded. He was seventy-two hours from the launch of what would be a miracle season.

20

"HOORAY FOR HANEY!"

The loud snap of the director's slate sent stuntmen and the actor Jimmy Cagney running up metal stairs and across steel service platforms. The clattering of the men's hard-soled shoes and the firing of pistols filled the air. While the actors scurried upward alongside a sixty-four-foot-high crude oil storage tank, the crew of sound men, camera operators, grips, and best boys carried out their tasks at the vacant Southern California oil refinery. The scenes shot on this night would be spliced with studio shots of Cagney shouting the film's signature line, "Made it, Ma! Top of the world!"

Since the second week of May, Raoul Walsh had been directing Cagney and Virginia Mayo in *White Heat* for Warner Brothers. Every project brought Walsh a mixture of invigorating reward and invariable stress, but this project also carried with it a unique degree of anxiety. At the end of each night's filming, the director and Mayo, the picture's female lead, would make a beeline for their cars. Once inside, they would switch on the radio, twisting the tuning dial or pressing a button. Both were yearning, straining for information, keen to find the familiar voice of the broadcaster who would tell them the score and just how the Hollywood Stars were doing.

Walsh had keen interest. He was an avid baseball fan and one of the Stars' celebrity investors. Mayo's case was entirely different. It was her husband, actor Michael O'Shea, who was the unabashed sports fanatic in their house. If the Stars' game was in town, O'Shea would likely be there, in which case Mayo would head to her church and help out with a fundraising project. For Walsh, however, the mere sound of the radio broadcasts would evoke unease, for his commitment to direct *White Heat* made him unable to get to games at Gilmore Field, just when the Hollywood Stars were winning like never before.

From the two-run home run Chuck Stevens belted to make Hollywood a 7–5 winner in its first game of the season to the three-hit shutout spun by Art Shallock to highlight the home opener fourteen days later, Hollywood won nine games, and Fred Haney's ball club gave notice that it had the material to be a contender for the 1949 Pacific Coast League pennant.

At their very first assemblage in spring training, Haney had insisted his players hustle. The new manager instilled a scrappy work ethic. The team's style of play gained the notice of the press, who labeled the Stars "Haney's Hustling Twinks." When Frankie Kelleher homered in a second consecutive game on April 19 and Jim Baxes joined him with a four-bagger, it capped a monumental 8–6 win over Oakland. It was a win that pushed the Hollywood Stars into first place for the first time in the Bob Cobb ownership era. "This team is full of fire," beamed Haney of his players.[1]

A grand slam by the twenty-year-old Baxes beat Oakland, 7–4, on April 28 and sent Hollywood into the month of May with a game-and-a-half lead over San Diego in the Pacific Coast League standings. "Fred Haney and his Hollywood Stars are the talk of the town," penned Braven Dyer in the *Times*.[2] And then, as if Hollywood's roster wasn't formidable enough, the Stars received another weapon, one who would confound opponents throughout the summer months: Willie Ramsdell.

For fourteen years Willie Ramsdell had been knocking around Organized Baseball. He had struggled to stick in the big leagues. The 1949 season was the second consecutive year that Ramsdell found himself demoted to the minor leagues once big-league clubs were made to reduce rosters from twenty-eight to twenty-five by May 1. A happy-go-lucky sort, Ramsdell employed a fastball that wasn't, a curveball that didn't, and a third pitch that was responsible for his nickname, "Willie the Knuck." Ramsdell's knuckleball had helped him enjoy twenty-win seasons three times in the minor leagues. It was a pitch that Brooklyn manager Leo Durocher had described as a ball bouncing on a rubber band. If anyone was apprehensive about Ramsdell's arrival, it was the two Hollywood catchers. They now had not one but two knuckleball pitchers to try to handle: Ramsdell and Pinky Woods. Hollywood's primary catcher,

Mike Sandlock, had been a shortstop early in his career, and his soft hands and reactive skills allowed him to deftly handle the floaters. Al Unser, on the other hand, "picked it up at the backstop," one teammate laughed.[3]

Haney sent Ramsdell to the mound for his first start on Wednesday night, May 8. An overflow crowd of 11,746 came to see the first-place Stars play the rival Angels. The outfield had to be roped off to create standing room for one thousand fans in front of the fence. By the end of nine innings, only two Angels batters had managed to time Ramsdell's dancing, darting knuckleball for hits. The newcomer had pitched Hollywood to a 6–1 triumph, and his effort was hailed by *Los Angeles Times* sportswriter Al Wolf as the "best performance of any Hollywood hurler to date."[4] By the end of the month, Ramsdell had won six consecutive games, Irv Noren was challenging for the Pacific Coast League batting lead, Baxes was drawing comparisons from his manager to Hall of Fame third baseman Pie Traynor, and Hollywood sat in front of the rest of the league by a full six games. It astounded both fans and some Hollywood players. "In spring training, I thought we'd be lucky to finish better than seventh," Jack Salveson said.[5]

Winning changed the tone at Gilmore Field. The celebrity crowd at Bob Cobb's wooden ballpark had largely been a subdued bunch in prior seasons. Now, they were the flint to the winning's spark that fanned flames of excitement all about the place. From his seat near the Stars' bat rack, Groucho Marx barked encouragement to each Hollywood player as he started toward home plate. At the first hint of a potential rally, Harpo Marx would leap to his feet and with his signature three-finger whistle prompt hand claps or cheers to spur the Stars on. Gail Patrick never missed a game. Her lucky rabbits' feet made many a Stars player swerve in her direction for a superstitious rub on their way to bat.

The passivity of the local fans and their habit of leaving in the late innings of night games ended on Tuesday night, June 7. Hollywood's closest challenger, the San Diego Padres, was the opposition. A first-inning strikeout of the Padres' Max West with two runners on base produced a startling roar. A running grab by Frankie Kelleher brought shouts and screams. Then, in the eighth inning with the score tied, 3–3, Kelleher shot a fly ball over the left-field wall for a game-winning home run that unleashed pandemonium all about the ballpark. "Our eardrums still feel as if Gene Krupa was beating out boogie-woogie on 'em throughout an

Few celebrities were bigger fans than the actress Gail Patrick. Here she greets Stars players before a home game in 1940. ***Courtesy of the author***

all-night jam session," wrote Al Wolf in the *Los Angeles Times*.[6] From that night forward, a fervor reverberated about the stands of Gilmore Field.

Not only had Hollywood been a bad ball club in 1948, but they were an unlucky one too. Of the 104 games they lost, 32 were by one run. Haney's hustlers had reversed that trend. The 1949 Stars prevailed in 35 one-run outcomes, all of which helped the club to sit seven games in first place by the end of June. "I don't know whether we're good or we're lucky, but as long as the Stars keep trying as hard as we are to be good, maybe we'll be lucky," Haney said.[7]

July brought accolades. Seven Stars were selected to play in the league All-Star Game. None was more heralded than the team's center fielder, Irv Noren. As a kid, Noren had on many a summer Saturday pedaled his bicycle sixteen miles from his home in Pasadena to Wrigley Field to watch Pacific Coast League ball. Now he was among the best players in the league. Noren's parents became fixtures at Gilmore Field. After each game they would take a moment to congratulate their son, then set out for their bakery, where they would work through the night to produce goods for the next day.

An eleven-game hitting streak at the end of June, during which he batted .500, pushed Noren to second in the Pacific Coast League batting race. His .355 average was .008 behind that of San Diego's Luke Easter. Noren achieved his success with a simple "see it and hit it" approach with the bat. "For a player of his experience, he is coming along faster than could ordinarily be expected," Haney praised.[8] After his hitting streak was snapped, Noren had five hits in his next eighteen at-bats before he was plunked on the right hand by a pitch and made to sit out for a week.

The celebrations of July gave way to a spate of calamity in August. The arrival of Branch Rickey Jr. to Gilmore Field unleashed a torrent of speculation. Rumors spread that Rickey was there to evaluate a player his father wanted in Brooklyn. Some sportswriters speculated that the player was Baxes, while others suggested it was Ramsdell. Haney assured fans and the press that Brooklyn wasn't plucking anyone. It did little to quell the worry.

No sooner had Rickey Jr. left Southern California when an even worse problem arose—injuries. A succession of key players went out of the lineup with a variety of ailments. Johnny O'Neil was spiked on a close play at second base and missed a week. Gene Handley injured his knee and was out for a month. Noren twisted his knee and missed three games. Glenn Moulder suffered from a painful finger blister. Chuck Stevens was spiked, sprained an ankle, tweaked his side, and then in a collision at first base he twisted a knee, which caused him to miss a handful of games and wear a knee brace once he returned. In Seattle, Art Shallock tore a ligament in his left side and was flown home to Los Angeles for treatment. Mike Sandlock had no sooner recovered from a stomach ailment when a foul ball left him with a fractured finger. The rash of injuries even involved the Stars' batboy, Elmer Ammons, who was struck by a foul ball and had to be hospitalized. Even Fred Haney was made unavailable for several games. The manager had to catch an emergency flight home from a road trip when his mother-in-law was seriously injured in an automobile accident.

Hitters slumped and invincibility waned. The ball club went into a tailspin. At that same time, Oakland got hot and made a charge. When the Oaks took five of seven games during a series with Hollywood, the Stars' once-mighty league lead was shaved down to just two games. Pitching made Hollywood able to hold Oakland at bay. On Saturday, September 4, Pinky Woods beat Sacramento to complete an almost unheard-of turnaround. After losing twenty games in 1948, Woods joined Eddie Erautt as one of the only twenty-game winners in Hollywood's history. The next day Willie Ramsdell stymied the Angels on a two-hitter. The win was Hollywood's ninety-fifth of the season, which equaled the team's single season record for wins. A crowd of 10,423 put the season attendance tally tantalizingly close to 500,000 and had Cobb working with architects on a plan to renovate and expand seating in Gilmore Field to 25,000.

Despite the win, the Hollywood clubhouse was morose. Smiles were scarce and jovial voices were sparse because in the ninth inning of the game, Jim Baxes had been injured and taken to the hospital. The rookie sensation had played every inning of every game and was tired. While trying to outrun a ball hit in the infield, he tripped over first base. Writhing on the grass in agony, Baxes muttered to the team doctor, Dr. Murray Small, that he felt a tearing of his stomach. Small confided to Haney his fear that Baxes may have broken a rib and torn muscles in his stomach area. Baxes spent the night in Park View Hospital, but when X-rays failed to show any broken bones and other tests did not reveal significant injury, Small released the All-Star. Baxes hurried to Gilmore Field, anxious to play in that night's game with San Diego. Haney, being cautious, refused and insisted Baxes sit on the dugout bench for a few nights.

Aspiration melded with preparation on the afternoon of September 12. Like a tantalizing carrot, the Pacific Coast League pennant had dangled in front of the Hollywood Stars for six months. When the manager and his players gathered at Municipal Airport in Los Angeles for their Western Airlines flight to San Francisco, one final road trip was all that stood between the team and its prize. Success had seen exultation burst from expectation. Players were shocked to see a thousand cheering fans amass to give the ball club a rousing send-off. The well wishes extended beyond cheering children and adults. Herb Wilkings brought the horn section from his orchestra. Cheerleaders led collegiate-style encouragement. A normally mundane road trip departure was made boisterous, if not inspiring.

The series in San Francisco was filled with drama. Four of the seven games were decided by a single run. One was won on a balk in the ninth inning. Another was lost in the eleventh. The Sunday doubleheader that would conclude the series became pivotal to the outcome of the pennant chase. Players were on edge. Following the Saturday night win, some had difficulty sleeping. Restlessness sent Chuck Stevens to the window of his hotel room at 3:00 a.m. As he gazed at the road below, a figure hunched over a pinball machine in the arcade across the street caught his eye. "It's Noren!" Stevens screeched. The noise woke the first baseman's roommate, who asked what the commotion was all about. "It's Noren," an astonished Stevens repeated. "He's down there playing pinball!"[9] The following afternoon Noren hiked his season tally for runs batted in to 119, second best in the league. George Genovese drove in two runs with a pair of doubles. Hollywood beat San Francisco, 10–3, in the first game of a doubleheader. When Willie Ramsdell mowed down the Seals on a two-hitter, and Kelleher and Noren drove in the runs to win the second game, 2–1, the pennant was practically in the bag. Oakland lost both games of its doubleheader against the Angels in Los Angeles, and with seven games left to play in the season, Hollywood held a four-game lead.

On the Stars' return they found Los Angeles teeming in pennant pursuit fanfare. The mayor had declared the week "Baseball Week" in Los Angeles. Banners that read "Come on Stars—Win that Pennant!" hung across busy Hollywood and Wilshire boulevards. Placards bearing the same slogan were displayed in dozens of store and shop windows. Large department stores incorporated the encouragement in their advertisements.

The first game of the final series of the season brought more than eight thousand fans to Gilmore Field. The throng cheered Pinky Woods, whose knuckleball frustrated Seattle and allowed just three hits in a 4–0 Stars triumph. The next night tension shrouded the ballpark. The Stars and Rainiers had battled to a standoff after nine innings. It was another half hour of play, and in the eleventh inning the crack of the ball hitting Frankie Kelleher's bat spiked the noise level as the winning run sprinted across home plate. While players showered, the news arrived that Oakland had lost in thirteen innings to Portland. The results meant that Hollywood could do no worse than tie for the Pacific Coast League pennant.

The evening of September 22 brought the Hollywood Stars to destiny's doorstep. Concentration superseded hijinks in what was a serious clubhouse. As each player buttoned up his flannel jersey and laced his spikes, he knew the significance of that night's game. Win, and Hollywood was the Pacific Coast League champion for the first time in the club's history. Though a few were tense, most of the players had good reason to feel confident. Theirs was the hottest team in the Pacific Coast League. The Stars had won nineteen of twenty-one games and swept five doubleheaders. If there were any doubters among the bunch, they were likely changed by reading Fred Haney's quote in the newspaper. "I think we're going to win it," the manager said.[10] Chuck Stevens's bases-loaded single in the first inning got the Stars going by scoring two runs. Over the next seven innings, however, fans were never able to get comfortable. Willie Ramsdell was not fooling the Seattle hitters. In the fourth inning, the Rainiers rallied to trim Hollywood's lead to one, 3–2. Anxiousness gave way to tension in the top of the seventh inning. Seattle put two runners on with just one out. A single to center field looked to one and all as though it would tie the game. But Irv Noren initiated perhaps the best defensive play of the season. He fired a strike to home plate. Mike Sandlock tagged the runner out, then rifled the ball to Jim Baxes at third base to complete a double play and end the inning.

Drama grew in the bottom of the eighth inning. This time it was Hollywood who put two runners on base. Ever the tactician, Haney pinch-hit Murray Franklin for George Genovese. Though Genovese already had two hits in the game, Haney considered the right-handed-batting Franklin to be a better match against the new Seattle relief pitcher,

Herb Karpel, who threw left-handed. The strategy paid dividends. Franklin smashed a Karpel pitch over the wall in left-center field. Delirious cheers celebrated the three-run home run, which broke the game wide open. Gene Handley followed the home run with a single, then Noren tripled him home. The four-run rally gave Hollywood a 7–2 lead.

In the top of the ninth inning, anticipation surged through the stands. With two outs, a fly ball to center field brought fans to their feet and sent euphoria rising. When Noren squeezed the ball in his leather mitt for the final out, Hollywood won, 7–4, clinching the first pennant of the Cobb ownership era. At least half of the 7,374 fans on hand spilled from the stands onto the field. Several revelers joined players to hoist Haney onto their shoulders and parade the Hollywood manager about the infield. "This is the greatest thrill of my life," Haney shouted.[11] Someone handed the skipper a folded cloth, and he knew exactly what it was for. Followed by the jubilant fans, Haney trotted to the flagpole beyond center field. Amidst joyful shouts and cheers Haney hoisted the makeshift Pacific Coast League pennant. The manager was momentarily taken aback by the sound of crying. "There's no wind, tonight of all nights," a fan sniveled. "The pennant won't fly."[12]

Late into the night, in nearby saloons and downtown dance halls, even in illicit area poker dens, the topic of chatter was Hollywood winning the pennant. A street dance not far from the ballpark turned into a pennant celebration once news of the final score was received. The next morning Pants Rowland told a reporter that he had never seen such an outpouring of joy to compare with the celebrating of the Stars' pennant-starved fans.

Hollywood blitzed through the first round of the Governor's Cup playoffs. Four wins in five games with Sacramento moved the Stars into the league finals. To their surprise, the opposition in the final would be not Oakland but San Diego. Fourth place in the regular season, the Padres had aligned with Bill Veeck's Cleveland Indians. After a strong start to the season, San Diego saw several of its better players, Al Rosen and Luke Easter among them, called up to Cleveland.

The Padres had regrouped and knocked off Oakland to win their playoff series, then won the first two games of the title series with the Stars. Once the games shifted to Gilmore Field, Hollywood's players found their city and ballpark a far different place than the palace of exuberance that flowed during the final week of the season. Apathy now reared its head. Just as a cold snap had blanketed Los Angeles, football

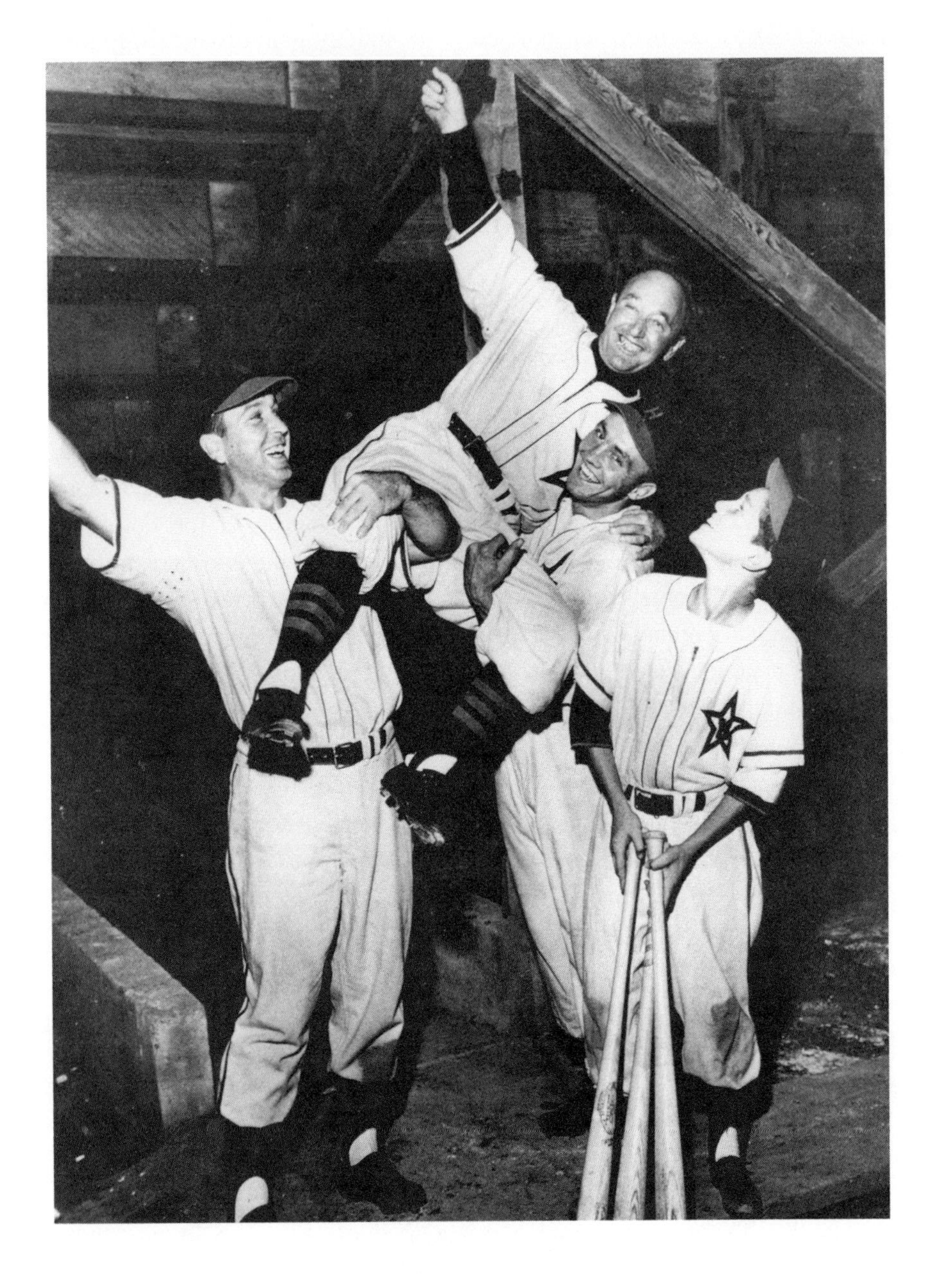

His players carry Fred Haney in celebration after winning the 1949 Pacific Coast League pennant. ***Courtesy of the Baseball Hall of Fame and Museum***

had snatched the attention of the city's sports pages. Some of the local newspapers had sent their baseball writers east to cover the World Series, while columnists devoted their space to the Rams or USC football. Scarcely three thousand fans, most of whom where bundled and shivering, saw Jim Baxes and George Genovese rap out three hits apiece to highlight a 7–4 win over San Diego. The following night, the turnstile count didn't even reach two thousand for a second Hollywood triumph. Accounts of the game were buried deep in the back of local sports pages behind football game stories and a large report about the World Series.

On Sunday, October 9, with Frankie Kelleher hitting his thirty-first home run of the season and Willie Ramsdell stumping San Diego's batting order, the Hollywood Stars won the Governor's Cup, 8–4. The next day the Broadway Department Store placed the Governor's Cup trophy in the window of its store at Hollywood and Vine, where a manager said it was "the best traffic stopper we have had in years."[13]

Haney struck an agreement to get players from the Brooklyn Dodgers. It brought Irv Noren to the Hollywood Stars. The outfielder was the 1949 Pacific Coast League Most Valuable Player. Here Noren receives his award from league president Clarence "Pants" Rowland. ***Courtesy of the Irv Noren Collection***

Sportswriters who covered the Pacific Coast League voted Irv Noren the league's Most Valuable Player. He had finished second in the batting race with a .330 average. Noren hit 29 home runs and drove in 127 runs.

So overwhelming was Noren's season that he received twice as many MVP votes as did the runner up.

The Stars celebrated amid the trappings of luxury at the Beverly Wilshire Hotel on Rodeo Drive. The victory party brought a throng. Throughout the night Fred Haney was continually pounded by enthusiastic backslappers. His right hand grew sore from being shaken. An ear-to-ear grin covered the manager's face. The line of well-wishers was so unending that Haney never had time to light a cigarette or sip his favorite bourbon and soda. The chatter made Haney oblivious to the singing of Gordon McRae, which filled the ballroom. Nor did the manager notice when Chuck Stevens slid behind the drums for a set, and later when Gordon Maltzberger accompanied the band with his harmonica. Across the room players boasted and laughed. They chattered about plans for their winnings. Each was to receive a cut of the $35,000 championship pot posted by the league. The lavish surroundings, the food and drink were all spoils of a miracle—a remarkable turnaround from sixth place in 1948 to a pennant one year later, thanks to an improvement of twenty-five wins. All about the room celebrities, fans, and players appropriately shouted, "Hooray for Haney!"[14]

Celebrities such as Ruth Warrick (left) joined the Stars' Irv Noren (center) and Mike Sandlock (right) to celebrate the 1949 championship with a lavish party. ***Courtesy of the Irv Noren Collection***

21

"IT'S FUNNY ABOUT KIDS"

During the spring of 1949, there was no more heralded baseball player in Southern California than a hard-throwing, seventeen-year-old high school pitcher by the name of Paul Pettit. During one stretch in his senior year, Pettit fired three consecutive no-hitters. So great was the interest in Pettit that administrators at his high school had to move bleachers from the football field to the baseball diamond to handle the large crowds that flocked whenever he pitched. Often in those crowds were Fred Haney and curious members of his ball club. Always in those crowds were scouts—dozens of them. Multiple scouts from every one of the sixteen major-league teams. The men jockeyed for favored status by helping Pettit's father chop wood and drying dishes for the pitcher's mother. None of them, however, was held in higher regard by Pettit and his family than the head scout for the Hollywood Stars, Rosey Gilhousen.

Ross "Rosey" Gilhousen was a personable fellow. He had grown up in Hawthorne, played ball at Compton Junior College, then spent two seasons playing the outfield in Class D ball before the onset of World War II caused many leagues at that level to cease operation. Gilhousen spent the war years working in a Los Angeles–area aircraft factory. He coached the factory's semipro team, the Northrop Bombers, to the Southern California semipro championships. It was at that time that Gilhousen began to dabble as a part-time scout for the Hollywood Stars. He learned tricks of the trade from Hollis "Sloppy" Thurston, who doubled as both a West Coast scout for the Pittsburgh Pirates and a Stars coach. Often their classroom was First Base, a bar Thurston owned on West Pico Avenue.

When Thurston resigned following the 1947 season, it was the thirty-two-year-old Gilhousen who received the promotion and was made Hollywood's head scout.

A jovial sort with thinning red hair, Gilhousen was a talker. His storytelling could be as riveting to the teenaged prospects he coveted as it was annoying to many of his fellow scouts. Rarely not in slacks, a jacket, and tie, with a fedora atop his head, Gilhousen carried with him a black book that contained the names of three thousand players whom he boasted of having seen on an annual basis. "It's funny about kids," he would say. "A boy may have every outward qualification. He may be able to run, throw, and hit. But we can't look into his head or his heart, and that's where we sometimes go wrong."[1]

Rosey Gilhousen could be immensely helpful—and he could terrorize. Gilhousen wasn't bashful about stopping a player to offer corrective batting tips. The scout routinely befriended and ferried players to games. Some would later admit that the scout scared them out of their wits by turning to eagerly tell a baseball story to his backseat passengers while blindly speeding down a freeway.

On taking the reins of the Hollywood scouting effort, Gilhousen expanded his team of scouts. Part-time scouts were enlisted and sprinkled about Southern California. Bird dogs were secured in other towns and cities around the state to provide tips and leads about prospects. It was one of those part-time scouts, Fred Millican, who first brought Paul Pettit to Gilhousen's attention.

All it took for Gilhousen was seeing Pettit pitch once and the scout was enamored. He invited the high school sensation and his best friend and catcher, Darrold "Gar" Myers, to Gilmore Field. On a tour of the ballpark the teens were introduced to the actor George Raft. Rather than feeling awe at meeting a famous actor, it was the female beauty on Raft's arm who left the boys speechless. A friendship grew between scout and players. Gilhousen opened his home to Pettit and Myers. The boys would ride their bicycles over after school to talk baseball and listen to the scout's stories. Gilhousen arranged for the teens to play amateur ball with clubs in Central California, with accompanying jobs in the area's farming community.

To Gilhousen, no player was unattainable. However, by the middle of Pettit's senior season, it became clear that the bonds of friendship would succumb to money. Paul Pettit had grown into a heralded talent, the best amateur player in the country. The bidding for his signature on a contract would go higher than ever before, far beyond the reach of the Hollywood Stars. Teams chased Pettit's high school teammates, too. Gilhousen convinced Gar Myers to reject a larger offer from the Detroit Tigers and sign with Hollywood. He gave the young catcher a bonus of $6,000. Six months later, in January 1950, Paul Pettit became the first player in baseball history to receive a six-figure signing bonus when he signed with the Pittsburgh Pirates for $100,000. Among the Pirates scouts who pursued Pettit was Babe Herman.

As 1950 drew closer, the population of Los Angeles continued to explode. Prior to World War II, the census figures totaled 1.5 million residents. Three years after the war, almost 2 million people called the area home. Along with the population, the numbers of talented amateur ballplayers in the area grew. In 1948 local American Legion leagues were filled by 225 teams and each year after, the leagues expanded. The nation's regard for Southern California's baseball talent was swelled by the renown for Paul Pettit and the success of the University of Southern California Trojans. In June 1948 the school earned the greatest prize ever won by an amateur team from the region. Made up of players from the area's high schools and American Legion programs, USC won the College World Series.

Throughout the Trojans' season, scouts were in hot pursuit of a half dozen of the team's top players. Hollywood fought hard to get its share. Gilhousen had befriended many of the Trojans' players through American Legion ball. The scout was aggressive in his pursuit of the team's center fielder, Gail Henley. Oscar Reichow and his assistant, Paul Clements, wooed the fleet outfielder over lunch at the Farmers Market. When Henley chose to sign instead with the Giants for a substantial bonus, Reichow groused, "We offered you more money!"[2] Four of the six coveted Trojans signed with major-league clubs. The other two, Dick Bishop and Bill Lillie, were signed by Gilhousen. Bishop helped the Stars right away, while Lillie was farmed out for development.

A plethora of high school talent brought scouts in droves throughout the spring and summer of 1949. Slick-fielding shortstop Eddie Bressoud was generating headlines at Washington High School. Billy Consolo and his pal George "Sparky" Anderson were the envy of scouts who followed Dorsey High. Large numbers of scouts watched Chuck Essegian and Norm Sherry whenever Fairfax High played.

When the graduating class had signed their professional contracts, only one Pacific Coast League club was successful in landing Southern California prospects. Gilhousen had convinced Sherry, Bill Pinkard, and Joe Potts to sign with the Stars.

Hollywood's dogged efforts were not limited to Southern California. In June 1949 Hollywood began its quest to sign one of the best pitching prospects in Northern California. The morning after his high school graduation, Wes Breschini was driven three hundred miles from his home in Gonzalez to Gilmore Field by one of Gilhousen's bird dogs for a tryout. The hard-throwing, 6-foot-3-inch fastball specialist impressed even Branch Rickey, who climbed from the stands for a closer look. When the Stars and Rickey made generous bonus offers, the teen turned it down. "I just graduated," he said. "I'd like to wait and start playing next spring."[3] No amount of persuading could change the pitcher's mind, and Breschini signed instead with the more accommodating Detroit Tigers.

Gilhousen's pursuit of top amateur talent followed a directive from the top. Not long after the calendar turned from 1948 to 1949, the Stars head scout was pushed by a different directive. By February 1949 the Stars were under pressure from community groups and media to sign an African American player. It was pointed out that two seasons had passed since Jackie Robinson debuted for the Brooklyn Dodgers. In April 1948 John Ritchey became the first African American to play in the Pacific Coast League with San Diego. Labor unions in San Francisco pressed the San Francisco Seals to sign a Black ballplayer. In Los Angeles, A. S. "Doc" Young, the sports editor for the *Los Angeles Sentinel*, did the same to the Hollywood Stars.

During his forays around Southern California, Gilhousen developed a network of high school, college, and semipro coaches. Each shared tips and insights about prospects Gilhousen should see. It was Joe LaCour, the coach of the Los Angeles Eagles, who urged the scout to have a look at Eddie Moore. The Eagles were an all-Black team in the Southern California semipro league. Their benefactor was the legendary jazz drummer Lee Young, who had reached prominence while playing for Count Basie and Duke Ellington. LaCour described a nineteen-year-old outfielder who had tremendous skills and good character. Moore, he said, was 5 feet, 11 inches and weighed 185. He could run, throw, and field better than most his age. Most of all, Moore could hit for power. LaCour added that the St. Louis Browns had been sniffing around and appeared to have interest.

It was late February, and the season was about to begin for Los Angeles City College, where Moore played. Gilhousen caught Moore's first game and came away impressed. He learned that the young player had shone at Jefferson High School, then been lured to Alabama by a scholarship to play football for Tuskegee Institute. Moore had returned home to help his mother and enrolled briefly at UCLA before settling at East Los Angeles Junior College. The more questions Gilhousen asked about the talented young man, the more impressed the scout became. He learned that Moore was not only looked up to by the youth at Ross Snyder Playground, where the children revered his baseball talent, but also at Morning Star Baptist Church, where he was a member of the choir and secretary of the Sunday school. Moore was a straight A student. In fact, Moore's schooling was being paid by a scholarship he had received from the Federation of Church Choirs.

Gilhousen invited Moore to Sawtelle Field, west of Los Angeles, where the Hollywood Stars were to hold a tryout. There, on February 17, in front of the Stars' manager and members of the front-office staff, Moore's skills stood out among a number of other hopefuls. Gilhousen became convinced and unleashed his persuasive efforts. He sat down with the ballplayer; his mother, Mrs. E. V. Moore-Holmes; and her husband of six months, Reverend C. W. Holmes, at their home on Maple Avenue. The scout explained why Eddie should sign the contract that he offered rather than hope for one from the local St. Louis Browns' scout. "Whatever you want to be, be the best," mother said to son.[4] Gilhousen succeeded.

Moore initially trained with Hollywood. It was determined that he was not ready to play at the Pacific Coast League level. Now that Hollywood controlled its own farm club in Billings, Montana, they had a place where they could develop Moore's talents. When the nineteen Mustangs players arrived in Billings to start the season, Eddie Moore was the only Black player. He was the only African American out of 160 players in the entire Pioneer League and the first ever to play in the league. During spring training Moore's teammates had taken a liking to the outfielder. When management fussed over what to do with Moore when they paired players to make up a motel rooming list, the team's catcher, Gar Myers, stepped up and said, "I'll room with Eddie."[5] Players fumed when, after a sixteen-hour bus ride from Billings to Salt Lake City, no motel or hotel in the city would provide Moore with a room. When the team entered a Salt Lake

City restaurant and were told, "Sorry, no Negroes are allowed in here," every player, without hesitation, turned and walked out.[6] Eddie Moore impressed in his first season of pro ball. He hit fourteen home runs for the Mustangs and batted .312. The decision was made to send him back to Billings in 1950 for more development, and it proved astute. Moore blossomed. He hit twenty-five home runs and batted .342.

Under Gilhousen's direction, the Stars staged tryout camps and clinics all over Southern California. The auditions drew in the hundreds. Clinics staged by the scout were popular and could lure as many as twenty-five entire high school teams. Frankie Kelleher replaced Babe Herman as the face of the Hollywood Rookie School. The Stars' slugger offered batting tips and used innovative gadgets to help unlock young players' talents. No sooner would Kelleher say, "Hey, you're pretty good," when Gilhousen might seize on the notice.[7] Whether a player was seventeen or just twelve, age was no deterrent to interest. The young player would be peppered with questions "How big is your father? How big is your mother?"[8] If Gilhousen liked the answers, the youngster's name would go into his black book to check on in the future.

Gilhousen's methods were evidence of just how aggressive the Hollywood Stars had become in pursuit of amateur talent. With the exception of the San Francisco Seals, no other club in the Pacific Coast League employed such tenacity in its quest to sign high school and college prospects. It was hoped that the effort to land young prospects would serve Hollywood well with an even bigger goal looming on the horizon.

22

"AREN'T THEY SEXY?"

One by one the players filed into the clubhouse. Their chatter echoed about the empty room. None had any idea why their manager, Fred Haney, had summoned them to the ballpark early on this Saturday. The first to arrive noticed the boxes that had been stacked neatly by Nobe Kawano, the Stars' clubhouse man, nearly a dozen of them.

Experience said that these types of summonses usually had to do with the way a team was playing. It often involved a manager's desire to say or do something drastic. Nothing that had happened thus far lent one to believe that any tirade, tongue lashing, or special workout was about to take place.

The Hollywood Stars 1950 season had begun with a great deal of fanfare. Opening Day renewed celebration of the team's 1949 pennant. Festivities began with a parade down Hollywood Boulevard at 3:30 in the afternoon. Once the crowd—which included such movie stars as Edward G. Robinson, George Burns, Harpo Marx, and Jack Benny—were in their seats, the pregame plaudits and awards took place. Trouble with the microphone on the field plagued the ceremony. It was salvaged only by the introduction of Miss Hollywood Stars, Betty Underwood, an attractive budding actress who had recently appeared in her first motion picture, *A Dangerous Profession*, with George Raft.

The team dropped their opener, 4–3, in ten innings, then came back the following night to win by the same score, also in ten innings. Yes, there had been errors and miscues in the first two games and, for that matter, in each of the four games. But as the players assembled as ordered on Saturday, none could come up with a reason that would merit a meeting such as this.

It was only after Fred Haney arrived and, together with Kawano, began to open the boxes that a few of the players made the connection to something they had read in one of the morning papers: "The Hollywood Stars are going to spring a big surprise today."[1] Haney reached into the first open box and proclaimed, "This is what we're wearing today."[2] The Hollywood manager pulled out a pair of short pants. Kawano next handed the manager a T-shirt, which Haney held up to show the players their new jerseys. That's when the grumbling began.

Chuck Stevens was first to complain. He was loud and he was angry, at least until Haney explained that the lightweight uniform would make him run faster. The shorts were white, pinstriped, lightweight flannel trunks that fell six inches above the knee. Inside were pouches for sliding

The Stars caused a stir throughout baseball in 1950 when they made short pants a part of their uniform. Pershing Mondorff, Chuck Stevens, Gene Handley, and Johnny O'Neill model for photographers. ***Courtesy of Larry Rubin***

pads. The jersey was a simple T-shirt made of very light rayon that weighed only one pound, six ounces. The idea had come from a column written by Braven Dyer in the *Los Angeles Times* in December following the 1948 season. "Why not hire a fashion expert from some movie studio to create something new in playing uniforms for the Twinks?" Dyer suggested.[3] It gave Fred Haney inspiration. "This isn't a gag," the manager insisted. "These outfits weigh only one-third as much as the old monkey suits, and when both are soaked in perspiration, the difference is still greater. It stands to reason that players should be faster wearing them—and that half step going down to first wins or loses many games."[4]

When game time approached and Fred Haney strode to home plate with his lineup card, he was met by the affable Bill Sweeney in hilarious splendor. The Portland manager wore an apron around his waist. A long wig with curls topped with a purple hat adorned his head. The man carried a small poodle under his left arm. Instead of handing the standard card with his starting nine to the umpires, Sweeney gave Haney a bouquet of pansies. The Stars' manager grinned broadly. He lapped up the hilarity of it all. From his box seat Groucho Marx hooted, "Aren't they sexy? They'll kill musical comedy."[5]

The usual cheers that greeted Hollywood's starting nine as they ran onto the field were seasoned with howls, insults, and laughter from the Portland dugout. Players waved handkerchiefs and cooed, "Yoo-hoo" and "Hubba-hubba." A Portland player hollered, "Hey sweetie, catch you after the game?"[6] Wolf whistles brought cries of laughter.

In the bottom of the first inning, Chuck Stevens was first to bat for Hollywood. When he narrowly beat out an infield hit, Haney turned to the fans and hollered, "He wouldn't have made it with the old unie on!"[7] Stevens added to his hit tally with a home run in the eighth inning to cap a 5–3 Hollywood victory.

The next morning, Delly Arnold, the team's receptionist, was pushed to a frenetic pace. It seemed as if almost everyone in Southern California was dialing WE-5151. Each caller, clearly motivated by newspaper photos of the Stars in their new short pants, asked if tickets were still available for that day's game. They were, and 9,269 gobbled them up and came away convinced the garb should become a staple. Their Stars won the first game of the Sunday doubleheader, 8–7, while wearing shorts. As if to confirm the opinion, when Hollywood switched to long pants for the second game, they lost, 4–3.

Within seventy-two hours of the unveiling, almost every major newspaper in the United States had made mention of Hollywood's new uniforms. Headline writers enjoyed a creative field day. "It's Daring—It's the New Ooh! Look," read the *Hollywood Citizen News*.[8] "Stars 'Fashion' 5–3 Win," topped the game story in the *Los Angeles Examiner*.[9] "Hollywood Stars Blossom Out," was the headline on page 1 of the *Los Angeles Times*.[10] The *Sporting News* devoted two full pages to the Stars' innovation. On its editorial page, the publication ran an entire column on the uniform breakthrough. "Leave it to Hollywood," the editorial began. "Accustomed as the community is to the eccentric dress of its movie actors and to seeing women parading on its streets in various stages of undress, perhaps it isn't so much of a novelty for its ballplayers to appear in unconventional uniforms in the Movie City." The publication added, "And the Hollywood uniforms are nothing less than a knockout."[11]

Frank Blair, the sports editor of the *Long Beach Press Telegram*, took the plaudits a step further when he wrote that Haney "may move into the Cooperstown Hall of Fame via a side door as one of the greatest men the game has ever produced."[12] Not every reporter shared the same view. On seeing Hollywood's players trot bare-legged onto Gilmore Field, L. H. Gregory, the sports editor of the *Portland Oregonian*, stomped out of the press box. "I can't stand covering such goings-on. I'm going home." He vowed to call Haney's team "the Bloomer Girls."[13]

Writers sought reaction from fashion experts. One even phoned the popular pinup model and actress Betty Grable, who smiled, "How could anyone have a bad word for shorts?"[14] Bob Cobb beamed, "This is the best thing that has happened to baseball since the automobile replaced the horse and buggy. It's the first change of baseball uniforms in 111 years."[15]

Hollywood's groundbreaking attire made the Stars the biggest draw in the Pacific Coast League. Curiosity and wonder built a phenomenon that lured more than 94,000 to the team's first eighteen games away from Gilmore Field. In late April, 61,000 came to gawk, heckle, and cheer during a seven-game series at Wrigley Field. The Stars' first 1950 visit to San Diego nearly eclipsed the Padres' attendance record for a series, and management in Sacramento reveled when more than 34,260 turned out to see the shorts-clad Stars during the June series in the state capital. The spectacle was not without complications. A near-capacity crowd in Oakland roared its approval when Hollywood took the field in their shorts. An inning into the game a cool evening breeze chilled the ballpark, which was not far from the shore of San Francisco Bay. Players beat a hasty retreat to the clubhouse for warm undershirts. Management in Portland gleefully rubbed their hands in anticipation of big crowds when the Stars appeared on the schedule. Delight turned to despair when the entire April series was rained out. Hollywood's first 1950 visit to Seattle drew an overflow crowd of 13,491. The city had endured record winter cold and still felt nothing akin to its usual springtime warmth. Most in the crowd were stunned and jeered in anger when Hollywood's players stepped from the dugout in long pants. "When it's hot," Fred Haney snapped after the Stars were booed and berated for nine innings.[16]

The Stars' fashion sensation grew beyond Hollywood. A junior college team in Sacramento adopted the radical garb. So, too, did the Marshall High School baseball team in Los Angeles. A Dodgers farm team in Valdosta, Georgia, chucked its flannels for shorts. The manager of the Fort Worth Cats was furious when management clad his players in green shorts with red striping. The McAllen Giants in the Class C Rio Grande Valley League stirred up interest in their last-place club by donning Haney's innovative attire, and the Miami Sun Sox changed from traditional uniforms to the Hollywood style as well. When players for the Class A Pueblo Dodgers convinced their front office to make short pants part of the uniform, manager Ray Hathaway shook his head. "The bench jockeys gave it to us real good," he said after the season ended.[17]

Manufacturers sought to cash in on the phenomenon. The Wilson Sporting Goods Company took out quarter-page ads in the *Sporting News* to promote the sale of the short pants and T-shirt uniform. A month later Rawlings Sporting Goods one-upped their competitor, buying an even bigger ad for the same purpose. In Brooklyn, Branch Rickey confessed he was considering short pants for the Dodgers. Hardcore fans were outraged. Some disparaged the Stars. Others groused that shorts belonged only on girls. For the staunchest of Hollywood's fans, the insults hurled from Brooklyn were the last straw. Moose McGreary, a gruff, muscular movie extra and regular in the Gilmore Field bleachers, barked, "The Stars ain't no sissy team."[18]

Expectations were high for the 1950 Hollywood Stars. A majority of the sportswriters who covered the Pacific Coast League pegged the team to win a second consecutive pennant. Throughout the winter Fred Haney was the most celebrated man in Los Angeles. He was honored by the mayor, feted by the Friars Club, and toasted at Kiwanis Club, Rotary Club, and sports luncheons and banquets throughout Southern California. At each he stoked the flames of expectation by proclaiming his Stars would once again be a good ball club. In April and May, they were. By June, things began to fall apart.

At the conclusion of June, the Stars were on top of the Pacific Coast League standings. They held a three-game lead over the Oakland Oaks. Then the injuries and slumps hit. First it was the flu. The virus swept through the Hollywood clubhouse, and for a stretch the Stars were forced to play shorthanded. On some nights two and three players were home, bedridden by illness. Next came injuries. A foot injury sent Chuck Stevens into a batting tailspin. Jack Salveson had been one of the best pitchers in the league through the first half of the season before injury kept him out for six weeks. Pinky Woods suffered a groin injury. His pride was wounded, too, by barbs from a sportswriter. Woods challenged the man to meet beneath the stands of Gilmore Field, where the pitcher dished out a pummeling. When Woods suffered a reoccurrence of the groin injury, the team sent him home for the remainder of the season.

Frankie Kelleher slumped. Jim Baxes did, too. Their struggles and the team's July slide from first to third made Haney realize that the sale of Irv Noren to the Washington Senators after the 1949 season had left an unfillable hole. "We have no pacemaker, no rally-around man such as Irv Noren was in '49," the manager lamented. "He hit in the neighborhood of .350 from start to finish and pulled the others along."[19]

Early in July the struggles of the ball club became a secondary concern to the health of Oscar Reichow. Not long after the pennant celebration had calmed in the winter of 1949, Reichow submitted his resignation to the board of directors. He had endured a series of health problems. While the board accepted Reichow's resignation, Bob Cobb did not want to see him go. He arranged for Reichow to broadcast the Stars' games on radio, a skill he had become renowned for in the 1930s with the Los Angeles Angels. KLAC also offered Reichow a daily baseball show.

By mid-June, however, Reichow's health deteriorated. He had to step aside from the microphone. It was then that the sixty-one-year-old became embroiled in a highly charged and emotional controversy. Reichow and his wife, Mable, had decided it was time to move to a smaller house. They sold their Leimert Park-area home to the first buyer who made an acceptable offer. It happened that the buyer was an African American couple. The sale outraged neighbors. Forty-two residents of the neighborhood, all white, campaigned to have Reichow removed from the air. They sued the Reichows for $185,000, the collective amount they claimed their property value fell by the integration of their neighborhood.

Three weeks later Reichow collapsed and was rushed to Queen of Angels Hospital. Doctors determined he had serious internal bleeding. An urgent call went out for blood donors. His physician, Dr. Laurin L. Wood, told reporters, "He let himself go for a week without realizing his critical condition."[20] For three days doctors worked to reverse the problem, but just after noon on July 8, Oscar Reichow died. Four days later tributes were paid. Two hundred mourners, some who had traveled all night from the East Coast, gathered in the chapel at Hollywood Cemetery. Reichow was praised for his baseball acumen and cited for his creativity and innovative ideas. A half dozen local sportswriters were pallbearers and laid Reichow to rest. That evening in Oakland, where the Stars were to play the Oaks, Hollywood's host paid respect with a moment of silence before the game.

Oscar Reichow's philosophies were fundamental to what the Stars practiced. The team's ticket sales strategies were a combination of Bob Cobb's belief in star power and quality and Reichow's experience as a club operator that taught three foundational schemes—to involve communities, which he did with civic nights; to recruit large businesses to be part of the Stars' activities; and to include and inspire youth.

The Stars constructed civic nights to evolve around recognition for a player. The chamber of commerce of the participating town would sell tickets, enlist local merchants to donate gifts, then fete the player in a pregame ceremony. Glendale honored Babe Herman several times during his six seasons with the Stars. Pasadena gifted Irv Noren a new television for being selected to play in the Pacific Coast League All-Star Game. On Fred Haney Day, the Hollywood manager received a new Ford station wagon. Chuck Stevens and Jack Salveson were showered with gifts by merchants from their hometown, Long Beach. Fans from Culver City presented Frankie Kelleher the gift of a new car. Companies such as Western Airlines were made to appreciate Gilmore Field as an ideal place to entertain their employees and celebrate corporate milestones. Programs designed to build children into future Stars fans were paramount. When Fred Haney became the Stars' broadcaster in 1946, he convinced Cobb and Reichow to launch a youth program. The result, Fred Haney's Knothole Gang, became hugely popular. Under the plan, youths sixteen and under would receive a membership card that enabled them to attend Saturday games for free. At the game, raffles were conducted for gifts such as whistles, caps, and bats. At some of the giveaway games, Bing Crosby, Gene Autry, Robert Taylor, and Clark Gable helped to distribute the booty. Pregame skills clinics were conducted, and the name of one knothole gang member was selected each Saturday to be the Stars' batboy the following weekend. By 1949 Fred Haney's Knothole Gang numbered six thousand members.

Season ticket holders received umpire horns, large megaphones with which to heckle the arbiters. They became a coveted item for sticky-fingered kids from the nearby neighborhood. Cobb enlisted friends from the entertainment world to help increase interest. Bud Abbott and Lou Costello performed their riotous "Who's on First?" routine between games of several doubleheaders. Joe E. Brown offered comedic shenanigans during pregame skits. Actors and singers brought renditions of "Take Me out to the Ball Game" to Gilmore Field. When the song's composer, Jack Norworth, was recruited to sing alongside Babe Herman, Cobb was startled to hear Norworth confess that he hated baseball.

Players were made part of the fun. When Gus Zernial and Joe Krakauskas became fathers during the 1948 season, the two were paired up in a diaper-folding competition. Krakauskas won and took home a trove of baby products as his prize. On Mother's Day, ladies received free orchids. A Dixieland jazz group, the Holly-hots, was formed to roam the stands and entertain between innings. Barbershop quartets and choirs were booked to enhance the game-night entertainment. A cheerleading squad was assembled to prance atop the dugout roof and coax noise from the Gilmore Field fans.

Reichow had been well acquainted with touring acts that worked the minor-league baseball circuit. He was quick to book them for performances before Stars games. Al Schacht, a former big-league pitcher and coach who had turned his gift for laughter into a traveling comedy act, packed the house. Johnny Price took batting practice while hanging upside down from an A-frame and caught fly balls in the outfield while riding in a jeep.

Then there was Cobb's unending quest for quality. Together with Danny Goodman, he forever searched for new food items that would impress fans. Prizes were put in bags of peanuts. For the 1950 season,

The Stars employed a cheerleading squad to enliven the crowd. They led cheers from atop the dugout roof at Gilmore Field. The cheerleader referred to as Smokey is Kathy Turner on the lower left. *Courtesy of Bill Turner*

mini donuts were added to the concession stand menu. They were baked in a glass oven in full view of the fans and sold six for ten cents for either plain or sugarcoated. Goodman introduced an electrocuted frankfurter that was zapped in a machine and boxed, untouched by human hands.

Following Reichow's resignation, Cobb hired Danny Menendez, the business manager of the Kansas City Blues. Menendez adopted flair. Weekly staff meetings were held to brainstorm and to concoct new ideas. Giveaway nights were staged that sent fans home from Gilmore Field with cars, appliances, food, and for guessing the season attendance, a trip to the World Series with Fred Haney and his wife.

Still, at the core of the Hollywood Stars was the reputation as groundbreakers. During the 1949 season and before they brought out short pants, the Hollywood Stars stirred controversy with another innovation. Among the hurlers on Fred Haney's pitching staff was one who infuriated both Danny Goodman and Bob Cobb. "Jack Salveson was a nice guy and a good pitcher," explained Chuck Stevens, who added, "Jack worked quick. His were quick games."[21] Jack Salveson knew his body. He knew that it would be ninety pitches before his legs would grow tired, his arm would fatigue, the curveball would flatten out and become hitable, and his fastball would lose its zip. To compensate, Salveson liked to work fast. Breakneck fast. He would tell his catchers to be back in the crouch and ready for the next pitch almost as soon as the throw to him had left their fingertips. Salveson sought to keep hitters off balance, to prevent them from getting set, drawing a bead on his release point, and getting a better look at the ball. A studious sort whose glasses provoked the nickname "Senator," Salveson would enlist a teammate in the dugout to keep a count of the number of pitches he had thrown during the game. Salveson's quick work kept teammates alert and on their toes. What made the former New York Giants pitcher successful, however, cost Goodman and Cobb a lot of money. Salveson worked so fast that fans didn't have a chance to go to the concession stands and buy food or drink. His games almost always concluded a half hour sooner than those pitched by anyone else on the Stars' staff.

When Goodman showed Cobb the decline in revenue during games that Salveson pitched, the men hit on an idea: an intermission. They proposed to pause the game for ten minutes during the fifth inning and let the groundskeepers regroom the infield dirt. When the Stars asked permission, George Trautman, head of minor-league baseball, rejected their request. "There is no provision in the playing rules for such an arrangement," Trautman said.[22] Cobb took the team's appeal to the rules committee. On March 3, 1949, the committee met in Sarasota, Florida, to review additions and revisions to the Rules Code for 1950. How to deal with balls that became lost in the ivy-covered walls of Chicago's Wrigley Field and uniformity of mitt specifications were discussed for hours. When Hollywood's request for a ten-minute intermission was raised, the idea was quickly vetoed. "If you want to try it and get the full consent of the Pacific Coast League, that's their headache," said Jim Gallagher, general manager of the Chicago Cubs.[23] Hollywood did and received permission on a trial basis. It worked out so well that by May 1950, even big-league teams had adopted the Hollywood Stars' intermission idea.

The legacy of the Hollywood Stars can be seen in many forms throughout professional baseball today. Perhaps the most recognizable thread to the Stars and Gilmore Field is the brief pause in games to groom the infield. It began at Gilmore Field in 1950. ***Courtesy of Jon Marley***

During the second half of the 1950 season, the Stars were in a battle not just for position but for money—$5,000 in prize money. That was the difference between what the league paid the third- and fourth-place clubs. By August they had fallen into third and were eight-and-a-half games behind first-place Oakland. Fred Haney's team had become so challenged to score runs that ten times during the season the manager employed the squeeze play. Starting the runner from third base as the batter bunted worked as a source of runs. During the final month of the season, Frankie Kelleher regained his batting stroke and went on a tear. In the team's final home game, Kelleher hit two home runs, but only 438 people were in the seats to see it. Kelleher's late surge made veteran observers wonder what might have been had he been this productive all season. The Stars' slugger finished with the best marks of his career—40 home runs, 135 runs batted in, and a .270 batting average. Despite his numbers, the team's goal of a repeat pennant would not be realized. The Stars finished the season in third place, fourteen games out of first. When asked what he planned to do once the season ended, Fred Haney sighed, "Sleep for a month."[24]

23

"THEY'LL SEE A LOT MORE MOVIE STARS THERE"

Car keys in hand, Sam Harris made his way through the kitchen of his Fairfax district home headed toward the family car parked in the driveway. His wife's three teenaged cousins were visiting from Chicago. The hands on the kitchen clock showed it was time to leave and pick the girls up. A daily task that had initially begun as drudgery had grown into routine. The family guests were starstruck. They wanted to be able to return home, tell their friends they had seen movie stars, and have the signatures scribbled in their autograph books to prove it.

Harris had told the girls about Lucy's, a small restaurant on Melrose Boulevard that was across the street from Paramount Studios. It was frequented, he explained, by movie stars. Harris suggested it might be an ideal place to fill their autograph book. The girls had made it part of their routine to spend hours there each day. As the man worked his way toward the front door of the family home, his young son Artie stopped him in his tracks. "Dad," the boy asked, "why don't you just send them to Gilmore Field? They'll see a lot more movie stars there!"[1]

From the day Bob Cobb telephoned several friends in the motion picture industry to invite them to invest in a baseball team, Hollywood's entertainment elite were interwoven into the fabric of the Hollywood Stars. The industry's biggest names—actors and actresses, directors and producers, singers and songwriters—were, like most Americans of the day, avid baseball fans. From the very first afternoon the Hollywood Stars played in Gilmore Field, the stars of the big screen, radio, and recordings made the local ball club their team of choice. They eagerly bought season tickets. The biggest names in Tinseltown cheered, heckled, and shouted displeasure from their box seats, just like fans from every walk of life. The giants of filmdom were as rabid in their admiration for Hollywood Stars players as the rest of America was for them. It was a reality that would impact Maria Stevens before she ever arrived in Los Angeles.

For the Stevenses the month of July 1948 had been a baseball roller-coaster ride. The family suffered extreme highs and discouraging lows. Not but a few days after her husband, Chuck, had ripped a double, one of only three hits the St. Louis Browns had managed off the Cleveland Indians' pitching ace Bob Feller, the Stevens household was made topsy-turvy. The Browns sold Chuck's contract to their farm team at San Antonio. The first baseman cried "raw deal," and insisted he would not accept the assignment. He had been batting .261 and argued, "I think I'm good enough to play major-league ball."[2] For three weeks Stevens stuck to his word. Then, on August 20, elation erupted in the Stevens household. The Hollywood Stars had bought the contract of the Southern California resident. While Chuck hurried to join his new ball club, Maria packed up their possessions and with their young daughter, Randall, boarded a train for Los Angeles. On the journey one passenger took particular delight in playing with the young girl. It was not until the train arrived at Union Station in Los Angeles that the passenger was recognized as the award-winning actor Spencer Tracy.

Once at Gilmore Field, Stevens became immersed in celebrity. Joe E. Brown and Pat O'Brien were among the first to welcome the new first baseman to the Stars. The Stevenses became regular diners at the popular Musso and Frank Grill. With the area of the diamond he patrolled just twenty-four feet from the first row of seats in Gilmore Field, Stevens conversed regularly with the box holders. "We got a young guy on third tonight whose arm is a little wild. Be careful," he said to the actor Jimmy Durante one night.[3] A few innings later, an errant throw sailed beyond Stevens's reach and struck the actor just as he was about to take a bite from a hot dog. Durante spent the rest of the game with bright yellow mustard stains all over his shirt. If Stevens heard a long "hello" spoken in a theatrical sounding voice, he didn't have to look to know that Frank Lovejoy was in his box. "Are you gonna hit any home runs tonight?" Lovejoy liked to ask.[4] Stevens's chats with one fan in particular—Jimmy

Stewart—grew into friendship. The first baseman called the film star "the General" long before the nickname stuck. Stevens accepted invitations from Stewart to golf. The first baseman and his wife were dinner guests in the Stewart home and also those of Cyd Charisse and Tony Martin, Frank Lovejoy and Joan Banks, and also the Bing Crosbys.

The Hollywood Stars' reputation nationally was affixed to its celebrity following. Some sports columnists in New York chided the Gilmore Field throng as being there only to be seen. While some, mostly lesser-known entertainers certainly were, such claims were far from the truth, at least where the big-name celebrities were concerned. The box office stars who frequented Gilmore Field were ravenous fans and ardent supporters of the Hollywood Stars. On many nights the very first fans in the ballpark were the famous husband-wife comedy duo George Burns and Gracie Allen, who would quietly take in batting practice from their box. Ronald Reagan rarely missed a game, and only his busy acting schedule could keep Humphrey Bogart away from Gilmore Field. "Baseball, it's my game," Bogart once said in a commercial, adding famously, "A hot dog at the game beats roast beef at the Ritz."[5] Alongside the famous often sat the infamous. The gangster Mickey Cohen enjoyed seats behind the Stars dugout. Players were told to smile politely, wave, and not shout back if Cohen or his bodyguards heckled them.

Chuck Stevens was far from the only Hollywood player to journey into Beverly Hills, Brentwood, or Bel Air to dine in the home of a movie star. Desi Arnaz and Ronald Reagan were among many entertainers who socialized with Stars players. During breaks from their busy filming schedules, Virginia Mayo and her husband, Michael O'Shea, enjoyed entertaining Stars pitcher George O'Donnell and his wife. It was not uncommon for Fred Haney's young grandchildren to scamper into their grandfather's den and find him "singing up a storm," with William Frawley or Bing Crosby.[6]

Between recording sessions or concerts, the popular singer Buddy Clark was a regular at Gilmore Field. Late in the 1949 season, Clark extended a dinner invitation to his two favorite players—Oakland second baseman Billy Martin and Hollywood shortstop George Genovese. Tragically, Clark was killed in a plane crash only forty-eight hours before the arranged get-together was to have taken place.

So rabid were Hollywood's motion picture fans that in 1939, when the Stars' Bill Cissell was fined $200 by the league for punching a sportswriter, Gary Cooper, George Raft, Barbara Stanwyck, Robert Taylor, and four film directors pitched in to pay the fine. When the club held its first bat day and gave away five thousand free Louisville Sluggers to children, Clark Gable, Gene Autry, Carol Lombard, Bing Crosby, and Barbara Stanwyck helped to pass out the souvenirs. Ronald Reagan and Mickey Rooney did guest stints calling action on radio broadcasts of Stars games. When a Little League team was recognized and one of its members awarded a new bicycle, the prize could not be found. A search found Groucho Marx gleefully riding in circles on the ballpark concourse.

During the 1950 season, KTTV arranged with Gail Patrick to host a thirty-minute interview show. It aired live after Stars telecasts on Wednesdays and Sundays. From her box seat on the first-base side of the ballpark, Patrick would conduct live interviews with players. One memorable show involved popular Angels first baseman Chuck Connors performing an ad-lib recitation of "Casey at the Bat." Patrick's show became popular and earned the actress considerable praise.

There were few celebrities more ardent in their support of the Stars than Patrick. Even after her divorce from Bob Cobb, she retained her box seat next to the Stars dugout. Patrick was hailed by sportswriters, fans, players, and their wives as the "first lady of baseball." At each game she clutched twenty-two rabbits' feet, one for each player. When it came their turn to prepare to bat, the more superstitious players would veer toward Patrick and rub the rabbits' feet for good luck. Patrick was also known for "parties, parties, parties," said the daughter of one Hollywood pitcher.[7] Together with her third husband, literary agent Cornwell Jackson, Patrick lived on a seven-acre gated estate in the La Brea Terrace area of Los Angeles. The couple hosted swim parties and barbeques for the players and their wives. It was not uncommon for players to receive a letter from Gail and Corny inviting them to a swim and dinner. "Bring your own Bikinis. We'll furnish the towels and thc Lux," Patrick would sign off.[8] Her fervent support was recognized following the 1939 season, when one writer actually gave Patrick his vote for Pacific Coast League Most Valuable Player.

Fred Haney's coach, Johnny Fitzpatrick, was almost always in a happier-than-usual mood whenever the comics George Burns, Groucho Marx, and Phil Silvers were in the ballpark. Fitzpatrick was a man who loved a good cigar. The three funnymen were quick to offer one whenever they were greeted by the coach. Players chided Fitzpatrick that he rarely, if ever, had to purchase a cigar between April and September thanks to the three comedians.

Admiration swung both ways. As eager as the celebrities were to entertain Stars players, the players liked to show appreciation to their luminary fans. One such occasion came on the sixty-sixth birthday of the silent film star William Farnum. Players surprised the star of 145 motion pictures with a large cake and song when he arrived at Gilmore Field.

Just which of Tinseltown's shining stars was its biggest baseball fan? That would likely depend upon which publication and entertainment columnist you read. Their consensus narrowed the field to three—Joe E. Brown, George Raft, and William Frawley. All three were regulars at Gilmore Field. None could say no to any request that came from the club. Frawley in private life was a gruff, sarcastic character. He was a prolific supporting actor who would perform in as many as eight films a year. There was no greater priority in his life, however, than baseball. A native New Yorker, Frawley had it written into his contract with Paramount Pictures that he could not be made to rehearse or shoot if the New York Yankees were playing in the World Series. When they were, he usually traveled to the games. During the Stars' first season under the Cobb ownership group, Frawley set up a Hollywood Stars Hall of Fame. He constructed and installed a decorative cabinet in the concourse area of Gilmore Field. Inside he placed the photograph of the Stars player who was voted Most Valuable Player of the season.

For all of his enthusiasm for the Stars and eagerness to help the ball club, Bill Frawley carried a demon that could bring Bob Cobb's blood to a boil: the bottle. Frawley's drinking caused problems for his acting career, and in 1941 it caused a rift in his association with the Hollywood Stars. During the final days of the 1941 season, a story broke in the *Detroit Times* that claimed Hall of Fame catcher Mickey Cochrane was to be named both manager and president of the Hollywood Stars. Cobb, Victor Ford Collins, and Oscar Reichow were caught completely off guard. Each told reporters there was no truth to the idea. Collins and Reichow investigated and found the source of the report was Frawley. The actor had apparently consumed one too many at an event at which Cochrane was present. Frawley extended the job offer and promised a handsome salary as well. Reichow sternly declared to reporters that Frawley had no authority to make any job offer on behalf of the Hollywood ball club, and the matter died.

Frawley was one of a very few celebrity supporters to overstep his bounds. George Raft drew the ire of some of the Stars' players when they learned that the actor would bet against them in his gambling group in the left-field grandstands. Dennis O'Keefe was forgiven for the occasional sedition. The star of *Follow the Sun* was a good friend of San Francisco Seals manager Lefty O'Doul and would don a Seals uniform and pitch batting practice to O'Doul's players whenever San Francisco came to town.

Mixing with entertainment greats had an intoxicating affect, and not just on the ball players. Their wives came to enjoy it, too. Some wrote home in almost giddy tones, telling family and friends about their conversations at the ballpark with Ginger Rogers or that Gail Patrick had fussed over and bounced their young child on her lap during a game. It was the sort of experience one might find difficult to give up. In the middle of a game in 1951, with her husband on the mound pitching, Donna Shallock was summoned to the Stars office. Fred Haney ducked in between innings and broke the news that her husband, Art, had just been purchased by the New York Yankees. "Who the hell are the New York Yankees? I'm not going!" she shouted as she left the room in a huff.[9]

Younger players and those who were new to the team were generally in awe of the celebrity fans. On joining the ball club, Dale Long spent a few nights in a hotel before he was able to find and move into an apartment. As he passed the hotel swimming pool one afternoon, he was approached by an attractive woman who asked if she could get a ticket to the evening's game. The requester was a young actress who had just signed her first contract with Twentieth Century Fox: Mitzi Gaynor. Rookies taking part in their first spring training would be awestruck by the sight of the renowned band leader Tommy Dorsey trotting onto the field in a Hollywood Stars uniform to take throws at first base. The popular singer Nat King Cole liked to do the same. Few who were there will ever forget how hard they laughed and slapped their thighs the day comic Jerry Lewis suited up and went through a training session with the Stars.

Then there were the girls. Glamorous box office stars dotted the crowd every night. A player might look up and do a double take, realizing it was indeed Susan Hayward who was hanging over the front of box 702. Teen boys had trouble concentrating on the game with Bing Crosby's wife, Dixie Lee, seated nearby. Aspiring actresses and models flocked in the hope they might be noticed by the many directors, producers, and casting directors who were fans. Young players became smitten. It didn't take long before Stars third baseman Jim Baxes was squiring attractive blonde actress Barbara Payton. "They'd see these lush-looking babes and cry, 'We've made the big leagues!'" laughed center fielder Gail Henley about his younger teammates.[10]

In time tourists, particularly those who were baseball fans, made Gilmore Field a place to visit on their vacation. Articles in newspapers all across the country and in the *Sporting News* had painted the enticing picture of the Stars ballpark as an ideal place to see a movie star. For many, some players included, the baseball setting at Beverly Boulevard, West Third Street, and Gardner Street was a place of fantasy. Yankee Stadium had its grandeur, Fenway Park evoked charm, but Gilmore Field offered unquestionably the most unique baseball environment anywhere in America.

24

"THIS IS MAJOR CLASS"

The camera shutters clicked. Bursts of light accompanied the popping of flashbulbs. Commotion began in earnest once Clarence "Pants" Rowland raised his right arm and waved papers. In the hand of the Pacific Coast League president was a list of demands his team owners had made to the commissioner of baseball. If each point was not agreed to, Rowland stressed, the men would withdraw their league from Organized Baseball, go outlaw, and declare it a third major league. "We have had the ambition for years to become a third big league," Bob Cobb said to a local sportswriter. "That is a goal quite possible to reach in the not-too-distant future."[1]

The September 1951 meeting represented the Pacific Coast League's fifth attempt to join the major leagues, a quest that had begun shortly after the end of World War II. Following the 1945 season, the Pacific Coast League applied to bring its eight clubs into the major leagues. On March 1, 1946, a hearing on the matter was held by a committee made up of general managers from American and National League clubs.

To many it seemed inevitable that the major leagues would plant a team or teams on the West Coast. No big-league club made its home farther west than St. Louis. In 1941 Donald L. Barnes, owner of the St. Louis Browns, first floated the idea of moving his ball club to Los Angeles. When Barnes arrived in the city in October, rumors began to fly. The head of a successful investment firm, Barnes simply smiled and said he was in Southern California to "enjoy the splendid climate."[2]

However, there was more to Barnes's visit than simple tourism. His Browns had been losing money for quite some time. Secretly, Barnes had been laying the groundwork to bring his American League club to Los Angeles for more than a year. Following the 1941 season, he had met privately with P. K. Wrigley and offered $1 million to buy the Los Angeles Angels and his ballpark, Wrigley Field. Bill DeWitt, general manager of the Browns, had clued the American League's schedule maker to his boss's actions. On December 6, sportscaster Bill Stern announced on his national NBC radio program that "one of the biggest baseball stories in twenty-five years" would break on "next Tuesday and concern an important city in the Pacific Coast League."[3] But the very next day, on December 7, 1941, Barnes's dream was ended by Japan's attack on Pearl Harbor. Two days later Barnes's plan was brought to a meeting of American League club owners in Chicago. For three hours the request was discussed. Barnes laid out how one of the biggest obstacles of a team in Los Angeles—travel issues—would be overcome. He displayed timetables and explained that a team could leave Chicago by train at 6:00 p.m. on a Sunday and be in Los Angeles by Tuesday morning. After playing games Tuesday, Wednesday, and Thursday, the club could be back in Chicago in time for a Saturday game. The ensuing vote of American League team owners was unanimous. Barnes's request was rejected. One baseball executive said the decision had much to do with world conditions but would likely be brought up again once the war had ended.

When the war ended, the Pacific Coast League worked to prevent the loss of its biggest market. The league asked a joint committee of big-league general managers on March 18, 1946, to consider all eight of its clubs for addition to the major leagues. The hearing ended with the promise of a thorough evaluation of the proposal. Throughout the summer, baseball's new commissioner, Albert "Happy" Chandler, visited PCL cities. He queried city leaders and business executives, inspected the ballparks, and took in games. On July 21, the commissioner spent the day with Bob Cobb, who squired Chandler along with the prolific film director David Butler before they watched the Stars take on the San Francisco Seals. Weeks later Bing Crosby boasted, "A third major league is just around the corner. Towns like Los Angeles, San Francisco, Oakland, and Seattle are potential gold mines."[4] In the middle of the 1946 World Series, the Pacific Coast League's enthusiasm was burst when gossip columnist Louella Parsons broke the news that movie mogul Louis B. Mayer was trying to buy a major-league team and move it to Los Angeles. In its October 16, 1946, edition, the *Sporting News* reported the St. Louis Cardinals to be that team. Vincent X. Flaherty, a sports columnist for the *Los Angeles Examiner*, served as Mayer's front man. Flaherty met with Happy Chandler, conducted a clandestine meeting with the owner of the Cardinals, and learned what steps the St. Louis Browns had taken in 1941 to try to move west. After the Cardinals won the 1946 World Series, the idea of relocation died. Reports surfaced that the Cardinals' owner had put a $3 million price tag on his ball club.

In December 1946 baseball's annual winter convention brought the game's executives and managers to Los Angeles. When the meetings ended, the city was still without a major-league team. The St. Louis Cardinals were not sold and the Pacific Coast League's application for major-league status was given a thumbs-down. The league received a list of reasons, the biggest of which was inadequate ballparks. Aside from Wrigley Field, none met major-league standards. The small parks meant smaller ticket revenues, which would make it difficult for a team to meet big-league cost obligations.

During the summer of 1947, the Pacific Coast League took another swing. "We are more enthusiastic than ever," Rowland declared, while conceding it might be three years before stadiums were renovated to meet standards.[5] Rather than the commissioner, baseball dispatched a committee to evaluate the idea. Ford Frick, president of the National League; Will Harridge, president of the American League; Frank McKinney, co-owner of the Pittsburgh Pirates; and Leslie O'Connor, general manager of the Chicago White Sox, toured the Pacific Coast League cities. During their visits it was pointed out that the Pacific Coast League had outdrawn the other top minor leagues, the American Association, and International League combined. Books were opened and finances shared. When the group arrived in San Francisco, Seals manager Lefty O'Doul declared, "This is major class."[6]

During baseball's fact-finding effort, the Pacific Coast League was caught completely off guard by a pronouncement from a Los Angeles politician. Leonard Roach, a member of the county board of supervisors, announced at a civic luncheon at the Hotel Biltmore that he had been meeting secretly with major-league club owners and had offered use of the Los Angeles Coliseum, a giant seventy-seven-thousand-seat oblong-configured stadium that was home to football and track and field but not

Cobb had powerful friends. He enlisted the help of California governor Earl Warren to try and boost the Pacific Coast League's quest for major-league status. Behind Warren in Cobb's Gilmore Field box is actor Bill Frawley. ***Courtesy of the Bob Cobb Family Collection***

designed for baseball. "I predict Los Angeles will have major league baseball in 1948," Roach told the gathering. He was quick to add, "I can assure you the Pacific Coast League will never attain major league status."[7]

When baseball convened its annual Winter Meetings at the McAllister Hotel in Miami, Victor Ford Collins introduced the Pacific Major League Agreement. The proposal to change the PCL to the Pacific Major League was first put to the forty-nine minor leagues for a vote. Bylaws required an approval of three fourths. The Pacific Coast League's quest fell short by just seven votes.

Before leaving for Miami, Happy Chandler had told reporters he would introduce a proposal for expansion. Under Chandler's idea, the American and National leagues would each add two teams to grow from eight to ten clubs. Prescott Sullivan of the *San Francisco Examiner* wrote that the San Francisco Seals, Oakland Oaks, Los Angeles Angels, and Hollywood Stars were the four ball clubs Chandler had in mind. The plan,

Sullivan wrote, was likely to be approved. But once all of the convention business had been conducted, neither Chandler's plan nor the relocation of a team to the Los Angeles Coliseum had come to fruition.

Whenever talk of a third major league arose, the question of talent shot to the forefront. "Why, there ain't enough major league ballplayers for three leagues," Babe Ruth once said about expansion, adding, "Who'd they use?"[8] The charge made Pacific Coast League team owners bristle. The minor-league draft had long been a bone of contention with the men. Under baseball rules, a player who had been with a minor-league club for four years was available to be drafted by major-league clubs. The fee for selecting a player was a fixed price of $10,000.

Men such as Bob Cobb argued that the draft robbed them of young players they had signed. Just as a player was becoming productive, he became eligible for the draft. Such was the case of Tod Davis, the touted shortstop Hollywood had signed as a teenager, only to subsequently lose in the draft to the Philadelphia Athletics. Brick Laws, who owned the Oakland Oaks, argued that the draft fee was unfair. He pointed out that he had purchased George Metkovich for $25,000 then later lost him in the draft for $10,000. Many in the Pacific Coast League argued that if their players were not subject to the draft, they could build teams that were better able to compete in the major leagues. On several occasions the Pacific Coast League offered proposals to change the draft rules. During the 1947 Winter Meetings they suggested the years of service be changed from four to six and that the selection price be increased from $10,000 to $25,000. The idea was rejected.

For four successive seasons following the war, Hollywood drew more than a half million fans. The attendance bonanza swelled the Stars' coffers. True to the board's commitment, money was poured into improvements to Gilmore Field. Better lighting was installed. The field was resodded. Bigger still, Bob Cobb hired architects to devise a way to expand the ballpark's seating capacity in order to boost the club's chances of joining the major leagues.

The initial idea called for extending the third-base side of the stands an additional one hundred feet. Cobb explained that this would add 260 box seats and 1,000 grandstand seats with backrests. Next, he proposed construction of steel bleachers behind the right-field fence. The bleachers would increase capacity by 4,000 and bring Gilmore Field's total seating capacity to 17,000.

Cobb was brimming with enthusiasm when he took the idea into Earl Gilmore's Fairfax Avenue office. He could not, however, have picked a worse time to present such a proposal. Gilmore's business was under assault from several directions. Competitors had undercut his gasoline prices. Losses had him in negotiations to sell a large portion of his oil business. Gilmore had developed plans to shift his business emphasis to oil exploration in Utah, Colorado, and New Mexico and to also launch a land development company. Added to Earl Gilmore's troubles was an assault from the city. After years of feuding, Los Angeles succeeded in annexing a portion of Gilmore's property. The move raised both Earl Gilmore's ire and his annual tax bill. Gilmore's move into land development made the onetime oil mogul reconsider use of his land. Offers came, some for small portions and others for larger parcels. Gilmore listened and pondered. When the football Rams relocated from Cleveland, Gilmore worked aggressively to make his stadium the team's home field. After the team chose to play instead in the Coliseum, Gilmore accepted the inevitable: that the onetime Olympic stadium would become the region's preferred outdoor sport and entertainment venue. Earl Gilmore thus accepted a development proposal and in 1952 demolished Gilmore Stadium.

A larger ballpark was key to the Hollywood Stars becoming part of the major leagues. Earl Gilmore politely listened to Bob Cobb's pitch to expand Gilmore Stadium. He periodically raised his black horn-rimmed glasses to rub his eyes. Throughout their conversation, Gilmore quietly calculated construction costs and return figures in his head. He estimated the price to build the addition to the ballpark would come to $250,000. Considering what the Stars were drawing and the 10 percent he received from each ticket sold, Gilmore determined it would take twenty-five years to get his money back. Once Cobb finished, Gilmore gave him a quick answer—no. Cobb was surprised at the pithiness. Retort and elaboration were not just fruitless but pointless. Cobb left the meeting frustrated and confused. It took time before clarity returned. Bob Cobb recognized that if his ball club were to survive, an entirely new ballpark would be required, and it would have to be in a completely different location.

By 1951 the idea of a major-league team in Los Angeles continued to gather steam. No region of the country was growing at a greater rate. The city boasted a population of 1.9 million. More than 4 million people lived in the county. P. K. Wrigley, owner of the Angels and the Chicago Cubs, said it was inevitable that the Pacific Coast League would gain major-league status. Lou Perini, the owner of the Boston Braves, favored adding two California teams to the American and National leagues. "Within twenty-five years, California will have more people than any state in the USA. Can the major leagues afford to stand still?" he asked.[9]

Bob Cobb's hope of gaining big-league stature may have been buoyed during the spring of 1951, when the Hollywood Stars became the first minor-league team to win two out of three exhibition games from the mighty New York Yankees. It was the first time the Yankees had trained in California. During one of the three mid-March games, an overflow crowd to see the World Series champions taxed the capacity of Gilmore Field. Joe DiMaggio was about to embark on his final big-league season, while a touted nineteen-year-old, Mickey Mantle, was on the cusp of his first. What role the Stars' success might add to the club's quest to join the big leagues was not stated. However, in the eyes of *Los Angeles Times* columnist Braven Dyer, beating the Yankees "might make the Twinks favorites for the Pacific Coast League crown."[10]

When Fred Haney's men began the 1951 season, change had come to the Stars clubhouse. Hollywood's twenty-year association agreement with the Brooklyn Dodgers had ended after just two. During the off-season, a power struggle had seen Branch Rickey pushed out of his role with the Brooklyn club. By late November Rickey was hired to run the Pittsburgh Pirates. Hollywood would follow him.

Bob Cobb's apprehensions about Rickey were now a thing of the past. The men had become great friends. Only a month before Rickey's change of teams, he and Cobb had been hunting on the Matt Tschirgi ranch southeast of Billings, Montana. "If the Old Man told me to jump off the roof of a twenty-story building, I'd do it in a second because I know he'd have made arrangements for me to land safely," Cobb said. "I hope I'm doing business with him forever."[11]

After Rickey's change of teams, Cobb notified Rickey's replacement, E. J. "Buzzie" Bavasi, of Hollywood's wish to end its arrangement with the Dodgers. Bavasi took a firm stance. The men negotiated and struck a deal that granted Hollywood's release from the agreement in exchange for several player contracts—eleven players in all. Among those who would strictly wear Dodgers colors in the future were three whom Hollywood's top scout, Rosey Gilhousen, had signed: Norm Sherry, Eddie Moore, and Gar Myers.

To observers who watched spring training, however, little had changed. Chuck Stevens and Gene Handley were beginning their fourth seasons. George Genovese had been bought back from Washington and Lou Stringer from Boston. In the outfield Frankie Kelleher was about to start his seventh season with the Stars, while George Smees and Ed Sauer returned for a second go-around. Jack Salveson, Art Shallock, and Pinky Woods were veterans on the pitching staff. Vic Lombardi was the lone starting pitcher to arrive via the Pittsburgh affiliation.

The significant newcomer was one who would turn into an unexpected surprise: Johnny Lindell. In the final weeks of the 1950 season, Haney traded Glen Moulder to the St. Louis Cardinals for Lindell. Lindell had been a heralded high school athlete at Arcadia High near Pasadena. He signed with the New York Yankees and reached the big leagues in 1941. When Joe DiMaggio entered the military in 1943, Lindell became a regular in the Yankees outfield and an All-Star. One year later, in 1944, he drove in 103 runs and batted .300.

DiMaggio's return from the war had pushed Lindell to the bench. The Yankees repeatedly offered him in trade but found no takers. When he stepped in for players who were injured, like Charlie Keller in 1947, Lindell played well. In 1949, though, Lindell suffered torn cartilage in his left knee during a collision at second base in a game with the Athletics in late May. In the early months of the 1950 season, Lindell struggled. Casey Stengel was now the Yankees' manager, and Lindell was not part of his plans. On May 17, Lindell was sold to the St. Louis Cardinals for $10,000. He was inserted in left field but hit a paltry .186 in 36 games, then was sent to the minor leagues. That's when Fred Haney pounced.

It was Haney's hope that Lindell might recapture his swing and that his bat would give the Stars a spark. But not long after he joined the Stars, Lindell approached his manager about a different role. He wanted to pitch. Lindell was originally signed by the Yankees as a pitcher. When he didn't throw hard, he was made an outfielder. Now, however, velocity would not be a factor. Lindell shared with Haney that he had been working on a knuckleball. During the final week of the 1950 season, Haney gave Lindell his chance. The result was remarkable. The veteran pitched a four-hitter. In the bottom of the eighth inning, Lindell hit Max West. An error by Jim Baxes allowed West to reach third base. West then scored when one of Lindell's knucklers got away from Cliff Dapper. Hollywood lost, 1–0, to San Diego.

By the time spring training began in February 1951, Haney had embraced the idea of Lindell as a starting pitcher. It was evidenced simply by the uniform he wore. During workouts, Haney had the pitchers wear white uniforms and clad the position players in gray. Lindell was issued whites. More proof that pitching was his future came when Hollywood's starting pitchers were grouped together for a publicity photo with RKO actress Mala Powers. One of the players in the photo was Johnny Lindell.

Lindell embraced his new role once the exhibition games began. He drew a start and pitched three scoreless innings against the Portland Beavers. When his former teammates, the New York Yankees, rolled into town, Lindell took added motivation to the mound in their exhibition meeting. Haney brought Lindell on in the sixth inning of a scoreless tie. For three innings, the Yankees flailed in frustration at their former mate's flutterball. In the ninth inning, an error put a man aboard. Lindell then walked a batter, and Cliff Mapes belted a double that scored the first two runs of the game. Phil Rizzuto then sent one of Lindell's floaters into the parking lot beyond the left-field fence. The Yankees won, 5–1.

Lindell pitched five innings of one-hit ball in an exhibition game against the White Sox, then drew the starting assignment in the first doubleheader of the season in Oakland. In the fourth inning, he left the game complaining of soreness in his right shoulder. It was an ailment that would keep Lindell out of action for the next three weeks.

His was not the only significant injury to affect the team. Frankie Kelleher developed a case of shin splints. Mike Sandlock suffered an injured hand. Bob Chesnes had a sore elbow. Without key players, Hollywood stumbled from the gate. By the end of the first month, the Stars were stuck in seventh place, well off the pace of the league's frontrunners.

May brought changes. Haney decided to put a bat back in Lindell's hands and told him that in games he did not pitch he would play right field against left-handed pitchers. To boost the pitching staff, Haney traded Ed Sauer to San Diego to get Roy Welmaker, a sixteen-game winner during the 1950 season. Welmaker became the first Black player on the Stars. The moves helped change the team's fortunes. When Frankie Kelleher hit three home runs in a game against the Angels, the feat sparked a six-game win streak that vaulted Hollywood into third place. Three weeks later the Stars were in second, only two games behind first-place Seattle.

Throughout the summer the specter of change loomed over the Hollywood Stars. Players were hearing the talk and reading newspaper accounts of the possibility of a Pacific Coast League jump into the big leagues. On July 30, the talk reached its highest level. Rather than the subject of a baseball committee, the concept was put before the United States Congress. The House Subcommittee on Monopoly Power launched hearings into several stated concerns about baseball. On the first day of questioning, Representative Patrick J. Hillings of California asked Hall of Fame outfielder Ty Cobb why the Pacific Coast League couldn't gain major-league status. The room was packed for Cobb's testimony. The sixty-four-year-old struggled to hear. He cupped a hand to his right ear, skirted the question, then finally acknowledged, "There are men that are more qualified."[12]

Ford Frick, president of the National League, followed Cobb and was harangued by the committee's chairman, Emanuel Celler (D-NY). "You can't keep this complete hold on major league status," Celler railed. When the questioning of Frick concluded, Celler said, "I would say that you and your colleagues are so inflicted with the idea of status quo that you are like people who ride in railroad cars backwards, you only see things after they have passed you by."[13]

While baseball's leaders were being peppered by Congress, the Pacific Coast League's team owners were crafting another plan of attack on the big leagues. But their two-day meeting became embroiled in contention and animosity. Paul Fagan, the new owner of the San Francisco Seals, was enraged by the repeated rebuffs from the major leagues. He urged his fellow club owners to withdraw from Organized Baseball immediately and operate as an independent league. Bob Cobb disagreed. "To break away would be suicidal at this time," he countered.[14] Cobb urged that the league concentrate its effort solely on gaining draft relief. The idea calmed Fagan, who agreed that draft relief was essential. Without it, he said, "I'll lock up Seals Stadium, and that's definite."[15] The question was how best to achieve it. Fagan returned to his belief in secession. He insisted that it was the best way for the league to get what it wanted.

The decision on whether to withdraw from the National Association was put to a vote. San Francisco, Oakland, Portland, and Sacramento were the ayes. Los Angeles, Hollywood, Seattle, and San Diego dissented. The four-four split evoked more discussion. A series of demands was agreed to. First, the men wanted the five major-league clubs that trained in California to cease playing exhibition games within a week of the start of the Pacific Coast League season. They wanted to put a stop to the daily radio broadcasts of major-league games into Pacific Coast League cities. The men felt those broadcasts hurt attendance. Their third demand was to exempt the Pacific Coast League from the draft of minor-league players. After much discussion it was decided not to press once more for major-league status. "Draft relief will be our first step toward becoming a major league," explained Oakland Oaks owner Brick Laws. "Given relief from the draft and an opportunity to build up an inventory of players, we could reach major league standards in a few years," San Diego Padres president Bill Starr elaborated.[16]

While the owners jockeyed to chart a successful course for the Pacific Coast League, the 1951 pennant pursuit whittled down to just two teams—the Seattle Rainiers and Hollywood Stars. Having climbed from seventh to second by the end of June, the Stars became firmly entrenched in the position but were unable to pare away Seattle's lead through the second half of the season. In September voting was announced for the Most Valuable Player Award. Seattle's Jim Rivera was the runaway winner. Johnny Lindell finished fourth, on the strength of 12 wins on the mound and a .292 batting average with 9 home runs. The Stars' knuckleball sensation was named the team's MVP and its most popular player. Fans showered the former Yankee with gifts on a night of tribute.

The final standings launched a four-team Shaughnessy playoff that involved Seattle, Hollywood, Portland, and Los Angeles. The Stars polished off Portland with ease. Seattle did the same with Los Angeles. The results pushed Hollywood into the Governor's Cup title series for the second time in three seasons. After Hollywood lost the first game of the best of five final, Johnny Lindell pitched them to a 4–1 win in game two. A thrilling end to game four saw Frankie Kelleher try to score from second base on a single in the bottom of the ninth and jar the ball loose from the Seattle catcher to produce a 4–3 win that forced a deciding fifth game.

Haney started Lindell on two days' rest. The thirty-four-year-old veteran pitched well through five innings and Hollywood led, 2–1. In the sixth inning, however, Seattle erupted. After a triple, a walk, and three singles, the Rainiers had scored four runs. Haney went to his bullpen, but no matter whom he brought to the mound, they could not quell the Seattle uprising. The Rainiers claimed the crown with a 9–2 triumph.

Once pennant revelry subsided, the men at the helm of the eight Pacific Coast League clubs turned their attention to the demands they would make at the Winter Meetings. During a special meeting, the men agreed with Bob Cobb's plan. They voted unanimously to press for draft relief with the threat to withdraw the Pacific Coast League from Organized Baseball if it was not given. Pants Rowland, the PCL president, triumphantly waved the papers that declared the league's position. Rowland's gesture made for impactful pictures.

Five weeks after the vote, Ford Frick, the new baseball commissioner, floated a plan for consideration by several high-ranking baseball men. Following the World Series, Frick held a six-hour meeting of the Major-Minor League Council. Frick proposed creation of an "open" classification for minor leagues that aspire to join the major leagues. Criteria were laid out for major and open classification clubs. Individual cities could not apply, only leagues. A league that sought major-league classification must have a population of 15 million. Each of its ballparks must have a seating capacity of 25,000. The league's member clubs would be required to have had a combined attendance of 3.5 million for three years prior to making its application.

At the Winter Meetings, the Pacific Coast League received good news at every turn. George Weiss, the New York Yankees' general manager, agreed to end his team's radio arrangements with the Mutual and Liberty networks that sent "Game of the Day" broadcasts into Pacific Coast League markets. The minor-league president adopted Frick's idea of a new open classification, the highest level of the minor leagues. It was promptly granted to the Pacific Coast League. An idea formulated by Victor Ford Collins to change draft rules was presented and adopted. It left the decision of draft eligibility up to the players. Separate contracts, one yellow and one white, would be offered. Players who did not wish to be drafted could sign a contract that was printed on yellow paper and expressed their draft declaration. If the player wished to be made available for the draft, he would be given a contract that was printed on white paper and contained a clause expressing his intentions. The proposal was agreed to by the Pacific Coast League and adopted by the National Association.

Three days after the Winter Meetings concluded, Frick convened a meeting of the American and National leagues at the Commodore Hotel in New York City. His proposed criteria for major and open classification leagues was agreed to, as were the requirements for promotion from an open-classification league to major-league status. "It is wonderful that the majors have seen fit to grant us the right to take a great step in the right direction," said a beaming Bob Cobb.[17]

Not all were impressed with baseball's action. Red Smith of the *New York Herald Tribune* wrote of Frick's move, "Its purpose is to rid Californians of the inferiority complex which characterizes all of them." Then Smith added an unmistakable dig at Bob Cobb: "especially those at the corner of Hollywood and Vine."[18]

25

"A FRANKENSTEIN WHICH MAY EAT ITS OWN"

The noise, or lack of it, was the first clue. That he didn't hear the buzz of a large crowd puzzled Bill Rivera. The Stars' new publicity director had pushed open the door to the team's office prepared to hear the roar of a big crowd and encounter the flurry that came with one. Instead, he was struck by the sparse number of people on the Gilmore Field concourse. By the time Rivera had reached the press box, he was in disbelief. In a matter of moments, the public address system would switch on and Jim Healy's voice would announce the starting lineups. When Healy reached the ninth and final spot in the Stars' batting order, the name of the focal point of the evening would burst from the loudspeakers. Rivera had telephoned the daily newspapers and all of the radio stations with the tip that Fred Haney planned to send Paul Pettit to the mound to pitch for Hollywood for the first time. The onetime area high school wunderkind was certain to pack Gilmore Field, or so Rivera felt. That it hadn't left the publicist stunned. As the umpires strode toward home plate to prepare for the start of the game, almost two-thirds of Gilmore Field's seats were empty.

Throughout the game Rivera remained puzzled. Here was Pettit, now a Pittsburgh Pirates prospect assigned to Hollywood, pitching against the defending Pacific Coast League champs. It was a Friday night. All the ingredients were in place for a surefire sellout. But where was everybody? Yes, the weather was chilly, but not in his wildest dreams did Rivera think that only 2,248 fans would come out to see the ballyhooed

$100,000 bonus baby pitch the Stars to a 5–3 win. It was not until several days later that Rivera, Bob Cobb, Victor Ford Collins, Fred Haney, and everyone else who scratched his head in bemusement at the smallish turnstile count learned the reason for it: television. In a region with 1,232,000 television sets, almost half of them on the evening of April 4, 1952, had been tuned to channel 9 to watch Paul Pettit make his Hollywood Stars debut. The revelation would leave executives at every level of baseball stunned. It was a viewership number almost equal to the 552,000 who regularly watched the most popular show on television, Milton Berle's *Texaco Star Theater*, on channel 4 each Tuesday night.

No team at any level of baseball, major or minor league, had embraced the burgeoning new medium of television like the Hollywood Stars. In May 1939 the meeting of Princeton and Columbia universities became the first baseball game ever to be televised. Three months later the same station that aired the college game, New York's WNBC, carried the Brooklyn Dodgers game against the Cincinnati Reds from Ebbets Field. It was the first television broadcast of a major-league game. Eight months after the Dodgers telecast on Opening Day of the 1940 Pacific Coast League season, an experimental Los Angeles TV station, KHJ, wheeled cameras into Gilmore Field. The actress Eleanor Counts and Hollywood manager Bill Sweeney welcomed viewers to the first live West Coast television broadcast of a baseball game. While some reporters and columnists called the telecast a "stunt," the response revealed otherwise. In Long Beach, thirty miles away from the ballpark, a merchant put a television set in his store window and tuned in the game. So many people stopped to watch that the crowd spilled from the sidewalk into the street and blocked traffic. Police were called to clear the congestion and let vehicle traffic resume. Bob Cobb had a set installed in the Brown Derby, and diners, both the curious and the enthusiastic, gathered around it to see how the Stars were doing.

In 1940 the medium was in its infancy. There were only three hundred television sets in Los Angeles. Still, the response persuaded the Stars and KHJ to air more games. Two days after the season opener, the KHJ crew again set up cameras in box seats on the first- and third-base sides of Gilmore Field. Throughout the season more games were beamed to the region.

Baseball's flirtation with television went on hiatus during the war years. Many television stations suspended broadcasting. Following the

Gail Patrick shows fellow actor Don Ameche the new television set at the Brown Derby restaurant in the spring of 1940. It was one of the first sets in all of Los Angeles and enabled diners to watch Hollywood Stars games. The Stars were the first minor-league team and the first club outside of New York City to televise games. ***Courtesy of the Bob Cobb Family Collection***

war, the game and the medium reconnected. In the fall of 1945, the Brooklyn Dodgers and New York channel WCBS began a series of discussions that would span more than a year and culminate in December 1946 with a deal to televise fifty of Brooklyn's seventy-seven home games during the 1947 season. Not to be outdone, New York Giants owner Horace Stoneham reached agreement with WNBT to put all of his team's home games on television. The arrangement netted the ball club $50,000.

Skepticism abounded throughout baseball. Naysayers predicted dire consequences at the box office. Lester Bromberg of the *New York World Telegram* called the Giants' decision to televise all of their home games, "a Frankenstein which may eat its own."[1] Robert Carpenter, the president of the Philadelphia Phillies, disagreed. "Once a man hears the roar of the crowd, he gets the itch to be there," Carpenter said. "Nothing can take the place of being there yourself."[2] Baseball got an answer to its dilemma on a night in late May 1947 in Jersey City, New Jersey. On one side of the Hudson River, the New York Giants were playing in the Polo Grounds. Television was carrying the game. Sixteen miles away on the opposite side of the river, the Jersey City Giants were playing to a paltry crowd in Roosevelt Stadium. When Charlie Stoneham, who ran the farm club, phoned his father with the attendance figures after the game, he reported that only 1,669 fans bought tickets. Jersey City's six hundred taverns, on the other hand, were packed with patrons to watch the telecast of the New York Giants' game from the Polo Grounds.

By tapping into television, the Dodgers and Giants initiated a domino effect. Management of the first television station to go on the air in St. Louis convinced the Cardinals to televise a smattering of home games. When WWDT began broadcasting in Detroit, Tigers games became a part of regular summer programming. In Chicago, P. K. Wrigley was curious about the budding medium. WGN had begun operation and was eager to televise Cubs games. After much consternation, the chewing gum magnate agreed to a deal. Wrigley, however, had many questions and decided to make his minor-league team, the Los Angeles Angels, a guinea pig of sorts. Unlike in New York, television was still in its infancy in Los Angeles. The first full-fledged commercial station in the city had only signed on the air in January 1947. That station, KTLA, agreed to televise four Angels home games per week during the 1948 season. Wrigley wanted to use the arrangement to experiment with such things as camera placement, shooting angles, and lighting.

Bob Cobb wanted to take the television plunge as well. He had a sizable obstacle, however, in Earl Gilmore. The ballpark owner forbade the Stars to put any of their games on television. The 1939 lease agreement between Gilmore and the Stars entitled the park owner to 10 percent of all gross receipts from tickets sold. It was Gilmore's belief that television would cut into the Stars' box office receipts. Throughout the 1948 season the two sides went back and forth on the issue. Under protest the Stars finally agreed to give their landlord one-third of any money they received for putting their games on television.

By 1949 seven television stations were on the air in Los Angeles. With three fledgling New York-based networks, CBS, NBC, and Dumont, yet to extend their cables to the West Coast, the Los Angeles-based stations were left to fill their airtime with local programming. The Pacific

Coast League schedule always had one of its two Southern California clubs at home every week of the season. This meant that from April through September there was a ball game every day or night of the week but Monday, which was the league's designated travel day.

An agreement was struck to put all of the Stars' home games on KTLA during the 1949 season. The station paid a fee of $20,000. During the team's first season on television, there were nights when lower-than-expected turnout left Bob Cobb to ponder the visual medium's influence. He concocted a scheme to test television's effectiveness. Crowds had been especially low for Friday night games. Cobb designated Friday, July 15, as Television Appreciation Night. The event was only publicized over the team's telecasts on KTLA. Details were not given to the newspapers. Jack Sherman was forbidden to mention the event on his radio broadcasts. On that night, Cobb, Danny Menendez, and many of the board members were startled to see 8,836 fans stream into Gilmore Field to thank, lavish praise, and pay tribute to the Stars' television broadcaster, Sam Balter. The crowd was almost triple what Hollywood had drawn for their previous Friday-night game.

Cobb believed the attendance drawbacks were only a short-term problem. He was convinced the new medium portended nothing but positives for the future. In an interview with Jack Hellman of *Hollywood Daily Variety*, Cobb expressed conviction that television would create new fans and that within five years Gilmore Field would be too small to accommodate them all.

Baseball represented more than just programming to the Los Angeles television stations. It was profitable. Advertising sales generated $192,000 in income for KTLA, and the station readily extended a proposal to carry every Hollywood home game again in 1950. The Hollywood board of directors agreed, but it didn't take long for problems to arise. The first struck on Opening Day. What was planned to be an extravaganza to celebrate the team's 1949 Pacific Coast League pennant was soured by the smallest Opening Day crowd in the entire league: 5,738. Only 2,440 came the next night. Cobb was put on his heels by accusations that television was to blame. "If you want any further indication of what television is doing to the world of amusements, have a look at the attendance figures for the first two games of the Hollywood club—a championship team backed by a championship parade, a Chamber of Commerce luncheon, and the best press any ball club ever got," wrote W. R.

Wilkerson in the *Hollywood Reporter.*[3] Cobb bristled at the criticism. "I think it's too early to tell," he told the *Los Angeles Times*. "When you start losing money, then it's time to worry. When the novelty of television wears off, say in one or two years, I think we will find that television has given us a great new audience of baseball fans. I sure hope so."[4]

Television set sales had mushroomed in the Los Angeles area. By the 1950 season, close to a half million homes now had sets. This was a substantial increase of 280,000 in just one year's time. By May, Hollywood's attendance was down by 20,000 from 1949. The board-projected attendance could wind up 100,000 shy of the 1949 total, which was a half million. Cobb conceded the figure "leaves us operating at a decided loss." Victor Ford Collins added, "Television is our most worrisome problem."[5]

On May 17, the Pacific Coast League held a special meeting to address the attendance problems of its members. Widespread belief in the league was that it had one culprit: television. Pants Rowland ordered clubs to give serious consideration to restricting telecasts to once per week for the 1951 season. The Hollywood board and front office staff weren't about to give in so easily. After brainstorming sessions, they chose the opposite route: an aggressive promotional plan to stop the decline of crowds. One of the ideas was to offer a special book of tickets with prize incentives. Fans could buy a book of four grandstand tickets for five dollars. The buyer's name was then entered into a drawing for prizes such as radios, televisions, and a trip to the World Series. The idea worked, along with several other schemes and a pennant-contending ball club, to help make Gilmore Field's box office staff busier. The final week of the season, however, would set off alarm bells up and down the entire Pacific Coast League.

On September 26, the Stars played Sacramento before a paltry turnout of 438 fans, the smallest ever to see a game in Gilmore Field. The following night only 569 people pressed through the turnstiles. Two nights later there were a mere 590 fans in the stands. Hollywood's final attendance for the 1950 season was 422,389, a decline of 80,000 off the 1949 total.

The downturn in attendance—and thus, revenue—sparked the ire of Earl Gilmore. Because television wasn't a popular medium in 1939, its potential revenues were not included in the Stars' lease agreement. Now Gilmore claimed that television was akin to radio, a medium that was covered in the lease. Thus, he felt entitled to a percentage of the rights fees that the team received just as he did from radio. Victor Ford Collins countered that television was a concession to which Gilmore had no claim. The retort angered Gilmore, who threatened action. He vowed to cut radio and television cables at the ballpark to prevent broadcasts. To show just how serious he was, Gilmore went to court and filed suit against the team. The Stars countersued. They asked a judge to stop Gilmore from preventing the broadcasts. Before the matter could reach the docket, the two sides reached a settlement: Hollywood offered to pay Gilmore 50 percent of any rights fee it received for television. Though he had demanded 75 percent, Gilmore conceded and accepted the ball club's offer.

Giving in to concerns from around the Pacific Coast League, Hollywood scaled back its television plans for the 1951 season. The Stars changed broadcasters to station KTTV and only aired Friday night games and the second game of Sunday doubleheaders. Any conviction that television was to blame for 1950s attendance plummet was put to rest at the end of the 1951 campaign. Despite the cutback in telecasts, Hollywood's attendance plummeted by another 30 percent. Fingers were pointed. The weather was blamed. The work of the Illinois schoolteacher who drew up the Pacific Coast League's schedule was ridiculed. A boring though championship-caliber club was criticized. Consensus was not reached, but television was not included in the reasons for the decline. Such was the board's belief in television that when station KHJ waved an offer of $75,000 to air all of Hollywood's 1952 home games, it was readily accepted.

Fred Haney's fourth season at the helm of the Stars brought together a core of returning veterans—Mike Sandlock, Chuck Stevens, Gene Handley, Frankie Kelleher, Johnny Lindell, Pinky Woods, and Art Shallock—and a group of Pittsburgh Pirates prospects who held promise. Dick Cole arrived to play shortstop. Paul Pettit was two years removed from being the most heralded high school hurler in the country. Injury had dulled his pitching skills, and the Pirates, who had for all intents and purposes given up on him as a prospect, farmed Pettit out to Hollywood. While Pettit offered abundant publicity fodder, another newcomer, Carlos Bernier, would present creative manna capable of offsetting any potential dent in ticket sales by television. A flashy prospect from Puerto Rico, Bernier had been selected from the Class B Tampa Smokers in the minor-league draft at the urging of one of Branch Rickey's chief lieutenants, Bill

Burwell. The twenty-three-year-old brought a bat with power, creative flair in the field, and a fleet pair of legs.

As Opening Day approached, a new man planned the annual spectacle. Danny Menendez had resigned his role as business manager to join a group that purchased the Toledo Mud Hens. Rumors had risen that Joe E. Brown's son, Joe L. Brown, would be Menendez's replacement. The younger Brown had been Hollywood's publicist before being poached by Branch Rickey to run Pittsburgh's New Orleans farm club. Rickey had other ideas for Brown, so Bob Cobb instead hired veteran minor-league executive Les Powers.

Powers dispatched the personable tavern owner Foghorn Murphy to grab his megaphone and ride on horseback through Santa Monica, Burbank, Glendale, and San Fernando, touting the Stars' season-opening game. The actor Frank Lovejoy agreed to be Opening Day master of ceremonies. The Kiwanis clubs provided an American flag that would fly over Gilmore Field throughout the season. Days before the lid-lifter, Powers was hit with a crisis. Marjie Millar, an attractive 20th Century Fox actress, had beaten out ninety-four other young women for the title of Miss Hollywood Stars 1952. Among Millar's duties was to fling the first pitch on Opening Day. As the day drew near, however, Powers could not find the girl. Dozens of phone calls went unanswered. Messages were unheeded. Newspapers ran stories about the missing actress. Powers was nearing a panic when he finally learned that Millar had been in the hospital recovering from an appendectomy. Assured that she had recovered and was fine, Powers went ahead with the Opening Day program as planned, and the pregame gala peaked with loud cheers for the strike hurled by Millar.

As Tom Harmon welcomed the viewers to channel 9 on behalf of sponsor Chesterfield cigarettes, Cobb and Rivera surveyed the stands with discontent. The turnout of 3,825 was less than half what both men wanted to see. They grumbled that across town more than 7,500 were cheering a championship boxing match taking place in the Olympic Auditorium.

The 1952 season was the Pacific Coast League's first as an open league. Twenty players in the league qualified under terms of service for the postseason minor-league draft. Of the twenty, nineteen had agreed to sign yellow contracts, which meant they did not wish to be drafted. Much to Fred Haney's chagrin, his team got off to a terrible start. The Stars lost seven of their first eleven games. Their wins came in somewhat dramatic methods: on Paul Pettit's impressive debut, a four-hit shutout of Seattle by Johnny Lindell, and a game-winning triple by the speedy outfielder Tommy Saffell in the bottom of the ninth against the Angels.

A subsequent five-game losing streak was snapped when Carlos Bernier slammed a home run in the eighteenth inning of a duel at Wrigley Field. Another batch of defeats came to an end when Haney employed his new bunt-and-drag strategy. During his first three seasons at the Hollywood helm, Haney had been what first baseman Chuck Stevens called "very safety first. Not a big-inning manager."[6] When the manager and his first baseman walked down the ramp toward the dugout, Stevens liked to josh, "Let's go out and kick the hell out of somebody tonight, and beat 'em, 2–1."[7] With the cast he had been given for the 1952 season, Haney decided to take advantage of the raw speed that Saffell and Bernier brought to the lineup. The two outfielders were given the green light to run once they got on base. He also put his players on notice that the bunt sign could be flashed on any count and at any time.

The change in strategy unleashed Carlos Bernier into stardom. On April 18, during a close game with Sacramento, Bernier walked, then stole second. After an out by a teammate moved the speedy outfielder to third base, Bernier raced home to score on a wild pitch. The next night, Bernier doubled, stole third base, then scored on a wild pitch to help Hollywood win, 2–0. During the doubleheader that concluded the Sacramento series, Bernier swiped three bases as the Stars swept both games.

The early losses had dropped Hollywood into seventh place. Haney's change of tactics and a seven-game hitting streak by Bernier strung together wins that vaulted the Stars into second, two and a half games behind San Diego. Pettit won five of his first six Hollywood starts. Three of Pettit's triumphs were by shutout. In mid-June, Johnny Lindell helped thrust the Stars toward the top of the Pacific Coast League standings. During a series in San Francisco, the veteran pitched Hollywood to a 2–1 win. The win was Lindell's tenth of the season, which was the best tally in the Pacific Coast League. Two nights later Haney wrote Lindell's name onto his lineup card as the Hollywood right fielder. The veteran went three-for-four with two doubles. A night later Lindell added a home run to his hitting binge.

The successful series sent Hollywood into San Diego with a shot to take over first place. Playing with greater confidence and vigor, Hollywood opened the series with a 5–3 win. Bernier highlighted the night with a triple, a run scored, and two runs driven in. Bernier's two singles and two stolen bases helped Hollywood take the third game, 7–4. On June 20, the talented Stars rookie had two hits, one of which was a double. He scored a run and led Hollywood to a 5–1 win, which vaulted them past the Padres and into first place. When the Stars padded their league lead by winning, 10–5, the following night, it was Bernier who earned the plaudits with two doubles, three runs batted in, and a stolen base. The Stars concluded their stay in San Diego by sweeping the Sunday doubleheader, 9–3 and 2–1. Bernier had three hits in the first game, while Johnny Lindell limited the Padres to four hits while winning his eleventh game of the season in the second game. Sportswriters asked if Haney's team was the Pacific Coast League's best in decades. San Diego manager Lefty O'Doul would only concede, "The Stars have the most over-all speed of anyone in the Coast League in years."[8]

The Stars' climb in the standings was fueled by a manager who was part master chess strategist and part riverboat gambler. Fred Haney's daring was exhibited by final-inning squeeze bunts that he had Chuck Stevens, Tommy Saffell, and even Frankie Kelleher execute, which won games. The crowd took to the daring strategy. It became almost a trademark of games to hear Bing Crosby's older brother Larry yell, "Bunt, Haney, bunt," night after night.[9] Shuffling the lineup became commonplace as well. Haney would alter his starting nine based upon the opposing pitcher. If a game was close in the late innings, it was not uncommon to see Haney pull the lumbering Kelleher for a faster Saffell and move Bernier from center to left field. "Platoons, pitching, and power seems to be the combination that has put the Stars up there at the top of the league," observed the *Times*'s Paul Zimmerman.[10]

Attendance at Gilmore Field improved considerably. Larger crowd counts quelled the naysayers. Still, television continued to bring occasional headaches—especially when the San Francisco Seals came to town. Their owner, Paul Fagan, bristled that the visitors' share of the gate was lower than in previous years. He blamed it on television and threatened to press the league to give visiting clubs a piece of the Stars' revenue from the visual medium.

Prior to the 1952 season, Cobb invested $50,000 into advertising and promotions. His aim was to avoid a repeat of the box office woes of 1951. Visits by the acrobatic baseball trickster Jackie Price and the Bob Roberts

Majorettes, giveaways of hats, and both family and ladies' nights contributed to hike turnstile counts by more than 20 percent. Nothing packed the house, though, like Paul Pettit. On June 27, a Friday night, fans poured off the number 4 Beverly Bus and the number 3 from Third Street. A steady stream of cars turned into the parking lot from Fairfax. By the time Pettit began to make his warmup throws, men were roping off an area in front of the outfield fence to create standing room. A thousand took advantage. Hundreds more turned away without reaching the entrance after hearing in the parking lot that there were no seats left.

The game began in a disquieting way. Pettit gave up three hits and a run in the first inning. After he received a piece of advice from Fred Haney, the popular hurler threw hitless baseball the rest of the night. Over one stretch, the former high school sensation retired fourteen Los Angeles batters in a row. Frankie Kelleher whacked a home run. Carlos Bernier swiped three bases, and the highlights of a 6–1 Stars win thrilled 12,682 fans, the team's largest crowd in four years.

Bernier had grown into a fan favorite. Young and old alike marveled at his base-running daring. The stolen bases thrilled. Feats like scoring from second base on a sacrifice fly drew awe. Bernier's flashy play brought almost as many nicknames as there were sportswriters who covered the Stars. He was called "the Comet" for his dynamic speed and "the Bandit" for his base running, while to youthful fans he was "Crash" for his frequent collisions with the outfield wall while making spectacular catches. Yet in the clubhouse and dugout at Gilmore Field, another attitude prevailed. Bernier's unpredictable temperament spawned detest for the outfielder among his teammates, who described the young player with adjectives that ranged from "naive" to "disgusting" and even "uncouth." When Hollywood's players paired up at the start of the season to form road trip roommates, none was willing to share a hotel room with Bernier. Fred Haney's problem was resolved when the easygoing Pettit agreed to be the outfielder's roommate. Bernier's natural skills were overshadowed by mental mistakes. He showed a lack of baseball savvy. Bernier attempted to steal bases with big leads, which was universally considered unsporting and could bring retaliation from opposing pitchers. Teammates would confront him. Fans in the box seats would hear shouting in the dugout, "Don't you ever do that again!"[11] What they could not see was that Chuck Stevens had Bernier by the collar as he shouted the message. When Bernier would disappear from the dugout then return with peanut shells on his uniform, heads would shake and eyes would roll. His teammates knew he had been trolling beneath the stands for gaps and holes through which he could look up the skirts of female fans.

By August the outfielder had swiped fifty bases. Every one of his swipes, though, came at a price. His lower legs, bared by the Stars' short pants, were scraped, cut, and bloodied. Bernier asked Haney if the team could ditch the short pants. His were good natured jibes at first but became serious pleadings as the season went on. In time, Haney came to agree. He slowly phased out the short pants, and a year later they were worn for the last time.

Carlos Bernier's speed and base-stealing skills sprouted promotional ingenuity. The idea to pit Bernier in a footrace against the Angels' fastest player, Bobby Talbott, was proposed. It was rejected by the Angels out of concern for injury. That did not stop the creative wheels from turning in the Stars front office. A scheme was concocted to put Bernier's running speed to the test. Its objective was to try to break a record for circling the bases. The gimmick buoyed what was usually a flat Friday night turnout. On August 15, curiosity pulled more than seven thousand fans to the ballpark. The track and field community was tapped for assistance. Three timers were supplied by the sport's local governing body, the Amateur Athletic Union. Fans were told that Bernier's goal was 13.3 seconds, a mark set in 1931 by Evar Swanson, who played for Columbus. Once Bernier bunted a ball pitched by a teammate, the timing devices began. Shouts of encouragement broke out as Bernier began his quest. With legs churning and arms flailing, the Hollywood sensation streaked from base to base. At each base the cheers grew louder. When Bernier's right shoe stomped on home plate, the timing devices clicked, and his time was soon announced—13.9 seconds. As he hunched near home plate, a broad smile filled Bernier's face. Unable to speak while he fought to catch his breath, the fleet Star was showered with gifts for his effort, $500 cash collected from fans, a new suede jacket, a Scotch cashmere sport coat, a $150 strand of pearls for his wife, dishes, and candy. It didn't take long once the ensuing game began for the cheers for Bernier to fade. After he reached base for the first time, Bernier swiped his fifty-fifth base of the season. Unbeknownst to Bernier, however, Len Ratto, the San Francisco shortstop, did not throw the baseball back to his pitcher. He kept it concealed. When Bernier obliviously strayed from second base, Ratto walked over and tagged him. Fans gasped on seeing the umpire raise his right arm to signal Bernier out. Carlos Bernier had been hoodwinked by the hidden ball trick.

A week after Carlos Bernier's try at a record, Johnny Lindell achieved a milestone. On August 18, he pitched Hollywood to an 8–3 victory over Sacramento to earn his twentieth win of the season. In the aftermath, Bob Cobb revealed that the Cleveland Indians, Boston Red Sox, New York Yankees, and Washington Senators had made offers to buy Lindell. "Sure, we'll sell Lindell," Cobb told reporters, "but not for cash—only for promising young players."[12]

Because of poor crowds and bad fall weather in past years, the Pacific Coast League had done away with its Shaughnessy playoff. The regular-season pennant winner would be crowned league champion. For most of the final two months of the 1952 season, Hollywood held a six-game lead over its closest pursuer, the Oakland Oaks. Neither the Oaks nor anyone else was able to cut into that advantage. On September 17, during the second game of their season-ending series in Portland, the Stars made their ascension complete. Tied 3–3 in the sixth inning, Hollywood rallied for three runs and beat the Beavers, 6–3. The win clinched the Pacific Coast League pennant. The Stars finished the 1952 season with 109 wins against 71 losses.

When the league's managers and the sportswriters were polled, they voted Johnny Lindell Most Valuable Player. He had compiled a 24–9 record with a 2.52 earned-run average. Carlos Bernier was chosen best prospect and the league's best newcomer. The flashy outfielder had equaled the league record for stolen bases with 65, almost double that of anybody else in the Pacific Coast League. Bernier finished third in the league with nine triples and fifth in hitting with a .301 batting average.

The propellers on Hollywood's last charter flight had barely stopped spinning when Haney and his players were whisked to the Beverly Wilshire Hotel for a lavish celebration. The Eddie Bergman Orchestra serenaded. Players, staff, and almost four hundred guests dined on filet mignon. Groucho Marx ignited the laughs. Gordon MacRae, Bill Frawley, and Virginia Mayo livened the evening. Studio heads and politicians offered backslaps and pumped the hands of the Stars' players.

The loudest roar of the night echoed about the room when Pants Rowland handed the large championship trophy to Fred Haney. True to his pledge, the team's former radio voice had turned the Stars into a winner. In Haney's four seasons at the helm, Hollywood had won the pennant twice and been to the finals of the playoffs once. His work to assemble talent and manage it in a way that brought out its best had much to do with the exuberance and revelry that echoed about the room.

Whatever initial apprehension Bob Cobb once held about Fred Haney as the Hollywood manager had long since evaporated and grown into a great friendship. The Cobbs were Uncle Bob and Aunt Sally to the Haneys' grandchildren. The Haneys were frequent diners at the Brown Derby. During the off-season Cobb and Haney often grabbed their shotguns and drove east to Indio to hunt quail or north to the Smith Ranch near Bakersfield for a weekend of duck hunting.

Fred Haney's career, like the fortunes of the Hollywood Stars, had been remarkably resurrected by the marriage. But the fervor that both had helped to unleash would soon be doused.

26

"RUN YOUR GUTS OUT!"

The last member of the orchestra had snapped his instrument case closed to officially end the championship party when it seemed the rumors began. In truth, they were actually first spoken in the fall of 1949, the sort of hitchhiker that normally rides with success. Worry struck some, angst rose in other corners, while a shrug of inevitability greeted the talk among those whose ear the rumor found. Fred Haney would not be back.

First as the friendly, likable voice on the radio, then as the man at the helm who at long last brought success to the Hollywood Stars, Fred Haney had become an endearing figure to fans of the ball club. In four seasons as Hollywood's manager, Haney had produced unrivaled success: two pennants and a trip to the playoff finals. It was October 2 when the rumor finally hit print. It first broke out of New York: Fred Haney was in line to become manager of the Pittsburgh Pirates. Six days later Haney strode into the Pirates' Forbes Field offices for meetings that included talks about the job. It was a full two months before the hiring was made official. "I hate to lose Freddy, but this nevertheless is a happy occasion," Bob Cobb said to Al Wolf of the *Los Angeles Times*.[1]

During the weeks and months that followed the 1952 season, Gilmore Field was rattled not by the seasonal Catalina eddy or Santa Ana winds, but by winds of change. Haney wasn't the only Gilmore Field staple fans would not see again. Three of the championship club mainstays—Johnny Lindell, Carlos Bernier, and Paul Pettit—would not return. Neither would catcher Mike Sandlock nor shortstop Dick Cole. All five players would follow Haney to Pittsburgh. The departures were orchestrated by one man, the newest influence in the Gilmore Field office and the club's newest shareholder: Branch Rickey.

The arrival of Rickey came from change to the hierarchy of the Hollywood Stars. At the end of World War II, the ownership structure of the Hollywood Stars had changed. The personal and professional ebb and flow that make up the cycle of life had seen inaugural investors bow out. On December 3, 1946, the Hollywood Baseball Investment Company was dissolved and replaced by a new ownership organization, the Hollywood Baseball Association. Cobb's fanciful policy that one could own just a single share in the ball club was scrapped. Two thousand shares in the new company were issued. Cobb, Victor Ford Collins, and George Young owned the majority of those shares. In the winter months that followed the 1950 season, beset by health issues, Young sold his 300 shares to Cobb for $200 per share. Only days before the 1952 season, Young's health deteriorated rapidly. He was rushed to St. Vincent's Hospital and passed away two days later. His role was not the only staple of the Stars' executive team to change. Just two months before Young's passing, Collins had elected to sell his 367 shares in the ball club. Cobb bought those shares, too, though he urged his friend and attorney to continue as president of the club.

In the years that followed Hollywood's 1949 tie-up with the Brooklyn Dodgers, Bob Cobb came to count Branch Rickey as a close personal friend. The men took duck-hunting trips to remote parts of Montana and went deep-sea fishing off the coast of Florida. They regularly talked baseball by phone and dined together whenever travel took Cobb to Pittsburgh or New York. It was on one of their visits, in August 1951, that Rickey first broached the idea of purchasing shares in the Hollywood Stars.

Discussions about the stock purchase went on for five months. During that time Al Wolf of the *Los Angeles Times* got wind that some form of negotiation was taking place. He wrote that Cobb was trying to convince the city of Los Angeles to turn over land in the San Fernando Valley, where Pirates owner John Galbreath would build a ballpark. The scheme was to culminate with Cobb and Rickey owning and operating a major-league team. As tantalizing as the idea might have been for those coveting big-league baseball in Los Angeles, the report just wasn't true. In January 1952, Branch Rickey became an investor in the Hollywood Stars. Rickey paid $87,500 for 325 shares in the ball club, ostensibly on behalf of his employer, the Pittsburgh Pirates. When the deal was made public, Cobb announced that the Pirates held a 16 percent stake in the Stars. Cobb owned 33 percent of the club's 2,000 shares and was now the majority shareholder. "I think his presence will be a great thing for the entire league too," Cobb enthused about Rickey's involvement. "In our quest for major league status we need all the good advice we can get."[2]

While Cobb was enthusiastic about the deal, the rest of the Pacific Coast League was not. Outrage erupted. Only days before the stock purchase was announced, directors of the Pacific Coast League had voted to bar working agreements with major-league teams and pledged they would not accept players on option from big-league clubs. "The 'Coast League must divorce itself 100 percent from the majors!" San Francisco Seals owner Paul Fagan railed.[3] What resulted was a ban on so-called house deals such as the one between the Chicago Cubs and Los Angeles Angels, which were jointly owned. News of Rickey's investment in the Stars set off a chain of anger-driven events throughout the league. One day after the transaction took place, Pants Rowland sent a cable to both the commissioner of baseball and the head of the minor leagues to ask that the men quash the Rickey purchase. "The owners disapprove of both the principle of the sale and the method," Rowland wrote.[4]

"The deal was made last August," Cobb countered. "It was made honestly and in good faith with everybody."[5]

Rickey was flummoxed. "I cannot understand it," he said. "It must be something personal."[6]

Six weeks after the transaction was announced, Pacific Coast League directors gathered at the Hotel Biltmore in Los Angeles to review the matter. After considerable discussion and debate, the purchase of Stars shares by Rickey and the Pirates was approved.

Through the turmoil, Cobb and Rickey sought a replacement for Haney. Dozens of names were raised in the newspapers. Only two men were serious candidates. It was rumored that Walter Alston, manager of the Brooklyn Dodgers' top farm team, the Montreal Royals, would get the job. In the end, it went to another manager in the Dodgers' farm system, Bobby Bragan. Bragan was a favorite of Rickey's. He knew how Rickey wanted players taught and teams managed. It was a hire that went completely against Bob Cobb's philosophy. In his hiring of Bill Sweeney, Oscar Vitt, Charley Root, Jimmie Dykes, and then Fred Haney, Cobb had sought a personality. Many of the men had local ties or were well liked by the local press, all of which helped generate publicity. Cobb's managers were big names who had big-league track records and were drawing cards for fans, especially the celebrity ones. Bobby Bragan was nothing like his Hollywood predecessors. He was not local, but an Alabamian. Al Wolf wrote in his column in the *Los Angeles Times* that the new Hollywood manager was "appallingly shy on showmanship."[7] Bragan had not managed at a level of baseball higher than the Class AA Texas League. The hiring of Bragan exemplified a growing reverence Bob Cobb held for Branch Rickey. "The outstanding baseball man in America," Cobb called his new partner, adding, "I'm proud to be associated with him."[8] Privately, fellow Pacific Coast League owners snickered at Cobb's gushing. Those who felt they had been burned in dealings with Rickey chided what they considered to be blind loyalty on Cobb's part.

Once the Stars checked into the Pickwick Hotel in Anaheim to begin spring training, both the manager's office and the roster had a decidedly Pittsburgh look to it. Gone were the mainstays of the pitching staff that had hurled Hollywood to the 1952 pennant. In their stead were four pitchers who were Pittsburgh property: George O'Donnell, Red Munger, Harry Fisher, and Junior Walsh. Frankie Kelleher was back for his ninth season with the Stars. Chuck Stevens returned for his sixth, but it would not be long before he was pushed off first base by a promising Pittsburgh product, Dale Long.

The new Hollywood manager's style was different from that of Haney's. "I like to grind 'em out," he explained. "Real baseball calls for speed and skill—the slide, the steal, the hit-and-run, the sacrifice."[9] It did not take players long to formulate the opinion that their new skipper was a taskmaster. "Fans don't come out to watch you trot to first," Bragan barked to a player one day. "They come to see you play. Run your guts out!"[10] During spring training Bragan tired of hearing his players grumble about the heat. The manager announced a fifty-dollar fine for the next player to gripe about the weather. When a sweat-soaked pitcher walked off the mound, wiped perspiration from his neck and groused, "Man it's hot," then saw Bragan, he quickly added, "just the way I like it!"[11]

Prior to Opening Day, more change came to the Stars' hierarchy. Bob Cobb was made president and general manager by the Hollywood board of directors. "Cobb is progressive and well qualified for his new responsibilities," said Victor Ford Collins, who was stepping down.[12] John Tanzola, an original stockholder, was voted secretary-treasurer. Bob Clements, assistant general manager of the Pittsburgh Pirates, was named vice president. Paul Jeschke was given the role of office manager, and Cecil B. DeMille was asked to continue his role as honorary chairman of the board.

The schedule maker sent the Stars on the road for eight games in San Diego to begin the season. New skipper Bragan was the hero in the opener. He put himself in the lineup as the catcher. In the ninth inning with two runners on, Bragan dropped a short fly ball in front of the center fielder that drove in the winning run in a 3–2 triumph. Branch Rickey arrived in town Thursday afternoon in time to see the Stars win four straight games. The final two wins during the stretch were memorable for vastly different reasons. In the Saturday encounter, Hollywood's 5-foot-8-inch right fielder, Teddy Beard, put on an epic hitting display. He had switched from a forty-two- to a thirty-six-ounce bat for the game and in the first inning got results in the form of a home run. Two innings later Beard came up with two men on base. The left-handed hitter shot another ball over the right-center-field fence. This one landed on Pacific Highway for home run number two on the day. In the fifth inning, Beard put another ball onto the highway to extend Hollywood's lead to 5–2. Beard led off the seventh inning and sent a scorcher over the wall in right-center field, just above the 375-foot marker, for his fourth home run of the game. In the ninth inning, Beard drew one more turn at bat. Enemy fans, all 2,919 of them, forgot partisanship and stood to applaud as the diminutive outfielder walked to home plate. The cheers pushed an impish grin on Beard's face. He stepped from the batter's box to acknowledge the crowd with a tip of his batter's helmet. Beard took two called strikes, then on the third offering unleashed a powerful swing that missed. Loud applause serenaded his walk back to the dugout. When he reached the bench, Frankie Kelleher grinned, "Just like I always thought, Teddy. You're just a flash in the pan."[13] In the press box, sportswriters frenetically typed game stories about the 6–5 Hollywood win and the new Pacific Coast League record for consecutive home runs in one game.

In the span of less than twenty-four hours, Beard and his teammates would plummet from the high of home-run-record euphoria to the depths of grief. That it came on the reverent occasion of Easter Sunday only added to the anguish. The season-opening series in San Diego had given several Stars the chance to once again see an old friend and former teammate, Herb Gorman. The outfielder had been a key player on Hollywood's 1949 pennant-winning team as well as during the next two seasons. Gorman was selected by the St. Louis Cardinals in the Rule 5 draft in December 1951. After a brief stint in the big leagues, Gorman was assigned by the Cardinals to San Diego for the 1953 season. Though he was a native of San Jose, Gorman and his new bride, Rosalie, had elected to make their home a stone's throw from Gilmore Field on Packard Street near La Cienega Boulevard.

Gorman was given his first start of the 1953 season in the Easter Sunday finale against the Stars. When he laced a double in his first turn at bat, the former Star engaged in good-natured ribbing from second base with his former teammate, Johnny O'Neil. In his second trip to the plate, Gorman doubled once again and this time tipped his cap to Kelleher in left field as he stood on the bag at second base. In the sixth inning, Gorman took his position in left field but soon after doubled over in pain. Buddy Peterson, the San Diego shortstop, heard Gorman holler for time-out. Sensing trouble, Peterson turned and sprinted toward his stricken teammate. When he reached Gorman, Peterson realized the trouble was serious. The shortstop waived his arms feverishly for the team trainer to come to the outfielder's aid. Coaches and teammates assisted Gorman from the field, but as he neared the dugout, the outfielder inexplicably broke away. He leaped over the retaining screen into the dugout then walked unaided up the tunnel to the clubhouse. Once Gorman reached the clubhouse, he collapsed. He was administered oxygen almost immediately. A physician who had been watching the game in the stands summoned an ambulance. In both dugouts Gorman's current and former teammates were shaken. Everyone in the ballpark could hear the wail of a siren fade into the distance and knew that it was rushing Gorman to Mercy Hospital. In the top of the ninth inning, the Stars' radio announcer, Mark Scott, was handed a note. He glanced at the paper and shuddered. His friend Herb Gorman had died. Players voted not to play the second game, and the fans filed silently out of the ballpark. Within forty-eight hours, an autopsy determined that Gorman had suffered a heart attack that was caused by a large clot in an artery. "He never complained, he never caused trouble—he just wanted to play. It's a terrible loss," San Diego manager Lefty O'Doul said somberly.[14]

A day off helped many of the Stars' players to come to terms with their grief. Tuesday, April 7, brought the first home game of the season, and though fans were filled with exuberance, sadness enveloped the Stars clubhouse. Usually lavish festivities that marked a home opener were kept short and simple. There was no celebrity first pitch, no pregame shenanigans, just the raising of the 1952 pennant, brief words from Bob Cobb, and the national anthem performance by the Holly-hots.

The Stars treated their fans to a power display. Hollywood's 10–9 win was the prelude to three more double-digit run tallies over the next four nights. The only night the Stars were held in check, few were there to see it. Many regulars of Gilmore Field were likely howling to the antics of the basketball wizards the Harlem Globetrotters, who were entertaining thirty-five thousand fans in the cavernous Los Angeles Coliseum. By the time the Stars had completed the second week of the season and roared through their series against the Oakland Oaks, they had won ten of their first fourteen games and held first place in the Pacific Coast League.

Two new fan favorites emerged during the early weeks of the 1953 season. George O'Donnell won his first six starts of the season to vault to the top of the Pacific Coast League pitching charts. The twenty-four-year-old from Illinois was from a close-knit farming family of thirteen children. As a teen he had traveled to St. Louis to try out for the Cardinals. When the club wanted to sign him but needed his father's signature on the contract, the O'Donnells loaded up their children and traveled to Sportsman's Park for the occasion. O'Donnell didn't throw exceedingly hard but was adept at changing speeds and had pinpoint accuracy. In a conversation with Frank Finch of the *Los Angeles Times*, Bragan called O'Donnell "one of the craftiest chuckers I've ever seen. He could put it through a knothole, I believe."[15]

Dale Long established himself as the biggest home-run threat in the Pacific Coast League. Fans could be grateful to his mother for that. A powerful 6-foot-4-inch, 210-pound talent, Long was prepared to sign a football contract with the Green Bay Packers when he was eighteen. His mother put her foot down and insisted he play baseball instead. By Memorial Day, Hollywood's fans were thankful for her intervention.

The Stars closed out the month of May by amassing a six-game win streak. Three of the wins were highlighted by home runs from Long. His seventh-inning blast broke a 2–2 tie and gave Hollywood a 3–2 win in the Thursday night game of the series against the Angels. On Saturday afternoon, Long lofted a shot over Wrigley Field's right-field bleachers to break a scoreless tie. Two innings later he doubled off the outfield bricks, then scored on a teammate's single as Hollywood won, 2–0. The next day he left fans in awe when he struck a ball that sailed an estimated 430 feet for a three-run home run to send Hollywood to a 5–4 victory.

Long's long-ball hitting streak continued once the Stars moved back into their own ballpark to host Seattle. His double decided the second game of the series. It gave Hollywood eight wins in eleven games. Three days later, Long's fourth home run in ten days propelled Hollywood past the Rainiers, 11–6, and Long into the league home run lead with 12. When the series with Seattle concluded, however, it was not Long's power hitting but an outburst over an umpire's call that the newspapers would be printing stories about. A crowd of 9,084 fans filled Gilmore Field for the doubleheader to conclude the series with the Rainiers. The two-man umpiring crew for the game included Gil Stratton, the motion picture and radio actor who had joined the Pacific Coast League's crew of umpires prior to the 1953 season. "I'm just nutty enough to want to be an umpire above all else," he had said prior to spring training.[16] During the eighth inning of the Sunday game, Stratton made a call on a close play at first base that sent the grandstand throng into a frenzy. Outraged fans hurled beer bottles and flung seat cushions onto the field. Play had to be halted twice to remove the debris. Amid the eruption from the field, Hollywood lost the game, 8–2.

It was not long before the outburst by the Gilmore Field fans was eclipsed by one even more volcanic. It may have taken the fans awhile to realize what Hollywood's players had learned in spring training—that Fred Haney's replacement was, in the term used in dugouts and clubhouses, a "red-ass." Stern, bombastic, volatile, fiery—each and every word combined to describe Bobby Bragan. It was a side of the Hollywood manager that particularly emerged when he became angry with umpires. His outbursts could make the explosive former Stars manager Bill Sweeney look like an altar boy by comparison. In truth, Bragan was a born ham. The man was a cutup who enjoyed teasing and playing pranks. "When in Rome, do as the Romans," he liked to chuckle of his Hollywood actions.[17] He saw his antics as part of his responsibilities, both to stick up for his players and to entertain the Hollywood fans. "There is nothing dull about daddy," his wife, Gwen, would tell their children.[18] Bragan's explosive umpire baiting reached an early peak during a series with San Diego, when he was ejected not once, but twice in one game.

The first inning hadn't been completed when Bragan became incensed that the base umpire, Bill Doran, called Hollywood's Tommy Saffell out on a stolen base attempt. The Stars' skipper plucked the wad of chewing tobacco from his left cheek and angrily flung it to the ground. He then stomped to the third base coaching box, where he plopped to the ground and, while seated, wrote something in the dirt with his index finger. In the top of the second inning, San Diego's manager, Lefty O'Doul, bent down to read what Bragan had written. O'Doul then turned toward the Hollywood dugout and rubbed his right index finger repeatedly over his left in the universal shame-on-you signal. Instead of returning to the coaching box for the bottom of the second inning, Bragan sent Hollywood's batboy, sixteen-year-old Dick Wisebard, to handle the chore. The umpires held up play until Hollywood complied with the rules and replaced the batboy with a coach. During the standoff, something Bragan uttered sent the home plate umpire, Ed Runge, charging toward the Hollywood dugout. Runge waved his right arm and ejected the Stars' skipper from the game. Bragan became obstinate. He refused to leave the field. The manager trotted to the first base coach's box. Fans howled with laughter. To umpires Doran and Runge, the matter was nothing to laugh at. Both used demonstrative body language to eject Bragan once again. The next day Pants Rowland cabled his admonishment of the Stars' field boss.

The league president's rebuke did little to quell Bragan's antics. Two weeks later a fiery outburst took ballpark beefs to a new level and saw the manager unconsciously hurt his team. The Stars had climbed back into first place and were playing second-place Seattle. Bragan had put himself in the lineup. While catching, he engaged in frequent jawing with Doran, who was the home-plate umpire. In the eighth inning, a call on a close play at first base that went against Hollywood made Bragan erupt in fury. He bolted onto the field after Doran. Following several minutes of vocal haranguing, Bragan trudged back to the Hollywood dugout. There, in his rage, the manager performed a baseball version of a striptease. First a chest protector flew from the dugout onto the field, then a cap, and that was followed by one shin guard and then another. Towels came next before the irate manager filled a towel with ice, wadded it up, and heaved it at Doran's partner, Runge. The missile narrowly missed striking the base arbiter. Doran ejected Bragan from the game.

The Stars' lone coach, Gordon Maltzberger, took over the managing duties. After Bragan's ejection, Hollywood tied the game. In the ninth inning, Maltzberger, who had been pitching, took himself out for a pinch-hitter. It was a decision that caused problems on two fronts. With Eddie

Malone now catching for the ejected Bragan, Maltzberger's use of Frankie Kelleher to pinch-hit meant Hollywood had no more reserves on the bench. It also meant that according to the rules, Maltzberger was out of the game and could not come onto the field whether it be to coach or speak to the umpires. The game wound up going extra innings. Seattle scored twice in the top of the eleventh inning to win, 5–3. The loss knocked Hollywood out of first place.

Pants Rowland was in Cincinnati at the major-league All-Star Game when he learned of Bragan's outburst. The PCL president was furious. Rowland suspended the Hollywood manager indefinitely. He fined Bragan $75. In a cable he admonished the manager for "childish antics and burlesque theatrics."[19] The suspension remained in force throughout Hollywood's six games in Portland and into the start of their series in Seattle. During that time, they encountered a catching crisis. Eddie Malone suffered a thigh injury. Dale Long, though left-handed, had catching experience. However, he was hobbled by a bad ankle. The team had to activate its bullpen catcher, John Deskin, who hadn't played competitively in two years.

Bob Cobb had not been a witness to Bragan's shenanigans. Nor had he been around to enjoy his team's ascension to first place. During the early weeks of the season, the Hollywood president's eighty-seven-year-old mother had suffered a stroke. Baseball and restaurant responsibilities were pushed to the side while Cobb provided care and support. The woman had been the source of Cobb's infatuation with baseball. She had run a team of Native American players from a local tribe during her son's youth in Montana. Cobb and his sister, Shellie, held out hope that their mother would rally, but on June 28, in the Knickerbocker Hotel suite that she had shared with her daughter for sixteen years, Martha Cobb passed away.

The Stars' surge toward a second straight league pennant included a feat never before accomplished in the team's sixteen-year history: a no-hitter. It was achieved by an unlikely candidate. Red Munger was a veteran of sixteen seasons in pro ball. His snapping curve and searing fastball had made him an All-Star three times in ten seasons with the St. Louis Cardinals. However, by the 1953 season he was just hanging on. Elbow troubles had diminished his skills. He was released by the Cardinals and sent to the minor leagues by the lowly Pirates.

On the Fourth of July, in the seven-inning second game of Hollywood's doubleheader with Sacramento, Munger fashioned a gem. The Texan set down the first twelve batters that he faced with ease. In the top of the fifth inning, however, Sacramento's Joe Brovia hit a groundball toward Monty Basgall that went right through the Hollywood second baseman's legs. Munger had his back turned to the scoreboard and didn't see the light go on to signify that the official scorer had ruled the play an error. After recording an out, Munger walked a batter. Bragan became concerned enough to send Gordon Maltzberger to the bullpen to warm up. A pitching change, though, wouldn't be necessary. For at least a day, Munger recaptured his sharp, biting curveball and induced Eddie Bockman to hit a ground ball to Basgall that was turned into a double play and helped the hurler out of further danger.

It was only after Munger was back in the dugout after the inning that he learned of the scorekeeper's ruling. He retired the Solons in order in the sixth inning, then got the first two outs with relative ease in the top of the seventh. Joe Brovia then hit a bounder toward Jack Phillips at third base. When the throw across the diamond retired Brovia for the final out of the game, Phillips was momentarily startled by the cheers from the stands and the sight of his teammates spilling from the dugout to congratulate Munger. The player had no idea that his teammate had just pitched a no-hitter.

By the end of July, Hollywood was in firm control of the Pacific Coast League title race. They took five of seven games from the Angels to build a six-game gap over second-place Seattle. Frankie Kelleher was almost singlehandedly responsible for three of the wins. Kelleher stroked a game-winning pinch-hit single in the ninth inning in the first triumph. The next night he belted a pinch-hit home run in the eighth inning that was the margin of victory. In the Sunday doubleheader, Kelleher drove in the first and last of Hollywood's runs in their 4–1 win. Over the next two weeks Hollywood extended its lead to ten games.

As the Stars' win tally grew, so too did the opinion of sportswriters and fans about Bobby Bragan. During the first half of the season, letters to the editor were dotted with "I don't like him," and "You can have Bragan."[20] One newspaper even led its game story by describing how a "fat fan bellowed dislike of Bobby Bragan."[21] After one particularly disheartening loss the manager came home to find a note from his wife that read, "I can't talk about it! Blow a five-run lead! You'll find wienies and navy beans in the oven. Good night."[22] By July all that changed. The Hollywood manager came to be described as "colorful" and hailed as a "favorite with fans all around the league."[23] Bragan rarely turned down a request to give a speech. By September he had spoken at forty-five different events and gatherings in and around Los Angeles. The manager regularly conducted a radio show with Mark Scott on which he fielded questions from fans. Bragan even won over Hazel Smith, a vociferous middle-aged woman who sat with her daughter, sister, and friend two nights a week in an area of the right-field grandstands the women called "Widows Roost." At first vocal in their unhappiness with the manager's antics, Smith and her companions would become some of Bragan's biggest fans.

Few fans knew of another side to the fiery manager. After games Bragan would retreat into Bob Cobb's office, where a large piano occupied a corner. Bragan would slide onto the bench and play to unwind. Though his mother had been a concert pianist, Bragan had no formal music training. He had been taught to play as a youth by a Black man in the employ of his family. The man, called Kelly, could only teach Bragan to play the black keys—the only keys he had been permitted to play. Bobby liked to make up songs for his children and friends. He said he relished playing after games because "it relaxes my soul."[24]

During the last week of August, Dale Long hit four home runs in a series with the Angels. The blasts pushed his league-leading total to thirty-two and gave boost to his MVP candidacy. They also helped to hike Hollywood's lead in the Pacific Coast League to 11 1/2 games. When the team took the field on Sunday, September 8, for a doubleheader with Oakland, the pennant was within its grasp. In the fourth inning of the second game, good news came across the Western Union ticker in the press box. Second-place Seattle had lost, 7–3, to Sacramento. The Rainiers' loss meant Hollywood had clinched the pennant. After the final out of the game, Bob Cobb bounded onto the field. He reached into the dugout and shook hands with Bragan, then lauded his manager as a miracle worker to reporters. The Stars had earned their third pennant in five years. Combined with their second- and third-place finishes during that time, the pennants gave Hollywood the most successful five-year span in the history of the Pacific Coast League.

With the title in the bag, Bragan set his sights on two achievements. One was accomplished on September 11, when he used Dale Long at all nine positions in one game. The slugger pitched the first inning. He walked four and flung a wild pitch but did not allow a run. In the second inning, Long caught. The left-handed Long used a right-hander's catcher's mitt. From the third through ninth innings, Long moved inning by inning through the four infield and three outfield positions.

Bragan's next objective was to see George O'Donnell win twenty games. The Hollywood pitching ace had been stuck on nineteen wins for two weeks. Bragan sent O'Donnell to the mound to start the first game of the doubleheader on the final day of the season. The tall, slender slinger pitched eight scoreless innings and did not walk a batter. But the one inning he was scored upon was disastrous. Oakland scored eight times in the third inning to thwart O'Donnell's quest and beat Hollywood, 8–7.

In the second game Hollywood scored eight times in the first inning to lead, 8–2. Thinking quickly, Bragan removed his starting pitcher. He then sent O'Donnell into the game in relief. The Hollywood manager knew that a starting pitcher could not get credit for a win unless he pitched five innings. O'Donnell pitched the final four innings. Hollywood won, 8–6, and O'Donnell received credit as the winning pitcher to earn his twentieth win of the season.

Once the attendance was recorded, 330,984 had cheered the team over the course of the championship season. The Stars finished with 106 wins. Dale Long was rewarded for his 35 home runs and 116 runs batted in with the Pacific Coast League's Most Valuable Player Award. In the clubhouse beneath the stands, players hollered, gulped beers, and laughed in celebration. In the manager's office, Bobby Bragan hurriedly packed his things. He had a plane to catch. A managing opportunity for a Cuban winter-ball team awaited. Inside the office of Bob Cobb, uncertainty awaited as well.

27

"A NATURAL"

The drive had taken Bob Cobb east on Sunset Boulevard, past Schwab's Pharmacy. He was oblivious to the throng of teenagers inside Wallich's who were lined up to buy the newly released forty-five of Bill Haley and the Comets' hit song *Rock around the Clock*. As Cobb passed La Cienega Boulevard, he glanced up at the marquee above Ciro's to see which performer had been booked. It was when he reached Grove Drive that Cobb turned the wheel to direct his Cadillac to the left and began the climb into the Echo Park area hills that surrounded a canyon known as Chavez Ravine.

The restaurateur had first come to this area in 1950 at the invitation of the chief of police. The man wanted to discuss catering. He sought Cobb's advice for setting up a kitchen and dining facility in the police academy, which sat near the north end of the hilly area. Their meeting led to an invitation to enjoy the shooting range. At least twice a week for the next few years, it was an invitation Bob Cobb heartily enjoyed.

The area's rolling hills, wild rose bushes, palm and eucalyptus trees may have measured just six miles from Cobb's Brown Derby office but felt another world away. The serenity offered a sharp contrast to the bustling streets and sidewalks of downtown Los Angeles to the south. Cobb's drives and shooting excursions with police officers brought a tranquility. More importantly, in Chavez Ravine, Bob Cobb saw the future.

Questions about the future of the Hollywood Stars took on a sense of urgency during the final weeks of the 1953 season. A letter that had arrived on Cobb's desk on August 11 from Don Stewart, president of the Los Angeles Angels, brought shock, if not anger. In it, Stewart declared that P. K. Wrigley would not grant the Stars an extension of the twenty-year waiver struck in November 1937 that had allowed the San Francisco Missions to encroach upon the Angels' territory and play in Southern California as the Hollywood Stars. Even though the Angels were receiving $40,000 per year from the Stars as part of the waiver settlement, they were prepared to let the agreement expire when the 1957 season came to a close.

Cobb protested. He sought to enlist support from fellow club owners and fight Wrigley's plan. Before he could do so, the Angels' owner dug his heels in for a fight. One week after his initial declaration, Wrigley served the Stars with a second notice that reaffirmed his stance. "We expected this club, after a reasonable time to find a home outside of our territory," Wrigley explained to Ed Prell of the *Chicago Tribune*.[1] The Stars' owner noted that his club and the Angels were the only two operations in the league to make money in 1953. Each drew their largest crowds when the other came to their ballpark. Cobb called Wrigley's declaration "a death warrant for the entire Pacific Coast League."[2]

Wrigley's position put Bob Cobb between a rock and a hard place. Already he was wary of the plans Earl Gilmore had for his land. With his oil wells now capped, Gilmore had begun to sell parcels of his property. In May 1950 Gilmore agreed to sell fifteen acres of his land to CBS for $2 million. The broadcast company had plans to use the site for a spectacular new home, "Television City." Included as part of the deal was the acreage where Gilmore Stadium stood. Already the once-popular stadium had been bulldozed away.

CBS had been a neighbor to Cobb at Hollywood and Vine. The network's employees and stars were regulars who had helped to make the Brown Derby a success. During a planning commission meeting in September 1950, the breadth of the CBS plan was revealed. It was learned that the broadcaster had also purchased options on two additional parcels of Earl Gilmore's land for future expansion. One was a four-acre site; the second parcel covered six acres. "Nobody knows how big this television industry is going to be. But we have to be prepared," said a spokesperson for CBS.[3] The oil magnate had it written into the purchase agreement that CBS could not exercise its option on the six-acre parcel until the fall of 1957, when the lease agreement with the current tenant expired. The site was Gilmore Field, and the Hollywood Baseball Association was the tenant.

The looming eviction from Gilmore Island and now the notice from the Angels made finding a new home an urgent matter. While Earl Gilmore and P. K. Wrigley may have been the heaviest weight on Bob Cobb's shoulders, an even tinier antagonist pumped greater fuel to the man's search for a new home. Cobb's secretary, Edna Ward, was working at her desk in the Stars' Gilmore Field office one morning. She happened to glance toward the switchboard and was struck by a normally white piece of wood that was now black. As she looked closer, she was certain she saw the wood move. A wider gaze about the office realized a stream of insects had marched to and up one side of her desk. The line of pests led to her typewriter. Ward let loose with a loud scream and ran from the office. An inspector found parts of Gilmore Field to be infested with termites. The ballpark was falling apart.

On the heels of Wrigley's second notice, Cobb flew to Phoenix. Convinced by local leaders that their town's ballpark could be expanded from four thousand seats to twenty-five thousand, Cobb took an option to buy the Class C Phoenix Senators, and the club was renamed the Stars. Advances in air-conditioning and the arrival of technology and manufacturing companies had sparked a population boom. The city now topped one hundred thousand residents and was growing at a 5 percent annual rate. Cobb announced that the Stars would operate the Arizona-Texas League club as one of its farm clubs. However, bigger plans were on his mind. Should Wrigley force the Stars out of Southern California, Cobb was prepared to petition baseball for the Phoenix territory.

While machinations constructed Phoenix as a potential future home for the Hollywood Stars, Bob Cobb's thoughts were never far from the spot where he ideally wanted to move his ball club. For three years he dreamed of a baseball mecca, one that would be the envy of the game and bring acclaim to Los Angeles. Cobb envisioned this palatial panacea rising from the hills seven miles west of Gilmore Field: Chavez Ravine. After his initial 1950 visit to the police academy and three weeks after Earl Gilmore had announced his deal with CBS, Cobb convinced Bill Schroeder, a local sportsman, to take a drive with him to see the Chavez Ravine site. As they walked a dirt road, the restaurateur pointed out where he pictured his ballpark in the 250-acre, *L*-shaped canyon. Around three hundred families had once called the area home before a proposed housing project had seen most move away in 1949. The project never got off the ground. Only a dozen or so families remained. Cobb pointed out to Schroeder that future plans called for four freeways to one day serve the area. The men agreed the site was "a natural."[4]

Cobb engaged a renowned local architect, Stiles Clements, to produce drawings for a sports complex. He insisted on a "super modern" ballpark with "a luxury setup with palm trees in the foyer, private cabanas where private parties could enjoy the game, swank restaurants, a nursery where mama can park the kids, an executive club where the fan can get a drink in comfort, an escalator where the old folks shoot up, a lanai where people can converge between double headers."[5] Clements was an architect of great acclaim in Los Angeles. His works included the El Capitan and Mayan Theatres, the Richfield Tower, and Coulter's department store. His design for Cobb's ballpark was dazzling.

Cobb displayed Clements's work in slick brochures. Over the next several days and weeks, he proceeded to bombard members of the city council with his idea. The barrage brought a meeting with the mayor, where Cobb proposed the city give him one hundred acres of land in Chavez Ravine. Cobb would then raise $8 million and with his associates build a new ballpark for the Hollywood Stars. Under Cobb's plan, the land and the ballpark would be deeded back to the city, and Cobb and his group of investors would take a ninety-nine-year tax-free lease at one dollar per year until the investors had recouped their money. Cobb added that the stadium would be built in such a way that it could be expanded to sixty thousand seats once the city was able to secure a major-league baseball team. "If we utilize Chavez Ravine the way it can be developed, it will gain for Los Angeles world-wide acclaim," Cobb told Jeane Hoffman of the *Los Angeles Times*.[6]

For almost three years Cobb worked vigorously to try to assemble support. His talk drew the attention of civic and elected leaders to the underdeveloped area. Curiosity grew to tepid support. Then, in the spring of 1953, the city's interest in Cobb's plan took a stark turn. Days before the 1953 baseball season was to begin, Lou Perini had stunned many in the game by moving his Boston Braves to Milwaukee. It was the first time in fifty years that a major-league team had changed home cities. To many in the game, this would not be an isolated move. It was common knowledge that the St. Louis Browns and Philadelphia A's were deeply in debt, and paltry attendance offered little hope of escape. Talk in baseball was rife that the only solution for both clubs would be to sell and move to a new home city. The rumors and the Braves' move spread belief among city leaders in Los Angeles that a big-league club in search of a new home was the city's best opportunity to gain a major-league team. That spelled bad news for the Pacific Coast League. Its quest to gain big-league status was now viewed by those in political office in Los Angeles to be little more than a pipe dream. From that point on, Bob Cobb received nothing but a cold shoulder.

Mayor Norris Poulson established a task force to study the possibilities for luring a major-league team. He wanted the group to determine the proper approach to take, how it could exploit those possibilities, and what the cost would be. He also sent a letter to the head of the Los Angeles Coliseum Commission to ask that a study be made of the viability of playing major-league baseball in the cavernous Olympic stadium. When local oil mogul Edwin Pauley agreed to fund the study, the Coliseum Commission voted unanimously to move forward.

Though rebuffed by the city, Cobb found an interested ear on the county board of supervisors. That body, it turned out, had been approached by Bill Veeck, who owned the St. Louis Browns. Veeck saw a move to Los Angeles as a solution to his ball club's problems. Roger Jessup, the senior member of the board, invited Cobb to a meeting at which baseball was the topic of discussion. The Hollywood Stars' president engaged in dialogue for almost an hour. He tried to dissuade the group from any interest in the Browns. "The St. Louis club is on the bottom," he said. "It is a money-losing proposition."[7] Cobb then advocated his sports center and urged the group to give the Pacific Coast League a chance to gain major-league status. Jessup was a self-made success in the dairy business and had an appreciation for successful, innovative businessmen. He raised the idea to offer land for Cobb's project that was not far from Griffith Park, near Riverside Drive and Los Feliz. In private, Cobb expressed his appreciation to Jessup. He insisted, however, there was no better site for a ballpark than Chavez Ravine.

Three times Cobb found his new ballpark hopes under threat, and three times in the year following the 1953 season he was able to breathe a sigh of relief. In September Veeck was pressured by the American League to sell the Browns to a group in Baltimore, and the team was moved to that city. Shortly before Christmas in 1953, the Coliseum Commission concluded its baseball study. Architects put the cost to construct necessary amenities and retrofit the stadium for baseball at almost $3 million. The potential expenditure drew thumbs-down from the commissioners by a vote of 7–1.

One year later, in November 1954, ninety-one-year-old Connie Mack, who was bedridden and so upset at the prospect of selling the team he had founded that he hadn't been able to eat for a week, signed the papers to part with his Philadelphia Athletics. The ball club was moved to Kansas City. In both cases, representatives of Los Angeles tried to lure the teams. The sale and moves of the two clubs elsewhere, however, put Los Angeles city leaders on the receiving end of sharp criticism. Del Webb, owner of the New York Yankees, pointed out that Baltimore and Kansas City came to meetings with cash and solid stadium plans. Los Angeles, he said, offered empty promises. It was reported that emissaries of the city came to league meetings and expressed half-truths. Supposed investors made vague promises. Paul Zimmerman, sports editor of the *Los Angeles Times*, blasted the city's efforts. "Major League baseball is inevitable for Los Angeles, but we'll have to buy, not beg or brag our way in," he wrote.[8] In a speech to supporters, Poulson attempted to deflect the criticism. He announced that he was working on a plan and had found the perfect place for a major-league baseball stadium in Los Angeles. It was Chavez Ravine.

On the field, Hollywood had again assembled a team that was the class of the Pacific Coast League. The 1954 season, however, did not start out that way. Bragan's players lost ten of their first twelve games and fell into sixth place. A hot streak in early May vaulted the Stars toward the top of the standings, and on May 15, they took over first place, where they stayed for the next three months.

With George O'Donnell in the big leagues with Pittsburgh, an unlikely ace emerged to lead the pitching staff. Mel Queen had once been a promising prospect in the New York Yankees organization. Following the 1952 season he had fallen down a flight of stairs and injured his back. Four months of treatment did nothing. A year later Queen took an off-season job in an airplane factory. He wielded heavy wrenches and manned a stress forming press. The daily tasks strengthened muscles in his back, and by spring training the pain had gone away. During spring training Queen altered his arm angle on his delivery. The change improved his control. Bragan rewarded Queen by naming him Hollywood's

Opening Day pitcher. He lost that game, 6–4, to Portland, but by the end of May, Queen had reeled off ten straight wins and led the league.

A ten-game win streak to end the month of May pushed Hollywood's lead to five and a half games. The Stars maintained that cushion through June and much of July. On its journey toward a possible third straight pennant, however, the team struck a few potholes. Queen suffered an elbow injury. His control faltered, and he lost six consecutive starts. The pitching staff was buoyed by a thirty-one-year-old rookie, Lino Donoso, whom a Hollywood scout had discovered pitching in the Mexican League. By mid-July, Donoso was among the best pitchers in the league, with a 15–3 mark. Red Munger, too, had also proven difficult to beat and was 15–4 headed into August. Neither player's ascendency would be sustained. During a road trip to Oakland, Donoso was rushed to a hospital with severe stomach pains and underwent an appendectomy. Three weeks later Munger was sidelined by an injured knee.

On August 5, Frankie Kelleher sat down in Bob Cobb's office and informed the Hollywood president of his decision to retire. Far and away Hollywood's most popular player for a decade, Kelleher was thirty-seven. His production had declined since his forty-homer season of 1950. Younger Pirates prospects had pushed Kelleher to the bench and a pinch-hitting role. Cobb proclaimed he would give Kelleher a night and set about making plans for a regal send-off.

The 1954 season brought Carlos Bernier back to Hollywood. He had spent the 1953 campaign with Pittsburgh but was hampered by leg injuries through much of the year. Bragan turned the speedster loose. He had no steal sign for Bernier, only a sign when he did *not* want the flashy outfielder to take a chance on the base paths. By August, Bernier led the league in base swipes, and his .313 batting average was among the best in the Pacific Coast League. Not only were Bernier's baseball skills mercurial, but his temperament was too. Whereas in his big 1952 season Bernier had a tendency to grumble and pout, now he was downright volatile and argumentative. Almost with regularity, Bernier flew off the handle at umpires' calls. He argued angrily and demonstrated his unhappiness with petulance.

Bernier was suspended five games in June for starting a fight, then fined for spitting at a fan in the box seats after being ejected from a game in Wrigley Field. Bragan urged Bernier to curb his outbursts. Bob Cobb took a paternalistic approach and counseled the outfielder that his temper, if unchecked, could hurt his career.

On the night of August 11, with two outs in the bottom of the eighth inning, Bernier took a called third strike and exploded into an epic rage. He initially stood silently and glared at the home plate umpire, Chris Valenti. The television cameraman kept his lens pointed at the pair. The enraged outfielder then bumped Valenti, who whipped off his mask and hollered that Bernier was out of the game. In the next instant, Carlos Bernier's lack of self-control would fulfill Bob Cobb's prophesy. The outfielder raised his left hand and slapped Valenti across the face. Gasps flew from among the 6,159 fans. Pants Rowland shot upright from his front row seat. From the on-deck circle, Jack Phillips raced toward his teammate. As the irate outfielder took another step toward the umpire, Phillips wrapped Bernier in a bear hug. Phillips tried to calm his teammate while he struggled to direct Bernier into the Stars dugout. Infuriated, Pants Rowland wasted no time in finding Cobb and Bragan under the stands. Bernier, he told them, was fined and suspended. Once the game ended, Bernier appeared in the doorway to the umpire's room. Valenti was startled to see him. Tears streamed down the ballplayer's cheeks. Over and over, Bernier repeated in broken English that he was sorry, so very sorry.

The next morning Rowland made official that Bernier was suspended indefinitely. He was also fined $75. With Bernier out for the remainder of the season and the pitching staff in tatters, Hollywood struggled to try to reach the finish line ahead of the other seven clubs in the league. Over each of the final four weeks of the season, the Stars' lead shrank.

Tension accompanied the players to Seattle and Portland for the final two weeks of the season. The pressure blanketed their wives as well. No sooner had the women seen the team off at the airport when they hatched a plan to relieve the pennant pursuit stress. The women were a close-knit group and often enjoyed activities together when the team was on the road. This time one thought it might be fun if they all dyed their hair a different color so that their husbands would come home to different wives.

On Thursday, September 9, in their final series of the season, the Stars were pummeled by the last-place Portland Beavers, 6–1. The defeat cut their league lead to only one game. Oregon rain kept the Stars at their hotel the next night and meant that the season would conclude with back-to-back doubleheaders on the weekend, a grueling spate of four games over two days. While Hollywood's players were playing cards and watching television, second-place San Diego beat the Angels at Wrigley Field, 6–0, to close to within a half game.

In the first game of the Saturday double header, seven Hollywood pitchers were tagged for 18 hits and 12 runs in a lopsided 12–1 defeat. The Stars rebounded to take the second game, 5–3, but received grim news from Los Angeles. San Diego had won again. Their 6–0 besting of the Angels pulled the Padres into a tie for first place headed to the final day of the 1954 season.

The final-day doubleheader began with a pitcher's duel. Lino Donoso and Mel Queen teamed to allow only one Beavers run. However, their teammates were unable to score, and the Stars lost. In Los Angeles, the Padres lost, 3–2. The two teams would enter their final game of the year in a first-place tie. In a must-win finale, Hollywood received the greatest pitching performance in its history. Roger Bowman was given the start. Only a day earlier he had been Hollywood's starting pitcher but was yanked from the game after giving up singles to each of the game's first four batters. Now, in the most important game of the season, Bobby Bragan was handing him the ball once again. It had been eight years since Bowman was a heralded eighteen-year-old signing of the New York Giants. His fastball at the time was compared to that of Bob Feller. But a shoulder injury and a hunting accident in which he shot himself in the pitching arm had funneled him to the minor leagues, where he now mixed a knuckleball and a changeup to try to get outs.

Bowman retired the side in order in the bottom of the first. His success brought relief. That he did it again in the fifth—and had done so for all five innings—brought drama. Hitter after hitter either flailed and missed at Bowman's offerings or hit one bounder after another to Hollywood infielders. As the twenty-first Portland batter came to the plate in the bottom of the seventh inning, the final inning of the Sunday doubleheader, the official scorer knew better than anyone else the sort of history that was being made. Nobody had walked or managed a hit, and no errors had been made. Bowman had struck out eight. Only one ball was hit out of the infield, a routine fly ball out to left field. The other twelve outs were ground balls to the infielders, just as the twenty-first was. It made Roger Bowman the first pitcher in Hollywood Stars history to throw a perfect game.

More importantly, Hollywood's 10–0 win was matched by the 7–2 victory San Diego registered over Los Angeles. After playing 168 games, Hollywood and San Diego had finished the 1954 season in a tie with 101 wins each. A coin toss sent the Stars to San Diego for a one-game playoff that would determine the regular-season champ. What was billed as sudden death was just that to Hollywood. Two long home runs by the Padres' Bob Elliott accounted for five San Diego runs. The Padres prevailed, 7–2.

The league had reinstituted its playoff system, but the results were abysmal for both the Stars and the league's bank account. Hollywood was swept by San Francisco, and with the attention of sports fans and media turned toward football, none of the three games managed to attract more than seven hundred to the ballpark.

The end of the season brought a disappointment that mixed with somberness to some of Hollywood's faithful. It was before the first game of the Stars' final home series that reality struck home and boyhood ended for many a youthful fan. Bob Cobb walked to a microphone near home plate. Together with Frankie Kelleher they announced the slugger's retirement. Amid the shower of vocal praise and weighty gifts, many fans were tugged by sorrow. For kids, it was an emotional good-bye to their hero. Ten-year-old Joe Harper was glum in his family's box seat. Neighborhood kids Marshall Barnes and Merv Williams were so transfixed watching through a crack and hole in the outfield fence that they weren't worried about Eddie, the cop. Big-league teams belonged to fans in other cities. To most young Southern California baseball fans, Joe DiMaggio was merely a name in the newspapers. Frankie Kelleher was real. Kelleher's power put everyone on the edge of their seat whenever he came to bat, especially when his home run prowess might tie or win a game in the late innings. Already the rest of the crew from the Hollywood heyday was gone. Chuck Stevens's six-year run had ended when he was sold to San Francisco. Johnny O'Neill had been sold to Oakland after five seasons as the Stars' shortstop. After six years as Hollywood's second baseman, Gene Handley was now in Class C ball. "I've got no more mileage on me to go any further," Kelleher said.[9] He was one week past his thirty-eighth birthday. He could feel the tap of Father Time on his shoulder whenever he had to chase a fly ball or when he swung and missed at a fastball. In ten seasons as a Hollywood mainstay, Keller had hit 232 home runs, second in the Pacific Coast League record book behind the 251 belted by Buzz Arlett.

Cobb surprised Kelleher. He brought the outfielder's parents on the field. He had flown them to Los Angeles from their San Francisco home. Gifts stacked as organizations and fans made presentations. The recognition culminated with Cobb handing Kelleher a set of keys to a new car, a station wagon. Cobb then proclaimed that no Hollywood Stars player would wear the number 7 ever again. It would be retired after ten seasons on Kelleher's back.

The ardent fan knew what the night represented: an end. Heroes of long standing would be no more. Any player with talent would spend just a season at Gilmore Field before heading off to Pittsburgh to help the woeful Pirates. As Frankie Kelleher walked out of Gilmore Field for the last time, there was a little less luster on the Hollywood Stars.

28

"THAT'S THE WRONG SANCHEZ"

The pace was faster. On this night, usually stern words carried an even more demanding tone. Fingers carefully moved flatware and glasses into proper position on the tables. Instructions were barked in the kitchen with a mixture of normal direction and unusual stress. The night was important. Excellence was paramount, even more so than usual for a restaurant synonymous with the glamour of Hollywood and the glitz of celebrity such as the Brown Derby. On this evening Bob Cobb's fourth restaurant, The Brown Derby on Los Feliz and Hillhurst near Griffith Park, was hosting a celebration—a special screening for the press of an episode of the popular television show *I Love Lucy*. The event was particularly special to Cobb, for it featured the Brown Derby.

Bob Cobb's restaurant had long been a particular favorite of the show's stars, the celebrity couple Desi Arnaz and Lucille Ball. When Ball gave birth to the couple's son in 1953, Desi Arnaz burst into the Hollywood Brown Derby to shout the news to a room full of diners. Another restaurant regular was William Frawley, the Hollywood Stars' shareholder who was a costar on the show as Arnaz and Ball's crotchety neighbor, Fred Mertz.

It was Arnaz who had approached Cobb with the idea to preview the show in his restaurant. Everyone had been elated once taping of the Brown Derby episode was completed. Titled "Hollywood at Last!" it features a starstruck Lucy having just arrived in Los Angeles and keen to see movie stars. She can think of no better place to do so than the Brown Derby. Over lunch in the restaurant, she recognizes William Holden, and hilarious hijinks follow. After the episode aired on February 7, 1955, it would come to be regarded as an iconic display of television comedy. A scene from the show would grace the cover of *TV Guide* magazine. Use of the restaurant as the setting for the episode would cement the Brown Derby's place as a staple of Hollywood glamour.

The *I Love Lucy* episode was not the Brown Derby's first brush with the bright lights and big cameras. Constance Bennett starred as a waitress at the Brown Derby in the 1932 film *What Price Hollywood?* In the 1945 movie *Mildred Pierce*, Joan Crawford's character tends bar in a scene filmed at the Brown Derby.

Featured even more than the Brown Derby in motion pictures and television shows were members of the Hollywood Stars. Films with a baseball theme were not uncommon in Hollywood. Joe E. Brown's baseball comedies, *Elmer the Great* in 1933 and *Alibi Ike* two years later, were successes for Warner Brothers. Beginning in the late 1940s the popularity of some of baseball's biggest stars drove a series of biopics that did well at the box office. Each time a baseball film went from proposal to production, producers and directors sought help to make their film as realistic as possible. That often brought a phone call to a member of the Hollywood Stars.

The phenomenon began in 1941, when Samuel Goldwyn received a pitch to make a film based on the life of New York Yankees star Lou Gehrig. Initially, he wasn't interested in doing the project. Goldwyn did not particularly like baseball films, but weeks after Lou Gehrig's death, he agreed to have lunch at the Brown Derby with Gehrig's widow, Eleanor; the late player's business manager, Christy Walsh; and Paul Gallico, a sportswriter who had written a screenplay for the film. After listening to their idea, Goldwyn was sold. He wanted a popular actor for the lead role. Gary Cooper was the first to be mentioned. Cooper was a hot commodity in the industry. He was being touted for an Academy Award for his work in *Sergeant York* and had signed to do Billy Wilder's *Ball of Fire* with Barbara Stanwyck.

Sam Wood was hired to direct the film, not just because of his talent but because he had played semipro baseball and understood the game. That understanding led Wood to express concern with using Gary Cooper in the lead role. Yes, the actor was athletic. He loved to ski and box. But Cooper had never played baseball. An even bigger problem was that

Cooper was right-handed; Lou Gehrig threw with his left hand and batted left-handed.

Once the entertainment and celebrity columnists wrote about the project, dozens of actors made a pitch for the leading role. Ed Barrow, general manager of the New York Yankees, urged members of his family to write letters to promote Eddie Albert for the part. Robert Preston, Billy Soos, and Johnny Mack Brown were considered because they batted and threw left-handed. Guinn Williams was called a dead ringer for the late Yankees' star. Celebrity columnist Hedda Hopper promoted Dennis Morgan. She pointed out that Morgan had played minor-league ball and was a left-hander. Goldwyn was not satisfied with any of the other candidates, and to support his gut decision, he conducted polls of both film and baseball fans. In both, Gary Cooper was the runaway favorite for the part.

On December 29, Cooper agreed to the project, and work to teach him baseball skills began. Bill Dickey, the Yankees' catcher, traveled to Montana, where he used snowballs to work with the actor on his throwing skills. Wood enlisted Lefty O'Doul to be a technical adviser. The San Francisco Seals' manager faced a herculean task. "You throw a ball like an old woman tossing a hot biscuit," he snapped in frustration at Cooper one day.[1] For batting lessons, Babe Herman was recruited. The training sessions were exasperating, if not futile. Finally, Wood hit on a solution. He would outfit Herman in a Yankees uniform and use the Hollywood Stars' outfielder in batting scenes. Herman's scenes would be shot from a distance, so the popular player would not be recognized.

Jack Salveson was cast as a pitcher in the film. In his role he was to hit Cooper in the head with a pitch. The prop department made a baseball out of cotton for the scene. It was easier to construct a cotton baseball than it was for the pitcher to throw it with any accuracy. It took seven takes before Salveson was able to plunk Cooper. "It just wouldn't go straight," Salveson complained.[2]

When *Pride of the Yankees* premiered in New York, ten thousand people attended screenings in forty-one cinemas around the city. It launched to much fanfare around the country. Once it had concluded its run, *Pride of the Yankees* was the seventh-most successful film of 1942, generating more than $8 million at the box office. In all, the film was nominated for ten Academy Awards.

During the fall of 1947, Goldwyn gave thumbs-up to another baseball movie. This project was the story of Monty Stratton, the former Chicago

White Sox pitching standout who lost his leg in a hunting accident yet made a remarkable pitching comeback. Jack Cummings, who was hired to produce the film, and Roy Rowlands, who would direct the picture, scoured Southern California diamonds for ballplayers. By the time the cast and crew were in place, nine members of the Hollywood Stars—Tod Davis, Frankie Kelleher, Johnny Lindell, Pinky Woods, Gus Zernial, Lou Stringer, Fred Millican, George Metkovich, and Chuck Stevens—received parts in the picture. Many scenes were shot in Gilmore Field. The entire Hollywood team walked the red carpet as special guests at the premier showing of *The Stratton Story* at the Egyptian Theatre.

When the film turned a profit of more than $1.2 million for Metro-Goldwyn-Mayer, its success spawned a string of biopics, dramas, comedies, and romance films with baseball themes. Many would involve the Hollywood Stars in one way or another.

Throughout the summer of 1949, Sam Bischoff tried to talk Jackie Robinson into doing a movie about his life. When Robinson finally agreed, it was with a stipulation. "He was a stickler for realism," said Al Green, the director.[3] The film was shot in Gilmore Field. Also in the summer of 1949, Columbia Pictures agreed to produce a baseball comedy called *Kill the Umpire.* William Bendix was cast in the lead role. Starring alongside Bendix was Bill Frawley. To ensure realism, director John Beck sought to cast real ballplayers. Frawley, unabashed Hollywood Stars fan that he was, arranged for ten members of the ball club—Kelleher, Stringer, Woods, Millican, Metkovich, Jim Baxes, Cliff Dapper, Irv Noren, Willie Ramsdell, and Jerry Priddy—to receive roles in the film.

It did not take the players long to figure out the business side of the motion picture industry. Each was paid by the day. When filming reached the final scene, a bit of enterprising mischief-making overtook Irv Noren. The scene called for Noren to make a throw from center field to third base. Instead, the Stars' centerfielder intentionally fired the throw high and over the head of the third baseman. When the director shouted "cut," players shot wry smiles at one another. Noren's wild throw meant they would have to come back the next day and do the scene all over again. More importantly, it meant each would receive another day's pay.

Not long after the 1951 season concluded, a number of Stars players were queried about doing yet another baseball film. Warner Brothers had agreed to do a picture about former St. Louis Cardinals' pitcher Grover Cleveland Alexander. Chuck Stevens, who had been snagged by a casting agent and given two cameo and two credited parts in films, signed on for a part in the film. Irv Noren, George Metkovich, Rowe Wallerstein, Lou Stringer, Pinky Woods, and Jerry Priddy also received roles. Frank Lovejoy, described by one newspaper columnist as "the incurable Hollywood Stars rooter," was hired to costar opposite Ronald Reagan and Doris Day as Rogers Hornsby, the Cardinals' manager.[4]

Once the picture *The Winning Team* was completed and shown in the summer of 1952, many of the Stars' players were unrecognizable even to their most ardent fans. Makeup artists hid them beneath beards and uniforms of the late 1800s. Critics noted that the use of so many pro ballplayers helped the film to achieve a strong sense of realism. So pleased was Alexander's widow, Aimee, at the outcome of the filming and the reviews in the press that she stopped by the *Los Angeles Times* to personally extend her thanks to the newspaper's entertainment writers.

Hollywood Stars games became vehicles to promote baseball films. Following release of *The Winning Team*, both Lovejoy and Reagan became involved in pregame activities. They handled first-pitch honors and took to the on-field microphone to urge fans to see their new motion picture.

Gilmore Field was also a convenient shooting location for non-baseball films. It was utilized in 1950 for the crime drama *711 Ocean Drive*. When considering places to film various scenes for *The Atomic City* in 1952, executives at Paramount Pictures pointed director Jerry Hopper three miles up the street to the Stars' ballpark. Several Hollywood players also received opportunities in non-baseball films. Pinky Woods was hired to teach Red Skelton to throw a baseball for his part in the film *Three Little Words*. Woods also was given a role in the picture. In 1951 Woods played the role of a policeman in *Father's Little Dividend*. That same year he was hired to coach Katharine Hepburn for a baseball scene planned for the movie *Pat and Mike*. The scene, however, was not used.

The growth of television as a medium brought with it many acting and appearance opportunities for Stars players. Dick Smith and his wife were contestants on the television game show *It Pays to Be Married* and left with $250 in cash and several prizes. George O'Donnell and Jack Phillips were each paid $100 to perform a baseball scene for the show *Dear Phoebe*. O'Donnell was to groove pitches to Phillips so that the first baseman could hit the ball out of Gilmore Field for a home run.

Not long after he moved his family into a house rented from the actor Arthur Treacher in Studio City, Bobby Bragan found that many of his neighbors worked in the entertainment industry. One extended an invitation to visit a taping of a Bob Hope project. To reach the studio, the Bragans had to traverse hilly, winding Laurel Canyon Boulevard. The drive left the manager's young daughter, Gwen, with an upset stomach. On their arrival at the sound stage, crew members warmly greeted the Bragans. The Stars' manager introduced his family. As the director made small talk with Bragan's young daughter, the girl suddenly clutched her stomach, jerked, and spewed her breakfast all over the director's shoes.

The path traveled by Mark Scott was not unlike the journey made by many of Hollywood's players. He honed his craft in a smaller town—Norfolk, Virginia—hoping to one day get a crack at performing on a bigger stage. In Scott's case his skill did not involve swinging a baseball bat or snapping off curveballs. His talent involved calling baseball games on the radio. When Scott and his wife, Dorothy, were married, he carried such a heavy volume of broadcasting commitments that the couple was unable to schedule a honeymoon. A year later heavy snow thwarted Scott's plans to take his wife and newborn daughter, Mary Jane, to visit family in Chicago during the Christmas holidays. As a consolation the Scotts traveled to Cuba. It would be a life-changing trip. While at the Hotel Nacionale, Mark Scott heard a bellboy page the publisher of the *Sporting News*. An avid reader of the publication, Scott sought out the man. When he shared his ambitions, Scott was told that the Hollywood Stars were looking for a radio announcer. Weeks later Mark Scott found himself seated in a booth in the Brown Derby. He fought to maintain calm, in disbelief that he was having lunch with Bob Cobb and one of the team's shareholders, the immortal crooner Bing Crosby. After the meal, Cobb and Crosby excused themselves. They went upstairs to Cobb's office to listen to a recording of Scott's work. Scott anxiously waited outside. When Crosby came out of the room, he gave Scott a wink and said, "Don't worry kid, you're in."[5]

Scott's work during the day giving scores and sports news on KFWB radio gave him a level of recognition in Southern California. Calling Hollywood Stars games bumped him into the celebrity category. Scott brought flavor and charm to his broadcasts. When he read a commercial for sponsors 7 Up, Scott would boost his young daughter, Mary Jane, onto his knee, then ask what she thought of the drink. "I yike it," the youngster would cutely chirp.[6] Scott's voice blared from car radios along Melrose Avenue, tabletop radios in offices, small transistor radios that kept mechanics company while they worked on cars, and large consoles where ardent fans such as Cecilia (DeMille) Harper kept score while she listened to every game that she was unable to attend.

Not long after an usher first pointed Scott to the broadcast position at the start of the 1952 season, he met and befriended many of the actors, directors, and producers who frequented Gilmore Field. In time these acquaintances would lead to casting opportunities in motion pictures and television programs. Stars mic-men had been convenient selections for roles as announcers long before Scott arrived in town. Sam Balter, the Stars' television broadcaster who had been a UCLA and Olympic basketball standout, played a broadcaster in *The Jackie Robinson Story.* Hollywood's radio voice prior to Scott, Jack Sherman, had received the part of an announcer in *The Pride of St. Louis*. Like Sherman and Balter, Scott was soon reading over scripts and rehearsing lines for parts. He was cast in the familiar role of a radio announcer in the popular film *The Kid from Left Field.* Scott did narration work on Lee Wilder's science fiction film *Killers from Space*. In *Hell's Horizon* he played an air force colonel. In *The Harder They Fall* he filled the role of an announcer. Scott also received parts in two television series, *Boston Blackie* and *Celebrity Playhouse*.

If some of Hollywood's players had grown accustomed to premieres and film hoopla, the launch of the 1955 home campaign felt normal. The first Gilmore Field contest of the season began with Hollywood aplomb. The chamber of commerce declared the day, April 12, "Baseball Day." They threw a luncheon at the Roosevelt Hotel to launch the new season. Once the meal and comments were complete, players piled into a caravan of cars for a parade to the ballpark. Leading the procession was Miss Hollywood Star 1955, a voluptuous Warner Brothers starlet named Jayne Mansfield. Each of the players shared a car with at least one young up-and-coming actress. Several businesses around the ballpark gave their employees the afternoon off so that they could enjoy both the parade and the ball game.

A turnout of 4,573 basked in warm afternoon sunshine at Gilmore Field. Going into the bottom of the ninth inning, however, the enthusiasm of the afternoon had quelled. Hollywood trailed Seattle, 5–4. A jolt of hope shot through the crowd when the Stars' new center fielder, Gail

Budding actress Jayne Mansfield was Miss Hollywood Stars 1955. Each year more than one hundred young actresses and models would compete for the title. ***Courtesy of the author***

Henley, walked. Jack Lohrke turned hope into enthusiasm by hitting a smash off the Seattle shortstop's mitt that rolled far enough away to allow Lohrke to reach first base with a single. The scene turned from calm to gusto as Carlos Bernier stepped to the plate. His single brought a roar from the crowd as Henley raced home with the tying run. Hand clapping and shouts that pleaded for a hit greeted R. C. Stevens. The big first baseman complied by smashing a pitch down the third-base line to bring in the winning run and complete an enthusiastic first day with a 6–5 triumph.

On the eve of the season opener, a poll of the managers of the eight Pacific Coast League clubs made Hollywood the team to beat for the 1955 pennant. Finishing on top would mean four consecutive regular-season first-place finishes for the Stars and four pennants in seven years. The team's first road trip was anything but smooth. It began with a turbulent flight to Sacramento. The bumpy ride knotted stomachs and frayed nerves up and down the aisle. "You heard of the champagne flight, haven't you? Well this is the knuckleball flight," Red Munger grumbled.[7] The rocky flight mimicked the Stars' early season play.

Pittsburgh Pirates prospects filled the Hollywood roster. It was a younger team than in the past and one whose talent Branch Rickey had badly misjudged. Following their dramatic season-opening win, the Stars spent the first two months of the season mired in last place. Rickey flew in from Pittsburgh to try to determine what was wrong. "I am completely mystified. It's worse than I thought," he told a reporter.[8]

Rickey shook up the roster. When replacements were dispatched, it brought calamity. Rickey promised to send Roberto Sanchez, a Cuban shortstop. When the player walked into the Stars' clubhouse, Bragan looked up and hollered, "That's the wrong Sanchez!"[9] An interpreter's mix-up at the Pirates' minor-league spring training complex had dispatched Panamanian pitcher Francisco Sanchez by mistake. Within twenty-four hours the mistake was straightened out: Francisco was sent to Billings and Roberto finally arrived.

In May, Bragan's frustration boiled over. He became incensed at an umpire's strike calls during the eighth inning of a game against the Angels, which the Stars trailed, 7–3. In the ninth inning the enraged Hollywood manager had enough. He sought to shine a spotlight on what he felt was poor umpiring. Bragan sent eight consecutive pinch-hitters to the plate and replaced each one before a single pitch could be thrown. Bragan had a ninth pinch-hitter ready to walk to the plate when the eighth, Clarence Buehller, swung before time was called. Had Buehller not hit into an easy out, the shenanigans would have continued. "All of those batters were used to show up the umpires who had already made a farce of the game," Bragan confessed.[10] Sportswriters called the antics "bush tactics," and the league admonished Bragan with a $50 fine.

Injuries took key performers out of the lineup. Second baseman Curt Roberts was hit in the forehead with a pitch and sidelined with a concussion. Bobby Del Greco suffered a leg injury. In addition to the injuries, acrimonious divorce proceedings that involved the Stars' right fielder, Lee Walls, filled the newspapers. A lawsuit also proved to be a distraction. A fan sued Stars outfielder Bobby Prescott, seeking more than $10,000 in damages for injuries she suffered when his errant throw hit her in the right eye.

In June, Hollywood went on a run that pulled them out of the Pacific Coast League's cellar. They won eighteen of twenty-three games to jump all the way into third place. Two months of tinkering had turned Red Munger's knuckleball into a formidable weapon, and the pitcher won six consecutive starts. The team's success pumped big crowds into Gilmore Field again. More than 9,000 cheered a 7–0 blanking of the Angels on June 9. The next night, 9,711 turned out. More than 10,000 roared with delight when the Stars swept a doubleheader from the Angels on June 12. After the series Angels president John Holland called Hollywood the team to beat. But the good times were short-lived. The Stars would lose six of seven to Portland, split a series with Sacramento, then split a series with the first-place San Diego Padres. When they lost four of six in San Francisco, the slide had become a freefall. The tumble took on embarrassing proportions. In the second game of a series with Oakland, Stars pitchers surrendered twelve walks, fourteen hits, and fifteen runs. In the team's worst loss of the season, 15–4, Bragan also lost his first baseman when R. C. Stevens suffered a knee injury.

Red Munger's pitching drew scouts from the New York Yankees. After he defeated Oakland for his fourteenth win of the season, the Yankees offered Bob Cobb $40,000 for the pitcher's contract. Cobb insisted Munger would not be sold for a penny under $50,000. The hard stance backfired when the Yankees declined to raise their bid and never called again.

In late August the team went on another upward surge. The winning once again pulled large crowds to Gilmore Field. A 5–3 win over the Angels was cheered by the largest crowd of the season: 12,151. So great was the overflow that 2,000 fans were made to watch the game while either standing or kneeling in front of the outfield fence. Hundreds more stood for nine innings behind the last row of grandstand seats.

A pennant fervor percolated as summer became fall. When Carlos Bernier slammed a two-run home run to cap a 3–0 win over the Angels on September 1, the Hollywood Stars had skied into first place. That, however, was to be the team's last hurrah of 1955. The Stars lost their next five games and quickly dropped three spots in the standings. Hope of another pennant grew faint, though it was still mathematically possible.

The team won two from Sacramento to keep hope alive. The second of the two wins, 10–6, was made possible by a five-run outburst in the tenth inning. But a 2–0 loss to the last-place Solons in the final game of the series dealt the Stars a crushing blow. They would enter the final series of the season, four games with second-place San Diego, sitting four games out of first place. Hollywood won the first game, 4–3, as Red Munger earned his twenty-third win of the season. The result created a three-team tie for second place between the Stars, San Diego Padres, and Los Angeles Angels. At the most inopportune time, though, the Stars suffered through one of their worst games of the season. The second game of the series was marred by errors, poor pitching, and a lack of hitting. Hollywood lost, 8–1, and was thus eliminated from any chance of winning the 1955 pennant.

When the Stars and Padres jogged onto the field to begin the doubleheader that would complete the season, the prize was second place. Drama built as the first game went ten innings. Bobby Del Greco ended the suspense when he clobbered a home run off the Signal Oil sign, a feat that made Hollywood victorious, 7–6, and netted the Stars' center fielder a $500 prize.

In the season finale, Hollywood went to the final inning trailing, 6–5. The noise at Gilmore Field rose when the Stars loaded the bases with nobody out. Fans shouted encouragement as Carlos Bernier came to bat. Their shouts became groans when Bernier hit a groundball that became a double play. Del Greco then struck out to seal defeat. By winning, San Diego earned second place. Seattle claimed the pennant. The Stars and Angels finished tied for third, which Hollywood later claimed by winning a playoff.

Once the season had concluded, packing was the overriding action in the Gilmore Field clubhouse. Bobby Bragan had a plane to catch for Cuba, where he had an assignment to manage a club in winter ball. Nobe Kawano put away the team's equipment for the winter. Players gathered belongings and prepared to head for home and off-season jobs. Mark Scott made the rounds to say his farewells. The Stars' radio broadcaster had another job to prepare for. He had lines to memorize and a part to study for. Mark Scott was the latest member of the Stars to be cast in a motion picture. Production was about to begin.

29

"IT WAS A GOOD CLEAN RIOT"

The tensions, intensity, and zealousness that erupted whenever the New York Giants and Brooklyn Dodgers met fueled a belief that theirs was the greatest rivalry in baseball. However, thousands in Southern California would vehemently disagree. To them, there was no rivalry with more antagonism or emotion in any sport in any city than that between the Hollywood Stars and Los Angeles Angels.

As Dick Hyland typed in his column in the *Los Angeles Times*, "Hollywood is poison to Los Angeles fans and vice versa."[1] The seeds of enmity between the Pacific Coast League adversaries were planted on February 16, 1939. To that date, William K. Wrigley's Angels had owned the Southern California sports landscape. The club was the biggest sports attraction in town. Ice hockey had tried and failed to make a go of things. Professional basketball was only a dream. Colleges and an American Football League team, the Bulldogs, pulled decent-sized crowds into Gilmore Stadium in the fall and winter. Boxing and auto racing had their followings, and the biggest of their events brought throngs.

From April through early October each year, the Angels ruled the roost. They were more than just the class of the Pacific Coast League and a winner of nine league pennants; the Angels were part of the fabric of the region. Uncles guided nephews onto trolleys in Long Beach and trekked to the Sunday doubleheaders. Fathers piled sons into the backseat of the family Plymouth, Ford, or DeSoto and made the drive from West Covina, Santa Monica, and Glendale. Working dads dropped sons off at the ballpark on a Saturday morning, then picked them up at the end of the day;

mothers did the same before embarking on an afternoon of shopping. Fathers and sons, drivers and passengers, bosses and employees debated whether Jigger Statz, Tuck Stainback, Jim Oglesby, Gene Lillard, Marv Gudat, Jimmy Reese, Carl Dittmar, Hugh McMillan, or the appropriately named pitcher Win Ballou was the best player on the Angels' remarkable 1933 championship team. To go to Wrigley Field was a treat. It was a big double-decked ballpark, just like those in the big leagues. In fact, to Angelinos, the Los Angeles Angels were the big leagues.

Nine weeks after Bob Cobb and his movie star backers bought the Hollywood Stars, Oscar Reichow was hired to run their ball club. Almost immediately David Fleming, who ran the Angels, kicked the Stars out of their eighth-floor office space in the Wrigley Field tower. Two days later, when Cobb and Victor Ford Collins called on Fleming to inquire whether the Stars might play in Wrigley Field while Gilmore Field was being completed, their request was sternly dismissed. "No love lost between the local clubs," wrote Mark Kelly in the *Los Angeles Examiner*. "All this makes for fine feuding and bigger gates."[2]

True to Kelly's forecast, both teams drew their largest crowds when they played each other. An eight-game series between the two in 1953 drew 91,384 fans. By comparison, during that same week the other thirty games in the Pacific Coast League lured a total of 49,040. Sportswriters dubbed the Angels-Stars rivalry the "Civil War Series." Beneath the clever moniker lived a level of detest and antagonism that could erode self-control and defy reason. A city championship trophy was created. It would be awarded at the final meeting of the two teams each season by the county sheriff, given to the team that had won the most games between the two during the year. Pride and even glee on receipt of the trophy was known to be accompanied by smugness and even outright derision.

By the time the two teams met for the first time in Hollywood's new park in 1939, the rivalry had warmed to a simmer. "The only rivalry at a stronger pitch than that between the players exists between the Hollywood and Los Angeles fans. They're rabid and they're hostile," Bob Ray declared in the *Los Angeles Times*.[3]

The ire of Gilmore Field loyalists was stirred by 15–13 and 7–0 losses in the first two games of that 1939 series. Hollywood's fans gained a reason to gloat two nights later, when Bill Fleming, nephew of the Angels' president, tossed a three-hit shutout, and Hollywood won, 6–0, before an overflow crowd of eleven thousand. In the Saturday game during the series, ire erupted when Babe Herman was hit on the wrist by an errant pitch. X-rays exposed a broken bone that would sideline the fan favorite for the rest of the season. During the Sunday finale, rage boiled over when an umpire's close call ended a potential Hollywood rally. Fans in the grandstands behind first base and down the right-field line erupted. Bottles cascaded, hurled in the direction of the umpire. Ushers scampered about to quash the outburst, and several fans were kicked out of the ballpark. The close proximity of Gilmore Field's stands to the players on the field sparked heated exchanges. Vows of retaliation spewed. After the game an irate fan sought revenge outside of the Angels locker room. When the subject of his fury emerged, angry words flew. The incident was ended by one punch from the player that flattened the enraged fan.

A degree of indignation would become a thread in the fabric of the rivalry from that day forward. During the teams' first meeting in Wrigley Field in 1940, fights broke out between rival fans in the stands. Following a 1942 game between the teams, Pappy Joiner had recorded the final out and pitched Hollywood to a 5–1 win over the Angels when the last batter he faced, Bill Schuster, began to jaw at the pitcher. Joiner spun Schuster with his right hand, then swung a left that caught the Angels' shortstop flush in the mouth and knocked him cold. Players from both clubs ran toward the incident. A handful of fans vaulted onto the field intent on joining the fray. Thinking quickly, the Gilmore Stadium electrician flipped the switch to shut off the ballpark lights. Darkness brought the mayhem to a halt before it could escalate into a melee.

Ushers and security men worked with heightened concern whenever the rivals squared off on the field. None, however, could have expected the unrest that broke out well before a June 1947 meeting of the Stars and Angels at Gilmore Field. A large Friday night crowd was planned for, but an unexpectedly large early rush filled the park beyond capacity more than a half hour before the game was to begin. Thousands more massed at the ticket booths, anxious to enter. Security workers and ballpark staff fought to slam shut the eight-foot-high entry gates. Those who were denied admission burst from irritation to rage. Shouted threats turned into action. Fans pushed and tugged at the chain-link gates to try to force them open. Scuffles broke out among Stars and Angels fans in the angry throng. Police were finally called to disperse the horde. The 11,286 who successfully made it inside saw the Stars drop an 8–6 decision in ten innings.

Arbiters faced far more wrath than in other games when a close or controversial call swung momentum in an Angels-Stars battle. During a 1952 meeting in Wrigley Field, an umpire's call on a close play at home plate sparked a heated argument by members of the Angels and their manager, Stan Hack. During the protest, fans hurled seat cushions, cups, wads of paper, and other debris onto the field. When the home plate umpire, Ed Runge, ejected Hack, three irate Angels fans leaped onto the field after the arbiter. Two of the men were quickly grabbed by ushers. One, however, punched Runge on the jaw, then wrestled the umpire to the ground. The Stars' Gene Handley dashed to the umpire's aide. While that was going on, four more fans ran onto the field before players and nightstick-wielding police stopped them. In the stands two women swung purses at each other before they were arrested and taken away to jail.

The anger and rage that had become inherent to the rivalry reached a violent crescendo during a two-week span in August 1953. The tide in the Pacific Coast League had turned. After two decades of dominance, the Angels watched Hollywood become the strongest club in the league. When the Stars and Angels met on August 2, Hollywood held a six-game lead in the standings. Overflow crowds stretched the capacity of Gilmore Field for every game of the series. A ballpark record of 13,153 roared its approval on Friday night. Almost 11,000 were in the stands for the doubleheader finale on Sunday afternoon. When the teams took the field for the first of the two Sunday games, Frankie Kelleher was a hitter on a hot streak. The man called "Mouse" because of his quiet nature had made plenty of noise by winning Friday and Saturday nights' games with pinch-hits. In the first inning of Sunday's first game, Kelleher put Hollywood on the scoreboard first with a run-scoring single. When he came to bat in the fourth inning, Angels pitcher Joe Hatton threw two balls in the direction of Kelleher's head. The Stars' slugger managed to twist his body and evade both pitches. Once he had gathered himself, Kelleher slammed the third pitch off the center-field wall and wound up on third base with a triple. Bobby Bragan rubbed salt in the wound by calling for a squeeze bunt. That the slow-footed Kelleher was able to score brought catcalls and heckling to the ears of the Angels' players as Hollywood took a 2–0 lead.

In the sixth inning, Hatton went after Kelleher again. This time he didn't miss. The Angels' pitcher directed a searing fastball into the middle of the slugger's back. Kelleher calmly laid down his bat, then walked briskly toward the mound. As the big man reached the pitcher, he reared back and belted Hatton. The blow caught Hatton square in the chest. Hatton flew backward at least three feet through the air, then landed on his behind. Fred Richards, the Angels' first baseman, attempted to wrap Kelleher in a bear hug. The Hollywood outfielder spun free and began raining punches on Richards, one of which decked the Angel. Players, coaches, and both managers rushed from their respective positions and dugouts. Rivals pushed, shoved, and wrestled. It was a full ten minutes before the brouhaha was brought under control. In the aftermath, teammates expressed shock at the actions of the normally mild-mannered Kelleher, more so than the voraciousness of the brawl. Kelleher was ejected from the game, the first ejection of his seventeen-year career.

When play resumed, Bobby Bragan sent Teddy Beard in to run for Kelleher. The outfielder moved to second base on an out. Then, on the next pitch, Beard took off for third. He made a hard slide and spiked the Angels' Murray Franklin on the left arm and chest. The pain of the twin gashes made Franklin drop the baseball. Furious, Franklin jumped on Beard and a second, more ferocious melee broke out. At just that moment, William Parker happened to step into his living room. The Los Angeles chief of police had spent part of the morning at the beach with his wife, Helen. As Parker turned on his television, he was startled to see the screen fill with images of brawling ballplayers. The stern, sometimes intense man with a bit of a temper quickly made for the telephone and ordered the department's riot squad to Gilmore Field. When Parker returned his attention to the television, Mel Queen was throwing a series of rights and lefts at Angels antagonists. Tommy Saffell was pummeling Murray Franklin. All around the infield Angels and Stars squared off and exchanged punches. Those who weren't, like Gene Handley and Gene Baker, were wrestling on the grass, legs kicking and spikes flailing. Chuck Stevens sought to play peacemaker and was caught by a punch from behind. Gordon Maltzberger tried to tug two combatants apart only to suddenly be knocked to the turf, become buried beneath a scrum, and feel a jagged edge from his broken glasses cut into his upper cheek.

It took time, but the umpires and managers were able to bring the brawling to a halt. Once play resumed, Hollywood went on to win the game, 4–1. As the Stars walked into their clubhouse, many were seething. Chuck Stevens became angry at seeing a man in street clothes standing near his locker. "Get him outta here," he yelled to Nobe Kawano, the clubhouse manager. The man turned and flashed a police badge. "I'm the captain of the riot squad," he announced.[4] The room went silent. Once the entire team was in the clubhouse, the man laid down the rules for the second game. No one was to leave the clubhouse but the nine players who were in the game, the manager, and the coaches. A player could leave only if summoned to pinch-hit, warm up in the bullpen, or enter the game as a substitute. Throughout the second game of the doubleheader, three uniformed police officers sat in each team's dugout while the bulk of players for both teams remained hidden from view beneath the stands. The second game was completed without incident. The Angels won, 5–3.

Following the second game, reporters pushed into the Stars clubhouse. They pressed Kelleher about his trek to the mound. "I just couldn't let it continue," he said calmly.[5] Wives and girlfriends waited anxiously outside the clubhouse door. When Maria Stevens spied her husband, she anxiously asked what had happened. "It was a good clean riot," Chuck Stevens laughed.[6] Sergeant Floyd Drender asked Hatton if he wanted to press charges against Kelleher and received an unequivocal no.

The next day, pictures and bold headlines of the fisticuffs covered almost two-thirds of the front page of several Los Angeles newspapers. By mid-afternoon, news arrived that fines had been assessed by the league. Five players were punished: three Stars and two Angels. Several players carried souvenirs of the melee. Fans who saw the Angels off at the airport for their flight to Seattle noticed that Bud Hardin had a slashed cheek and one eye was swollen shut. Bandages covered deep cuts on Murray Franklin's left arm and chest. At Gilmore Field, Gordon Maltzberger bore cuts on his face. Teddy Beard hobbled about from a badly twisted knee. Eddie Malone had a spike wound on his leg.

Across town the switchboard operator at Wrigley Field was kept busier than usual. Hundreds of callers phoned from the beginning to the end of business hours. Each was anxious to make ticket reservations for a specific game. The Stars and Angels were to meet up again in three weeks' time. It was already a game that nobody wanted to miss.

In the ensuing days the melee was the biggest story in baseball. Newspapers big and small, from the *New York Times* to the *Walla Walla Bulletin*, ran large headlines and photos of the brawl. *Life* magazine devoted three full pages to the fight. When the newspaper in the Los Angeles suburb of Culver City reported that Kelleher had been fined $100, readers contributed money to cover his fine.

The return meeting of the teams in Wrigley Field brought stern warnings from both the league president and the chief of police. Both insisted players be on their best behavior. Hoping that they weren't was what brought the largest crowd in all of minor-league baseball that season—21,440—to Wrigley Field. During the eight games in the series, not a single terse word was hollered nor a punch thrown. The only blow dealt was to Hollywood's pennant pursuit when the Angels won four of the eight games.

Given the added revenues their games generated, the clubs explored the idea to play a series in the Los Angeles Memorial Coliseum. "We'd not only draw 40,000 for a Sunday but prove whether the place is adaptable for baseball," said John Holland, president of the Angels.[7] Exploration didn't take long. It was quickly decided that the cost was prohibitive and the conditions were not acceptable.

At least some degree of hostility coursed through every Stars fan toward the Angels, and vice versa. Stars fans were made to feel apprehensive about attending games in Wrigley Field, as were Angels fans about entering Gilmore Field. Animosity ran deep. One such example involved two preteen fans from the neighborhood near Gilmore Field. The mother of one had entered her son in Fred Haney's Knothole Gang, not realizing the boy was a staunch Angels fan. When one Sunday the son's name was drawn to be the Stars' bat boy the following weekend, the youth steadfastly refused to accept the prize. Instead he offered it to a pal, and young Barry Weinstock, a devoted Stars fan, cherished the experience for a lifetime.

During the middle of the 1954 season, enmity once again erupted between the two clubs. It broke out during a Sunday doubleheader. Volatility ripped through the 13,576 fans in Wrigley Field. Rival fans had been fighting in the grandstands, which pulled a dozen police officers and ushers to stop the unrest. On the field Carlos Bernier attempted to steal second base in the top of the fifth inning and was called out. Angry at what he felt was an unnecessarily hard tag, Bernier kicked at Angels shortstop Bud Hardin. Hardin took exception. He swung a haymaker that missed, then pounced on the Hollywood outfielder. As their scuffle broke out, Hardin's teammates Gene Mauch and Bob Unser soon joined the fray. Mauch threw and landed four punches. Dale Long of the Stars came to his teammate's aide and began wrestling with Unser on the grass. More players ran to the dispute, and soon there was pushing and shoving between several Stars and Angels around the diamond. Police abandoned the mayhem in the stands to assist the umpires and break up the fighting on the field. Bernier was ejected from the game. As he began to make his way toward the Hollywood dugout, Bernier was chided by fans. He made an obscene gesture. Bill Sweeney, the Angels' manager, admonished the outfielder, who cursed at him. The response made Sweeney's temper flare, and the two began to jaw. When Bernier finally exited the field and stepped into the Hollywood dugout, his temper had hardly cooled. All it took was a sarcastic comment hollered by Angels first baseman Dixie Upright to ignite another shouting match. Bernier's verbal shots grew so caustic that an enraged Upright abandoned his position to run toward the Hollywood dugout. He wanted to get at the mercurial outfielder. One of Bernier's teammates grabbed a bat and moved to intercept the irate Angel. Several teammates reacted quickly and managed to stop both players before things could grow worse. As the umpires worked to ease the tension on the field, the ushers had their hands full in the grandstands. Pockets of small fights broke out. With the help of the police, the ushers managed to kick several instigators out of the ballpark and finally restore calm.

Feuding wasn't limited to the field or the stands. It even involved the radio announcers for the two clubs. On learning that Angels broadcaster Bob Kelley had lampooned Bernier on air and blamed him for starting the fight, Hollywood mic-man Mark Scott shot back with a scathing retort. Scott took aim at Bill Sweeney during a broadcast. He lambasted the Angels' manager, criticized him for his remarks, and called Sweeney "a rabble rouser."[8]

In the days after the Bernier-Hardin brawl, letters appeared in the area's newspapers that chastised the Stars for their brawling behavior. One sportswriter noted that Stars players had drawn nine fines from the Pacific Coast League in the 1953 and 1954 seasons, far more than any other team in the league. He also noted that the "trouble is due to the red-hot rivalry with Los Angeles. No such feud exists elsewhere in the league."[9] Hollywood pitcher Ben Wade took it a step farther: "Best rivalry I've ever seen, even better than the Dodgers and Giants."[10]

30

"YOU'RE LOOKING AT SOMETHING SPECIAL"

As the player spun across the infield dirt in Gilmore Field, his movements were considered wizardry to some, hailed as pure magic by others. Teenaged ballplayers watched in wonder and former players from all levels simply marveled. None had ever seen someone play second base the way the nineteen-year-old coal miner's son did for the Hollywood Stars during the spring and summer of 1956. "We have a second baseman who'll be the greatest within three or four years," Bob Cobb predicted.[1] "He is pure dynamite on double plays," praised his manager.[2] Portland's manager, Tommy Holmes, was more succinct: "He's amazing."[3] From spring training at La Palma Park in Anaheim into the start to the season, Bill Mazeroski's play was a ray of sunshine that pierced the shroud of rain and foggy days that had unexpectedly dampened the arrival of a new baseball season.

The 1956 season came after four months of hubbub fueled by change in Pittsburgh. At the conclusion of the 1955 season, the Pirates fired Fred Haney. For the second time, Pittsburgh turned to the Hollywood Stars for a new manager. Bobby Bragan was hired to replace Haney. In November, Bob Cobb shared with reporters that two men were finalists to be the Stars' manager, Andy Cohen and George Genovese. Genovese was a former Hollywood shortstop who, like Cohen, had enjoyed success managing in the Pirates' farm system. Only days later the search changed course. On November 10, the Portland Beavers announced that Clay Hopper would not return as their manager. Hopper was a favorite of

Branch Rickey. A fifty-three-year-old Mississippian, Hopper had managed for Rickey for twelve years in the St. Louis Cardinals' farm system and nine years in the Dodgers' organization. Upon learning of Hopper's availability, Rickey pushed Cobb to hire the man. Two weeks later Cobb sent word from the minor-league meetings in Columbus, Ohio, that Hopper would indeed be the new Hollywood manager.

The roster Hopper was given was unlike any that had taken the field at Gilmore Field before. It represented the complete surrender of the Hollywood Stars to Branch Rickey. All of the players were young prospects. The average age of the Stars was twenty-three. Only five players returned from the 1955 team. One of the returnees was Paul Pettit, but in a very different role. Pettit, whose pitching promise had been ended by a debilitating elbow injury, was done with the mound. The Pirates had converted him to a first baseman and outfielder.

It raised more than a few eyebrows when Cobb proclaimed, "This will be one of our best Hollywood teams."[4] Few who saw the team in spring training could agree. By the start of exhibition games, it was the naysayers that were proven right. Errors dotted losses. Eight were committed in a single game with Sacramento. When the manager received a player from Pittsburgh who had set the California League record for errors the previous season, Al Wolf wrote in the *Los Angeles Times* that "they may reactivate Manager Clay Hopper's ulcers."[5]

In a quest for positive publicity, Cobb brought the voraciously read entertainment columnist Hedda Hopper to the ballpark to pose for pictures with her namesake Clay. When a photographer asked that the two swap hats, the manager looked at the writer's wide-brimmed floral trimmed bonnet and said, "This picture's gonna set my career back thirty years"—to which Hedda Hopper replied, "What do you think it will do to mine?"[6]

Sportswriters warned the new manager about the Stars' penchant for slow starts. They pointed out that the ball club in recent seasons caught fire in midseason, only to fall short of a pennant. As strong as the Pacific Coast League stacked up for the 1956 campaign, a slow start could spell doom for the Hollywood Stars, the writers predicted.

Through the first month of the season, Hollywood's play was so bad that Cobb relished the unprecedented three rainouts that kept the gates to Gilmore Field closed. By the end of the first month of play, the Stars were dead last in the Pacific Coast League. When June arrived, the Stars had improved one place in the standings, to seventh.

Branch Rickey Jr. made repeated trips to the West Coast to survey the problem. The results saw players shuttled weekly, and in some cases daily, between the Stars, the Pittsburgh Pirates, the Pirates' New Orleans farm club, and even their farm club at Mexico City. When Carlos Bernier, Dick Smith, and R. C. Stevens rejoined the Stars, play improved.

Amid the turmoil was a gleaming gem: Bill Mazeroski. Teammates couldn't get over the improvement the nineteen-year-old had made since the 1955 season. Mazeroski chalked it up to gaining both fifteen pounds and confidence over the winter. His newfound assurance came, he said, from playing against more experienced players in winter ball in the Dominican Republic. Fans marveled. Never had they seen someone play second base the way the young Pirates prospect did. "He's without a peer in this league at the double play," Hopper said to Frank Finch of *Sporting News*.[7] Indeed, the Pirates prospect turned double plays with lightning speed. Teens were amazed at how, rather than catch feeds from his shortstop in his glove, Mazeroski stopped the ball with the backside of the mitt to quicken his ability to throw to first base. Fans insisted that Mazeroski's hands were so quick you could not see him make the transfer of the ball from glove to hand. Teammates called him "No Touch."[8] One said, "You're looking at something special."[9]

Mazeroski had improved with the bat from 1955. He hit in streaks. A dozen games with success would give way to six without. By the end of June, though, he was Hollywood's leading hitter and was seventh in the Pacific Coast League with a .320 batting average.

In mid-June, as had become custom, the Stars went on a hot streak. They won fifteen of sixteen games to vault from the depths of the standings into third place. George O'Donnell had rejoined the club and aided the team's strong play by reeling off seven consecutive wins. It was then that Branch Rickey showed up at Gilmore Field, and the press had a pretty good idea why.

In Pittsburgh the Pirates were struggling. Bobby Bragan asked for help. Rickey no longer ran the club. He had been forced out, serving in a consulting capacity to his replacement, Joe L. Brown. Rickey's arrival at Gilmore Field during the first week of July gave rise to the opinion that Mazeroski's days with the Stars were numbered. Indeed, on July 6, the Pirates announced that they were bringing the Stars' sensation up to the big leagues. Clay Hopper told reporters that the Pirates were getting "a master at the double play."[10]

From that point on, Hollywood's upward surge in the standings stalled. While they remained in third, the margin between the Stars and the first-place Angels widened. Injuries took a toll. By the time the season ended, Hollywood would endure a spate of injuries like nothing they had ever experienced before. In all, thirty players would spend time on the disabled list.

The aches and ailments ranged from the usual—ankle sprains, muscle pulls, and spike wounds—to the inexplicable, all of which produced exasperation and perplexity. Hollywood's promising pitching staff was reduced to rubble by injuries. A ligament injury put Bob Purkey's knee in a cast. Art Murray underwent surgery to remove bone chips from his elbow. Joe Trimble was sidelined by a tendon injury in his shoulder. After pitching a one-hit shutout in April, then a three-hit shutout in May, Ben Wade suffered a shoulder injury and could pitch only after receiving injections to relieve the pain. Hugh Pepper spent time in the hospital with a concussion from a collision when he tried to steal home. Injuries grew from the frustrating to the bizarre. During a game with Sacramento, the Solons' batter fouled a ball off of his foot. As he hopped around home plate in pain, the player involuntarily flailed his bat around. It whacked the Stars' catcher, Bill Hall, in the head and knocked him out. In August, Hall stepped on a bat and suffered a severe ankle sprain. This occurred ten days after another Hollywood catcher, Danny Kravitz, did the same thing and incurred the same injury. Desperate for catching help, the Stars purchased the contract of a thirty-five-year-old player-manager from a Class C club to fill in behind the plate for the remainder of the season. The Stars lost their third baseman when Gene Freese tripped and fell at the swimming pool at his apartment complex and cut his heel badly on a sprinkler. Tragedy shook the Stars as well. Within days of each other, Bill Garber and Dick Smith hurriedly left the team grief-stricken by the death of infant children.

The lack of a pennant contender, poor early season weather, and competing sporting events at times during the summer undercut attendance. The Stars endured one of the biggest drops in turnstile count in the Pacific Coast League. Rather than bemoan their plight, Cobb and Stars business manager Paul Jeschke taxed ingenuity to try to generate fan interest. A partnership was struck with Thrifty Stores. The chain bought twenty-five thousand tickets. Any fan who purchased a ticket was given one for free. Four newspapers agreed to run ads that would enable readers to buy two tickets for the price of one for a one-week series. The Stars staged an on-field dog show, gave away trips to Las Vegas, and held a home run hitting contest between players and an egg toss challenge that involved the pitchers. "Grocery Night" filled the park with fans who hoped to take home one of one thousand baskets of free food, toiletries, and cigarettes. A contest to create a new theme song generated more than one thousand entries, including one from a ninety-two-year-old man who was serving a life sentence in prison for train robbery. Further brainstorming sessions created the $100,000 Throw. The contest involved a seven-foot-high board placed on second base during a break in the game. In the center of the board was a hole, 3.3647 inches in diameter, barely bigger than a baseball. Three fans were selected during each game and given the chance to try to win $100,000. All they had to do was throw a regulation baseball from home plate through the hole. During the first week of the contest, none of the fifteen fans to attempt the throw so much as managed to hit the board.

The Stars' hitting futility rivaled that of the contest's flinging fans. Over the final month of the season, Hollywood faded and fell into fourth place. Over a stretch of ten games during the malaise, the Stars scored a paltry fifteen runs. They ended the season in fourth, twenty-two games behind the pennant-winning Angels. As the newly crowned champs celebrated in the Cocoanut Grove nightclub across the street from the original Brown Derby, Clay Hopper bemoaned his ball club. "This is probably the weakest hitting club I ever managed," he said.[11] Hopper declared he would probably retire from baseball. Four weeks later he did.

31

"HOME RUNS ARE MY BUSINESS"

In the realm of baseball hero worship, youth and teens who grew up in Pacific Coast League cities were not unlike those anywhere else in the country. Hero worship was a part of their upbringing. While baseball-crazed kids in most towns pined for and even imitated Stan Musial or Mickey Mantle, youths who lived in Southern California turned their idolatry in a different direction—to their favorite member of either the Hollywood Stars or Los Angeles Angels.

By the 1957 season, the toast of Los Angeles was undeniably Steve Bilko. A prodigious home run hitter, Bilko was a stocky twenty-six-year-old who had failed in six trials with the St. Louis Cardinals dating back to 1949. When the Cardinals sold him to the Chicago Cubs, Bilko was then assigned to the Angels. Once in an Angels uniform, the first baseman found Wrigley Field's dimensions to be perfectly suited for his swing. In his first season the right-handed slugger drove balls over the left-center-field wall at such a rate one columnist suggested residents of the apartment building across the street wear mitts when they sat down for dinner. Bilko slugged 37 home runs in the 1955 season. He drove in 124 runs, batted .328, and was voted Most Valuable Player in the Pacific Coast League. In 1956 Bilko threatened the league home run record. He finished 5 shy, with 55 and 164 runs batted in. With a batting average of .360, he earned the league Triple Crown as the leader of the three major statistical categories. Once again, sportswriters voted Bilko the league MVP. By the spring of 1957, Steve Bilko was the most popular athlete in Los Angeles, so popular that his name had been immortalized by one of the of the top comedy shows on television. Emmy Award–winning writer and producer Nat Hiken was constructing a show for CBS around the talents of comedic actor Phil Silvers. Hiken crafted eight possible themes for the show. In one, Silvers was to be a minor-league baseball manager. In another, he would play a finagling army sergeant. CBS selected the army theme. When pressed to give the central character a name, Hiken, at Silvers's urging, chose that of the most popular athlete in town. The scheming sergeant would be forever known as Sergeant Bilko.

As spring training was winding to its close and about to merge into Opening Day of the 1957 season, Bob Cobb was excited to learn he would get a Bilko of his own. News reverberated about La Palma Park in Anaheim, where the Stars were training, that the Pittsburgh Pirates had assigned Dick Stuart to Hollywood.

As heralded as Steve Bilko was, Dick Stuart held the title as the most prolific home run hitter in all of professional baseball. The previous summer he had slugged sixty-six with the Pirates Class A farm club in Lincoln, Nebraska. The tally was six more than Babe Ruth's major-league record for home runs in a season, though six shy of the minor-league record seventy-two that Joe Bauman hit for the Roswell Rockets in 1954.

Stuart checked out of the Bradford Hotel in Fort Myers, Florida, and quickly caught a flight to Southern California. On arriving, the new Star spewed predictions—that Hollywood would win the league and do it thanks to his hitting, that he would lead the league in home runs, that he would one day be a star in the big leagues. When a reporter asked how many home runs he would hit for Hollywood, Stuart answered, "Whatever it takes to lead the league."[1]

Elation in the Hollywood camp to gain both a slugger and potential box office bonanza was matched only by the relief among the Pittsburgh Pirates to be rid of Stuart. As much as Stuart could excite a crowd with prodigious home runs, he exasperated his manager with fielding that was more pathetic than prolific. "The goshawfulest fielder I've ever seen," Bobby Bragan called Stuart.[2] "The only thing his glove is good for is swatting flies," said a teammate.[3] Stuart struck out more than he made contact—a league-record 171 times in 141 games with Lincoln in 1956. Moreover, managers and teammates accused Stuart of putting himself above the team. "Never played with a player who was more about himself and less about the team," said Paul Pettit, who played with Stuart in Mexico City for part of the 1955 season.[4] More than once at Lincoln,

Stuart was caught in right field with his glove under his arm and cracking peanut shells during play. During a Western League game in 1956, Stuart had implored an umpire to throw him out of the game. The slugger pleaded that a girlfriend was arriving in town, and he had to go and pick her up. It was the power, however, that made so many men in the Pirates' organization overlook the annoyances that came with having Dick Stuart on a ball club.

The twenty-four-year-old received a clean slate from Cobb when he joined the Stars. The assignment to Hollywood represented a homecoming to Stuart. During the off-season he lived in Culver City, seven miles southwest of Gilmore Field. In Stuart's first workout with Hollywood, he lined a pitch from Clyde King, the new Hollywood manager, over the forty-foot-high bleachers that were 464 feet from home plate. "My best pitch too," King laughed.[5] Later that day in an exhibition game, Stuart sent a ball 450 feet into the center-field bleachers.

It was under the lights of Lane Field in San Diego that curiosity erupted into fervor. An eagerness enveloped the Stars as they checked out of their spring training headquarters, the Disneyland Hotel, and bused to San Diego to begin the 1957 season. In the second inning on opening night, Stuart's name was announced to the crowd. Fans who had heard tales of his exploits heckled the newcomer. "Hey Elvis," one barked, "where are your sideburns?"[6] One hundred twenty-seven miles to the north, ardent Stars fans who twisted the knob to tune their Zenith, Westinghouse, or Packard Bell radios to 790 perked their ears at the sound of bat-and-ball contact. The voice of Hollywood's play-by-play announcer, Mark Scott, rose in volume with his standard home run call of: "Fly ball. Deep to left. Way back. Way back, and *gone*, a home run!" Stuart's drive had sailed 385 feet and landed in the left-field stands. Two innings later Scott described yet another Stuart home run. This one soared 350 feet and again fell into the left-field bleachers. In the dugout teammates sat in stunned silence. It wasn't about the distance of the blast; it was the conquest. Veteran Stars had never before seen a player outmuscle the ten- to fifteen-mile-an-hour winds that blew in off the bay and manage to put a ball in Lane Field's left-field bleachers. Stuart's blasts helped Hollywood to victory, 4–1.

Above the *Los Angeles Times* story of the Stars' 4–1 win following the second day of the season read a large headline: "500-Foot Homer Hit by Stuart."[7] The prodigious newcomer's third home run in two days had knocked Steve Bilko from the headlines. When Stuart slugged two more home runs the following night, one sportswriter labeled Hollywood's right fielder "the cocky clouter from Culver City."[8]

Five consecutive Hollywood wins were overshadowed by Dick Stuart's exploits when the Stars arrived home from San Diego. The brash young home run hitter was awash in celebrity. He tooled around town in a new car, an Olds 98. It seemed the ball field was the only place that Stuart did not wear sunglasses. He became a member of the Screen Extras Guild Union and got bit parts in a movie, *D-Day: The 6th of June*, and on two television shows, *Navy Log* and *Badge 714*. Every autograph that he signed was accompanied by the number of his home run record, 66. When the actress Jayne Mansfield asked, "How come you get your name in the paper more than me?" Stuart shot back, "You didn't hit no 66 homeruns!"[9]

Stuart was fussy about his bats. He didn't want anyone else to touch the thirty-three-ounce Babe Herman model that he swung. He was particular about just how they were handled, so much so that Buzzy Richardson, the Stars' batboy, took to wrapping Stuart's lumber in Turkish towels.

When the Stars met the Angels during the second week of the season, photographers posed Stuart and Bilko. The two pointed their bats at one another akin to soldiers aiming rifles. They chatted during batting practice. "Seems like a nice fellow," Bilko said to a teammate. On hearing a comment by one of the Angels, Stuart said, "If you want to be a great hitter why don't you study my batting technique."[10]

It was during the series with the Angels that Stuart's hitting skills faltered. By the time the series had ended, any excitement about Dick Stuart's future was clouded in doubt. More than seven thousand fans came out to see Hollywood's home opener. They left disappointed, both in the outcome, a 5–3 loss to the Angels, and in their new hero. Stuart struck out twice, walked, and had a single but failed to hit a home run. The next night the Angels triumphed again, 3–1, and Stuart struck out two more times.

Prior to the third game of the series, celebrated photographer Phil Bath was on the field snapping shots of Stuart. "You sign with MGM or Paramount?" shouted Windy Wade, the Angels' center fielder.

"Paramount," Stuart shot back.

The Stars hoped that prolific slugger Dick Stuart (right) would challenge the Angels' Steve Bilko (left) for power-hitting supremacy in the Pacific Coast League in 1957. In May, with his strikeouts far outnumbering home runs, Stuart was sold to Atlanta. ***Courtesy of Howard Ballew, Los Angeles Public Library Photo Collection***

"Well good. From the way you're hitting you're going to need a new racket," Wade laughed.[11]

The jibes were good-natured. Stuart and several Angels players called the same LaBrea-area hotel home and often dined together. Outsiders, however, weren't wrong to believe that humility and Dick Stuart traveled in different stratospheres. His arrogance was the stuff that sparked tempers and pushed men to the edge of fights, particularly in bars. The aggrieved weren't just opponents but sometimes agitated teammates and even obnoxious fans. Such was the anger Stuart could produce that not even his hulking 6-foot-3-inch height and 210-pound build could diffuse a foe's venom. "I don't want to fight," Stuart would say when challenged. Then after a pause he would add, "I'll arm wrestle."[12] In almost every case Stuart would pin his foe's hand to a table or bar top in less than a second.

The early season series with the Angels saw the hero's mantle returned to its previous owner. In the finale, Steve Bilko homered twice. His first smacked off of an ad for the soft drink 7 Up to net a $100 prize. Bilko's second home run was a grand slam. It helped the Angels score ten runs in an eighth-inning rally as they romped past Hollywood, 15–5. The final score was only one part of the humiliation endured by the Stars. They were beaten in all five games against the Angels. While Bilko was cheered for his heroics, Stuart struck out sixteen times in forty-three turns at bat.

As April neared its end, Gilmore Field's prince was becoming a pauper. Strikeouts at the plate and errors in the field became the story of Stuart's nights. Pitchers "had him upside down," said a teammate.[13] They threw him curveballs in fastball counts, didn't give him good pitches to hit, and grinned mischievously as the slugger flailed at bad balls. Along the way rival pitchers figured out Stuart's weakness and exploited it repeatedly. Anything thrown letter-high or slightly above was simply too tempting for Stuart to lay off. With a slight uppercut to his swing, Stuart stood little chance to make contact unless, as one columnist cracked, he were to stand on a crate.[14]

When Portland arrived for a series at Gilmore Field, Clyde King decided to drop Stuart from fourth to sixth in the batting order. He wanted to take pressure off the slumping slugger. The next night Stuart's struggles would put him on the bench. He began the night in the starting lineup but struck out twice to give him twenty-four whiffs in seventeen games. By the time the eighth inning rolled around, Hollywood trailed Portland, 3–2. It was then that King's patience in Stuart ran out. The Stars' skipper sent Paul Pettit to pinch-hit, and the onetime wunderkind doubled to tie the game. Two innings later Hollywood loaded the bases. Pettit came to bat and promptly singled to win the game, 4–3. When he met with sportswriters after the game, King announced a change to his starting eight. Paul Pettit, who had made a remarkable transformation from sore-armed pitcher to good-hitting outfielder, would be Hollywood's right fielder. Stuart, whose average was a trifling .229, was relegated to the bench.

The manager instructed Stuart to make adjustments to his hitting mechanics. Stand farther away from home plate, he urged. King insisted Stuart shorten his long swing. Pettit, meanwhile, celebrated his opportunity to play. He slugged three home runs in a week and became the new media darling, the subject of interviews and invited by television channels to appear on their baseball shows.

On May 5, the Stars met their archrivals in Wrigley Field. A crowd of almost sixteen thousand filled the large ballpark. Stuart could only watch from the dugout as former Angel and current actor Chuck Connors presented the Tony Lazzeri Trophy to Steve Bilko for being the 1956 Pacific Coast League home run champion. The game result added further insult: Hollywood lost, 11–1.

Stuart's struggles brought tension. News that King had benched the slugger was not well received in Pittsburgh. Word came down from Branch Rickey Jr. that Stuart was to play. The manager complied, but the results didn't change. Stuart's strikeout tally grew, while his hits and home runs did not.

One morning while on the 20th Century lot, Stuart was approached by director Leo McCarey. The man held a bat and proceeded to tell Stuart about his own high school hitting prowess. McCarey offered Stuart some batting tips. The beleaguered Star listened politely. He thanked the man but with a modicum of disgust. That night Stuart struck out four times. "He must not have been listenin'," McCarey told a colleague the next day.[15]

For Dick Stuart, things plummeted from bad to worse. He was served with divorce papers by his wife. After strikeouts, fans would hurl beer bottles at him. Though Stuart led the Pacific Coast League in home runs with six, he had struck out thirty-two times in seventy-two turns at bat. Just thirty days into the season, Dick Stuart's time in Hollywood came to an end. On May 11, the Pittsburgh Pirates arranged for the Atlanta Crackers of the Class AA Southern Association to take Stuart. When King broke the news, the tall, handsome ballplayer broke down and cried. He threatened to quit baseball, then said he would go to Canada and play semipro ball. Before he left Gilmore Field for good, Stuart visited the pressroom, where he personally thanked the sportswriters for what they had written about him. He told the men that he would one day lead the major leagues in home runs, then bid farewell by saying, "Home runs are my business."[16]

32

"I'LL SEE YOU AT CHAVEZ RAVINE"

Dick Willis yearned for the nights when his mother's brother would drop by the house for dinner. Between bites, the twelve-year-old would prod his Uncle Ralph about the chances of big-league baseball coming to Los Angeles. Few were more in the know than Uncle Ralph—Ralph Carson to the rest of the world. The man owned the largest advertising agency in town, and he used it to try to lure a big-league team to Los Angeles.

Ralph Carson's specific target was the Brooklyn Dodgers. He was shameless in his pursuit. Carson used every trick in the book to boost Los Angeles. One that drew particular attention was the rainout billboard. Whenever and wherever the Dodgers were rained out, Carson swiftly erected a billboard in the city. Its message told Walter O'Malley that it was sunny and warm in Los Angeles. "You're going to get the chance to see major-league baseball very soon," the ad executive assured his nephew one night. "But Dickie, it's going to take away your childhood."[1]

Ralph Carson, like many baseball fans, knew that Angelinos were wedded to their Angels or Stars. He knew the childhood staples for kids in the Fairfax district: riding bicycles to Gilmore Field on game nights, hovering behind the outfield fence in hopes for a batting practice ball to be socked over the wall, anxiously hoping to hear one's name called out during a Sunday game as winner of the batboy for a game contest. So deep was the devotion to the team that the area boys knew who the power hitters in the Pacific Coast League were and would routinely abandon their spot behind the left-field wall and dash toward the eucalyptus trees behind right field when it was Luke Easter or Max West's turn to hit. The neighborhood boys knew just from the rattling sound when a pepper game had sent a baseball over the interior center-field fence and in front of the secondary wall that supported the batter's eye and scoreboard. They treasured the one boy in their circle of friends who was small enough to crawl beneath the secondary fence and snatch the pearl-white prize.

Such fans were the kids from the surrounding neighborhoods that they knew the days and times when Stars players would have a steam at the Turkish baths on Melrose and Poinsettia. On those days the kids would wait in the parking lot with their mitts, a bat, and a baseball. The players would oblige with a few throws and even a lesson or two on how to stand in against a back-bending curveball.

Admiration for the ball club and its players took many forms. For some youths it involved the cherished autograph received after extending a program or ball from the stands. One youth bonded with Rugger Ardizoia by swapping his comic books to the pitcher for baseballs. Players were a staple of the community. Frankie Kelleher opened a health club not far from the ballpark. Roger Bowman started an upholstery shop near Inglewood. Youths could boast of buying their first pair of cleats from Eddie Malone, who worked as a salesman at United Sporting Goods. If a housewife wanted kitchen appliances, Pots and Plans in Beverly Hills was a good place to go. It was owned by Stars center fielder Tommy Saffell. Marvin Gudat owned the El Texano Café in Burbank, and Lou Stringer refereed high school basketball games in the winter.

It wasn't just baseball that drew neighborhood boys to Gilmore Field. Stan Cline, for one, was fascinated by the growing medium of television. The admiring preteen would hang around the production truck that was parked outside the ballpark. Cline would offer to help the broadcast crew lay cables and lug equipment on game days, then once inside would remain in Gilmore Field to watch the game for free. When the calendar flipped to 1957, however, those interests and bonds were about to be broken. It would come at an emotional price.

Bob Cobb had entered the new year on a high note. The year 1956 had ended somberly, with the November passing of Cobb's longtime friend Victor Ford Collins, who had succumbed to a series of strokes. To fill the vacancy, Cobb proposed Branch Rickey be appointed chairman of the board of directors of the Hollywood Stars. Rickey had been pushed out of his role as president and general manager of the Pittsburgh Pirates. During the Stars' annual board meeting in the first week of the new year, Cobb put the idea of Branch Rickey as board chair to a vote. Three weeks past his seventy-fifth birthday, Rickey lit a cigar to celebrate an election win.

Six weeks into the New Year, headlines in the six Los Angeles newspapers sent bomblike reverberations through the Gilmore Field offices. Walter O'Malley, owner of the Brooklyn Dodgers, had purchased both the Los Angeles Angels and Wrigley Field. Rickey, Cobb, and everyone who worked in the Stars front office knew what the deal meant. The Dodgers were likely coming to Los Angeles.

O'Malley had actually pulled off an ingenious swap. He had traded the Dodgers' Fort Worth, Texas, farm club to P. K. Wrigley for the Angels.

Following the 1956 season, the Hollywood Stars' board of directors elected Branch Rickey chairman of the board. Behind Rickey from left to right are Bob Clements, vice president; Paul Jeschke, business manager; and Bob Cobb. ***Courtesy of Los Angeles Public Library Photo Collection***

That was only part of the deal. Having recently sold both Ebbets Field in Brooklyn and La Grave Field in Fort Worth, O'Malley used proceeds from the sales to buy Wrigley's Southern California ballpark. "I'm tired of being called the 'fly in the ointment,'" Wrigley said of the deal. "I feel we are giving Los Angeles a better chance for major league baseball."[2]

Cobb's time was running out. His lease with Earl Gilmore was due to end on December 31, 1957. While CBS concentrated its construction efforts on other areas of Gilmore's land, it would only be another year or two before they would want the parcel where the ballpark stood.

The 1957 season began with Cobb's usual praise for a new manager along with the Stars' prospects for success. Clyde King was a Rickey protégé, a former Brooklyn Dodgers pitcher who believed his pitching staff had the arms to compete for Hollywood's fourth pennant in nine years.

A week before Opening Day the Boston Red Sox flew into town to conclude a series of exhibition games in California. New owners of the San Francisco Seals, the Sox had played two games in San Francisco and agreed to games with Hollywood and the Los Angeles Angels. The crowd at Gilmore Field would have exceeded capacity had late arrivals not been dissuaded by a full parking lot and gone home. A thunderous roar filled the air in the top of the third inning, when Ted Williams launched a towering home run over the right-field fence. His blast was the highlight of a 3–0 Boston win. The Stars front office staff smiled smugly twenty-four hours later when it was revealed that the Angels had drawn far fewer fans than Hollywood for their game with the Red Sox.

Once the 1957 Pacific Coast League season began, it seemed that whatever could go wrong for the Hollywood Stars did. On opening night, the team's shortstop, Dick Smith, and second baseman, Spook Jacobs, collided while chasing a pop fly. Both were carried from the field on stretchers and taken by ambulance to a hospital. Smith suffered a broken jaw that was wired shut. Jacobs was left with a fractured skull. Neither would play again for almost two months.

Two weeks later, umpires were forced for the first time to call off a game at Gilmore Field due to thick fog. The heavy mist rolled in over the right-field fence just as the game was about to begin. By the fourth inning, fans were unable to read the numbers on the scoreboard. Five minutes later sportswriters in the press box could no longer make out second base. Al Somers, the umpire-in-chief, halted play for forty-three minutes, then decided waiting any longer was pointless. The game simply could not go on.

Gilmore Field was beginning to show wear. Nineteen years of use had stripped it of its shine. It was no longer the jewel that had dazzled fans back in 1939. Now when kids scampered to the railing to seek autographs, the floorboards sagged beneath their feet. Where high school players were once wowed by the chance to play in the Stars' park, now they heard their coaches call the place a dump. In the early innings of one game, a discarded cigarette started a fire in the padding at the base of the backstop. It sent ushers dashing for extinguishers to prevent catastrophe. Even Bob Cobb admitted that his ballpark "should have been condemned."[3]

On the field the club teased more than it gratified. After all the hype, Stuart flopped and was shipped out. R. C. Stevens initially filled the power void. Paul Pettit's hitting was a revelation. On the mound, two local products, Bennie Daniels from Compton and Red Witt from Long Beach, were stellar. In late April and again in early May, the Stars leapfrogged the Angels into first place. By the middle of May, however, they had fallen into fourth, where they would stay for much of the summer.

Injuries, not a lack of talent, were again the team's biggest problem. Carlos Bernier fractured his right thumb. Stevens sprained his back. Emil Panko fractured his left ankle. By the end of April alone, Hollywood had seventeen players nursing injuries. Their situation became so desperate, they signed former Detroit Tigers first baseman George Vico, who had been out of Organized Baseball for two years and was working for the local water company. Before Vico agreed to sign, he extracted a promise that he would play only in games that did not interfere with his job. So bad was the injury problem that King was forced to play a left-handed-throwing first baseman at third and rotate a starting pitcher and backup catcher in right field.

On Sunday, April 28, there was much to smile about at Gilmore Field. The box and grandstand seats were occupied by 4,058 fans, who cheered Hollywood to a pair of wins over Portland, 7–2 and 2–1. But quietly, Bob Cobb was steamed. Norris Poulson, the mayor of Los Angeles, took in the two games. Poulson, who was a native of Portland, chose to sit behind the visiting team's dugout and root against the Stars. That's not all that made Cobb hot under the collar. He had been angered by recent comments in which the mayor knocked the Stars and the quality of Pacific Coast

League baseball. As fans filed out of the ballpark, Cobb cornered the mayor near a concession stand. Their voices rose, tinged with anger. Fans who noticed Cobb move toward Poulson craned their neck to try to hear what was being shouted. "I paid my way in as a fan and, as such, have a right to express my opinions," Poulson was heard to holler. When word of the spat reached reporters, the men scurried to Cobb for comment. "Oh, it was nothing," Cobb insisted. "He's a really good guy."[4]

Two days later, inevitability introduced itself when Walter O'Malley landed in Los Angeles. Ostensibly, the Dodger owner's visit was to meet the people who ran his minor-league club and see the team play. In reality, O'Malley's visit involved much more. He wanted serious answers. He hoped the visit would lay the groundwork for a move out of Brooklyn and make Los Angeles the Dodgers' new home.

While a long line of politicians sought to meet with O'Malley, the first man the Dodgers' owner insisted on meeting was Bob Cobb. They spoke privately in O'Malley's hotel suite. Cobb laid out his grandiose idea for Chavez Ravine. O'Malley peppered the Stars' president with questions. "You have given me more information in five minutes than I received from all of the politicians combined in the past eight weeks," the Dodgers' owner said.[5]

After his sit-down with Cobb, O'Malley's visit became a blur of meetings and tours. The politicians filled day two. On Thursday, May 2, Captain Sewell Griggers, head of the sheriff's department's aero squad, flew O'Malley over Chavez Ravine and pointed out traffic patterns on the freeways and city streets below. O'Malley's meeting with heads of the Los Angeles Coliseum dampened their enthusiasm. Negativity and concern filled his response to almost everything they showed him. The dimensions of the playing field were the biggest problem. A left-field fence just 230 feet from home plate, O'Malley pointed out, was 20 feet shy of the minimum distance required by Major League Baseball. The stadium's lack of box seats furrowed O'Malley's forehead. That, he rumbled, would cost his Dodgers significant income.

Friday, May 3, was filled with wall-to-wall meetings: a breakfast meeting with business leaders and more sit-downs with the mayor, city council members, and county supervisors. The Dodgers' owner made clear to everyone he met that he would build the stadium at his own expense. What he wanted from city leaders was land—Chavez Ravine, to be specific—and for the land to be made ready, with roads and parking lots constructed so that his construction team could go to work. That night, during a meeting in O'Malley's suite at the Statler Hilton Hotel, city leaders agreed to the Dodgers' owner's demands in a memorandum.

No sooner had O'Malley's plane taken off for New York on Saturday, May 4, when Poulson hiked the enthusiasm of local baseball fans when he shared with reporters, "If the Dodgers come, it'll be next year."[6] Three weeks later the National League gave both the Dodgers and the New York Giants unanimous approval to move their clubs if they saw fit. The vote would trigger a summer of negotiating and gamesmanship. In New York, city and borough leaders made counteroffers, none of which persuaded O'Malley to stay. Across the country Poulson's projection that it could cost $11 million to satisfy O'Malley set off bickering. City council members and supervisors argued that the Dodgers should make Wrigley Field or the Coliseum their permanent home, even though O'Malley had made very clear that neither was acceptable.

Inevitability seeped into Stars fans. Their team was playing on borrowed time. This would be the end of a remarkable run. Fathers like Marty Claire and Jule Wilk had fostered a love of baseball in their children through father-son treks to Gilmore Field. The Wilks had come for the first time in 1951. That day, eight-year-old Woody became a dyed-in-the-wool Carlos Bernier fan when he saw the speedster evade a rundown play by diving between an infielder's legs. Now, the father counseled his teenaged son that "day in and day out you have not seen major-league baseball. When you see the Dodgers, you will notice the difference."[7]

While Bob Cobb was pleased that big-league ball would soon come to his adopted hometown, he stewed at the effect all the attention on the Dodgers was having on revenue at Gilmore Field. "Major League talk has murdered Pacific Coast League attendance," he said.[8] Cobb pointed out that the myriad column inches local newspapers devoted almost daily to stories about the Dodgers were robbing his club of publicity.

Throughout the summer, politicians in Los Angeles haggled about the money involved to acquire and prepare Chavez Ravine for the Dodgers. Others, who sensed a lack of unanimity at City Hall, tried to get in on the act. The town of Buena Park, twenty miles south of Los Angeles, pitched its freeways and fast-growing population. The effort to woo O'Malley moved Cobb to predict that one day Southern California would be home to two major-league clubs. He drew snickers when he said he thought that Anaheim might one day make a good place for that second team.

Shrouded by Dodgers speculation and negotiation, the Hollywood Stars sat firmly ensconced in fourth place in the Pacific Coast League standings. Lost amid the anticipation of Major League Baseball's arrival were stellar seasons by Red Witt and Paul Pettit. Honing a curveball helped to vault Witt to the top of Pacific Coast League pitching prospects. By mid-August he had set a Pacific Coast League record, amassing 50 2/3 consecutive innings without allowing an earned run. "He's got all he needs to be a great one," boasted his manager.[9] After scouting Witt, former Washington Senators manager Charlie Dressen said, "I wish we had him. He could win in the majors right now."[10] Pettit would finish with 20 home runs, 31 doubles, 102 runs batted in, a .284 batting average, .382 on base percentage, and a .456 slugging percentage. "Gosh how that guy has worked," San Francisco Seals manager Joe Gordon said to Braven Dyer of the *Los Angeles Times*. "He never quits trying. He's a sound hitter now. I hope he makes it."[11]

As the season reached its final weeks, reminiscing became as much a favored activity as contemplation. An old-timers' game celebrated the Stars' and Angels' past. Tod Davis belted a two-run home run to make the former Stars 3–1 winners over the ex-Angels. And any farewell between the Stars and their archrivals was not going to be fond. In what everyone felt might be the final series the two teams ever played against each other, tempers erupted into yet another wild melee. The brouhaha took place in the Saturday game of the series. After a Hollywood home run that put the Stars ahead, Angels pitcher Tom Lasorda threw his next pitch up and in on the Stars' batter, Spook Jacobs. On the very next pitch, Jacobs pushed a bunt up the first base line. To the astonishment of all, Lasorda raced to the first base line and threw a flying block on Jacobs. "We had no idea why," Paul Pettit said afterward.[12] Players rushed onto the field from both dugouts. All around the infield players squared off and were pushing and shoving; some even threw punches. The most heated combatants were Jacobs and Angels second baseman Sparky Anderson. Umpires worked feverishly for ten minutes before they were finally able to quell the tiff.

The next afternoon the two teams met for the final time. Close to nine thousand fans turned out despite threatening skies. When the doubleheader ended, light showers failed to generate more moisture than that in the eyes of many staunch fans. Hollywood's 6–3 win in the first game was the 260th in the twenty-year rivalry. The 6–2 victory posted by the Angels in the second game was their 293rd. In all, the Angels won the City Cup eleven times. Hollywood won the majority of their meetings in nine seasons.

Emotions rippled about Gilmore Field two weeks later when the Stars brought the curtain down on baseball in their homey park. The evening began with a raucous national anthem by the Hollywood Legion Post 143 Tootlers, Tweeters, and Thumpers. Paul Pettit's long home run over the right-field wall sent loud cheers thundering from the stands. In the fifth inning, the usual pause to regroom the infield brought out a microphone and Ab England, the president of the Hollywood Chamber of Commerce. England launched into a heartfelt tribute to Bob Cobb. As he concluded his remarks, he pointed to Cobb, who was seated in his box near the Stars dugout, then urged the fans to show their appreciation. Everyone, all seven thousand, stood and cheered. As the applause grew, Cobb broke down and cried.

While it was Cobb who received the deserved plaudits, Hugh Pepper was in the center of the spotlight. By the time Cobb had settled back in his box seat, the talk was of the Hollywood pitcher who had yet to allow a hit. Big moments were nothing new to the twenty-six-year-old Mississippian. As a college football standout at Southern Mississippi, Pepper's sixty-six-yard touchdown run had been a highlight of the school's biggest win ever, an upset of fifth-ranked University of Alabama. In 1954 he had been the sixth overall selection in the NFL draft but spurned the Pittsburgh Steelers for a $20,000 bonus offer from the Pittsburgh Pirates. Injury and inconsistency had taken the shine off Pepper's grand prospect status. Now, with nudges in both dugouts and whispers in the stands giving rise to a developing no-hitter, the stocky right-hander successfully retired all three Seals in the sixth, then again in the seventh. Pepper's fastball was lively, "the liveliest it's been all year," said his catcher, Bill Hall, after the game.[13] Again San Francisco batters failed to get a hit in the eighth inning, and when play began in the top of the ninth inning, the emotion of the final game in Gilmore Field was eclipsed by the drama of a no-hit game. To thunderous cheers, Pepper set down the first two batters in the ninth. A crack of ball on bat, however, brought the crowd to a still silence then a gasp when Ed Sadowski hit a fastball back up the middle that rolled into center field for a single that spoiled Pepper's gem. Standing atop the canvas first base bag, Sadowski doffed his cap and bowed toward the Hollywood dugout. From the top step, Clyde King waved his arms with rage toward Sadowski. Fans angrily booed. "What are they doing?" nine-year-old Steven Kipnis asked his father, Sol. "They don't like each other," was the sharp reply.[14] When the next batter, Marty Keough, was retired to end the game, the Stars celebrated Pepper's one-hit, 6–0, victory near the pitcher's mound. Fans released their jubilation by flinging seat cushions onto the field. Once the noise died and the players had retreated to the clubhouse, fans began to silently file out of the ballpark. Many were, as one said, "really saddened" knowing it was for the last time.[15]

The departing red taillights on the cars that exited the parking lots took with them habits, bonds, and desires that would never again be relished. In the ensuing days a somberness would pervade the community, if not other areas of Southern California. Never again would young Frankie Freudenthal's mother, a German refugee, walk him to Gilmore Field from their home on Oakmont Street, then sit in the grandstands and knit while the boy cheered the Stars. Gone would be the Chance family drives from Compton to meet up with their friends, the Meroloffs, for dinner and a game at Gilmore Field. No more would the neighborhood boys hover behind the outfield fence for home run balls that some would use for pickup games and others would sell for a quarter.

During the final two weeks of the 1957 season, Hollywood was on the road. The most fervent of Hollywood's fans would plant themselves in front of radios each night. Mark Scott's broadcasts on KFWB were the lone remaining link to the ball club. Sadness among the avid was lessened when Paul Pettit hit a two-run home run, a grand slam, and drove in ten runs in a 20–2 romp past Seattle on September 11. Then, on Sunday September 15, the final day of the season, Pettit homered in the eleventh inning to make Hollywood 9–8 winners in the first game of the doubleheader. After a brief intermission the Stars beat the Rainiers, 5–4, to complete the doubleheader sweep in the final game they would ever play. A third-place finish, seven games behind the pennant-winning San Francisco Seals, was how the Stars would bring down the curtain.

Minutes after the final out was recorded, Mark Scott signed off the air for the last time. He let the phone company know the broadcast was complete and their line was no longer needed. An hour later Nobe Kawano packed up the last of the Stars' uniforms and for the final time latched shut the equipment trunk, then headed for the airport.

Attention now would turn to the Dodgers and Walter O'Malley's decision. Bob Cobb decided not to be around for it. He instead traveled to Reno, where he competed in the National Skeet-Shoot Championships, then on to Montana for a week of pheasant hunting and trout fishing.

In Los Angeles, contentious debate raged in the halls of local government. Facing a deadline imposed by O'Malley, the city council voted on October 7 to give him 304 acres in Chavez Ravine in exchange for title to Wrigley Field. The vote was 10 to 4. The following afternoon, Poulson received a Western Union telegram that read, "Get your wheelbarrow and shovel. I'll see you at Chavez Ravine."[16] It was signed Walter F. O'Malley. The Dodgers were coming to Los Angeles.

33

"WE ARE AT A LOSS"

The Pacific Coast League was in a hair-tugging, forehead-pounding state. Its two biggest markets, Los Angeles and San Francisco, were gone. Three of its member clubs—Hollywood, the Los Angeles Angels, and the San Francisco Seals—had to move. Under the rules of baseball, the Dodgers were now owners of the Los Angeles market. The Giants, who had also announced plans to leave New York, subsequently filed paperwork to move to San Francisco and thus claimed rights to that baseball territory. No team was thrown into greater chaos by the moves than the Hollywood Stars.

Like the Dodgers, who had acquired the Los Angeles Angels, the Giants grabbed San Francisco's Pacific Coast League club. Horace Stoneham, owner of the Giants, had arranged to swap top farm clubs with the Boston Red Sox. The Giants would take title to the San Francisco Seals in exchange for the Giants' club in the American Association, the Minneapolis Millers. Ownership of their own Pacific Coast League farm clubs gave the Dodgers and Giants a large degree of control in the say of where those clubs would move to.

Concerned that the pursuit of new cities by the Stars, Angels, and Seals may encroach upon other leagues' territories and incur damage claims, the Pacific Coast League insisted it coordinate matters. The Dodgers were perfectly willing to follow the league's direction and move the Angels to Spokane, Washington. Stoneham publicly stated that he was happy to move the Seals wherever the league wished. In reality, however, Stoneham was plotting to move the team just where he wanted, which would throw a wrench in the Hollywood Stars' plans.

For two years Bob Cobb had made regular trips to Phoenix to determine whether the city was a viable landing spot for the Hollywood Stars. His initial efforts to stake legal baseball claim to the city hit trouble soon after it began. Weeks after he took an option on the Class C team in Phoenix in the fall of 1954, Cobb met with the city's mayor. He sought to lay groundwork that would make Phoenix the spring training home for the Hollywood Stars. It was a quest Stoneham was not about to let happen. The New York Giants owner had a winter mansion in the Phoenix suburb of Scottsdale. His ball club held its spring training in Phoenix. When Stoneham learned of Cobb's exploration, he exercised political muscle. The Giants' owner offered to sign a ten-year lease to make Phoenix the spring training home for his club. His proposition came with a caveat: exclusive use of the city's lone ballpark, Municipal Stadium, which he got.

Cobb's tie-up with the class C Phoenix club was part of a long-term plan to study the area. He told confidants that when that day came, he would exercise his right under the deal to buy the Phoenix ball club, which would bring with it the territorial rights. Cobb would then move the Stars to the desert oasis. Unfortunately, the arrangement with the Phoenix Stars soured quickly. Early in the 1955 season, relations between the Hollywood front office and a prickly business manager for the Phoenix club grew antagonistic. By late summer it was apparent that despite a successful season, the Phoenix Stars would lose considerable money. This made the relationship incompatible. Prodded by his business manager, the owner of the Phoenix Stars severed ties with Hollywood at the end of just one season.

As September 1957 neared, Cobb's need to find a new home for the Stars was pressing. Things around him were happening fast, and pressure was mounting. Unbeknownst to Cobb, Horace Stoneham had clandestinely pulled strings to plant his farm team in Phoenix. On August 21, the day after he signed papers in the mayor's office in San Francisco, Stoneham flew to Phoenix. There he persuaded the owner of the Phoenix Stars to sell his ball club. Once the transaction was complete, Stoneham held territorial rights to Phoenix. He informed the PCL's president, Leslie O'Connor, that Phoenix would unequivocally be the Seals' new home.

Stoneham's manipulations dealt Bob Cobb a staggering blow. "We certainly want to stay in business," he told reporters. "We will try every way possible to stay in baseball."[1] With board members and backers insisting the Stars remain close to Los Angeles, Cobb was running out of options. Suitors lined up to court the team. Tacoma, Salt Lake City, Dallas, Houston, Edmonton, and even Mexico City cabled or phoned to express interest. "The Mexico City people made Cobb a tremendous offer," said a PCL spokesperson.[2] The league felt the city was too far away to warrant serious consideration. Cobb was perplexed. He consulted Branch Rickey, but their discussions failed to bring clarity to the muddied predicament. "We are at a loss as to where to go to stay in business," Cobb said.[3]

Rumors flew that Anaheim would be the Stars' destination. "We believe that the Anaheim area is growing fast enough to warrant a possible move there," said the Stars' vice president, Bob Clements.[4] The thought had merit. Anaheim had been the Stars' spring training base for six years. Since Cobb's friend and Hollywood season ticket holder Walt Disney had opened his theme park, Disneyland, in 1955, the population of Anaheim surged by more than 500 percent to almost one hundred thousand. Still, Cobb quashed the rumor and remained adamant that Anaheim was not a viable option.

When owners of the eight Pacific Coast League clubs gathered in Sacramento on November 1, their goal was to put plans in place for the 1958 season. One man, D. Patrick Ahern, threw the meeting into disarray. Ahern was a large man with a big idea. Since fulfilling his service in World War II, Ahern had been director of the Veterans Service Center. An avid baseball fan, he had run the largest American Legion baseball tournament in Southern California and was the state commissioner of American Legion baseball. Following election to the Long Beach City Council on his third try in 1954, Ahern became a strong proponent of the plan to invest $400,000 into construction of a ballpark, Blair Field, within the city's Recreation Park. With the Stars suddenly in search of a new home, Ahern traveled to Sacramento in hopes of landing a tenant for his city's new ballpark.

Ahern spent half an hour in front of the team owners. He could see the expressions on the men's faces and knew they were surprised and also impressed by what he was telling them. The councilman showed telegrams from mayors of six cities: Lakewood, Downey, Compton, Norwalk, Bellflower, and Paramount. Each urged the league to put a team in Long Beach and pledged their support. Emil Sick, who owned the Seattle Rainiers, asked about the population of Long Beach and its surrounding communities. Like many in the room, he was surprised when Ahern answered that Long Beach and two suburbs, Lakewood and Signal Hill, totaled 420,000 residents and that 1,350,000 lived within a ten-mile circle. Ralph Kiner, the San Diego Padres' general manager, questioned the seating capacity at Blair Field. Ahern answered that it would not be hard to increase it to 9,000.

The meeting had no sooner broken up when Cobb pulled Leslie O'Connor aside and told the PCL president that he was interested in Long Beach. He was not alone. Ahern's presentation made Buzzie Bavasi, the Los Angeles Dodgers' general manager, reconsider moving the Angels to Spokane. "The minute we place a club in Long Beach, that's the minute we start saving money," Bavasi said.[5]

O'Connor told Hank Hollingsworth, the executive sports editor of the *Long Beach Independent Press Telegram*, that the league's directors were "definitely interested in Long Beach. I can say that Long Beach is front and center because of its bid today."[6] As interested as the Dodgers were, one league director told Hollingsworth that the city's best shot at landing a team was the Hollywood Stars.

A committee was assembled to reorganize the league. O'Connor appointed the owner of the Portland Beavers and general manager of the Seattle Rainiers to join him in the task. The league's future would be discussed at the baseball Winter Meetings in one month's time. While they worked, Cobb went back to his board and pondered. He told the men that they may have to offer the Dodgers 5 percent of all revenues in order to play in the team's territory. As Cobb and the Hollywood board contemplated, the work of O'Connor's committee sent up ominous signals. A shift of power was taking place within the Pacific Coast League. For decades, six of the eight teams in the league had been based in California, which left the Seattle Rainiers and Portland Beavers in a voting minority. That was undergoing change. The Oakland Oaks had been sold and moved to the Canadian city of Vancouver. Spokane sought a team, as did Salt Lake City. An extreme reshaping of the Pacific Coast League was in the making. Change could put five of the eight clubs in the Northwest, which would pare the travel costs of those five northern clubs and forge greater geographic rivalries.

A week before the Winter Meetings, Cobb and the Hollywood board could see the inevitable. Their hand was being forced. On November 24, Cobb threw in the towel. He telephoned O'Connor with news that he and the board had decided to put the Stars up for sale. He phoned Ahern with the news as well. "I have two restaurants that take up too much of my time, so I would like to get out of baseball entirely right now," Cobb explained to Hollingsworth. When asked what he would sell the Stars for, Cobb replied, "It could be priced in the neighborhood of $225,000."[7]

Ahearn quickly assembled a group of five investors, four of whom had previously owned the Riverside club in the Class C California League. Two days after Cobb had announced his intent to sell, the Long Beach group flew to the state capital and filed articles of incorporation for their Harbor Baseball Club. The prospective buyers sent engineers to evaluate the lighting system at Gilmore Field with an idea to buy it for the new Long Beach ballpark. Cobb cautioned Ahern and the prospective investors about the climate within the league. He explained that the decision about who could buy his team and where the Stars were moved might be out of his hands and rest solely with the league. Ahern replied that it was a chance he was willing to take.

Settling the relocation of the Stars and extracting damages from Walter O'Malley and Horace Stoneham were the top priorities when team owners arrived at the baseball Winter Meetings in Colorado Springs on December 2. By the end of the first day, O'Malley and Stoneham had agreed to pay the Pacific Coast League $900,000 for invading its largest markets. The moneys would be paid out over three years and split among the remaining six teams. Hollywood would receive $150,000. Negotiations to resolve the Hollywood Stars' dilemma would be far more complicated.

Bob Cobb was insistent that he would not budge from his $225,000 asking price for the Stars. He explained that the sale covered contracts for eight players and affixed the $40,000 waiver price as their value. The buyer would take possession of the Stars' baseball equipment and could also have the stadium lighting system from Gilmore Field. "The San Diego franchise went for $300,000 without assets equal to ours," Cobb explained.[8]

Nicholas G. Morgan, a Utah oilman, headed the Salt Lake City effort. He flew into Colorado Springs and presented Cobb with an offer of $150,000 for the Stars. Morgan then left so hurriedly that fellow team owners nicknamed him "Swifty." Negotiations between Cobb and Morgan quickly bogged down. The unbending stance of the two men moved O'Connor to contact Ahern. The PCL president asked if the Long Beach investors would guarantee an annual attendance of two hundred thousand fans. "Why should Long Beach have to guarantee such attendance?" Ahern angrily replied.[9] The councilman noted that it was a figure many of the league's members had failed to achieve in the just completed season.

Cobb threatened to sell to the Long Beach group if Morgan failed to raise his offer. Unfortunately, O'Connor had told a number of sportswriters that the league had reservations about Long Beach, specifically its proximity to Los Angeles and the adverse effect the Dodgers' radio and television broadcasts as well as their advertising efforts could have on a club so close. He had also made known that directors wanted a team in Salt Lake City. Several of those sportswriters shared the information with Morgan, who called the Stars' president's bluff. "Cobb's franchise is not worth any $225,000," Morgan insisted. He smugly boasted that Cobb "will accept our offer or wind up in Mexicali."[10]

Clyde Perkins, who owned the Portland Beavers, negotiated with Morgan behind Cobb's back. At Perkins's behest, on the fourth day of the Winter Meetings, a power play was executed. Discussion to approve new cities for San Francisco, the Los Angeles Angels, and Hollywood came to the forefront. The topic elicited considerable argument, primarily about Hollywood. Minutes turned to an hour, then two, and in time reached an excruciating fourth. Dialogue was dotted with acrimony. Cobb was pressured to drop his asking price. Fellow directors criticized the Hollywood president for asking too much. Others claimed he was impeding not only the Pacific Coast League's plans but those of three other minor leagues that would be affected by the moves. As things raged, there came a point when Cobb excused himself to tend to a business matter. Once the Hollywood Stars' president was out of the room, a motion was made to bring a vote to the floor to approve Phoenix, Spokane, and Salt Lake City as new member cities for 1958. Ralph Kiner argued against it. He could see what was happening: Directors were making an end run to get what they wanted. Kiner favored Hollywood's move to Long Beach. Without a PCL team in Los Angeles, his San Diego Padres would be isolated and face much higher travel costs. Kiner, however, found himself alone. When directors cast their vote, Rosey Ryan, the new business manager of the Giants' farm club, sided with the majority, as did the Angels and Sacramento. The Solons' owner would later confess that he wanted Long Beach kept available as a possible relocation site should he continue to lose money.

When Cobb returned to the room and learned what had happened, he was speechless. The vote had included a deadline to complete the sale of his ball club. It robbed him of any negotiating power with the Salt Lake City group. Indeed, when Morgan learned of the vote, he insisted to reporters that it meant acceptance of his $150,000 offer. Perkins cajoled the Salt Lake City group to raise their offer, which it did, to $175,000. Left with no alternative, Cobb accepted "so that nobody could accuse me of stopping baseball's progress." Privately Cobb groused, "They had me as the villain."[11] The Long Beach investors never got a chance to present a formal offer to Cobb or the league. Following a midnight press conference, O'Connor conceded that directors from the Seattle, Portland, and Vancouver clubs were steadfastly against Long Beach from the beginning.

The inevitable had become reality. The end. While many in Southern California celebrated the arrival of big-league baseball, a malaise permeated Hollywood's longtime fans, who lamented the demise of their Stars. A little more than a week after the sale was agreed to, several of the team's most ardent fans arranged for a hotel banquet room where they staged a Christmas party for Stars employees and players. About a dozen players who called Southern California home attended. "They were real sad to see the Stars go," Paul Pettit told a friend. "They put on a nice event and gave us some very nice gifts."[12]

On December 19, eleven days after the nineteenth anniversary of Cobb's purchase of Herbert Fleishhacker's ball club, Morgan and his attorney strode into the Hollywood Brown Derby. Tables were turned. Unlike on December 8, 1938, it was Cobb who was being forced to sell by factors far beyond his control. Along with Jeschke and Cobb's attorney, Frank Kanne Jr., the group squeezed into a booth. Leslie O'Connor joined the men. All around them was conviviality. Cobb was reflective. "Baseball," he explained, "is like life. It brings a new challenge every day. You have your headaches, but you also have your fun." With a broad grin Cobb added, "I'd do it all over again."[13]

Christmas spirit flowed about the famous restaurant. It was in stark contrast to the mood of Jeschke, Kanne, and Cobb. Agreement papers were laid out on the table. Cobb's scan of the typewritten pages represented the final seconds of arguably the most innovative, glamorous, and perhaps glorious run in the history of minor-league baseball. Morgan and Kanne watched as the Stars' president picked up a pen. Then, an instant later, the swoosh of ink across the bottom of the page brought an end to the spectacular life of the Hollywood Stars.

34

"THOSE WERE THE HALCYON DAYS"

What began as a murmur had risen to an energetic buzz. Now, as the clock neared the noon hour, the noise level bordered on a low roar. Happiness to the point of jubilation filled the room. Business leaders rubbed shoulders with wide-eyed baseball fans. Smiles radiated. Red, white, and blue bunting along with streamers of pennants hung from the ceiling. A large banner read, "Welcome Los Angeles Dodgers," and beneath it an even larger banner covered the wall behind the head table. It read, "Greatest Catch in Baseball!"

October 28, 1957, was a red-letter day for the city of Los Angeles, proved by the smiles and prideful posture of the men about the room. This was the day the city stepped into the big leagues and welcomed Major League Baseball.

By the time the voice of Joe E. Brown boomed from the dais, more than 1,100 people had filled the ballroom at the Statler Hilton Hotel. The comedic actor and, on this day, event emcee evoked cackles with a handful of jokes. The laughter became applause when Brown introduced the many baseball celebrities who were in attendance—Casey Stengel, Leo Durocher, and the umpire Beans Reardon. Brown then introduced the man of the hour: the owner of the Dodgers, Walter O'Malley. A thunderous applause grew as O'Malley rose. "Mister Toastmaster," the Dodgers' owner began, "you have done a fine job. But you must be charged with an error. You failed to introduce Bob Cobb!"

If bitterness was expected of Bob Cobb, there was none. He became an unabashed booster of the Dodgers. Cobb helped members of the Stars' staff—Edna Ward, Nobe Kawano, Tony Tuso, Danny Goodman, and Howard Lorenz—to land jobs with the Dodgers. He worked to get a ballot measure passed to allow construction of Dodger Stadium to proceed. Once the 1958 season began, Cobb organized buses to take diners from his restaurants to Dodgers games. When the Dodgers won the pennant in 1959, one full-page ad in the *Los Angeles Times* offered congratulations. It was from Bob Cobb and his Brown Derby restaurants.

It has been more than six decades since Bob Cobb sold the Hollywood Stars and exited baseball, but his fingerprints remain on the game. His idea to pause play in the fifth inning and drag the infield so fans could hurry to the concession stands is now common practice at every major- and minor-league game. Cobb's 1953 vision of an ultramodern ballpark with cabanas, a restaurant, and a private club is commonplace in the twenty-first century. In the 1950s, Cobb's was a lone voice arguing the benefits of putting home games on local television. Today, such telecasts are commonplace around Major League Baseball. So, too, is flying by charter, something the Hollywood Stars initiated in 1946, ten years before New York Giants and Pittsburgh Pirates did it. Though short-lived, short pants were a box office smash. In 1972 the Chicago White Sox brought the fashion statement to the major leagues. White Sox owner Bill Veeck called them Hollywood Shorts.

The minor league that Cobb proposed and with Oscar Reichow helped to launch—the California League—has sent more than twenty-seven hundred players to the major leagues. Fourteen graduates are in the Hall of Fame. No team in the Pioneer League has enjoyed more success through the years than the Billings Mustangs. The team that Cobb created in 1948 has won fifteen league titles since its inception. During the 2007 season, a pair of Illinois filmmakers produced a documentary, *Cobb Field, A Day at the Ballpark*. It earned three Emmy Awards.

While Tod Davis reached the major leagues with Philadelphia, few of the teens Hollywood signed fulfilled their potential. Bill Barisoff returned from World War II with a sore shoulder. Eddie Erautt joined the Cincinnati Reds, then suffered a shoulder injury. Clint Hufford fell off a ladder, and the damage to his shoulder brought his career to an end. Eddie Harrison chose to pursue a business career rather than return to baseball. After working in the film lab at Paramount Studio during the day and folding linen at the Roosevelt Hotel at night, Harrison caught on with a commercial real estate firm, the Beaumont Company, and later bought the firm.

Bill Gray left baseball to join an uncle and open a men's clothing store. Bill Gray's Men's Wear flourished on Santa Monica Boulevard for several decades.

After baseball Frankie Kelleher worked in public relations, then opened a tool sales company in Stockton, California. "He was the most wonderful, kind gentleman I have ever known," said his daughter-in-law, Denise Kelleher.[1] Irv Noren's big season with Hollywood led to an eleven-year career in the big leagues. "How lucky was I?" he reflected.[2] In 1971 he became a coach with the Oakland A's. Away from the game Noren owned a bowling alley, a liquor store, and two sporting goods stores. He invested in racehorses and spent many a summer afternoon at Del Mar Racetrack near San Diego. During his six seasons with the Stars, Chuck Stevens was both a popular and productive ballplayer. "It was the best thing that ever happened to me," he reminisced.[3] After his playing career ended, Stevens spent thirty-eight years assisting former players, umpires, coaches, and managers beset with difficulties as secretary of the Association of Professional Baseball Players of America. Once in the big leagues, Bill Mazeroski fulfilled the predictions of greatness bestowed by Bob Cobb and others. Eight times he was awarded the Gold Glove for fielding excellence. In 1960 he socked a dramatic game-winning home run in the bottom of the ninth of Game 7 of the World Series to help Pittsburgh win its first title in thirty-five years. In 2001 Mazeroski was inducted into the Baseball Hall of Fame.

A year after his celebrated flame-out with Hollywood, Dick Stuart spent ten seasons in the big leagues with Pittsburgh, Boston, Philadelphia, the New York Mets, and the Los Angeles Dodgers and Angels. Fielding woes plagued Stuart throughout his career. It was a trait that brought him such nicknames as "Stonefingers" and "Dr. Strangeglove." When the Pittsburgh Pirates held a reunion of their 1960 World Series team, Stuart did not attend. It was reported that he skipped the event because the Pirates would not provide him with first-class airfare. Injuries limited Carlos Bernier's big-league career to a single season. It was theorized that Bernier's temper outbursts may have been the product of frequent headaches from a beaning he suffered during his first season in pro ball. On April 6, 1989, Carlos Bernier was found hanged in his home in Puerto Rico. Authorities listed the cause of death as suicide.

Hollywood became a career for some former Stars. Buzz Knudsen became a legendary sound engineer and the winner of Academy Awards for his work on *Cabaret*, *The Exorcist*, and *E.T. the Extra-Terrestrial*. Director John Landis said of Knudsen, "He was one of those guys who directors really sought out because they knew he would elevate the film."[4] Rowe Wallerstein was assistant director and production manager for such successful television shows as *Mannix*, *The Wild Wild West*, and *Quincy*. In the fall of 1959, Mark Scott helped to develop a television show that would pit major-league sluggers against each other in a home run hitting competition. The project, *Home Run Derby*, came to fruition in April 1960 and was a hit. In July, as talks for a second season were underway, Scott suffered a fatal heart attack in his sleep. "Mark loved sports and especially baseball," said his widow, Dorothy. "His motto and famous last words after his baseball game broadcasts and his sports radio shows were, 'Whether you win or lose, be a good sport.'"[5]

Hollywood had few fans who were more devoted to the team than Gail Patrick. Despite her divorce from Bob Cobb, Patrick remained a fixture at Gilmore Field. In 1947 Patrick married literary agent Cornwall Jackson. Among her new husband's clients was Erle Stanley Gardner, author of the popular *Perry Mason* legal novels. Patrick felt the stories had great potential for the growing medium of television, but Gardner was not interested. Frequent talks softened the man. He agreed to partner with Patrick to produce the television adaptation of *Perry Mason*. For nine years *Perry Mason* was a ratings winner. Gail Patrick was lauded for her work as one of television's first female producers.

Gilmore Field stood for a little over a year after the Stars moved to Salt Lake City. During that time the Los Angeles Rams utilized the vacant venue for practices. In January 1958 CBS exercised its right to buy the land the ballpark stood on, and Earl Gilmore hired workers to tear the place down. Almost forty years later, construction workers at the CBS site stumbled upon the Gilmore Field dugouts, buried in a field.

In the years that followed the departure of the Hollywood Stars to Salt Lake City, Bob Cobb focused his professional efforts on his Brown Derby restaurants. Baseball, competitive shooting, and outdoor sports remained a passion, as did the role of doting grandfather. The Southern California chapter of the Baseball Writers' Association circled April 2, 1970, on the calendar for a season-opening luncheon. As part of the program, the organization planned to present a special civic award to Cobb. Two weeks before the event, organizers began to receive RSVPs. Venue and meal preparations were in place when, on Saturday, March 21, startling news was received. Bob Cobb had succumbed to cancer. He was seventy-one. Cobb's widow, Sally, received nine hundred condolence letters. "The Brown Derby," Lois Dwan of the *Los Angeles Times* wrote, "became one of the best-known restaurants in the country. The Hollywood Brown Derby brimmed with glamour during its great days. It never faulted on service and served some dishes that were never better anywhere. Bob Cobb will be remembered for his Cobb salad. It is hoped he is also remembered as a really nice guy."[6]

The Hollywood Brown Derby continued for another fifteen years, but it wasn't the same. The studios had abandoned the area. Celebrities no longer flocked. General Mills bought the recipe for the restaurant's famous sponge cake. The mastermind of the Brown Derby's salad dressings, chef Robert Kreis, took his recipes national under the label of Good Seasons. In April 1985 the celebrated Brown Derby on Vine Street ceased operations.

For many, like Jim Hardy, the Hollywood Stars and Gilmore Field came to represent not just cherished memories but a special time. From his hiring as Hollywood's first ballboy in 1939, Hardy had risen to prominence. He shone as a football standout at Fairfax High, was Most Valuable Player of the Rose Bowl in 1945 for USC, and earned Pro Bowl honors in the NFL for the Los Angeles Rams. At the age of ninety-two, a tinge of giddiness accompanied Hardy's telling of being stopped by the voice of Edna Ward in the parking lot after a game: "How come you haven't come into the office to pick up your check?" Hardy, taken aback, stammered, "You mean, I get to do this, *and* I get paid for it?"[7] Or when he injured his back and Bob Cobb sent his personal physical to the Hardy home, after which Gail Patrick dropped by and insisted Hardy's parents send her the bill. Then there was the exhilaration whenever Bob Kahle would urge the teen to take the third baseman's place during batting practice, rubbing elbows with the great Babe Herman, a "funny, funny guy."[8] Then, of course, there was the nightly parade of movie stars and celebrities into Gilmore Field, a source of awe that put the teen "in hog heaven."[9] Few nights, though, evoked more excitement than the night "my pal," Eddie Harrison, debuted for Hollywood at the age of seventeen.[10]

For an afternoon the storytelling brought a return to nirvana. The reflections were a vessel on a journey. They carried Hardy to a time when an adolescent matured into manhood through exposure to and association with the uniqueness of innovation, the motivation instilled by accomplishment, and the inspiration derived from greatness. Just as they did for Hardy, the qualities that made the Hollywood Stars a unique and groundbreaking baseball team also lent themselves to the maturation of the region and the growth of professional baseball. With a voice energized by his blissful return to cherished years, Hardy concluded wistfully, "The Greeks said it first, but those really were the Halcyon days."[11]

NOTES

1. "YOU CAN SELL IT OUT OF A HAT"

1. Lois Dwan, "Trying on the New Derby," *Los Angeles Times*, 19 February 1975.
2. Lois Dwan "Roundabout," *Los Angeles Times*, 21 September 1969.
3. "Quality and Service Stressed at Derbies," *Los Angeles Times*, 16 June 1967.

2. "NOT WITHOUT ME"

1. Bob Hunter, "Hollywood Putting $200,000 into Park," *Sporting News*, 19 January 1939.
2. Dick Farrington, "Fanning with Farrington," *Sporting News*, 18 January 1940.
3. James Bawden, "Dream Factory Time: Gail Patrick," *Films of the Golden Ages*, 29 April 2014.
4. Farrington, "Fanning with Farrington," 18 January 1940.

3. "WHOLLY OWNED BY HOLLYWOOD PEOPLE"

1. Bob Ray, "The Sports X-Ray," *Los Angeles Times*, 1 August 1939.
2. "Lang Suit Lost by Fleishhacker," United Press International, 6 December 1937.

3. Bob Hunter, "Hollywood Putting $200,000 into Park," *Sporting News*, 19 January 1939.

4. "GO IN AND GET A UNIFORM"

1. Oscar Reichow, "Reichow the Original Landis Man Pays Tribute to His Choice," *Sporting News*, 18 November 1920.
2. Ibid.
3. John Sheridan, "Back of the Home Plate," *Sporting News*, 10 February 1920.
4. Oscar Reichow, "Cubs a Happy and Confident Lot as They Start for Camp," *Sporting News*, 4 March 1929.
5. Mark Kelly, "Scribbled by Scribes," *Los Angeles Examiner,* 2 March 1939.
6. Charles Maher, "A Dodger Lineup You Don't Hear Much About," *Los Angeles Times*, 15 July 1973.
7. Scott Ostler, "Remembering Babe Herman," *Los Angeles Times,* 1 December 1987.
8. Frederick G. Lieb, "Inside the Game's Most Famous Deals," *Sporting News*, 27 April 1944.
9. Ostler, "Remembering Babe Herman."
10. Lieb, "Inside the Game's Most Famous Deals."
11. Hedda Hopper, "Public Affection Makes or Breaks Film Stars," *Los Angeles Times*, 19 March 1939.
12. John B. Old, "Ballyhoo Building Will Include Films," *Sporting News*, 6 September 1945.
13. Bob Ray, "The Sports X-Ray," *Los Angeles Times*, 8 December 1938.
14. Bob Ray, "The Sports X-Ray," *Los Angeles Times*, 10 February 1938.
15. Ibid.
16. Bob Hunter, "Bob Cobb Ends 20 Years' Service to the Game," *Sporting News*, 8 January 1958.
17. Jim Hardy, telephone interview, 14 October 2017.

5. "PLAY BALL!"

1. Bob Ray, "Stars Outslug Angels in 10–9 Opener," *Los Angeles Times*, 2 April 1939.
2. Bob Ray, "The Sports X-Ray," *Los Angeles Times*, 3 April 1939.

3. Bob Ray, "Herman Signs," *Los Angeles Times*, 1 April 1939.

6. "A FEW STEPS AHEAD OF THEM"

1. Chuck Stevens, telephone interview, 10 February 2018.

2. J. G. Taylor-Spink, "Caterer Cobb Garnishes the Game with New Ideas," *Sporting News*, 28 December 1939.

3. Ibid.

4. "'Orphaned' Hollywood Ball Team to Bring Back Glamour at Picturesque New Stadium," *Van Nuys News*, 2 March 1939.

5. Taylor-Spink, "Caterer Cobb Garnishes the Game with New Ideas."

6. Ibid.

7. Bob Ray, "Stars Route Rainiers in New Park by 9–4 Score," *Los Angeles Times*, 4 May 1939.

8. Taylor-Spink, "Caterer Cobb Garnishes the Game with New Ideas."

7. "CLEAN UP THAT MOUSE TRAP"

1. Bob Hunter, "Bob Cobb Ends 20 Years' Service to the Game," *Sporting News*, 8 January 1958.

2. Ibid.

3. Artie Harris, telephone interview, 4 August 2015.

4. "Actress Accuses Idle Husband," *Los Angeles Times*, 25 January 1940.

5. "Goddess of Chance Disrupts Marriage," *Los Angeles Times*, 29 May 1940.

6. George Genovese, interview, 27 January 2010.

7. "Baseball Gaming Scandal Hinted," *Los Angeles Times*, 18 November 1940.

8. "Antigambling Drive on at All Coast Parks," *Los Angeles Times*, 6 July 1941.

9. Paul Zimmerman, "Sportscripts," *Los Angeles Times*, 12 September 1946.

10. John B. Old, "Bad Foot Again Kicks Camilli out of Lineup," *Sporting News*, 17 August 1944.

8. "WE'RE BOTH IRISH"

1. Dick Hyland, "Fans, Officials in Uproar over Gilmore Field Fight," *Los Angeles Times*, 22 March 1940.
2. Ibid.
3. Ibid.
4. Ibid.
5. Bob Hunter, "Kress and Tiger Tie up Pictured in Hollywood," *Sporting News*, 14 September 1939.
6. Dick Hyland, "Behind the Line," *Los Angeles Times*, 9 June 1941.
7. Paul Zimmerman, "Sportscripts," *Los Angeles Times*, 20 April 1957.
8. "Gail Patrick Files Suit for Divorce from Cobb," *Los Angeles Times*, 29 October 1940.
9. Ibid.
10. Ibid.
11. Ibid.
12. "Gail Patrick Wins Divorce from Baseball Club Official," *Los Angeles Times*, 15 November 1940.
13. Ibid.

9. "THE COAST LEAGUE HAS BEEN FAST ASLEEP"

1. J. G. Taylor-Spink, "Caterer Cobb Garnishes the Game with New Ideas," *Sporting News*, 28 December 1939.
2. Bob Ray, "The Sports X-Ray," *Los Angeles Times*, 29 June 1939.
3. Paul Zimmerman, "Seraphs Outslug Hollywood Stars for 8–6 Margin," *Los Angeles Times,* 6 July 1940.
4. Bob Ray, "The Sports X-Ray," *Los Angeles Times*, 17 July 1940.
5. Bob Ray, "Stars Open Seal Series," *Los Angeles Times*, 27 August 1940.
6. Bob Ray, "Stars Stage Wild Rally to Break Even with Seattle," *Los Angeles Times*, 26 August 1940.
7. "Stars Say Cincy's Action Forced Dropping Riverside," Associated Press, 1 July 1941.
8. "Pacific Coast League Notes," *Sporting News*, 3 July 1940.

10. "A DAY THAT WILL LIVE IN INFAMY"

1. Scott Michael Rank, "WWII Multimedia Timeline," History on the Net, http://www.historyonthenet.com.
2. Library of Congress, transcript of speech by Franklin D. Roosevelt, 8 December 1941.
3. John B. Old, "Hollywood Seeks Major Tie-up and AA Players," *Sporting News*, 4 December 1941.
4. Sam Greene, "Success of Tigers' Transfusion Rests with Bloodworth," *Sporting News*, 18 December 1941.
5. Al Wolf, "'Carry On' Is Keynote of Coast League Clubs," *Los Angeles Times*, 18 December 1941.
6. Shirley Povich, "Stay in There and Pitch—FDR," *Sporting News*, 22 January 1942.
7. Tom Treanor, "The Home Front," *Los Angeles Times*, 19 January 1942.
8. "All Hollywood Mourns Popular Actress' Death," *Los Angeles Times*, 18 January 1942.
9. Ibid.
10. Hedda Hopper, "Hedda Hopper's Hollywood," *Los Angeles Times*, 2 February 1942.

11. "A SWEET PROSPECT"

1. Braven Dyer, "Shieks Lose Billy Gray," *Los Angeles Times*, 20 February 1942.
2. Braven Dyer, "Stars Seek Campbell for First Base Post," *Los Angeles Times*, 15 March 1942.
3. "Stars Offered Five Pirates," *Los Angeles Times*, 22 January 1942.
4. Braven Dyer, "Babe Herman Says He's Through with Baseball," *Los Angeles Times*, 13 March 1942.
5. Paul Zimmerman, "Sport Postscripts," *Los Angeles Times*, 7 February 1942.
6. George Genovese, interview, 28 January 2010.
7. Ibid.
8. Jim McConnell, "Then and Now: A Star Was Born during World War II," *Los Angeles Daily News*, 10 May 2010.
9. Scott Ostler, "Remembering Babe Herman," *Los Angeles Times*, 1 December 1987.

10. "Root 'Thinking Over' Bid from Hollywood," *Los Angeles Times*, 3 February 1942.
11. "Root Joins Hollywood Ball Club," *Los Angeles Times*, 7 February 1942.
12. Eddie Erautt, interview by Dick Dobbins, 23 April 1997.
13. Ibid.
14. "Stars Sign Boy Pitching Wonder," *Los Angeles Times*, 7 March 1942.
15. Dyer, "Stars Seek Campbell for First Base Post."
16. Eddie Erautt, interview by Dick Dobbins.

12. "THE TERRIBLE TWINKS"

1. John B. Old, "Patriotic Air Prevails at Hollywood Opener," *Sporting News*, 9 April 1942.
2. Paul Zimmerman, "Sport Postscripts," *Los Angeles Times*, 9 May 1942.
3. Ibid.
4. Dorothy McWhirter, telephone interview, 19 December 2017.
5. Al Wolf, "Kalin Hits Three Homers as Stars Win," *Los Angeles Times*, 28 June 1942.
6. "Erautt's Demon with His BB Gun," *Los Angeles Times*, 24 May 1942.
7. "Local Baseball Moguls Ready to Play in '43," *Los Angeles Times*, 6 August 1942.

13. "WE FELLOWS WILL WIN THIS FIGHT!"

1. Steve George, "Coasters Shout Down Graham Shutdown Idea," *Sporting News*, 13 August 1942.
2. John B. Old, "Root Moves in as Hollywood Ousts Os' Vitt," *Sporting News*, 4 March 1943.
3. Lee Dunbar, "The Bull Pen," *Oakland Tribune*, 16 February 1942.
4. "Charley Root to Head Stars," *United Press*, 26 February 1943.
5. "Joe E. Brown Spreads Laughter in War Zone," *Los Angeles Times*, 20 March 1943.
6. "Southland's Navy Day Speakers See Victory," *Los Angeles Times*, 28 October 1942.
7. "Hollywood Prexy Counting on 'Teen Age' Players," *Sporting News*, 27 August 1942.
8. Braven Dyer, "The Sports Parade," *Los Angeles Times*, 7 April 1943.

14. "DON'T WORRY ABOUT HIM"

1. Braven Dyer, "The Sports Parade," *Los Angeles Times*, 9 April 1944.
2. John B. Old, "Taught by Dad, Young Pitcher Twinkles for Hollywood Stars," *Sporting News*, 18 May 1944.
3. Clint Hufford, telephone interview, 4 April 2017.
4. Ibid.
5. Ibid.
6. Al Wolf, "Hufford Blanks Suds, 1–0, 10 Innings," *Los Angeles Times*, 14 April 1944.
7. Old, "Taught by Dad, Young Pitcher Twinkles for Hollywood Stars."
8. Ibid.
9. Ibid.
10. "Stars Hopes Center on Cantrell," *Los Angeles Times*, 21 February 1945.
11. Al Wolf, "Stars Call D-Day Game, Play Tonight," *Los Angeles Times*, 7 June 1944.
12. Al Wolf," Sportraits," *Los Angeles Times*, 30 March 1944.
13. Al Wolf, "Angels and Stars Get Even Break," *Los Angeles Times*, 10 September 1944.
14. Al Wolf, "Sportraits," *Los Angeles Times*, 15 May 1944.

15. "DIDN'T WE MAKE A FORTUNE?"

1. Al Wolf, "Sportraits," *Los Angeles Times*, 22 April 1945.
2. Ibid.
3. Robert Walsh, telephone interview, 5 March 2020.
4. Al Wolf, "Twinks Return, Start Padre Series Tonight," *Los Angeles Times*, 15 May 1945.
5. Al Wolf, "Babe Herman Back to Dodgers," *Los Angeles Times*, 4 July 1945.
6. John B. Old, "Anything Can Happen and Does in Hollywood," *Los Angeles Times*, 12 July 1945.
7. Art Ryon, "Word of Peace Brings Bedlam in Los Angeles," *Los Angeles Times*, 15 August 1945.
8. John B. Old, "Film Funsters Fete and Rib Last-Place Hollywood Club," *Sporting News*, 4 October 1945.

16. "THE BOY WONDER"

1. John B. Old, "Coast Camps Overflow with Prewar-Sized Squads," *Sporting News*, 21 February 1946.
2. John Cavalli, telephone interview, 8 March 2019.
3. John B. Old, "Coast Clubs at Axe Swinging Stage," *Sporting News*, 21 March 1946.
4. John B. Old, "Ole Os Is Seeing Stars," *Sporting News*, 12 March 1942.
5. Emmons Byrne, "Oaks Blank Twins in 12th," *Oakland Tribune*, 1 May 1946.
6. Edgar G. Brands, "Majors Back Chandler's Authority over Game," *Sporting News*, 20 December 1945.
7. Dan Daniel, "Air Travel Adds to Unrest among Players," *Sporting News*, 23 May 1946.
8. Ibid.
9. "Collins Denies Report Dykes to Boss Stars," *Los Angeles Times*, 25 May 1946.
10. John Cavalli, telephone interview, 8 March 2019.
11. Lee Dunbar, "On the Level," *Oakland Tribune*, 23 May 1945.
12. Ibid.
13. Stan Baumgartner, "Coast Loop O.K., but Dykes Dreams of Return to Big Top," *Sporting News*, 23 October 1946.
14. Braven Dyer, "The Sports Parade," *Los Angeles Times*, 6 June 1946.

17. "THE BUSINESS IS NOT FOR SALE"

1. Dan Daniel, "Hank Hints He'd Like to End His Career as a Yankee," *Sporting News*, 1 January 1947.
2. Al Wolf, "Sportraits," *Los Angeles Times*, 10 February 1947.
3. John B. Old, "Hollywood Gives Five Star Program," *Sporting News*, 18 September 1941.
4. Braven Dyer, "The Sports Parade," *Los Angeles Times*, 18 April 1947.
5. Clint Hufford, telephone interview, 30 November 2017.
6. Ibid.
7. Al Wolf, "Sportraits," *Los Angeles Times*, 16 March 1947.
8. John B. Old, "Dykes Goes on Limb for Davis," *Sporting News*, 23 April 1947.
9. Braven Dyer, "The Sports Parade," *Los Angeles Times*, 13 May 1947.

10. Braven Dyer, "Dykes Hopes for Better Twink Pitching," *Los Angeles Times*, 2 July 1947.
11. "Woods Claims New Arm," *Sporting News*, 16 August 1945.
12. Dick Hyland, "The Hyland Fling," *Los Angeles Times*, 7 June 1948.

18. "GIVE 'IM MY REGARDS WHEN YOU SEE HIM"

1. "Babe Ruth Here, Raps Major League Baseball," *Los Angeles Times*, 2 May 1948.
2. John B. Old, "Surgery Planned to Restore Babe's Voice to Normalcy," *Sporting News*, 12 May 1948.
3. Don Jewell, "$100,000 Capital Near for Saddling Billings Mustangs," *Sporting News*, 28 January 1948.
4. "'Welcome Mustang' Dinner Draws 600 Fans," *Billings Gazette*, 4 May 1948.
5. "Baseball Park Name Changed," *Billings Gazette*, 15 April 1948.
6. Old, "Surgery Planned to Restore Babe's Voice to Normalcy."
7. "Secret Kept from Ruth," *Sporting News*, 25 August 1948.
8. Old, "Surgery Planned to Restore Babe's Voice to Normalcy."
9. Al Wolf, "Twinks Tackle Ducks Tonight at Gilmore," *Los Angeles Times*, 24 August 1948.
10. Jack Geyer, "Twinks Capture Nightcap after Losing Opener," *Los Angeles Times*, 9 August 1948.
11. Al Wolf, "Sportraits," *Los Angeles Times*, 8 June 1948.
12. "8-Year Old Gives Dykes Tips on How to Trim Waist," *Sporting News*, 3 September 1947.
13. George Genovese, interview, 11 August 2011.
14. John B. Old, "Dykes Steps Down, Stringer Up on Stars," *Sporting News*, 8 September 1948.

19. "LET ME HAVE IT FOR THREE YEARS"

1. Frank Finch, "Baseball World Pays Tribute to Fred Haney," *Los Angeles Times*, 9 January 1958.
2. Al Wolf, "Sportraits," *Los Angeles Times*, 11 September 1947.
3. Chuck Franklin, telephone interview, 23 February 2019.
4. "Haney Rejects Job," *Independent*, 6 November 1948.

5. Paul Zimmerman, "Sportscripts," *Los Angeles Times*, 1 December 1948.

6. Paul Zimmerman, "Sportscripts," *Los Angeles Times*, 13 November 1948.

7. "Haney Hailed as New Hollywood Hope," *Sporting News*, 24 November 1948.

8. Frank T. Blair, "Frankly Speaking," *Long Beach Press-Telegram*, 24 November 1948.

9. Al Wolf, "Sportraits," *Los Angeles Times*, 21 November 1948.

10. Dave Lewis, "Webfoots Request Championship Go," *Independent*, 16 November 1948.

11. Bob Hunter, "Bob Cobb Ends 20 Years' Service to Game," *Sporting News*, 8 January 1958.

12. Ibid.

13. Ward Morehouse, "Cobb's Brown Derby Off to Branch Rickey," *Sporting News*, 14 October 1949.

14. John B. Old, "Stars' New Pilot Ribbed as Honor Guest at Dinner," *Sporting News*, 8 December 1948.

15. Ibid.

16. Irv Noren, interview, 22 March 2018.

17. Ibid.

18. Ibid.

20. "HOORAY FOR HANEY!"

1. Frank Finch, "Haney's Hustling Twins Hand San Diego Third Loss, 13–6," *Los Angeles Times*, 3 April 1949.

2. Braven Dyer, "Sports Parade," *Los Angeles Times*, 21 April 1949.

3. Darrold "Gar" Myers, telephone interview, 15 January 2018.

4. Al Wolf, "Stars Pin Twin Loss on Angels," *Los Angeles Times*, 9 May 1949.

5. Braven Dyer, "Sports Parade," *Los Angeles Times*, 5 June 1949.

6. Al Wolf, "Sportraits," *Los Angeles Times*, 8 June 1949.

7. Frank Finch, "Haney Says: Hurling and Hustle Makes Twinks Tick," *Los Angeles Times*, 27 May 1949.

8. Ned Cronin, "Noren Shining Proof of Sparkle Added to Stars by Dodger Tieup," *Sporting News*, 25 May 1949.

9. Chuck Stevens, telephone interview, 10 February 2018.

10. Fred Delano, "In the Spotlight," *Long Beach Press-Telegram*, 20 September 1949.

11. Al Wolf, "Twinks Grab Pennant with 7–4 Triumph," *Los Angeles Times*, 23 September1949.

12. Sandy Oster, telephone interview, 5 August 2019.

13. John B. Old, "Display of Governors' Cup Hollywood Traffic Stopper," *Sporting News*, 5 October 1949.

14. John B. Old, "Party for Haney—Hollywood Style," *Sporting News*, 26 October 1949.

21. "IT'S FUNNY ABOUT KIDS"

1. Jack Geyer, "Baseball Scout Rosey Gilhousen Eyes 3000 Prospects Every Year," *Los Angeles Times*, 5 August 1953.

2. Gail Henley, telephone interview, 10 October 2018.

3. Wes Breschini, telephone interview, 28 March 2019.

4. A. S. Young, "Dodgers Sign Ed Moore, Claude Butler for Farm Club," *Los Angeles Sentinel*, 3 March 1949.

5. Darrold "Gar" Myers, telephone interview, 15 January 2018.

6. Ibid.

7. Arlo Engel, interview, 12 January 2018.

8. Ibid.

22. "AREN'T THEY SEXY?"

1. Al Wolf, "Twinks Down Beavers 5 to 3," *Los Angeles Times*, 31 March 1950.

2. Chuck Stevens, telephone interview, 10 February 2018.

3. Braven Dyer, "Sports Dots and Dashes Served for the Masses," *Los Angeles Times*, 19 December 1948.

4. Braven Dyer, "Haney Steals Again—Presents Stars in Shorts," *Sporting News*, 12 April 1950.

5. Virginia MacPherson, "'Briefies' Will Kill Musical Comedy, Says Groucho," *United Press*, 3 April 1950.

6. Ed Cereghino, telephone interview, 25 July 2018.

7. Dyer, "Haney Steals Again—Presents Stars in Shorts."

8. Ibid.

9. Ibid.

10. Ibid.

11. "Hollywood Catches National Game Short," *Sporting News*, 12 April 1950.

12. Frank T. Blair, “Frankly Speaking,” *Long Beach Press-Telegram*, 3 April 1950.

13. “Tremendous! Stupendous! Colossal! Stars in Shorts!” *Sporting News*, 12 April 1950.

14. John B. Old, “Hollywood Can Take Anything—Except Criticism from Brooklyn of Its Shorts,” *Sporting News*, 12 April 1950.

15. Ibid.

16. John Brougham, “Stars Wear Longies—Short Change Seattle,” *Sporting News*, 12 April 1950.

17. “Pueblo’s ‘Hollywood’ Garb Gets Western Loop Okay,” *Sporting News*, 21 June 1950.

18. Old, “Hollywood Can Take Anything—Except Criticism from Brooklyn of Its Shorts.”

19. Al Wolf, “Sportraits,” *Los Angeles Times*, 21 September 1950.

20. “Reichow May Need Donors,” *Los Angeles Times*, 5 July 1950.

21. Chuck Stevens, telephone interview, 10 February 2018.

22. “Stars Will Continue Fight for Okay on Intermission,” *Sporting News*, 16 February 1949.

23. Stan Baumgartner, “Changes in Rules Favorably Received,” *Sporting News*, 16 March 1949.

24. Al Wolf, “Sportraits,” *Los Angeles Times*, 21 September 1950.

23. “THEY’LL SEE A LOT MORE MOVIE STARS THERE”

1. Artie Harris, interview, 19 March 2017.

2. Chuck Stevens, telephone interview, 10 February 2018.

3. Ibid.

4. Ibid.

5. Skip Wollenberg, “Baseball Revives, Updates Commercials Starring Frawley, Bogart,” Associated Press, 15 October 1986.

6. Chuck Franklin, telephone interview, 19 July 2018.

7. Mary Sarty, telephone interview, 10 January 2019.

8. Gail Patrick Jackson, letter to George Genovese, 16 July 1951. TR

9. Art Shallock, telephone interview, 11 July 2010.

10. Gail Henley, telephone interview, 22 March 2017.

24. "THIS IS MAJOR CLASS"

1. Joe King, "'We'll Be Big Time Our Way'—Asserts Hollywood Official," *Sporting News*, 25 March 1953.

2. John B. Old, "Visit of Barnes Revives Major Invasion Talk," *Sporting News*, 22 October 1942.

3. J. G. Taylor-Spink, "O.B. Ready to Spark War Morale Again," *Sporting News*, 11 December 1941.

4. "Bing Favors Third Major," *Sporting News*, 15 September 1946.

5. John B. Old, "Coasters Get Hearing from Major Group," *Sporting News*, 21 March 1946.

6. Dan Daniel, "Mr. San Francisco Speaks His Piece," *Sporting News*, 1 January 1947.

7. Al Wolf, "Roach Predicts Major Baseball Here Next Year," *Los Angeles Times*, 17 July 1947.

8. Al Wolf, "Sportraits," *Los Angeles Times*, 5 October 1947.

9. George C. Carens, "12-Club Major Loops Urged by Perini," *Sporting News*, 25 April 1951.

10. Braven Dyer, "Sauer's 2 Homers Spark Stars to 4–3 Win over Yanks in 10th," *Los Angeles Times*, 22 March 1951.

11. Ned Cronin, "Cronin's Corner," *Los Angeles Times*, 16 October 1957.

12. Jack Walsh, "Territorial Rights Spotlighted at Probe," *Sporting News*, 8 August 1951.

13. Ibid.

14. Larry Jackson, "Paul Fagan Belts Rowland for His Opposition to Bolt," *Sporting News*, 8 August 1951.

15. Prescott Sullivan, "Fagan Says He'll Lock Park If Coast Draft Fight Fails," *Sporting News*, 18 July 1951.

16. John B. Old, "Coasters Believe Inquiry Will Aid Draft Relief Plea," *Sporting News*, 8 August 1951.

17. "Major League Plan Would Assist PCL," *Los Angeles Times*, 15 November 1951.

18. Red Smith, "Views of Sports," *Sporting News*, 19 December 1951.

25. "A FRANKENSTEIN WHICH MAY EAT ITS OWN"

1. Lester Bromberg, "Television Detours Jersey's Fans from Parks," *Sporting News*, 2 June 1948.

2. Stan Baumgartner, "Talk Not Cheap to Phils," *Sporting News*, 8 January 1947.

3. W. R. Wilkerson, "280,000 TV Sets Nearby, Attendance Dips, Hollywood May Cancel Television," *Sporting News*, 2 April 1950.

4. Braven Dyer, "TV Blamed for Empty Seats at Gilmore Field," *Los Angeles Times*, 1 April 1950.

5. John B. Old, "Stars Trying Ticket-Buying Prize Contest for TV Fans," *Sporting News*, 3 May 1950.

6. Chuck Stevens, telephone interview, 10 February 2018.

7. Ibid.

8. John B. Old, "Stars Are Meteors in Star-Filled Race," *Sporting News*, 2 July 1952.

9. Dick Hyland, "Hyland Fling," *Los Angeles Times*, 10 September 1952.

10. Paul Zimmerman, "Sportscripts," *Los Angeles Times,* 25 June 1952.

11. Chuck Stevens, telephone interview, 10 February 2018.

12. John B. Old, "Lindell, Ex-Yank Flyhawk Stars on Coast as Pitcher," *Sporting News*, 4 August 1952.

26. "RUN YOUR GUTS OUT!"

1. Al Wolf, "Fred Haney Signs One-Year Contract to Manage Pirates," *Los Angeles Times*, 12 December 1952.

2. Al Wolf, "Pirates Buy Interest in Holly Stars," *Los Angeles Times*, 18 January 1952.

3. Frank Finch, "Stars Deal Okayed; New Rule Adopted," *Los Angeles Times*, 26 February 1952.

4. Al Wolf, "Sales of Stars' Stock Opposed by PCL Teams," *Los Angeles Times*, 26 January 1952.

5. Ibid.

6. Al Wolf, "Rickey Hurt by Reaction of Coasters," *Los Angeles Times*, 19 February 1952.

7. Al Wolf, "Sportraits," *Los Angeles Times*, 15 April 1953.

8. "Fireworks on Star-Rickey Deal Seen at PCL Confab," *Sporting News*, 20 February 1952.

9. Al Wolf, "Sportraits," *Los Angeles Times*, 12 March 1953.

10. Gwen "Cissie" Bragan Walden, telephone interview, 17 May 2018.

11. Ibid.

12. John B. Old, "Bob Cobb Big Cog in Stars, Named Prexy," *Sporting News*, 1 April 1953.

13. Jack Geyer, "Boxer Willhoit Entertains at Grid Writers Luncheon," *Los Angeles Times*, 7 April 1953.

14. "Herb Gorman Rights to Be in San Jose," *Los Angeles Times*, 7 April 1953.

15. "'Guided Missile' O'Donnell Displays Radar Aim on Hill," *Sporting News*, 24 June 1953.

16. Frank Finch, "Gil Stratton Finally Reaches Goal as Coast League Umpire," *Los Angeles Times*, 24 March 1953.

17. Gwen "Cissie" Bragan Walden, telephone interview, 17 May 2018.

18. Ibid.

19. "Bragan Fined $75 for Bat Boy Incident," *Los Angeles Times*, 1 July 1953.

20. Al Wolf, "Sportraits," *Los Angeles Times*, 18 July 1953.

21. Al Wolf, "Stars and Seals Split Slugfest," *Los Angeles Times*, 11 May 1953.

22. Jeane Hoffman, "Bobby Bragan Mild, Tame When He's Home," *Los Angeles Times*, 23 June 1953.

23. Jack McDonald, "All Pilots Expected to Return for 54," *Sporting News*, 2 September 1953.

24. Jeane Hoffman, "It Turns Out That Bobby Bragan Is Twinks' Answer to Liberace," *Los Angeles Times*, 26 April 1955.

27. "A NATURAL"

1. Ed Prell, "No Chance for Major Shift to Coast Now, Says Wrigley," *Sporting News*, 16 September 1953.

2. Al Wolf, "Cubs Refuse to Renew Territorial Agreement with Stars," *Los Angeles Times*, 5 September 1953.

3. "Gilmore Stadium Sold to CBS for TV City," *Los Angeles Times*, 25 May 1950.

4. Jeane Hoffman, "Bob Cobb Favors 2 Major League Franchises in LA," *Los Angeles Times*, 7 June 1957.

5. Ibid.

6. Ibid.

7. "Cobb Hits at Plan to Secure Browns," *Los Angeles Times*, 26 August 1953.

8. Paul Zimmerman, "Sportscripts," *Los Angeles Times*, 15 October 1954.

9. Al Wolf, "Sportraits," *Los Angeles Times*, 12 August 1954.

28. "THAT'S THE WRONG SANCHEZ"

1. Richard Sandomir, "Reversing Course on Reports about a Classic," *New York Times*, 8 February 2013.
2. "Obituary," *Sporting News*, 25 January 1975.
3. Hedda Hopper, "Movie Caps Career of Star Athlete," *Los Angeles Times*, 14 May 1950.
4. Braven Dyer, "Sports Parade," *Los Angeles Times*, 2 July 1952.
5. Frank Finch, "Illness, Injuries and Page Boy Put Broadcaster in His Job," *Sporting News*, 27 April 1955.
6. Mary Jane Dante, telephone interview, 10 September 2018.
7. Jack Geyer, "Solons Host Stars Today in Opener," *Los Angeles Times*, 5 April 1955.
8. Al Wolf, "Marshall's Grand Slam Ruins Stars," *Los Angeles Times*, 20 May 1955.
9. "Name's the Same, but Stars Learn Size, Position Differ," *Sporting News*, 27 April 1955.
10. "8 Pinch-Hitters for Batter, Bragan's Umpire—Reprisal," *Sporting News*, 11 May 1955.

29. "IT WAS A GOOD CLEAN RIOT"

1. Dick Hyland, "Hyland Fling," *Los Angeles Times*, 30 August 1953.
2. Mark Kelly, "'Feud' Build-up in Los Angeles," *Sporting News*, 2 March 1939.
3. Bob Ray, "The Sports X-Ray," *Los Angeles Times*, 26 June 1939.
4. Chuck Stevens, telephone interview, 10 February 2018.
5. "Ump Says Statement by Bragan Is False," *Los Angeles Times*, 5 August 1953.
6. Chuck Stevens, telephone interview, 10 February 2018.
7. "Angels Study Plan to Shift Twink Series to Coliseum," *Sporting News*, 29 August 1956.
8. John B. Old, "Bill Sweeney, at Luncheon, Answers Blast of Aircaster," *Sporting News*, 30 June 1954.
9. Braven Dyer, "Sports Parade," *Los Angeles Times*, 20 June 1954.
10. John Schulian, "Of Stars and Angels," *Sports Illustrated*, 21 June 1993.

30. "YOU'RE LOOKING AT SOMETHING SPECIAL"

1. Braven Dyer, "Sports Parade," *Los Angeles Times*, 9 April 1956.
2. Dick Hyland, "Hyland Fling," *Los Angeles Times*, 3 May 1956.
3. Frank Finch, "Mazeroski Billed by Stars for Rookie of the Year Honors," *Sporting News*, 27 June 1956.
4. Dyer, "Sports Parade."
5. Al Wolf, "Sportraits," *Los Angeles Times*, 13 March 1956.
6. Jeane Hoffman, "Hoppers Congregate on Baseball Field," *Los Angeles Times*, 10 April 1956.
7. Finch, "Mazeroski Billed by Stars for Rookie of Year Honors."
8. Artie Harris, telephone interview, 7 July 2018.
9. Gail Henley, telephone interview, 10 October 2018.
10. John B. Old, "Pirates Ship Four to Stars, Obtain Trio from PCL Club," *Sporting News*, 11 July 1956.
11. John B. Old, "Pacific Coast League," *Sporting News*, 12 September 1956.

31. "HOME RUNS ARE MY BUSINESS"

1. Frank Finch, "Debonair Dick Stuart Predicts Big Year for Stuart with Stars," *Los Angeles Times*, 4 April 1957.
2. Don Bryant, "Stuart to Take It Easy on HRs, Seek Bat Title," *Sporting News*, 26 June 1957.
3. Paul Pettit, telephone interview, 18 November 2017.
4. Ibid.
5. Jack Geyer, "Stars Bombard Beavers for 22 Hits, 17–3 Win," *Los Angeles Times*, 6 April 1957.
6. Gail Henley, telephone interview, 17 November 2017.
7. Frank Finch, "Angels Shade Stars, 3–2, before 6228*,"* *Los Angeles Times*, 20 April 1957.
8. Jack Geyer, "Dick Stuart Slams Two More Homers," *Los Angeles Times*, 14 April 1957.
9. Mark Harris, "The Man Who Hits Too Many Home Runs," *Life*, 2 September 1957.
10. Frank Finch, "Angels Top Stars, 3–1 before 5921," *Los Angeles Times*, 19 April 1957.
11. Finch, "Angels Shade Stars, 3–2, before 6228."
12. Paul Pettit, telephone interview, 18 November 2017.

13. Ibid.

14. Cronin, Ned. "Cronin's Corner," *Los Angeles Times*, April 24, 1957. C3.

15. Ned Cronin, "Cronin's Corner," *Los Angeles Times*, 7 May 1957.

16. "Dick Stuart Says He May Return to Hollywood—to Make Movies," United Press International, 12 June 1957.

32. "I'LL SEE YOU AT CHAVEZ RAVINE"

1. Artie Harris, interview, 14 August 2019.

2. Ben Foote, "'Game Benefits from Occasional Shakeup'—P. K.," *Sporting News*, 27 February 1957.

3. Sid Ziff, "The Inside Track," *Sporting News*, 5 September 1956.

4. "Stars Cobb and L.A. Mayor in Verbal Exchange at Park," *Los Angeles Times*, 15 May 1957.

5. Rube Samuelson, "O'Malley Kept Busy Looking, Listening on His Visit to Coast," *Sporting News*, 15 May 1957.

6. Frank Finch, "Bums May Arrive in 1958—Poulson," *Los Angeles Times*, 5 May 1957.

7. Woody Wilk, interview, 11 June 2018.

8. "Major Talk Killing PCL Games, Says Cobb," United Press International, 3 June 1957.

9. Frank Finch, "Witt Shuts Door on Rivals, Opens Gate into Majors," *Sporting News*, 14 August 1957.

10. Frank Finch, "Here's the Pitch," *Los Angeles Times*, 25 July 1957.

11. Braven Dyer, "Sports Parade," *Los Angeles Times*, 5 September 1957.

12. Paul Pettit, telephone interview, 11 November 2018.

13. Frank Finch, "Pepper Wins Stars' Finale on 1-Hitter," *Los Angeles Times*, 6 September 1957.

14. Steve Kipnis, telephone interview, 6 March 2018.

15. Ibid.

16. Carlton Williams, "Mayor Signs Dodger 'Ticket' to LA," *Los Angeles Times*, 9 October 1957.

33. "WE ARE AT A LOSS"

1. Robe Samuelson, "Rube-Barbs," *Pasadena Star News*, 13 September 1957.

2. Hank Hollingsworth, "L.B. Citizens May Buy Hollywood Franchise," *Long Beach Press-Telegram*, 25 November 1957.

3. Jack McDonald, "'Throw Us a Life Preserver' PCL Plea to Majors," *Sporting News*, 12 June 1957.

4. "Cobb Quashes Report Stars Moving to Anaheim, "*Sporting News*, 11 April 1956.

5. Hank Hollingsworth, "Sports Merry-Go-Round," *Long Beach Independent Press-Telegram*, 1 December 1957.

6. Hank Hollingsworth, "PCL 'Interested' in Long Beach Bid," *Long Beach Press-Telegram*, 2 November 1957.

7. Hollingsworth, "L.B. Citizens May Buy Hollywood Franchise."

8. "Cobb Took Buck Drubbing to Aid Realignment," *Sporting News*, 11 December 1957.

9. Hank Hollingsworth, "4 Stipulations Must Be Met before Long Beach Can Bid on Stars," *Long Beach Independent*, 10 November 1957.

10. Hank Hollingsworth, "Salt Lake, Spokane, Phoenix Join PCL," *Long Beach Press-Telegram*, 3 December 1957.

11. "Cobb Took Buck Drubbing to Aid Realignment."

12. Paul Pettit, telephone interview, 18 November 2017.

13. Rube Samuelson, "Western Sector in Each Major, Bob Cobb's Idea," *Sporting News*, 18 September 1957.

34. "THOSE WERE THE HALCYON DAYS"

1. Denise Kelleher, interview,10 January 2019.

2. Irv Noren, interview, 22 March 2018.

3. Chuck Stevens, telephone interview, 10 February 2018.

4. Dennis McLellan, "Robert 'Buzz' Knudsen, 80; Won Academy Awards for Sound Mixing on 'Cabaret,' 'The Exorcist,' and 'E.T.'," *Los Angeles Times*, 8 February 2006.

5. Dorothy Scott, e-mail interview. 10 September 2018.

6. Lois Dwan, "Roundabout," *Los Angeles Times*, 29 March 1970.

7. Jim Hardy interview, 14 October 2017.

8. Ibid.

9. Ibid.

10. Ibid.

11. Ibid.

BIBLIOGRAPHY

All game information is drawn from two sources: editions of the *Los Angeles Times* and the *Sporting News*.

"8 Pinch-Hitters for Batter, Bragan's Umpire—Reprisal." *Sporting News*, 11 May 1955.
"8-Year Old Gives Dykes Tips on How to Trim Waist." *Sporting News*, 3 September 1947.
"Actress Accuses Idle Husband." *Los Angeles Times*, 25 January 1940.
"All Hollywood Mourns Popular Actress' Death." *Los Angeles Times*, 18 January 1942.
"Angels Study Plan to Shift Twink Series to Coliseum." *Sporting News*, 29 August 1956.
"Antigambling Drive on at All Coast Parks." *Los Angeles Times*, 6 July 1941.
"Babe Ruth Here, Raps Major League Baseball." *Los Angeles Times*, 2 May 1948.
Barisoff, Bob. In discussion with the author, 13 January 2018.
"Baseball Gaming Scandal Hinted." *Los Angeles Times*, 18 November 1940.
"Baseball Park Name Changed." *Billings Gazette*, 15 April 1948.
Baumgartner, Stan. "Changes in Rules Favorably Received." *Sporting News*, 16 March 1949.
———. "Coast Loop O.K., but Dykes Dreams of Return to Big Top." *Sporting News*, 23 October 1946.
———. "Talk Not Cheap to Phils." *Sporting News*, 8 January 1947.
Bawden, James. "Dream Factory Time: Gail Patrick." *Films of the Golden Ages*, 29 April 2014.
"Bing Favors Third Major." *Sporting News*, 15 September 1946.
Blair, Frank T. "Frankly Speaking." *Long Beach Press-Telegram*, 24 November 1948.
———. "Frankly Speaking." *Long Beach Press-Telegram*, 3 April 1950.
"Bragan Fined $75 for Bat Boy Incident." *Los Angeles Times*, 1 July 1953.
Bragan Walden, Gwen "Cissie." In discussion with the author, 17 May 2018.
Brands, Edgar G. "Majors Back Chandler's Authority over Game." *Sporting News*, 20 December 1945.
Breschini, Wes. In discussion with the author, 28 March 2019.
Bromberg, Lester. "Television Detours Jersey's Fans from Parks." *Sporting News*, 2 June 1948.
Brougham, John. "Stars Wear Longies—Short Change Seattle." *Sporting News*, 12 April 1950.
Bryant, Don. "Stuart to Take It Easy on HRs, Seek Bat Title." *Sporting News*, 26 June 1957.
Byrne, Emmons. "Oaks Blank Twins in 12th." *Oakland Tribune*, 1 May 1946.
Byrnes, Edd. In discussion with the author, 16 May 2018.
Carens, George C. "12-Club Major Loops Urged by Perini." *Sporting News*, 25 April 1951.
Cavalli, John. In discussion with the author, 8 March 2019.
Cereghino, Ed. In discussion with the author, 25 July 2018.
Chance, Joel. In discussion with the author, 24 July 2018.

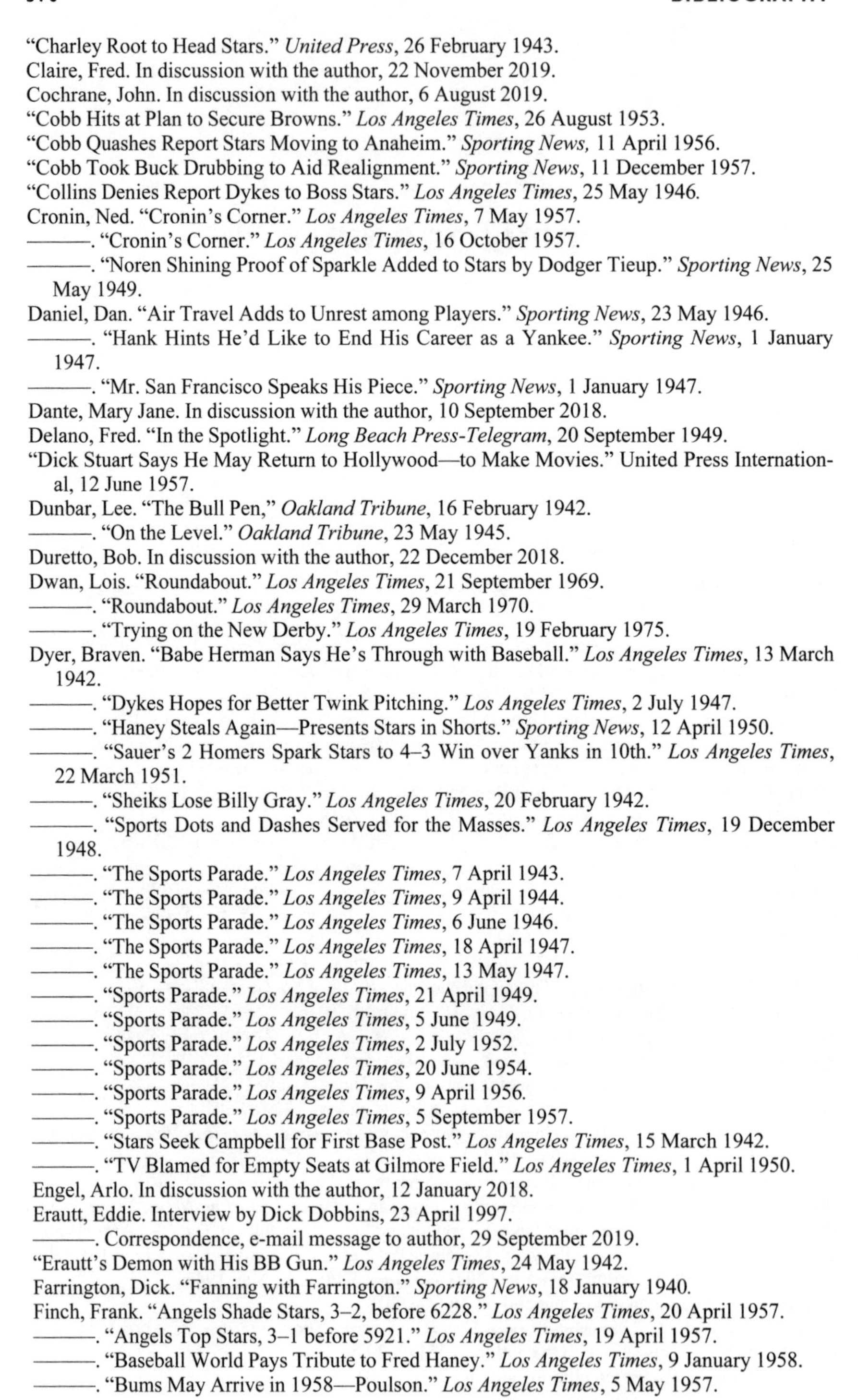

"Charley Root to Head Stars." *United Press*, 26 February 1943.
Claire, Fred. In discussion with the author, 22 November 2019.
Cochrane, John. In discussion with the author, 6 August 2019.
"Cobb Hits at Plan to Secure Browns." *Los Angeles Times*, 26 August 1953.
"Cobb Quashes Report Stars Moving to Anaheim." *Sporting News,* 11 April 1956.
"Cobb Took Buck Drubbing to Aid Realignment." *Sporting News*, 11 December 1957.
"Collins Denies Report Dykes to Boss Stars." *Los Angeles Times*, 25 May 1946.
Cronin, Ned. "Cronin's Corner." *Los Angeles Times*, 7 May 1957.
———. "Cronin's Corner." *Los Angeles Times*, 16 October 1957.
———. "Noren Shining Proof of Sparkle Added to Stars by Dodger Tieup." *Sporting News*, 25 May 1949.
Daniel, Dan. "Air Travel Adds to Unrest among Players." *Sporting News*, 23 May 1946.
———. "Hank Hints He'd Like to End His Career as a Yankee." *Sporting News*, 1 January 1947.
———. "Mr. San Francisco Speaks His Piece." *Sporting News*, 1 January 1947.
Dante, Mary Jane. In discussion with the author, 10 September 2018.
Delano, Fred. "In the Spotlight." *Long Beach Press-Telegram*, 20 September 1949.
"Dick Stuart Says He May Return to Hollywood—to Make Movies." United Press International, 12 June 1957.
Dunbar, Lee. "The Bull Pen," *Oakland Tribune*, 16 February 1942.
———. "On the Level." *Oakland Tribune*, 23 May 1945.
Duretto, Bob. In discussion with the author, 22 December 2018.
Dwan, Lois. "Roundabout." *Los Angeles Times*, 21 September 1969.
———. "Roundabout." *Los Angeles Times*, 29 March 1970.
———. "Trying on the New Derby." *Los Angeles Times*, 19 February 1975.
Dyer, Braven. "Babe Herman Says He's Through with Baseball." *Los Angeles Times*, 13 March 1942.
———. "Dykes Hopes for Better Twink Pitching." *Los Angeles Times*, 2 July 1947.
———. "Haney Steals Again—Presents Stars in Shorts." *Sporting News*, 12 April 1950.
———. "Sauer's 2 Homers Spark Stars to 4–3 Win over Yanks in 10th." *Los Angeles Times*, 22 March 1951.
———. "Sheiks Lose Billy Gray." *Los Angeles Times*, 20 February 1942.
———. "Sports Dots and Dashes Served for the Masses." *Los Angeles Times*, 19 December 1948.
———. "The Sports Parade." *Los Angeles Times*, 7 April 1943.
———. "The Sports Parade." *Los Angeles Times*, 9 April 1944.
———. "The Sports Parade." *Los Angeles Times*, 6 June 1946.
———. "The Sports Parade." *Los Angeles Times*, 18 April 1947.
———. "The Sports Parade." *Los Angeles Times*, 13 May 1947.
———. "Sports Parade." *Los Angeles Times*, 21 April 1949.
———. "Sports Parade." *Los Angeles Times*, 5 June 1949.
———. "Sports Parade." *Los Angeles Times*, 2 July 1952.
———. "Sports Parade." *Los Angeles Times*, 20 June 1954.
———. "Sports Parade." *Los Angeles Times*, 9 April 1956.
———. "Sports Parade." *Los Angeles Times*, 5 September 1957.
———. "Stars Seek Campbell for First Base Post." *Los Angeles Times*, 15 March 1942.
———. "TV Blamed for Empty Seats at Gilmore Field." *Los Angeles Times*, 1 April 1950.
Engel, Arlo. In discussion with the author, 12 January 2018.
Erautt, Eddie. Interview by Dick Dobbins, 23 April 1997.
———. Correspondence, e-mail message to author, 29 September 2019.
"Erautt's Demon with His BB Gun." *Los Angeles Times*, 24 May 1942.
Farrington, Dick. "Fanning with Farrington." *Sporting News*, 18 January 1940.
Finch, Frank. "Angels Shade Stars, 3–2, before 6228." *Los Angeles Times*, 20 April 1957.
———. "Angels Top Stars, 3–1 before 5921." *Los Angeles Times*, 19 April 1957.
———. "Baseball World Pays Tribute to Fred Haney." *Los Angeles Times*, 9 January 1958.
———. "Bums May Arrive in 1958—Poulson." *Los Angeles Times*, 5 May 1957.

———. "Debonair Dick Stuart Predicts Big Year for Stuart with Stars." *Los Angeles Times*, 4 April 1957.
———. "Gil Stratton Finally Reaches Goal as Coast League Umpire." *Los Angeles Times*, 24 March 1953.
———. "Haney Says: Hurling and Hustle Makes Twinks Tick." *Los Angeles Times*, 27 May 1949.
———. "Haney's Hustling Twins Hand San Diego Third Loss, 13–6." *Los Angeles Times*, 3 April 1949.
———. "Here's the Pitch." *Los Angeles Times*, 25 July 1957.
———. "Illness, Injuries and Page Boy Put Broadcaster in His Job." *Sporting News*, 27 April 1955.
———. "Mazeroski Billed by Stars for Rookie of Year Honors." *Sporting News*, 27 June 1956.
———. "Pepper Wins Stars' Finale on 1-Hitter." *Los Angeles Times*, 6 September 1957.
———. "Pacific Coast League." *Sporting News*, 12 September 1956.
———. "Pirates Ship Four to Stars, Obtain Trio from PCL Club." *Sporting News*, 11 July 1956.
———. "Stars Deal Okayed; New Rule Adopted." *Los Angeles Times*, 26 February 1952.
———. "Witt Shuts Door on Rivals, Opens Gate into Majors." *Sporting News*, 14 August 1957.
"Fireworks on Star-Rickey Deal Seen at PCL Confab." *Sporting News*, 20 February 1952.
Flaherty, Vincent X. "Quotes." *Sporting News*, 12 June 1946.
Foote, Ben. "'Game Benefits from Occasional Shakeup'—P.K." *Sporting News*, 27 February 1957.
Franklin, Bob. In discussion with the author, 25 February 2019.
Franklin, Chuck. In discussion with the author, 23 February 2019.
"Gail Patrick Files Suit for Divorce from Cobb." *Los Angeles Times*, 29 October 1940.
"Gail Patrick Wins Divorce from Baseball Club Official." *Los Angeles Times*, 15 November 1940.
Genovese, George. In discussion with the author, 27 January 2010, 28 January 2010, 11 August 2011.
George, Steve. "Coasters Shout Down Graham Shutdown Idea." *Sporting News*, 13 August 1942.
Geyer, Jack. "Baseball Scout Rosey Gilhousen Eyes 3000 Prospects Every Year." *Los Angeles Times*, 5 August 1953.
———. "Boxer Willhoit Entertains at Grid Writers Luncheon." *Los Angeles Times*, 7 April 1953.
———. "Dick Stuart Slams Two More Homers." *Los Angeles Times*, 14 April 1957.
———. "Solons Host Stars Today in Opener." *Los Angeles Times*, 5 April 1955.
———. "Stars Bombard Beavers for 22 Hits, 17–3 Win." *Los Angeles Times*, 6 April 1957.
———. "Twinks Capture Nightcap after Losing Opener." *Los Angeles Times*, 9 August 1948.
"Gilmore Stadium Sold to CBS for TV City." *Los Angeles Times*, 25 May 1950.
"Goddess of Chance Disrupts Marriage." *Los Angeles Times*, 29 May 1940.
Greene, Sam. "Success of Tigers' Transfusion Rests with Bloodworth." *Sporting News*, 18 December 1941.
"'Guided Missile' O'Donnell Displays Radar Aim on Hill." *Sporting News*, 24 June 1953.
"Haney Hailed as New Hollywood Hope." *Sporting News*, 24 November 1948.
"Haney Rejects Job." *Independent*, 6 November 1948.
Hardy, Jim. In discussion with the author, 14 October 2017.
Harper, Joe. In discussion with the author, 16 April 2018.
Harris, Artie. In discussion with the author, 4 August 2015, 19 March 2017, 7 July 2018, 14 August 2019.
Harris, Mark. "The Man Who Hits Too Many Home Runs." *Life*, 2 September 1957.
Harrison, Bruce. In discussion with the author, 17 October 2017.
Henley, Gail. In discussion with the author, 22 March 2017, 17 November 2017, 10 October 2018.
"Herb Gorman Rights to Be in San Jose." *Los Angeles Times*, 7 April 1953.

Hoffman, Jeane. “Bobby Bragan Mild, Tame When He’s Home.” *Los Angeles Times*, 23 June 1953.

———. “Bob Cobb Favors 2 Major League Franchises in LA.” *Los Angeles Times*, 7 June 1957.

———. “Hoppers Congregate on Baseball Field.” *Los Angeles Times*, 10 April 1956.

———. “It Turns Out That Bobby Bragan Is Twinks’ Answer to Liberace.” *Los Angeles Times*, 26 April 1955.

Hollingsworth, Hank. “4 Stipulations Must Be Met before Long Beach Can Bid on Stars.” *Long Beach Independent*, 10 November 1957.

———. “L.B. Citizens May Buy Hollywood Franchise.” *Long Beach Press-Telegram*, 25 November 1957.

———. “PCL ‘Interested’ in Long Beach Bid.” *Long Beach Press-Telegram*, 2 November 1957.

———. “Salt Lake, Spokane, Phoenix Join PCL.” *Long Beach Press-Telegram*, 3 December 1957.

———. “Sports Merry-Go-Round.” *Long Beach Independent Press-Telegram*, 1 December 1957.

“Hollywood Catches National Game Short.” *Sporting News*, 12 April 1950.

“Hollywood Prexy Counting on ‘Teen Age’ Players.” *Sporting News*, 27 August 1942.

Hopper, Hedda. “Hedda Hopper’s Hollywood.” *Los Angeles Times*, 2 February 1942.

———. “Movie Caps Career of Star Athlete.” *Los Angeles Times*, 14 May 1950.

———. “Public Affection Makes or Breaks Film Stars.” *Los Angeles Times*, 19 March 1939.

Hufford, Clint. In discussion with the author, 4 April 2017, 30 November 2017.

Hunter, Bob. “Bob Cobb Ends 20 Years’ Service to the Game.” *Sporting News*, 8 January 1958.

———. “Fans, Officials in Uproar over Gilmore Field Fight.” *Los Angeles Times*, 22 March 1940.

———. “Hollywood Putting $200,000 into Park.” *Sporting News*, 19 January 1939.

———. “Kress and Tiger Tie up Pictured in Hollywood.” *Sporting News*, 14 September 1939.

Hyland, Dick. “Behind the Line.” *Los Angeles Times*, 9 June 1941.

———. “Fans, Officials in Uproar over Gilmore Field Fight.” *Los Angeles Times*, 22 March 1940.

———. “The Hyland Fling.” *Los Angeles Times*, 7 June 1948.

———. “Hyland Fling.” *Los Angeles Times*, 10 September 1952.

———. “Hyland Fling.” *Los Angeles Times*, 30 August 1953.

———. “Hyland Fling.” *Los Angeles Times*, 3 May 1956.

Jackson, Gail Patrick. Letter to George Genovese. 16 July 1951.

Jackson, Larry. “Paul Fagan Belts Rowland for His Opposition to Bolt.” *Sporting News*, 8 August 1951.

Jewell, Don. “$100,000 Capital Near for Saddling Billings Mustangs.” *Sporting News*, 28 January 1948.

“Joe E. Brown Spreads Laughter in War Zone.” *Los Angeles Times*, 20 March 1943.

Kelleher, Denise. In discussion with the author, 10 January 2019.

Kelly, Mark. “‘Feud’ Build-up in Los Angeles.” *Sporting News*, 2 March 1939.

———. “Scribbled by Scribes.” *Los Angeles Examiner*, 2 March 1939.

King, Joe. “‘We’ll Be Big Time Our Way’—Asserts Hollywood Official.” *Sporting News*, 25 March 1953.

Kipnis, Steve. In discussion with the author, 6 March 2018.

“Lang Suit Lost by Fleishhacker.” United Press International, 6 December 1937.

Lewis, Dave. “Webfoots Request Championship Go.” *Independent*, 16 November 1948.

Lieb, Frederick G. “Inside the Game’s Most Famous Deals.” *Sporting News*, 27 April 1944.

“Local Baseball Moguls Ready to Play in ’43.” *Los Angeles Times*, 6 August 1942.

Maalen, Terry. In discussion with the author, 8 February 2019.

MacPherson, Virginia. “‘Briefies’ Will Kill Musical Comedy, Says Groucho.” United Press, 3 April 1950.

Maher, Charles. "A Dodger Lineup You Don't Hear Much About." *Los Angeles Times*, 15 July 1973.
"Major League Plan Would Assist PCL." *Los Angeles Times*, 15 November 1951.
"Major Talk Killing PCL Games, Says Cobb." United Press International, 3 June 1957.
McConnell, Jim. "Then and Now: A Star Was Born during World War II." *Los Angeles Daily News*, 10 May 2010.
McDonald, Jack. "All Pilots Expected to Return for 54." *Sporting News*, 2 September 1953.
———. "'Throw Us a Life Preserver' PCL Plea to Majors." *Sporting News*, 12 June 1957.
McLellan, Dennis. "Robert 'Buzz' Knudsen, 80; Won Academy Awards for Sound Mixing on 'Cabaret,' 'The Exorcist,' and 'E.T.'" *Los Angeles Times*, 8 February 2006.
McWhirter, Dorothy. In discussion with the author, 19 December 2017.
Morehouse, Ward. "Cobb's Brown Derby Off to Branch Rickey." *Sporting News*, 14 October 1949.
Myers, Darrold "Gar." In discussion with the author, 15 January 2018.
"Name's the Same, but Stars Learn Size, Position Differ." *Sporting News*, 27 April 1955.
Noren, Irv. In discussion with the author, 22 March 2018.
"Obituary." *Sporting News*, 25 January 1975.
O'Donnell, Dennis. In discussion with the author, 18 June 2018.
Old, John B. "Anything Can Happen and Does in Hollywood." *Los Angeles Times*, 12 July 1945.
———. "Bad Foot Again Kicks Camilli out of Lineup." *Sporting News*, 17 August 1944.
———. "Ballyhoo Building Will Include Films." *Sporting News*, 6 September 1945.
———. "Bill Sweeney, at Luncheon, Answers Blast of Aircaster." *Sporting News*, 30 June 1954.
———. "Bob Cobb Big Cog in Stars, Named Prexy." *Sporting News*, 1 April 1953.
———. "Coast Camps Overflow with Prewar-Sized Squads." *Sporting News*, 21 February 1946.
———. "Coast Clubs at Axe Swinging Stage." *Sporting News*, 21 March 1946.
———. "Coasters Believe Inquiry Will Aid Draft Relief Plea." *Sporting News*, 8 August 1951.
———. "Coasters Get Hearing from Major Group." *Sporting News*, 21 March 1946.
———. "Display of Governors' Cup Hollywood Traffic Stopper." *Sporting News*, 5 October 1949.
———. "Dykes Goes on Limb for Davis." *Sporting News*, 23 April 1947.
———. "Dykes Steps Down, Stringer Up on Stars." *Sporting News*, 8 September 1948.
———. "Film Funsters Fete and Rib Last-Place Hollywood Club." *Sporting News*, 4 October 1945.
———. "Hollywood Can Take Anything—Except Criticism from Brooklyn of Its Shorts." *Sporting News*, 12 April 1950.
———. "Hollywood Gives Five Star Program." *Sporting News*, 18 September 1941.
———. "Hollywood Seeks Major Tie-up and AA Players." *Sporting News*, 4 December 1941.
———. "Lindell, Ex-Yank Flyhawk Stars on Coast as Pitcher." *Sporting News*, 4 August 1952.
———. "Ole Os Is Seeing Stars." *Sporting News*, 12 March 1942.
———. "Party for Haney—Hollywood Style." *Sporting News,* 26 October 1949.
———. "Patriotic Air Prevails at Hollywood Opener." *Sporting News*, 9 April 1942.
———. "Root Moves in as Hollywood Ousts Os' Vitt." *Sporting News*, 4 March 1943.
———. "Stars Are Meteors in Star-Filled Race." *Sporting News*, 2 July 1952.
———. "Stars' New Pilot Ribbed as Honor Guest at Dinner." *Sporting News*, 8 December 1948.
———. "Stars Trying Ticket-Buying Prize Contest for TV Fans." *Sporting News*, 3 May 1950.
———. "Surgery Planned to Restore Babe's Voice to Normalcy." *Sporting News*, 12 May 1948.
———. "Taught by Dad, Young Pitcher Twinkles for Hollywood Stars." *Sporting News*, 18 May 1944.
———. "Visit of Barnes Revives Major Invasion Talk." *Sporting News*, 22 October 1942.
"'Orphaned' Hollywood Ball Team to Bring Back Glamour at Picturesque New Stadium." *Van Nuys News*, 2 March 1939.

Oster, Sandy. In discussion with the author, 5 August 2019.
Ostler, Scott. "Remembering Babe Herman." *Los Angeles Times*, 1 December 1987.
"Pacific Coast League Notes." *Sporting News*, 3 July 1940.
Pettit, Paul. In discussion with the author, 18 November 2017, 11 November 2018, 18 November 2017.
Povich, Shirley. "Stay in There and Pitch—FDR." *Sporting News*, 22 January 1942.
Prell, Ed. "No Chance for Major Shift to Coast Now, Says Wrigley." *Sporting News*, 16 September 1953.
"Pueblo's 'Hollywood' Garb Gets Western Loop Okay." *Sporting News*, 21 June 1950.
"Quality and Service Stressed at Derbies." *Los Angeles Times*, 16 June 1967.
Ray, Bob. "Herman Signs." *Los Angeles Times*, 1 April 1939.
———. "The Sports X-Ray." *Los Angeles Times*, 10 February 1938.
———. "The Sports X-Ray." *Los Angeles Times*, 8 December 1938.
———. "The Sports X-Ray." *Los Angeles Times*, 3 April 1939.
———. "The Sports X-Ray." *Los Angeles Times*, 26 June 1939.
———. "The Sports X-Ray." *Los Angeles Times*, 29 June 1939.
———. "The Sports X-Ray." *Los Angeles Times*, 1 August 1939.
———. "The Sports X-Ray." *Los Angeles Times*, 17 July 1940.
———. "Stars Open Seal Series." *Los Angeles Times*, 27 August 1940.
———. "Stars Outslug Angels in 10–9 Opener." *Los Angeles Times*, 2 April 1939.
———. "Stars Route Rainiers in New Park by 9–4 Score." *Los Angeles Times*, 4 May 1939.
———. "Stars Stage Wild Rally to Break Even with Seattle." *Los Angeles Times*, 26 August 1940.
Reichow, Oscar. "Cubs a Happy and Confident Lot as They Start for Camp." *Sporting News*, 4 March 1929.
———. "Reichow the Original Landis Man Pays Tribute to His Choice." *Sporting News*, 18 November 1920.
"Reichow May Need Donors." *Los Angeles Times*, 5 July 1950.
"Root 'Thinking Over' Bid from Hollywood." *Los Angeles Times*, 3 February 1942.
"Root Joins Hollywood Ball Club." *Los Angeles Times*, 7 February 1942.
Rubin, Laurence. In discussion with the author, 12 March 2019, 9 August 2019.
Ryon, Art. "Word of Peace Brings Bedlam in Los Angeles." *Los Angeles Times*, 15 August 1945.
Samuelson, Rube, "O'Malley Kept Busy Looking, Listening on His Visit to Coast." *Sporting News*, 15 May 1957.
———. "Rube-Barbs." *Pasadena Star News*, 13 September 1957.
———. "Western Sector in Each Major, Bob Cobb's Idea." *Sporting News*, 18 September 1957.
Sandomir, Richard. "Reversing Course on Reports about a Classic." *New York Times*, 8 February 2013.
Sarty, Mary. In discussion with the author, 10 January 2019.
Schulian, John. "Of Stars and Angels." *Sports Illustrated*, 21 June 1993.
Schwepe, Robert. In discussion with the author, 20 July 2018.
Scott, Dorothy. Correspondence, e-mail message to author, 10 September 2018.
"Secret Kept from Ruth." *Sporting News*, 25 August 1948.
Shallock, Art. In discussion with the author, 11 July 2010.
Sheridan, John. "Back of the Home Plate." *Sporting News*, 10 February 1920.
"Southland's Navy Day Speakers See Victory." *Los Angeles Times*, 28 October 1942.
Smith, Red. "Views of Sports." *Sporting News*, 19 December 1951.
"Stars Cobb and L.A. Mayor in Verbal Exchange at Park." *Los Angeles Times*, 15 May 1957.
"Stars Hopes Center on Cantrell." *Los Angeles Times*, 21 February 1945.
"Stars Offered Five Pirates." *Los Angeles Times*, 22 January 1942.
"Stars Say Cincy's Action Forced Dropping Riverside." Associated Press, 1 July 1941.
"Stars Sign Boy Pitching Wonder." *Los Angeles Times*, 7 March 1942.
"Stars Will Continue Fight for Okay on Intermission." *Sporting News*, 16 February 1949.
Stevens, Chuck. In discussion with the author, 10 February 2018.

Sullivan, Prescott. "Fagan Says He'll Lock Park If Coast Draft Fight Fails." *Sporting News*, 18 July 1951.
Taylor-Spink, J. G. "Caterer Cobb Garnishes the Game with New Ideas." *Sporting News*, 28 December 1939.
———. "O.B. Ready to Spark War Morale Again." *Sporting News*, 11 December 1941.
Treanor, Tom. "The Home Front." *Los Angeles Times*, 19 January 1942.
"Tremendous! Stupendous! Colossal! Stars in Shorts!" *Sporting News*, 12 April 1950.
Turner, Bill. In discussion with the author, 10 April 2019.
"Ump Says Statement by Bragan Is False." *Los Angeles Times*, 5 August 1953.
Van Ornum, John. In discussion with the author, 12 January 2017, 19 January 2018, 31 January 2019.
Walsh, Jack. "Territorial Rights Spotlighted at Probe." *Sporting News*, 8 August 1951.
Walsh, Robert. In discussion with the author, 5 March 2020.
"'Welcome Mustang' Dinner Draws 600 Fans." *Billings Gazette*, 4 May 1948.
Wilk, Woody. In discussion with the author, 11 June 2018.
Wilkerson, W. R. "280,000 TV Sets Nearby, Attendance Dips, Hollywood May Cancel Television." *Sporting News*, 2 April 1950.
Williams, Carlton. "Mayor Signs Dodger 'Ticket' to LA." *Los Angeles Times*, 9 October 1957.
Wolf, Al. "Angels and Stars Get Even Break." *Los Angeles Times*, 10 September 1944.
———. "Babe Herman Back to Dodgers." *Los Angeles Times*, 4 July 1945.
———. "'Carry On' Is Keynote of Coast League Clubs." *Los Angeles Times*, 18 December 1941.
———. "Cubs Refuse to Renew Territorial Agreement with Stars." *Los Angeles Times*, 5 September 1953.
———. "Fred Haney Signs One-Year Contract to Manage Pirates." *Los Angeles Times*, 12 December 1952.
———. "Hufford Blanks Suds, 1–0, 10 Innings." *Los Angeles Times*, 14 April 1944.
———. "Kalin Hits Three Homers as Stars Win." *Los Angeles Times*, 28 June 1942.
———. "Marshall's Grand Slam Ruins Stars." *Los Angeles Times*, 20 May 1955.
———. "Pirates Buy Interest in Holly Stars." *Los Angeles Times*, 18 January 1952.
———. "Rickey Hurt by Reaction of Coasters." *Los Angeles Times*, 19 February 1952.
———. "Roach Predicts Major Baseball Here Next Year." *Los Angeles Times*, 17 July 1947.
———. "Sales of Stars' Stock Opposed by PCL Teams." *Los Angeles Times*, 26 January 1952.
———. "Sportraits." *Los Angeles Times*, 30 March 1944.
———. "Sportraits." *Los Angeles Times*, 15 May 1944.
———. "Sportraits." *Los Angeles Times*, 22 April 1945.
———. "Sportraits." *Los Angeles Times*, 10 February 1947.
———. "Sportraits." *Los Angeles Times*, 16 March 1947.
———. "Sportraits." *Los Angeles Times*, 11 September 1947.
———. "Sportraits." *Los Angeles Times*, 5 October 1947.
———. "Sportraits." *Los Angeles Times*, 8 June 1948.
———. "Sportraits." *Los Angeles Times*, 21 November 1948.
———. "Sportraits." *Los Angeles Times*, 8 June 1949.
———. "Sportraits." *Los Angeles Times*, 21 September 1950.
———. "Sportraits." *Los Angeles Times*, 12 March 1953.
———. "Sportraits." *Los Angeles Times*, 15 April 1953.
———. "Sportraits." *Los Angeles Times*, 18 July 1953.
———. "Sportraits." *Los Angeles Times*, 12 August 1954.
———. "Sportraits." *Los Angeles Times*, 13 March 1956.
———. "Stars and Seals Split Slugfest." *Los Angeles Times*, 11 May 1953.
———. "Stars Call D-Day Game, Play Tonight." *Los Angeles Times*, 7 June 1944.
———. "Stars Pin Twin Loss on Angels." *Los Angeles Times*, 9 May 1949.
———. "Twinks Down Beavers 5 to 3." *Los Angeles Times*, 31 March 1950.
———. "Twinks Grab Pennant with 7–4 Triumph." *Los Angeles Times*, 23 September 1949.
———. "Twinks Return, Start Padre Series Tonight." *Los Angeles Times*, 15 May 1945.
———. "Twinks Tackle Ducks Tonight at Gilmore." *Los Angeles Times*, 24 August 1948.

Wollenberg, Skip. "Baseball Revives, Updates Commercials Starring Frawley, Bogart." Associated Press, 15 October 1986.
"Woods Claims New Arm." *Sporting News*, 16 August 1945.
Young, A. S. "Dodgers Sign Ed Moore, Claude Butler for Farm Club." *Los Angeles Sentinel*, 3 March 1949.
Ziff, Sid. "The Inside Track." *Sporting News*, 5 September 1956.
Zimmerman, Paul. "Seraphs Outslug Hollywood Stars for 8–6 Margin." *Los Angeles Times*, 6 July 1940.
———. "Sport Postscripts." *Los Angeles Times*, 7 February 1942.
———. "Sport Postscripts." *Los Angeles Times*, 9 May 1942.
———. "Sportscripts." *Los Angeles Times*, 12 September 1946.
———. "Sportscripts." *Los Angeles Times*, 13 November 1948.
———. "Sportscripts." *Los Angeles Times*, 1 December 1948.
———. "Sportscripts." *Los Angeles Times,* 25 June 1952.
———. "Sportscripts." *Los Angeles Times*, 15 October 1954.
———. "Sportscripts." *Los Angeles Times*, 20 April 1957.

INDEX

ABOUT THE AUTHOR

Dan Taylor is a former award-winning television sportscaster and currently a member of the television broadcast team for the Fresno Grizzlies of the Pacific Coast League.

He is a member of the Society for American Baseball Research and contributes to their biography project. He is also a member of the Pacific Coast League Historical Society.

This is the fourth book produced by Dan Taylor. His prior works include *Fate's Take-Out Slide*, in collaboration with George Genovese (2017); *A Scout's Report: My 70 Years in Baseball* (2015); and *Rise of the Bulldogs* (2009).

He resides in Fresno, California.